About th

George Simon Budge was born in Plymouth, Devon in 1947. He was educated at Efford Secondary Modern School. George by his own admission said "My schooldays were like going to a shop to buy bread, and coming out of the shop with an empty bag". George was not an academic pupil at school, but he did enjoy History and Geography. George was a creator and excelled in Woodwork and Metalwork, hence when George left school he worked as Architectural and Structural Engineer for five years. George then followed the path of his destiny, working as an HGV driver for most of his working life.

Dedication

I dedicate this book to all the innocent civilians who have died and have suffered at the hands and actions of the evil perpetrators who have no regard or any values for human life, or the innocent civilians of conflicts around our world.

I would also like to mention the late Mr Richard Telling (Area Manager of Crown Paints). Mr Telling was responsible for giving me six months leave from Crown Paints to serve with the Red Cross in the former Yugoslavia.

George Budge

MISSION OF MERCY

AUSTIN MACAULEY
PUBLISHERS LTD.

A CIP catalogue record for this title is available from the British
Library.

ISBN 978 1 78455 419 4 (Paperback)
ISBN 978 1 78455 424 8 (Hardback)
ISBN 978 1 78455 423 1 (E-Book)

www.austinmacauley.com

First Published (2015)
Austin Macauley Publishers Ltd.
25 Canada Square
Canary Wharf
London
E14 5LB

Acknowledgments

At the time of my mission I was in full-time employment with Crown Paints. My manager; Mr Richard Telling granted me six months' unpaid leave to carry out my mission. I would therefore like to thank all the Crown Paints staff for their kindness and support during and after my mission.

 I would also like to thank Samantha Eastwood for all her help and advice with this book. Finally, I was fortunate and honored to serve my mission with Red Cross volunteers from all over the world. We all shared a precious moment in time and worked together with a common goal of Decency, and Humanity. May also thank all the Red Cross and Red Crescent staff, past and present. If it wasn't for the Red Cross and Red Crescent staff, the suffering we witness on our TV news reports would be a hundred times worse.

CHAPTER ONE

The Death of Yugoslavia

Whilst under the leadership of Tito, Yugoslavia's six republics, Slovenia, Croatia, Bosnia, Macedonia, Montenegro and Serbia, stood together in brotherhood and unity. Even after Tito's death in 1980, Yugoslavia stood together sharing the very values that he had taught their people. However, in 1987 a flame of destruction was lit in the province of Kosovo.

In the past Serbia had dominated Yugoslavia; Tito gave the provinces of Vojvodina and Kosovo the power to self-rule as a way to cut the size of Serbia in proportion to the other Yugoslavian republics. In Kosovo the Serbian people were in a minority when compared with the Albanians. The Serbs in Kosovo felt threatened, they were always outnumbered by the Albanians, particularly when it came to any disagreements. Demonstrations by the Serb population, and civil unrest, had become a regular occurrence in Kosovo.

The President of Serbia, Ivan Stambolić, was becoming concerned with the tensions in Kosovo. He decided to send his right-hand man, Slobodan Milošević, to calm the situation and remind the population of the brotherhood that Tito had installed in Yugoslavia.

In hindsight, the President never could have known that the man he had sent to Kosovo to bring peace was about to be the catalyst for one of the most devastating civil disputes of the decade. Milošević arranged a meeting with the Serb Communist Party leaders in Kosovo as a diplomatic reminder of the republics' previous unity. Whilst the meeting was taking place, a crowd gathering outside became agitated and started throwing stones at police chaperoning the proceedings. The police, who were mainly Albanian, responded with force, taking their batons to the rioters.

The commotion outside began to interfere with the meeting, the Serbs feeling that they were not getting any concessions in Kosovo. When Milošević and the Communist Party leaders came outside to calm the restless crowd, lies and deceit began pouring from the people's mouths. The rioters told Milošević that the police had started to beat them without any provocation. Insisting that the Albanians were always beating the Serbian residents and trying to drive them out of Kosovo.

Swept into a Serb Nationalist ploy, Milošević told the crowd that steps would be taken to secure their people's safety in the province, unaware that the crowd had intentionally provoked the Albanians.

The Albanian leader in Kosovo, Azem Vllasi, explained to Milošević that the Serbs had manipulated the situation in Kosovo, greatly exaggerating their woes in order to gain sympathy. Unfortunately, Milošević, choosing to believe his eyes rather than fact, was not prepared to accept Vllasi's warning.

Back in Belgrade Serb television covered the events in Kosovo, omitting the stone throwing that provoked the police. The Serbian President was appalled at the way Milošević had handled the situation in Kosovo, enough that he even accused Milošević of breaching party policy; Stambolić had sent him to Kosovo to calm the tensions, not to stir up trouble by embracing Serb nationalism. In retaliation the people of Belgrade began filling the streets, chanting in support for

Milošević. They had taken him into their hearts, seeing him as a leader that would fight for the Serbian people, upholding their rights and values.

At a meeting in Belgrade, Milošević maliciously canvassed for the Serbian Communist Party delegates to oust the President by accusing him of trying to create a dictatorship over the people. President Stambolić denied the accusations, telling the delegates that he had acted in good faith by sending Milošević to Kosovo as a mediator for the Albanians and Serbs. He launched his own accusation, that Milošević was fuelling hatred and division between the different peoples of Kosovo.

Milošević told the Serbian Communist Party that the President had let the Serbs down in Kosovo and he should go. Milošević pushed the delegates for a vote and, due to the growing support for Milošević, President Stambolić was unanimously voted out of office. Thus launching Milošević on a crusade to take over Yugoslavia. The Serbs looked on Milošević as their savior, a man that could give them a better future.

You could compare some of the events in Yugoslavia to Germany in the thirties. It is impossible to understand why countries like Yugoslavia, in the wake of recent histories, manage to make the same mistakes – surely they did not have a death wish?

Milošević turned to the Serbian provinces of Vojvodina and Kosovo, since these provinces could still vote against Serbia – along with the other republics of Slovenia, Croatia, Bosnia, Macedonia and Montenegro. He used the people to force the leaders of Vojvodina, Kosovo and Montenegro out of their political seats, swaying the votes by implying that old representatives did not act in the people's best interests, 'The people must be obeyed!' he implored.

Milošević used his growing influence to install his own men into powerful positions – underpinning his insidious monopoly over these now vulnerable provinces. By the beginning of 1989 Milošević was in control of half of Yugoslavia.

In Kosovo the Albanians hit back when the miners led a general strike; they wanted their former leader, Azem Vllasi, returned to power. He wanted the Serbs and Albanians to live and work together in the fashion that Tito had bred: in brotherhood and unity. However, Milošević was very angry at these latest developments in Kosovo. He accused Vllasi of being behind this rebellion against him and, in retaliation, Milošević asked the Yugoslav state council to grant him emergency powers in Kosovo.

The Bosnian President Raif Dizdarević, and the Slovene leader Milan Kučan, were both concerned that Milošević intended to punish the striking Albanians; concerned what that might do to the federation. Especially when Milošević said, 'We Serbs will act in our own interests, if this violates the Yugoslav constitution we do not care!'

Kučan walked out of the state council meeting fearing that, after he was finished in Kosovo, Milošević would soon be turning his attention Slovenia.

Kučan returned to Slovenia to speak with his people and told them that the strikers in Kosovo were defending the rights of Albanians, and of Yugoslavia as a whole. Serbian television stations picked up a feed from the Slovenian television stations, which the Serb television chief decided to show to the Serb people. Serb television reported Kučan as a traitor in his speech to the people, calling it deliberately provocative in the defending of the Albanian Kosovians. The broadcast brought the Serb people of Belgrade onto the streets in protest of the statement made by the Slovene leader. The following day the Serbs in Belgrade were given the day off to march the streets chanting "Slobodan!" in support of their rising leader.

With half of the population of Belgrade on the streets supporting him, Milošević now felt he was in a position to give the president of Yugoslavia an ultimatum. Either the President gave him the powers he wanted, or the President would have to deal with the crowd in Belgrade. Milošević made it very clear *he would not be responsible for the actions of the crowd.*

Faced with serious Serb blackmail, the President decided to speak to the mass crowd in Belgrade. He warned them of the dangerous road they were taking, reminding them of Tito's legacy of unity and that their actions would surely lead the people into unwanted conflict. Despite the President's efforts to encourage common sense in the protestors, he failed to satisfy the crowd in Belgrade. He returned to the Communist Party Council to recommend that the power of the Yugoslavian Army be given to Milošević, on the grounds that a million Serbs could not be ignored.

As Milošević addressed the waiting crowd in Belgrade the crowd shouted for the arrest of Kosovian/Albanian leader, Azem Vllasi. Milošević replied, 'No force on earth can stop the people of Serbia, and those who plot against Yugoslavia will be arrested and punished!'

Following this Vllasi was arrested and jailed. All dissent was crushed when the Yugoslav army entered Kosovo. However, it was the tiny republic of Slovenia that first turned on the Serb giant. They had been enjoying a new freedom of speech against the old communist system. Franci Zavrl, the editor of youth magazine *Mladina*, adopted a satirical look at the events in Belgrade; Milošević was even ridiculed in several articles. The Yugoslav Defence Minister took advantage of military manoeuvres in Slovenia telling Milan Kučan, "You must clamp down on your press", but Kučan took no action on the press as their State Prosecutor deemed that no illegal material had been published.

The editor of the *Mladina* was shown the transcript from a documented meeting supposedly held in Belgrade. The document accused *Mladina* of being financed by the CIA, and that Kučan was harbouring rebel revolutionaries. The editor published extracts from the secret party transcript, meaning that *Mladina* had now broken the law in Yugoslavia, and because of this Kučan bowed to Belgrade pressure authorising the secret police to arrest Janez Janša, the Defence Correspondent at *Mladina*. Upon searching Janša's house they found a *secret army document*. With the case getting too hot to handle, Kučan had no choice but to hand the case over to Yugoslav Intelligence.

Whilst Janša was in custody he was questioned and threatened with fifteen to thirty years in prison if he did not cooperate with the Secret Police; they also threatened to stand him against the wall and shoot him. Yugoslav Intelligence managed to get enough evidence to arrest some of the *Mladina* reporters; they were ready to make an example out of these rebellious Slovenes.

However, when Yugoslav Intelligence tried to implement a law it backfired, with anti-army and anti-Yugoslav demonstrations erupting in Slovenia.

Kučan's next move was to change the constitution in an attempt to keep the Serbs of Belgrade out of Slovenia affairs. Milošević in turn threatened to rally in the Slovene capital, where he would inform the Slovenian people that their leader was a traitor to the provincial brotherhood of Yugoslavia. It was becoming clear that Milošević would stop at nothing to get his own way.

The Serb Party activists in Kosovo planned a trip to Slovenia to drum up support against Kučan; but with Kosovo being at the opposite end of the country, the activists would have to travel through Croatia, which shared the same border as Slovenia. Kučan found an ally when neighbouring Croatia refused to let the Serb Party activist across the border from Serbia in order to access Slovenia. The police did not have too much trouble with the few local Serbs who turned out to demonstrate. It seemed Milošević would have to try something else in order to defeat Kučan's Slovenia.

The instrument he chose was the Yugoslav Communist Party Congress, which was held in Belgrade in 1990, whose delegates stood for their national anthem of brotherhood and unity. It was clear this congress had been summoned by Milošević to crush the Slovenes, but Slovenia had welcomed the congress as an opportunity to make amendments to the Yugoslav constitution. Unfortunately, every time an amendment was put forward by the Slovenes most of the delegation voted against it. Slovenia had only one hope to save this congress from turning into a farce.

The Yugoslav's second largest republic of Croatia and their delegation leader, Ivica Račan, took to the platform. He told the delegates *let us all show a bit more tolerance before we make this congress a mockery*. The tension at the congress was rising by the minute, with the mighty Serb nation behind Milošević who would *dare* vote *against him*?

Ciril Ribičič, a Slovene delegate, took the platform to announce to congress *under these circumstances we will have to leave the Communist Party of Yugoslavia*; and the Slovene delegates duly walked out of congress.

There was a pause in congress following the Slovene walkout. Milošević was very concerned about how the Croatian delegates might react. For the first time Milošević looked worried, with his charm having deserted him, but his worries were not without foundation. When the head of the Croatian delegation, Ivica Račan, announced that *Croatia could not accept a Yugoslavia without the Slovenes*, and then the Croatian delegates also took their leave from the congress.

CHAPTER TWO

The Road to War

With the flames of nationalist destruction reduced to an ember in Kosovo, sparks were drifting across other areas of Yugoslavia like uncontrollable forest fires. The collapse of communism in the two largest federations of Serbia and Croatia had brought about a sudden wave of nationalism; Milošević being the first to inflame that nationalism.

On Palm Sunday 1990, the newly elected President of Croatia, Franjo Tuđman, addressed a rally in Croatia's capital Zagreb. In his address he seemed to compare himself with our dear Lord Jesus Christ, when he said, "On this day Christ triumphantly came to Jerusalem, he was greeted as the messiah. Today our capital is the New Jerusalem. Franjo Tuđman has come to his people."

Tuđman's arguably insensitive speech only further infuriated the Serb population in Croatia. In the dusty Croatian railway town of Knin, the police force was run by the Serbs; and it was here that those sparks of tension finally lit the fuse of war...

The Serbs had raw memories of last Nationalist to take rule of Croatia. The Croats had been allies of Adolf Hitler's during World War II, and they were therefore responsible for the deaths of over 100,000 Serbs. When Tuđman spoke of nationalism in Zagreb, kissed and embraced the Croat checkerboard flag, it was like waving the Nazi swastika in the face of the Serbian people.

After the televised celebrations of Tuđmans election speech, a Serb police inspector named Milan Martić was so outraged he felt the time had finally come to protect Serb interests in Knin. At a meeting with Serb activists, Martić said, "We serve the Serb people; we will not obey this vile Croat government."

When Tuđman witnessed the unrest on television he sent his ministers down to Knin to deal with the rebel police, seeing that the situation bore all the hallmarks of the recent problems in Kosovo. The Mayor of Knin, Milan Babić, was also a Serb, as well as a dentist in the town; but I would be very surprised if many Croat's attended his surgery after the unrest in Knin!

The Mayor prepared a reception committee for the Croat ministers. It was not to be a friendly welcome, in fact he ordered his Serb party activists to rally people in the streets hoping to intimidate the ministers from Zagreb. Perica Jurić, the Croatian Interior Minister, tried to quell the unrest in Knin. At a meeting with the police and the Serb party activist he said, "Every policeman has the right to his own political views."

After he had finished speaking there were furious replies came at him from all directions. It was clear to Jurić that it was not just the police protesting about the nationalist approach in Zagreb, but the whole Serb nation. The ministers were getting more worried as the meeting progressed, they could hear the restless crowd yelling outside.

Jurić's colleagues talked amongst themselves. There was a whisper of *promise them anything to get us out of here in one piece*. They feared there was a lynch mob amassing outside and, without the help of the police, the Serbs of Knin would never have let them out alive. The Police Chief and Mayor got great satisfaction seeing the ministers from Zagreb squirm for their lives. The Police Chief joked, *I believe Percia Jurić went to the toilet about ten times in the couple of hours the ministers were here, perhaps it was something he ate*. The Police Chief and the Mayor had turned the protest outside into a full rebellion. That was the end of Croat authority in Knin.

The Police Chief was given the task of building up the defence force in Knin, he wanted to arm the police, or at least get the protection of the Yugoslav Army. For the Serb revolt to be successful in Knin they would need the support of Belgrade, the capital of Serbia and Yugoslavia. Milošević was more than happy to stoke the flames of unrest in Croatia. Knin's rebel Mayor, Babić, had become a frequent visitor to Belgrade, wanting Milošević to provide military support for a revolution in Knin.

In 1990 Serbia held the chairmanship of the Yugoslav State Council, and the State Council had the power to give orders to the Army. The chairman, Borisav Jović, was a very close friend to Milošević and was duly appointed to take care of *the situation in Knin*. The Serb population in Croatia demanded the Council take action to stop Croatia going independent. The last time Croatia had gone independent was under the Nazis in World War II; a period in which they had committed mass genocide against the Serbs – with that in mind we could perhaps understand their fears.

Federal Police Minister, Peter Gračanin, advised the Knin delegation in Belgrade how they could organize their rebellion. He told them to put up barricades and to get hold of what weapons they could, so that they could patrol the streets day and night and guard against attacks from *the fascists who run Croatia*. Babić did not get a specific promise of help from Belgrade; but it was left in no doubt that the capital would do whatever possible to protect the Serbs in Croatia.

The Serb delegation returned to Knin to set their next plan in action, and they were armed with much more than just advice from Belgrade. The Serbs in Knin began to set up roadblocks, television networks from Belgrade quick to play on the fears of their Serb brothers. There were televised interviews of Serb policeman saying they were scared, and *we*

Serbs must protect ourselves because we have learnt from the past… we must stop history repeating itself.

The crisis in Knin came at the height of the tourist season. Tourism was a vital source of income for the Croat Government and the Serbs had deliberately blocked the vital road and rail links that supplied the Croatian holiday resorts of Split and Dubrovnik.

Franjo Tuđman, the President of Croatia, was about to open the European Athletic Championships in the Croatian town of Split. However, with the unrest spreading at a rapid pace, a lot of damage could be done to the credibility of Croatia as a holiday destination. The President faced a dilemma: should he act against the rebellious Serbs in Knin? He could face the mighty wrath the Yugoslav Army marching against him and Croatia. Inevitably he ordered the Croat police to send special forces that would disarm the rebel Serb police in the city.

Interior Minister, Perica Jurić, had travelled to Knin with colleagues to negotiate a peaceful settlement. He was given the task to organize helicopters to fly special forces to Knin and restore law and order, feeling it was his duty and right after he and his colleagues had been humiliated at the Congress earlier that year. The rebellion began spreading like wildfire when the Serb rebels knew they had support from Belgrade.

President Tuđman knew if he did not act his country would be overrun by Serb rebels, so he gave the final order. Three police helicopters crammed with special forces took off from Zagreb to rendezvous with ground units and launch an attack on the rebel Serbs. Air traffic control was told that the helicopters would be carrying equipment and supplies to the holiday resorts of Split and Dubrovnik, but within ten minutes after take-off they received an anonymous tip-off about the operation the airborne helicopters were really planned for. Air traffic control alerted the Yugoslav Army informing them about the airborne helicopters and the planned assault on the rebel Serbs in Knin.

11

General Andrija Rašeta of the Yugoslav Army was ordered to scramble two MiG Jet fighters to intercept the helicopters and order them to return to their base, or they would be shot down. The MiG jets flew effortlessly over and around the three helicopters, demonstrating to the occupiers that it would be all too easy to shoot them down. One of the MiG pilots radioed to the helicopter commanders the threat of what would happen should they choose not to return home. Intimidated, the helicopters returned to Zagreb.

President Tuđman was furious at the Yugoslav Army's intervention; it was becoming clear that their support lay with the rebels in Knin and there was more to this crisis than met the eye. The President telephoned the head of the Yugoslav State Council, Borisav Jović, in a rage. "This is a catastrophe!" he roared, accusing the Yugoslav State Council of undermining a democratically elected body, and demanding to know if the State Council was trying to overthrow Croatia's government.

Jović denied any part in a conspiracy against Croatia, telling President Tuđman that the State Council had not ordered the helicopters to return to base. He assured Tuđman that air traffic control had ordered the helicopters to return to Zagreb for technical reasons. Round one to the Serbs.

The Serbs had claimed an area of Knin as their own mini Serbia, declaring it as a no-go area for the Croats. Croat television dubbed the rebellion in Knin as the *revolution of the logs*, referring to the Serb log roadblocks, and made cartoon characters portraying Serb rebels as stupid drunken louts. It was an attempt to laugh off the situation in Knin and mock the Serb rebels, but it was no laughing matter for President Tuđman. He had been elected to rebuild and restore Croat pride, but the Serbs were making a fool of him, and there was not a lot he could do about it. That was until a Croat Government minister called General Špegelj approached the President, warning him that Croatia would need to act if they were to save their pride and dignity. However, it seemed the President had no chance of getting support or weapons from the Yugoslav Army in order to protect his people. *We must find other means to arm our Police*, agreed President Tuđman as he gave the general authorization to make the necessary enquiries.

Špegelj approached the US Ambassador, Warren Zimmermann, asking for weapons to improve the police force in Croatia. However, as an Ambassador for the entire Yugoslavian nation, Zimmerman did not hesitate to recommend to Washington that they refuse the order for weapons. Arming the Croatian police force would only lead to the weapons being used to suppress the Serbs.

Therefore General Špegelj took his business elsewhere, approaching Budapest to make a deal with Hungary. Croatia bought a consignment of weapons and, when the cheque had cleared, they sent two lorries to collect the weapons from Budapest.

The head of Intelligence for the Yugoslav Army, General Aleksandar Vasiljević, had received a tip-off through authorities at the border; it was suspected an attempt to smuggle arms into Croatia was about to take place. General Vasiljević placed a surveillance team in place at the border but when two lorries arrived he could not be sure if they were carrying arms. However, his suspicions were raised when he saw that senior Croat police officials had gathered at the border in force to ensure the lorries got through. Prompting Yugoslav Military Intelligence to begin a major operation to discover who was behind the smuggling at the Yugoslav/Hungarian border.

Army agents started asking questions in Budapest. Aggressive measures were being taken against the Croats. A concerned government minister in Croatia called Slavko Degoricija said, "If we can't bring arms into Croatia by plane, ship, or lorry then we must use private cars," and that is exactly what they did! Although some were caught, more than enough got through. Only the Army of the Yugoslav Federation would be capable of stopping the Croats.

A display of force was televised throughout Yugoslavia to remind the people not to mess with the Serbs. The Yugoslavian High Command had to face the fact that the Croatian Government was equipping itself to form a rival army. Admiral Branko Mamula, advisor to the Yugoslav Defence Minister, said, "It is our duty to act against the arms smuggling of any State, this is a rebellion against Yugoslavia, an internationally recognized nation."

The problem was that these arms smugglers were the democratically elected government of Croatia. It would be politically dangerous to arrest them. The Yugoslav Military Intelligence decided not to act, but to observe the situation on a daily basis.

In the beginning of January 1991 an order was issued throughout the federation, although its intended recipients had been the Croats. It read: *All illegally held weapons must be handed in within ten days*.

Croatian ministers were openly defiant against the order, Stjepan 'Stipe' Mesić said, "What are we to do? Part of Croatia is in rebellion. Should we import two lorry loads of pens? Then we could write letters to the Serbs in our country asking them not to attack us. No chance, I have a message for the Serbs. The Croat flag will soon fly again in Knin!"

Stipe Mesić then phoned Belgrade and spoke to the chairman of the Yugoslav State Council Borisav Jović. He requested that Jović write down the following ultimatum, in case the State Council failed to receive the strong feelings of the Croat Government. He went on to say, "If the Yugoslav State Council did not back down and withdraw the order of giving up weapons:

"(1) Croatia would recede.

"(2) They would ask the United Nations to intervene.

"(3) They would walk out of all aspects of the Federation."

Jović scoffed, "These arms smugglers had the cheek to ask for UN protection, this could lead to war."

Fear swept through Zagreb, crowds rallied in the capital's main square and prayed for peace believing they were about to be attacked by the whole Yugoslav Army. President Tuđman called an emergency session of his parliament. He said, "The use of force against Croatia will be treated as a threat to our republic. We will view any attempt to repress Croatia as an act of enemy occupation."

During the session an invitation arrived from Belgrade; Tuđman and Stipe Mesić were asked to attend a meeting of the Yugoslav State Council and the Yugoslav Army Leadership.

The Croatian President's ministers were in tears, begging him not to travel to Belgrade, as rumors had spread claiming if the President and Mesić went to Belgrade they would be arrested. Tuđman was insistent when he said, "We have no choice. I must go to Belgrade to negotiate a peaceful settlement to this national crisis."

He was confident that even if he was thrown in prison, or murdered, it would prove to the world that Belgrade and the Serbs were attacking freedom of speech and democracy in Croatia.

The Yugoslav State Council was the highest and most powerful authority in Yugoslavia. It was also the only body able to give the order for the Yugoslav Army to act against Croatia should they refuse to hand over their illegal weapons. On the evening of the 25th January 1991, the Yugoslav State Council met to decide Croatia's fate; each of the Republics would have a chance to vote. Croat Council member, Stipe Mesić, arrived in Belgrade for the meeting before his President; although he could well have been testing the water to see how dangerous his road was in Belgrade. Due to this the meeting began without the Croatian President.

Mesić immediately rejected all proposals requesting Croatia to conform to the Yugoslavs' State Council's wishes. For some of the Council members it was obvious the

Yugoslav Army would have to be sent into Croatia; yet for others it was not that clear cut. The Council members continued to argue late into the night.

The head of the Yugoslav Military Command then made a request for a break in the meeting, which the Council members agreed to. Apart from the Serb Chairman, the rest of the Council members were not aware that the break had been called to deceive them into watching the evening news on television. The State Council, along with the rest of Yugoslavia, found themselves watching a news broadcast showing footage of the chief Croat arms buyer, General Špegelj, discussing terrorist organizations within Croatia – footage that had been recorded without either of the participant's knowledge. General Špegelj, who was talking to two men in the film, was witnessed saying, "In this military district the Yugoslav Army have 9,000 officers, they also have 18,000 soldiers that cover Slovenia, Croatia, and parts of Bosnia. We now have 80,000 men armed with Kalashnikovs."

The Yugoslav Military Intelligence having made the film had also intercut the footage with statements from the Croatian President where he denied that Croatia had been smuggling weapons illegally; which contradicted what General Špegelj had previously said in the film. Even more damning, the General Špegelj went on to say, "You have got to understand we are at war with the Yugoslav Army."

After watching the news the State Council members reconvened, only now you could cut the atmosphere with a knife! The Council Chairman, Borisav Jović, reveling in the discomfort that Croat Council member Stipe Mesić was now feeling. The rest of the Council members were numb with disbelief; they had just witnessed what appeared to be evidence of Croatia's elected participants plotting treason. In an attempt to soft soap them, Mesić admitted some bits of the film might be genuine, but he insisted the majority of the film had been doctored in order to discredit the Croat Government. With modern technology anything was possible. He went on

16

to suggest the film was a plot to overthrow the government and should be disregarded completely.

When President Tuđman finally arrived at the meeting, instead of responding to the much talked about film, he issued a warning to the Defence Minister – *the General would have to answer for any bloodshed*. Tuđman and the Serb Council members were at one another's throats until the early hours. The Serbs thought the film would make the Croat Government back down, and cause the Croat people to disown Tuđman and his government. After a very long and tiring debate the Yugoslav Military Intelligence tactics seemed to work; President Tuđman made a promise to the State Council that he would allow the Yugoslav Army access to arrest anyone implicated in the smuggling of arms in Croatia.

Tuđman returned to Zagreb a very tired man. When he spoke to the media he was not sure how his people would receive him after seeing the incriminating film. He did not disclose the promise he made whilst in Belgrade, instead choosing to ensure them that *the Croat people can sleep peacefully and will not wake up to find tanks in their streets*. However, when Tuđman came to give his address to the people in Zagreb Square, he was in for the surprise of his life. His people's fear of attack had given way to nationalist celebration. The people chanted *we will not give up Croatia*!

Safely on home ground Tuđman withdrew the promise he had made in Belgrade, and passed a law giving his ministers immunity against any arrest for arms smuggling. In the meantime General Špegelj, who had been seen *plotting treason*, made an appearance on Croat television to defend himself and answer questions regarding the contents of the film – stating that footage in question was a *total fabrication*. Although, on leaving the television studio, the General set out to discover who had given him away. Only two people could have betrayed him: one was a man he trusted totally; and the other was a close family friend. He had been filmed whilst trying to persuade two Yugoslav Army officers to steal weapons for Croatia. One of them, though a Croat and a close family friend, had decided to put the interests of the Yugoslavian nation before the needs of his home state. He had hidden a video camera inside his television set to film and record the meeting that took place with General Špegelj. The rest was history after Yugoslav Military Intelligence got hold of the film and overdubbed their own version of events.

Television makers in Croatia embarked on a campaign to mock the Serb nationalist movement, once again depicting them as stupid in cartoons. Certain characters were amusingly animated sawing the branches off trees whilst sitting on the same branch; and the Croats got away with it, at least for the time being.

President Milošević had now declared himself as the guardian of Yugoslavia. He persuaded the generals of the Yugoslav Army to mobilize themselves in readiness to disarm Croatia, but they would require an order from the State Council representing all the republics before they could march on Croatia.

At the same time that the State Council was due to meet, to discuss the possible intervention of the Yugoslav Army in Croatia, there was a demonstration in Belgrade led by students wanting more freedom of speech for the press. It was this demonstration that provided Milošević with a chance to impress upon the State Council how the Yugoslav Army could be used to quash growing unrest. Despite the demonstration being peaceful, Milošević chose to see it otherwise. He called Borisav Jović and told him there was chaos in the streets of Belgrade, going on to suggest they might need to use the army to restore public order. Milošević knew he could rely on his most trusted friend to get the Yugoslav Army involved in the situation, and also with a view to using the Yugoslav Army in Croatia. He was also aware that his close friend was the State Council Chairman and he could persuade fellow members to vote in favour for the use of military force, except those from Slovenia and Croatia. Unfortunately for him, the Chairman was not having much luck in persuading the Council members to endorse the use of the army. In fact the Council felt the student demonstration was very peaceful and any military intervention would cause unwanted trouble in the capital.

Milošević decided to take drastic measures to persuade the State Council that the Army needed to be involved, sending in the police ordering them to use tear gas on the protestors. The demonstration quickly descended into mayhem as police and demonstrators fought in the streets of Belgrade. Now that the protest had gotten *out of control*, the Chairman was able to get the majority of his fellow State Council members to vote in favour of using the Army to prevent further protests or vandalism in the city. The Yugoslav Army Chief of Staff, General Blagoje Adžić, phoned the Serb police minister to tell him *when the Army arrives send in your police... order them to attack the demonstrators, go for them, and beat them until you're exhausted!*

Milošević appeared on television to justify the intervention of the Yugoslav Army. He said, "Today in Belgrade our biggest asset was in danger, the threat to peace. Serbia will use all legal means to oppose the forces of chaos."

Now here was a man who was prepared to make an example out of his own people, just to show the Croats that he was not a man to be messed with. Milošević had got the army tanks out of the barracks once, now he could take the next step by deploying them in Croatia.

Chairman Jović went on television to announce to all the other Council members that there would be a meeting of the Presidency Supreme Command; although the Slovene Council member refused to attend. The Croat Council member, Stipe Mesić, felt it his duty to attend if he was to have any hope of talking to his fellow Council members around to Croatia's point of view in the whole situation. When the Council members arrived they were escorted to military buses. They were told that the meeting had been moved to Army Headquarters, but some Council members felt this was merely a ploy to intimidate them, and to make them see it was a very serious situation. Only the Serb Chairman and the Minister of

Defence knew what was going on as the Council members arrived for the meeting on the 12th March 1991.

Chairman Jović called on the Yugoslav Defence Minister, General Veljko Kadijević, to address the Council members and to put forward his proposal. "An insidious plan has been uncovered to destroy Yugoslavia," he announced. "Stage one is civil war. Stage two is foreign intervention, and Stage three is puppet regimes being set up throughout Yugoslavia."

The minister went on to propose a nationwide state of emergency, but Croat Council member Mesić was not prepared to accept the proposal. He knew that using the Yugoslav Army was just Milošević's way to enlarge Serbia, and that would mean war. Mesić desperately tried to bring the generals back to reality, wanting to make them see the crisis was not all the fault of Croatia. The Defence Minister replied, "If you don't order action you will destroy the federation."

The moment of decision had come.

Chairman Jović required the support of five out of the eight voting members. The voting procedure did not follow that of a secret ballot; instead each member in turn would say *Yes* or *No* to the proposal. The tension around the large circular table, as each member cast their vote, was palpable.

The first two votes registered *No* against the proposal of action against Croatia, but the next two votes registered *Yes* for action. With voting poised at 2–2 it began to look like a tense football match as the voting carried on like a see-saw, 3–2, 3–3. Eventually the vote was almost balanced with those in favour of action: 4; those against: 3. The Serb Chairman required a *Yes* vote from the last voting member, Bogić Bogićević, the Bosnian Council member. Bogić was Serb, but he represented a Bosnian population made up from Muslims, Croats and Serbs. In the event of a civil war breaking out in Yugoslavia, it would be Bosnia who would stand to lose and suffer the most. In mind of this he told his fellow Council members, "It is my duty to prevent civil war at any price and I feel this crucial proposal should be discussed in more depth before voting."

The Chairman was getting very frustrated with Bogić. He started shouting, "What is your problem? Vote just vote!" and there was a deadly silence as they waited for Bogićević to vote. Finally he replied, "At this moment in time, this proposal is counter-productive, therefore I am voting against the proposal."

Final whistle 4–4. The disgruntled chairman closed the meeting, with Bosnia having prevented Milošević from using the Yugoslav Army against Croatia; but Milošević was always one step ahead of everyone else in his game of cat and mouse. He later announced on television that *Serbia* would be *withdrawing its members from the State Council.*

He went on to say, "Serbia used to think the State Council did its job properly, this illusion is now dead. It's better to face the truth than delude ourselves."

Milošević was now trying to destroy the supreme authority in Yugoslavia, which controlled the High Command of the Yugoslav Army. The High Command could say that they no longer had a civilian authority commander, which would allow them to take the decision to disarm the Croats. That was the formula Milošević needed to give him carte blanche to launch a war against Croatia, but it was unsure how the West might react to a move like this.

Borisav Jović called for a meeting with the US Ambassador, Warren Zimmermann. Zimmerman made it very clear to Jović that the West was very anxious that force not be used in Croatia. To which Jović replied, "Does all the states in the USA have their own Army?? Therefore how can you tolerate each of our federation having their own Army in Yugoslavia ? That being the case, how can you expect us not to react when the Croats are trying to build their own Army?"

Jović came away from the meeting with the Ambassador aware that there would be direct pressure on the Yugoslav authorities, and a possible intervention from the Western powers, if civil war were to break out in Yugoslavia.

Chairman Jović consulted with the General Kadijević and between them they decided to go to Moscow to seek support for their planned action. Whilst in Moscow Jović and the minister met secretly with the hard-line communists who ran the Soviet Ministry of Defence. He asked, "If Yugoslavia were to take action against Croatia by force in order to seize illegal weapons, would Russia defend us even if the West intervened?"

The Soviet Defence Minister gave Jović a secret document, containing information from intelligence reports, which showed that the Yugoslav Army could safely ignore Western warnings regarding intervention in Yugoslavia. Confident they could now act in complete safety, Milošević and Jović returned to the Yugoslav military headquarters, ready to launch the military action they had planned together.

At the State Council meeting just under a week earlier the Defence Minister, General Kadijević, had made his intentions very clear when he said, "If the State Council do not order us into action, we will act on our own merit," but, now that the time had finally come to act, his fellow conspirators were in for a nasty shock.

When he was approached and briefed on the forthcoming action against Croatia the General hesitated, starting to make excuses and looking for reasons not to take action against Croatia. His main concern was the reaction from the West, and the possibility that his military intervention would be seen as a coup, which he feared would make the crisis in Yugoslavia worse. In his heart he wanted to save Yugoslavia, but would not use the army to do so – it was more than his conscience could bear. For these reasons he could not give the order for the Army to march on Croatia.

Once again a twisted turn in events caused a checkmate against Milošević; except this time it had been his own general who was turning out to be all mouth and no action, dashing his plans. Over the next few weeks President Tuđman openly flaunted the new weapons in his rebel Army's possession. A mass parade of military strength took place in Zagreb and President Tuđman told his Army that *Croatia was embarking on the road to independence, and the troops at this parade should know that the Croat nation will rise as one if we have to defend our sovereignty.*

On the 15th April 1991 Milošević seemed to accept the inevitable. He called for a summit with Tuđman to work out how to carve up Yugoslavia between them; but this was a summit of ill intentions. Once again Milošević was just playing political games with Tuđman and the Serb leader had other, more insidious plans.

Milošević decided to change his tactics, deploying troops in the Serb areas of Croatia, anticipating his actions would provoke the Croats to war – through which he could trample them and take over those tempestuous territories. Two weeks later all hell broke loose and the war began in Croatia. Unfortunately good and innocent civilians often suffer when mighty armies intend on killing not only each other. They feel they have the right to take away the chance of life given by God to women and children. No cause on earth is worth that...

CHAPTER THREE

War of Independence

The Republic of Croatia had declared itself independent from Yugoslavia, alone it pleaded to the world for recognition. Croatia's President Tuđman declared, "We call on all parliamentary democracies to recognise the will of the Croat people to join the society of free and independent nations."

Behind their smiles, Croatia's leaders were nervous that Serbia, Yugoslavia's biggest republic, would crush them and their ambition to leave the federation.

The neighbouring republic of Slovenia also declared independence on the same day. Though the Slovenes were more daring, immediately removing Yugoslav customs officials from their borders with Italy and Austria. *Yet could Yugoslavia let its richest and most western republic go without a fight?*

On the 26th June 1991 Slovenian President, Milan Kučan, inspected the military parade, yet always aware he might soon have to use his troops to defend Slovenia. When President Kučan returned home after the ceremony he started to write his speech for the Congress that would be meeting the following day. He was interrupted by a telephone call from his aide, and was informed that Yugoslav Army tanks were on the move in Slovenia. Milan Kučan contacted General Rašeta demanding an explanation as to why tanks were active in Slovenia so early in the morning? General Rašeta reassured the President that the Yugoslav Army had no plans to attack and that he had been misinformed regarding the tanks – yet tanks *were* on the move in Slovenia.

President Kučan summoned his cabinet to the Presidential Offices to decide whether to fight the Yugoslav Army. Kučan informed his cabinet of the possibility that war with the remaining Yugoslavian nation could be on their doorstep, but he was not sure if Slovenia was prepared for military action.

The President's cabinet sat at the table with their heads bowed. The Minister of Defence, Janez Janša, said of the meeting, "*We could not look each other in the eye. Nobody said a word.*"

The Slovene Police Minister, Igor Bavčar, commented, "*It felt like an eternity, but the silence lasted just a few minutes. None of the ministers wanted to commit themselves to the crisis that Slovenia could be facing. The President proposed the republic of Slovenia would take all necessary measures to defend our independence against the Yugoslav Army.*"

The Cabinet backed the President's proposal, although they were not aware that the Yugoslavian Army's intentions had only been to regain the border posts that Slovenia had assumed charge of.

The Yugoslav Army did not expect any resistance and so deployed 2,000 untried conscripts who were split up into smaller groups for their tasks. What should have been a formality for the Yugoslav Army units turned into a nightmare with Slovenia having mobilized over 35,000 police and militia.

The Yugoslav Army had completely miscalculated the situation, putting their 2,000 *raw* recruits in a vulnerable situation. Their troops depended on supplies, their barracks and ports were separated from their stores. The Slovene Army cut off all their supply routes by blocking every major road in the country. Thousands of Yugoslav troops relied on the Slovene infrastructure and were now trapped in their barracks without supplies; and with a giant Slovenian army surrounding them.

A day before the Yugoslav Army had been there to protect the Slovenes, yet just twenty-four hours later they were hostages. On television, one such Yugoslav soldier was interviewed at his post:

Reporter, "How are you?"

Soldier, "How the hell do you think I am?"

Reporter, "Do you understand your assignment?"

Soldier, "All I know is that they keep shooting at us."

Reporter, "Who is shooting at you?"

Soldier, "The Slovene's, who do you think?"

Reporter, "What is the conflict about?"

Soldier, "Supposedly Slovenia are trying to secede from Yugoslavia and we are trying to stop them."

Yugoslav Colonel Milan Aksentijević had served in Slovenia for forty years. He watched helplessly as his dedicated life's work was shattered within twenty-four hours. The Colonel said, "We were completely wrong-footed. I could not believe a Slovene soldier would shoot at my men or me. I thought the country we all served was invincible. It is now obvious that I was naive."

The Colonel spoke with a dying passion, and it was clear to see that the crisis was breaking his heart. The Yugoslav Army tried to push through the Slovene barricades with tanks, but no sooner had they cleared one barricade another would spring somewhere along the same road. They began airlifting supplies by helicopter to aid the encircled soldiers, but the Slovenes threw down another the gauntlet. Police Minister, Igor Bavčar, said, "I could not have made it any clearer to the Yugoslav Army Generals. You fly your helicopter over our capital and we will be forced to shoot it down."

The Yugoslav Army ignored the Slovene threat and sent in their helicopter with supplies anyway. Colonel Aksentijević recalled, "The moment our helicopter was hit we heard the explosion, we felt it hit the ground. The pilot, who lay dead amongst the twisted wreckage, was a Slovene serving in the

Yugoslav Army. That was a very harsh blow and that was the moment I realised it was all over for Slovenia to be a part of Yugoslavia."

Milan Kučan had a surprise meeting with Serbian President, Slobadan. Kučan told Milošević that it would be better if Slovenia left Yugoslavia, being allowed to secede from the Union. However, in return the Serb President made Kučan a tempting offer. Milošević was prepared to agree to Slovenia leaving Yugoslavia, if Kučan agreed to support Milošević in allowing Serbs all over Yugoslavia to secede from *their* republic and rejoin the Serb motherland.

Milošević took Kučan by the arm in a way of reassurance, to let Kučan know that he could trust him. Except Kučan did not trust Milošević. Jokingly Kučan said, "Give Milošević your finger and he will take your arm off, so you cannot ever relax and trust him."

Milošević told Kučan, "We both know what is going to happen. You Slovenes want to leave Yugoslavia so let's make a deal. We can re-write the constitution, and extend the right to secede not just to the republics, but to all ethnic groups throughout Yugoslavia." Yet Kučan felt he could not risk everything on a mere verbal promise from Milošević.

The crisis in Yugoslavia was beginning to cause a great deal of concern throughout Europe. In Luxemburg European Community (EC) leaders attended a summit meeting. They were keen to show they could handle the trouble in their own back yard without intervention from America. The Slovenian pilot who lost his life carrying bread to feed the hungry soldiers, put the crisis in Yugoslavia at the top of their agenda. The EC sent three foreign ministers on a rescue mission to persuade Croatia and Slovenia to reconsider their ambitions for independence, if only for the sake of peace in Yugoslavia. The ministers hoped the rebel republics would listen to reason in return for international recognition at a later date. The Foreign Minister from Italy, Gianni De Michelis, supported Croatia and Slovenia's declarations of independence; but that support meant nothing without the EC's formal recognition.

De Michelis suggested a cooling-off period of three months before talks officially began for independence.

Since Slovenia was now classed as a *war zone*, the meeting was held in Croatia, despite it being just as much of a war zone and no more safe than Slovenia. Gianni De Michelis said, "It was bizarre, President Tuđman was making his international debut, he expected us for dinner but we did not arrive until three a.m. Nevertheless, Tuđman was determined to make a good impression and play the perfect host, so at three a.m. we all sat down to a full state dinner. Manners would have been better served if he had allowed his guests to have a good night's sleep followed by lunch the following day, but in the early hours of the morning the courses kept coming. There was propriety, ceremony and etiquette, and yet we had a crisis on our hands. When the Slovene President arrived the atmosphere changed. European opinion had made President Kučan the eye of the storm. Kučan looked nervous; he could not face all the food at that time of the morning. He had not slept for days, and it showed."

Kučan had talks with European ministers on other occasions before the meeting in Zagreb Croatia. Jacques Poos, European minister for Luxemburg, asked Kučan, "Are you feeling unwell?"

Kučan replied, "How can I be well, my Country is at war."

However, the EC ministers soon had something to celebrate. The Slovenes agreed to a ceasefire and to negotiations on the future of the republics. The EC ministers began patting one another on the back, albeit prematurely; they had reason to believe they had stopped the war in Yugoslavia. Within a couple of days the Yugoslav Army and the Slovenes resumed the fighting and the Yugoslav soldiers were bearing the brunt of it.

Colonel Aksentijević felt the position of the Yugoslav Army in Slovenia had become intolerable. He decided the time had come to make his feelings known at headquarters. He approached the general on duty to ask, "What is going on?

Are we an Army or not? Do something to support your troops, our boys are being killed and we are losing helicopters. If we are the Yugoslav Army we should act, if we are not we should retreat."

A decision had to be made back in Belgrade. The Minister of Defence proposed to the State Council that they launch a massive military attack. Branko Kostić, Yugoslav State Council member for Montenegro, asked the Defence Minister, "What do you mean, a massive attack on Slovenia?"

The Defence Minister replied, "We would use the Air Force , artillery and tanks to bring Slovenia to its knees." The head of Army Intelligence, General Vasiljević said, "We could take absolute control in twenty-four hours, and we would make all the necessary arrests; but we must expect heavy casualties."

The State Council members were about to authorize military action on a large scale against Slovenia. All they required was the support from their most powerful republic: Serbia. Yet the Council was in for a big shock in this unpredictable see-saw of a conflict. Serb Council Chairman, Borisav Jović, said, "I will put it bluntly. We did not want a war with Slovenia. Serbia had no territorial claims in Slovenia, and it was an ethnically pure republic with very few Serbs living in Slovenia. Serbia could not care less if Slovenia left Yugoslavia, and I propose that the Yugoslav Army be withdrawn from Slovenia to the new border."

The State Council members looked at each other with extreme amazement and were lost for words. This was a bolt out of the blue. Once again the Serb regime changed course in their unpredictable political stance. Perhaps the Slovene President could have trusted Milošević after all…

The head of Army Intelligence, General Vasiljević, could not believe his ears saying, "We are soldiers you know, that was an order from our supreme command not a proposal. But it is not for me to argue."

Reluctantly General Vasiljević carried out the order and withdrew the Yugoslav Army from Slovenia, thus putting an end to the conflict in Slovenia, as Serbia's ambitions lay elsewhere.

Milošević and his friend Jović were in agreement that the Yugoslav Army would have been overstretched fighting in Slovenia and Croatia, not to mention the prize of Bosnia, which was always present in the back of Serbia's collective political mind. With the Slovenes out of the way, they could dictate terms to the Croats. The Serb President had now laid his cards on the table and asserted his legitimate interest in Croatia.

Italy's foreign minister, Gianni De Michelis, recalled the night Milošević had a private meeting with him. He said, "I remember Milošević being very forthright in the way he viewed the crisis in Yugoslavia. He told me Croatia couldn't just walk out of Yugoslavia as 600,000 Serbs live in Croatia. If we grant the Croat people the right to leave Yugoslavia then they cannot deny others the right to make their own choice. If the Serbs wanted to stay in Yugoslavia, then the 600,000 Serbs and their land in Croatia must become part of Serbia, or we will not let the Croats leave Yugoslavia without a fight."

In the Croatian town of Vakovar, close to the Serbian border, was where the real war for Yugoslavia would begin. Serb nationalists had already seized control of a dozen Croat villages, it was their intention to link them together across the border as a way extend the Serbia territory well into Croatia. To do this the Serbs would expel the Croats from these villages and claim the land as part of Serbia, and this *pure Serb mini state* would then join the motherland. This was the first step to a new Yugoslavia run by Serbia whose borders would expand deep into Croatia and Bosnia. Extremist allies of Milošević set about provoking a conflict between Serbs and Croats.

Serb nationalist leader, Vojislav Šešelj, addressed a rally saying, "We Serbs are in danger. Croat fascist hordes attacked women and children!"

In 1991 Serb nationalist leaders launched a massive campaign to recruit volunteers, who would then be sent to the *danger zone* in eastern Croatia. The man whose job it was to stop such intrusion was the east Croat Police Chief, Josip Reihl-Kir. He commanded 1,000 armed men – Croatia's only military force in the eastern district. Although, Josip Reihl-Kir refused to take the path of confrontation, doing all he could to make sure Serbs and Croats went on living and working together in peace. Whenever the Serbs put up a roadblock Josip Reihl-Kir would drive to the roadblock, get out of his car and open his coat to reveal to the rebel Serbs that he was unarmed. Usually he was able to persuade them to take down the roadblock, but Josip Reihl-Kir had an opponent in the local party leader. The Croat party leader was as extreme as any of the extremist in Serbia and he did not like the *softly, softly* approach that Josip Reihl-Kir had adopted.

Reihl-Kir's wife, Jadranka, said of him, "Our party boss showed up at the police station with a delegation of government ministers from Zagreb. They told my husband to take them to Borovo Selo. Borovo Selo is a suburb of Vukovar, the main city on the Croatia bank of the Dunar. It was a prime target for the Serb nationalists. In the city the population was a mix of Croats and Serbs, but the suburb was mostly Serb, and the Serb extremists erected barricades to keep the Croats out. My husband had to drive through thick fog to take the party leader and the ministers to Borovo Selo. When they arrived his passengers started to unload some boxes from the bank of my husband's car. My husband was shocked to see them assemble a rocket launcher."

Reihl-Kir was amazed when they fired three rockets into Borovo Selo. The first was on target, hitting a tractor being used as a roadblock. The second rocket veered off into a cornfield, and the third rocket hit a house in the town. This act of provocation had been committed by some of President Tudman's closest political partners.

Jadranka Reihl-Kir continued, "My husband was very concerned about the events in Borovo Selo, and decided to voice his disapproval to the Police Minister for Croatia, Josip Boljkovac. He told him about the attack in Borovo Selo, and asked who was responsible. The group was led by a man called Susak, who had recently returned from exile in Canada, a leader of the Croat Party's extremist wing. The Deputy Minister for Police was also present at the attack in Borovo Selo."

This midnight rocket attack did nothing to intimidate the Serbs in Borovo Selo, who looked to Belgrade for protection. The Serb nationalist leader was approached and asked to send volunteers and the Serbs in Borovo Selo demanded around-the-clock protection. Milošević's police gave the volunteers weapons.

The Serbs in the Vukovar suburb seized two unpopular Croat policeman when the Croats tried to hit back. Two buses heavily armed with Croat police drove confidently down the main street into the Serb stronghold, and straight into an ambush. Gunfire raged from the bus, and return fire could be heard hitting fiercely into the bus. It was touch and go for half an hour, before the Serb volunteers quashed the attack. The fight left twelve Croat policemen lying dead and twenty-two wounded.

The media were quick to report the events in the Vukovar suburb. That night Croatia exploded into an anti-Serb and anti-Yugoslavia fury. The crowds burned the Yugoslav flags, deeming these flags to be a symbol of Serbia. The crowd chanting *Croatia! Croatia! Croatia!* into the early hours of the morning. Croatian President, Franjo Tuđman, appeared on television announcing that, "In the light of this situation in Vukovar I have instructed the Minister of Police to mobilise police reservists into the crisis territories. We will defend every inch of Croatia."

As Croatia and Serbia slid towards an all-out war, the extremists took charge in the dwindling republic. A war party close to President Tuđman was determined to put an end to the peacekeeping efforts of their own Police Chief, Josip Reihl-Kir, and made it their mission to get rid of him. His wife, Jadranka, recalled her husband's fears. She said, "My husband went to see the Croat Police Minister to tell him he was at the end of his tether and that he felt he was finished. He asked the Minister to help him before he was killed. He requested a transfer to the capital where he was prepared to accept any job offered to him. The Minister told Josip to grow up and gave him a whisky to calm him down. Whilst my husband sipped his whisky he asked the Minister to save him. The Minister asked my husband, 'Who is after you?' My husband told the Minister, 'Since our last meeting' when he informed him of events in the rocket attack in Borovo Selo, other members of Tuđman's cabinet soon found out about his visit the office and felt the local party chief was now devising a way of getting rid of him. He also felt Susak, the leader of the Croat Parties extremist wing, was pulling the strings to eliminate him.

"The Police Minister agreed to transfer my husband to the capital. On the day my husband and I were about to leave for the capital he received a telephone call reporting a roadblock incident. My husband drove out to Tenja to calm the situation. He was lured to one of his own police checkpoints. The commander of the checkpoint was curiously absent from his post. A man called Gudely stood in my husband's way. Gudely pointed his Kalashnikov at my husband's car and fired his whole magazine into the car. My husband was hit with sixteen fatal bullets and murdered by his own people. That was his reward for all the months of hard work and effort keeping the peace between the Serbs and Croatia. His killer was a reserve policeman. The absurd thing was a couple of days earlier Gudely went to see my husband and asked to be issued with a weapon for protection on the police checkpoints. My husband issued him with a Kalashnikov. With that Kalashnikov he murdered my husband in cold blood."

Listening to this interview with Josip Reihl-Kirs' widow Jadranka was very emotional. We are all aware of the faces of good and evil in this world of ours. I pray to God that this man Josip Reihl-Kir be remembered for the good in his heart, and for trying to keep the peace between Serbia and Croatia. Josip

Reihl-Kir paid a heavy price for his actions, the ultimate sacrifice: his life.

God rest his soul…

Two days later, a column of tanks twenty miles long set off from Belgrade, heading straight for the Croat border. They flew the Yugoslav flag, but increasingly it was beginning to look like the personal army of the Serb President, Slobadan Milošević. The Yugoslav Army generals claimed that they were neutral peacekeepers, and their mission was to protect Serbs that lived in the Croatian countryside, but evidence showed otherwise. Despite this the Serb media backed them up their supposed *good intentions* with heavily biased reports. One such report on television showed a woman hanging out her washing with a Kalashnikov draped over her shoulder as she told the reporter, "The Croats are all over the place. I carry my gun for protection, even when I tend to my pigs. It is a crying shame, shame on the Croats."

One of the Yugoslav Army officers sent to the Croat boarder was Colonel Ratko Mladić – a butcher of human rights and ethnic cleanser who would later command the Serb army in Bosnia – to this day he is still wanted for war crimes and genocide in Bosnia. When he was interviewed on television, he used these worthless words, "I serve the Socialist Federated Republic of Yugoslavia. My brother officers and I protect all nations and nationalities"; but the Croats were soon to find out how uneven Mladić and his henchmen were.

When Mladić arrived at a small village near Knin called Kijevo, there was a Croat population blocking the road to Serb villages. The Croats in Kijevo refused to let the Serbs supply settlements, which lay just behind their village. Mladić ordered the area Serb commander, Milan Martić, to issue an ultimatum to the Croat police to relinquish their post in Kijevo or face an onslaught from the Yugoslav Army. When they refused Colonel Mladić ordered regular Yugoslav Army units into action, where they pounded the Croats into submission with air strikes and artillery.

Once again Mladić was interviewed on television where he said, "In Kijevo we fired on legitimate military targets. We did not destroy a single house simply for the sake of it."

Once the Yugoslav Army had completed their task, the local Serbs walked into Kijevo and there was nothing the Croats could do to stop them, they had been outgunned by the mighty Yugoslav Army. Several houses laying in ruin due to the bombardment, but the Yugoslav flag was raised in Kijevo with celebration from the Serbs, and the Yugoslav Army went on to seize Croat town after Croat town. The Serbs may have had the heavy guns, but were faced with a slight problem. The Yugoslav Army had barracks in most Croat towns, but when they arrived at these barracks they found them empty of supplies. Secretly Croats had besieged the camps and taken all of the supplies.

The Croats only had a small Army, so President Tuđman had to pick carefully the area in which to make a stand against the Serb/Yugoslav Army. He decided to protect Vukovar, and to the cities that lay directly behind it. If the Serbs walked into Vukovar it would be a disaster for Croatia, so they threw everything they had into defending it. The Yugoslav Army in Vukovar was mainly made up of conscripts, which had already been hit by a rush of desertions. Milošević bolstered the Yugoslav Army with his forces made up of gangs of nationalist thugs. The Serbs looked on Vukovar as the key stronghold for the Croat *fascists*; they were sure that *when Vukovar fell to the Serbs, the fascists would be finished.* The regime in Serbia was convinced these nationalist thug volunteers would play a big part in the fall of Vukovar, because they knew exactly what they were fighting for.

Serbia provided a barracks to train the volunteers and they did everything in their power to supply uniforms, weapons and transport to help the volunteers. The volunteers were made up ofcriminal gangs and fanatical Serbs who believed in nothing but the Serb cause. When these men were ready they would be sent to the front line. One such man was Dragoslav Bokan, he later went on to Croatia to teach Ideology, but for the meanwhile had ended up as a commander on the front line. He believed that since his country Serbia was at war, it was his duty as a Serb nationalist to fight against the Croat fascists. He said, "You must know where you stand. Are you a hero or a coward? Will the world look on you as a war criminal or a righteous warrior? Will your nation honour you or shame you as a deserter?"

When the Serb paramilitaries, better known as evil thugs, seized the village of Lochean in eastern Croatia, which had a population of 1,500, they left a gruesome calling card to serve as a warning to all Croats who dared stand in their way. When the Croat Army retook the village they found forty-eight civilians had been executed. They had been shot in the face and eyes, and some had been killed with an axe blow to the head. There was evidence found of people having been burnt alive. A brutal scene of bodies was left on display as a warning to the Croats.

The terror inflicted in Lochean was a calculated move aimed at driving the whole Croat population from the area, and it was here it became known as *ethnic cleansing*. Serbs were the chief perpetrators of this heinous crime but, in time, all sides of the war would have no value for innocent civilian life, not even of women and children.

The European Community had allowed three months to settle the crisis in Yugoslavia, and only two months had passed before violence had escalated. All six Yugoslav republics were summoned to talks aimed at solving the crisis.

At the talks President Milošević opened the debate stating, "The Yugoslav crises started with the Yugoslav brotherhood members wanting to leave the Federation of Yugoslavia first of Slovenia and then Croatia."

Croatian President, Franjo Tuđman, replied, "Croatia had every right to leave Yugoslavia because Serbia had torn up the constitution."

Lord Carrington, the British representative and an EC peace negotiator, could clearly see considerable difficulties in negotiations. He decided to have a meeting with the leaders that really mattered in the crisis, namely Tuđman and Milošević. He got them around the table and started talking to them about the future of Yugoslavia. Milošević insisted that, "If the Croats had the right to an independent state, then the Serbs had the right to make the same choice! Serbs in Croatia must have the right to join Serbia – equal treatment, human rights, and no discrimination. That is why Serbia supports the Serbs outside Serbia."

Lord Carrington asked Milošević *if he was prepared to accept the independence of Croatia.* Milošević agreed to Lord Carrington's proposal; just to make sure the President understood Lord Carrington's proposal, he was asked several times! Lord Carrington set out to turn this verbal agreement into a plan for all of the republics in Yugoslavia to live together in peace. But was Milošević serious about Lord Carrington's proposal?

The European foreign ministers were not sure. The Foreign Minister for Germany, Hans-Dietrich Genscher, said, "It was perfectly clear to me that the Serbs were buying time to prepare for their next onslaught."

The Germans had good reasons for their doubts. The Serbian generals were not impressed with the European Commission's peace plan; there was instant defiance as the Serbs began shelling the ancient Croatian city of Dubrovnik. When Milošević returned to Belgrade from The Hague, his generals offered him a quicker way to end the war and they had everything planned to the last detail.

It was their intention to seize Zagreb with a two-pronged attack. The Yugoslav Army General of Staff, Života Panić, said, "In forty-eight hours we could take Zagreb. That would be the end of Croatia."

Such an open campaign would carry the risks of sanctions against Serbia. Milošević called for a meeting with his war cabinet, which also included their allies from Montenegro.

The President of Montenegro, Momir Bulatović, said, "We could either accept the peace plan the EC was drafting or keep fighting and risk outside intervention."

Serbia's representative, Borisav Jović, said, "If we chose an all-out war with Croatia, they would call on Germany, Austria, Hungary and God knows who else for help. We do not have allies like that. Russia told us they could not help us if we go to war with Croatia."

Milošević made it clear the peace plan Lord Carrington was drawing up would allow Serbia to get what it wanted. Bulatović said, "When all was said and done it was obvious we had to accept the Carrington peace plan."

The peace plan proposed by Lord Carrington was the democratic attempt by the EC to tackle Yugoslavian problems. Had it been successful it might have averted the bloodshed to come, not only in Croatia, but in Bosnia also. Lord Carrington sent the draft peace plan to all the republican presidents of Yugoslavia prior to a conference. Carrington did not want any last minute surprises, so he opened the conference not long after he had issued the draft peace plan to presidents of each republic.

He gave President Milošević of Serbia the first chance to address his conference on the peace plan. After Milošević had read the final draft on behalf of Yugoslavia, it was evident that he was far from happy with the final peace plan. He objected to the draft proposal on the grounds of a *slight change to the verbal agreement* that had been accepted by the republics at an earlier meeting.   In this version of the draft it stated that all the republics would be granted sovereignty and independent status; which meant Milošević would lose his hold on the remaining republics, and the territories from those republics. Prior to this Milošević had verbally agreed to Croatia having their independence because he assumed he'd be reclaiming the parts of Croatia that belonged to the Serbs who presently lived there.

Milošević said, "Let me tell you, the documents put before us are absolutely unacceptable for Serbia. The reason is simple; if we sign this document we will be accepting their proposal to dissolve Yugoslavia with a single stroke of the pen. They have no right to expect us to do that."

Milošević was willing to compromise when it came to the Serb population in Croatia, but was adamant to keep Serbs in the other republics together. Milošević had ambitions of Serbia expanding its border not only into Croatia but also to its ally Montenegro; although the *big prize* was Bosnia, which was home to over a million and a half Serbs. If he let these republics go independent, how would Serbia achieve its goal to become the major republic in Yugoslavia? He wanted a state for all Serbs, one that would give them supremacy over all the other republics.

After Milošević finished speaking, Lord Carrington asked each republican state president around the table if they were prepared to accept the peace draft he proposed. One by one the presidents of each republic approved Lord Carrington's plan.

Milošević could see the Yugoslav Federation, where all his Serb brothers could live, shrinking before his eyes; soon Serbia would not have another republic to stay federated to. The Serb President knew he would be safe if just one other republic voted to stay in Yugoslavian federation.

Milošević was sure he could rely on his ally Momir Bulatović, President of Montenegro; but he was wrong. President Bulatović said *he could see no flaw in the peace plan, it enabled them to secure their own interests. It protected the interest of the other republics. It was an excellent peace plan to stop the war in Yugoslavia.*

When Montenegro's President accepted the plan, it was a slap in the face for Milošević.

A person could hear a pin drop in the silence that followed, Milošević looked sullen, his stern face told the full story. The Serb President could not sit still; he was confused and nervous like a man about to face a firing squad.

Milošević skulked out of the meeting with his tail between his legs, but upon his return to Belgrade, he alerted his power base. He told them that the plan proposing to split Yugoslavia into independent states had been accepted, and this move would further fragment the Serb nation. Serbs would end up scattered among several republics, and the Serb people would be in mortal danger. Councilman Jović felt this was the worst crisis the leadership had had to face since the elections.

Milošević spent the next few days plotting his next move. He had no choice, but to make the President of Montenegro, Momir Bulatović, change his mind and vote against Carrington's plan. That night the President's phone in Montenegro never stopped ringing. Calls from the political heavies from Serbia interrogating President Bulatović, asking if *he was really a traitor to the Serb people*? All night Montenegro received all kinds of threats, and later on Serb television it was announced that the Montenegro peoples' party had called for Parliament to reconvene for an emergency debate. Their President was willing to revisit his decision to accept the proposal of the Carrington draft peace plan.

In the Montenegro Parliament, the President's opposing party was quick to attack his decision to accept the peace draft. They stated that his actions were a *national betrayal*, and for that reason they could not accept Carrington's proposal. In his own defence the President responded and said, "Does good government in Montenegro entail lavish obedience to Serbia? If so why do we have our own government? Is Montenegro a Serb satellite?"

Hearing about the President's comments in his Parliament, Milošević summoned the Montenegro leader to his office in Belgrade. He asked President Bulatović directly, "What were you offered to betray your friends in Serbia? How much were you paid to abandon Yugoslavia?"

The Yugoslav Army intelligence had gathered some information that Gianni De Michelis, Italy's Foreign Minister, held a powerful incentive for the President of Montenegro to abandon Serbia.

The enticement was an important aid program worth thirty to forty billion lira. For the tiny republic of Montenegro that was big money, and the President was interested to start economic relations with the European Commission. Bulatović saw Italy as Montenegro's way into Europe; but Milošević had hard evidence that Montenegro would not be the only beneficiary of this *aid account* offered by Italy. In fact, evidence suggested that President Bulatović himself would personally benefit if he accepted the Carrington peace plan.

It meeting in Belgrade was very rough for the Montenegrin President. He was grilled like a criminal before finally admitting his involvement in this scandalous activity. Poor Momir was pouring with sweat as he confirmed that he had secret talks with Italy's Signor De Michelis.

Milošević gave the President of Montenegro a choice, either he faced a public scandal and political ruin, or send a letter to Carrington voting *No* to the draft peace plan. Milošević even went to the trouble of preparing a written text for President Bulatović to sign, which he promptly sent to Lord Carrington. As soon as he signed the letter, the Serbs stopped calling the President of Montenegro a traitor, but the Carrington peace plan was now effectively dead and buried.

Milošević could now focus on finishing his war with Croatia; the Serbs had secured most of the Croatian territory they wanted, but the city of Vukovar stubbornly held out. The Serb high command sent its top general, Života Panić, for the final assault on Vukovar. The General decided not to fight house to house, but would take Vukovar with heavy bombardment. Vukovar was an old city, many houses were built with flimsy materials, and with artillery and rockets the Serbs had hoped to take Vukovar in a matter of days. The Croats made the Serbs fight for every inch of Vukovar!

Croatian President Tuđman judged the city of Vukovar was all but lost but the city still had a big role to play. Croatia had only one friend in Europe, and that was Germany; but they required the sympathy of other European countries. Croatia was almost alone in the world searching for recognition, until the Serbs closed in on Vukovar. The people of Vukovar were dependent on a thin trickle of supplies and those deliveries were quickly drying up!

A Croat commander called Mile Dedaković decided to appeal personally to his President. He set off to walk through the encircling Serb Army lines; he was lucky the fog came down and there was light rain. Keeping his head down he made his way through the cornfields with a small body of men and, after thirteen hours he made it to Zagreb; although two of his guards were killed on the way.

At the short meeting Dedaković pleaded with the President that heavy artillery and supplies be sent to enable his men to fight off the Serbs in Vukovar. President Tuđman told his commander that the minimum necessary to supply his Army and the people of Vukovar would authorised, but when the commander returned to the front line no heavy weapons or supplies had arrived.

Following the start of the Serb bombardment in Vukovar, the Croats held the city for two months. Just before Vukovar finally fell to the Serbs, commander Dedaković went before the press accusing his leaders of sacrificing Vukovar to gain international sympathy. He told the press, "I am not saying the President did not send the supplies and heavy weapons I requested to hold on to Vukovar, but the fact remains we did not get any."

With the Serbs about to take Vukovar it gave the German Foreign Minister, Hans-Dietrich Genscher, a powerful argument within the European Community. Genscher fought hard for the EC to recognise the independent states of Slovenia and Croatia. The debate was fierce, but the result was better than Germany could have hoped for. The EC was prepared to recognise Slovenia and Croatia as independent states, if a European Community Mandate and Human Rights issues were accepted within these States.

Finally Vukovar fell to the Serbs – Serbia now controlled one third of Croatia; but there was a cost. Between the two sides there were 15,000 dead and 500,000 refuges.

In March 1992, UN troops moved into Croatia to protect innocent civilians from Human Rights abuses; but through this the United Nations effectively found itself protecting the Serb gains in Croatia. In the meantime Croatia began to rebuild its Army, and Serb forces prepared for their next target, Bosnia.

CHAPTER FOUR

The Gates of Hell

The Bosnian Parliament was in fierce debate; high on the agenda was the crisis spreading throughout Yugoslavia. Half of the Yugoslav Republic had gone for independence and now it was time for the Bosnians to decide. Radovan Karadžić issued a black warning saying, "I warn you, you will drag Bosnia down to hell, you Muslims are not ready for war, and you could face extinction if you travel down that road."

The Bosnian President, Alija Izetbegović, replied to Karadžić warnings and said, "Bosnia won't stay in a Yugoslavia run by Serbia, and I won't let Bosnia be a part of a greater Serbia. Mr Karadžićs speech and his behaviour here today show why we cannot remain as part of Yugoslavia. I sense a looming inferno in Mr Karadžić's voice. It felt as if the gates to hell had opened and we were all scorched by the tongues of flame."

President Izetbegović was a Muslim, but he did not speak for all Bosnians. The Bosnia/Serb leader, Radovan Karadžić, represented one third of the Bosnian population, and they wanted Bosnia to stay in Yugoslavia, as it was where most of the Serbs lived. Karadžić responded, "We created a situation in which Bosnia was doomed. Nearly every Serb wanted to stay in Yugoslavia, but the Muslims and the Croats wanted out."

President Izetbegović called for a referendum the discussions surrounding independence. In Sarajevo, Muslims, Serbs and Croats had lived together in peace for centuries; but now they had to choose a future.

No one but the Serbs wanted Karadžić's future for Yugoslavia. The majority population of Muslims and Croats supported President Izetbegović and supported his vote for independence. The President intended to complete Bosnia's recession from Yugoslavia as soon as possible, but in his heart he knew that Bosnia too could be on the verge of civil war. However, he did not expect Bosnia was on the verge of genocide. It was not long before the tension exploded and this time it was not the Serbs to show the aggression.

The President's own Muslim people lit the fuse that turned Bosnia into a bloodbath. It happened as the guests arrived for a Serb wedding. A personal feud between the groom's father and a Muslim ended when the Muslim turned up at the wedding armed and fired two shots into the groom's father, killing him outright. That night the Serbs hit back. Gunmen erected armed barricades all over Sarajevo, as they searched and intimidated every Muslim who approached to cross the barricade.

The Serb National Party in Sarajevo demanded that the Bosnian Government stop seeking international recognition for their independence. Neither the Bosnian police nor the Green Berets, who were the Muslim paramilitaries, were strong enough to take on the Serbs. The Muslim leadership decided to withdraw from any confrontation with the Serbs, at least for the time being. If it had come to street fighting the Muslims could not have won in those parts of Sarajevo that they had erected barricades. The streets of the capital fell into the hands of the rival militia: the Muslims held the city centre and the Serbs much of the rest of Sarajevo, including the strategic heights around the city where they placed heavy weapons. The people of Sarajevo saw war looming, and begged their leaders to prevent it at all costs.

On Yugoslav TV news, on the 3rd March 1992, they reported Karadžić and President Izetbegović had caused the crisis in Bosnia and, as the ethnic leaders, they were both responsible if war erupted in Bosnia. After the news report the people wanted the two leaders to meet for a peaceful outcome to the crisis and their political phones did not stop ringing. After a great deal of public pressure they agreed to meet at the Yugoslav Army Headquarters in downtown Sarajevo. At the meeting the atmosphere was icy, with national feeling strained to the point of no return.

Federal Army Commander for Bosnia, General Milutin Kukanjac, said, "They were shaking their fists in each other's faces and accusing each other of all kinds of political failures. This went on for an hour before I managed to calm Izetbegović and Karadžić to a point of constructive communication; they finally found a way to defuse the crisis. They agreed to protect the citizens with joint patrols that would be run by the Federal Army and the Bosnian Police."

President Izetbegović thought that civil war in Bosnia had been avoided, but despite talks Karadžić had not really backed down. He knew that his patrons Serbian President, Slobodan Milošević, and Croatian President, Franjo Tuđman, were making ambitious plans to carve up Bosnia. Tuđman felt the three ethnic peoples in Bosnia could form a confederation, all three would then be happy, if not Bosnia should be partitioned.

At the Presidential Palace in Zagreb, Tuđman initiated a series of secret meetings between the Bosnian Serbs and Bosnian Croats. Parliamentary speaker, Stipe Mesić, said, "I witnessed Bosnian Serbs and Bosnian Croats agree to carve up Bosnia between themselves without any consideration for the Muslim community."

The frontier was agreed along the Neretva River, which runs across the south of Bosnia. After the meeting Tuđman endorsed the agreement and, by supporting a partition of Bosnia, the risk of a three-way war with each of the ethnic groups fighting one another.

Karadžić travelled to Belgrade to report to President Milošević. He could not hide his delight when told the President that everything was now in place to take over a large part of Bosnia. Milošević and Karadžić could not care less if Bosnia were recognised by Europe, Milošević saying, "Caligula proclaimed his horse a senator, but the horse never took his seat. Izetbegović might get recognition for Bosnia, but he will never have a state."

Milošević now fully controlled the Yugoslav Army, but he was too clever to use it against Bosnia; he adopted a more devious approach.

Milošević and his advisor, Borisav Jović, knew that if Bosnia became recognised in Europe, and he sent in the Yugoslav Army, Serbia would be seen as the aggressors by the outside world. Milošević and Jović talked it over without consulting anybody else and realised their plan would require them to pull a fast one. They decided that, because the Yugoslav Federal Army was already in Bosnia helping the police to keep some kind of order, they would transfer every Bosnian Serb from the Yugoslav Federal Army stationed in Bosnia to Serb units in Bosnia. This would provide Radovan Karadžić with an army of 80,000 soldiers, who were fully trained and equipped, and Milošević could then deny any responsibility by the Serbian republic. However this way he still kept his hands on the controls in Bosnia.

In Belgrade the Serb leadership promised to pay all the costs for the Serb units in Bosnia, since the Bosnian Serbs did not have a state budget to fight against the government, and the officers leading their men to fight in Bosnia had to be paid. Milošević also offered his own Serb paramilitaries, who had been armed by his secret police and led by extremist Serb nationalists with a reputation for terrorising the civilian population, and ethnic cleansing. Serb paramilitary commander, Vojislav Šešelj, said, "Milošević and his generals did not give us orders, they just requested for my fighters in certain areas and we would never let them down."

The first place Milošević sent the paramilitaries was Bijeljin. The Serbs wanted absolute military control there as it offered a strategic crossroads to northeast Bosnia. The heavily armed Serbs captured the city in three days, then they rounded up the local activist in the Muslim Party. The paramilitaries invited a media photographer along to witness one man, a Muslim, pleading for his life. The photographer caught him in the last moments before he was shot; it appeared the presence of a photographer did not stop further executions. It appeared the paramilitaries were proud of their actions, their attitude never carrying any remorse, even boasting that they were *ridding this earth of scum*.

Bosnia's President Izetbegović said. "To start with we were getting contradictory reports. It was hard to believe that they had killed civilians. I have made a vow; the terrible scenes in Bejeljina must never be repeated. So I call upon every citizen of Bosnia Herzegovina, not just my own people the Muslims, but also the Bosnian Serbs and the Bosnian Croats. Truly I mean all the people of Bosnia. We must support our Bosnian police and the Militia to defend our state against the ethnic aggression of Serbia'.

On the 5th April 1992, the citizens of Sarajevo took to the streets for a non-violent demonstration demanding peace. They saw the city's tradition of tolerance, with more mixed marriages than anywhere else in Yugoslavia, at mortal risk. They occupied the Parliament chamber chanting, *Bosnia, Bosnia, Bosnia!* A speaker said, "Our Government has abandoned us. The people must take charge. Down with the Government!"

They opposed the Muslim nationalism, and the leaders Izetbegović and Karadžić. Karadžić could see the demonstration from his office window in the Holiday Inn, which was just across the street from where it took place. He saw the crowd challenge his right to divide Sarajevo and attempt to march on his headquarters, and decided to telephone the Serb guard. Karadžić told them to get ready to sort out the activists. Despite a peaceful protest, his men opened fire at the demonstrators and six people were killed.

In the city centre, long an Izetbegović stronghold, police reasserted control and arrested the Serb snipers who fired at the demonstrators near Karadžić's office. Izetbegović and his followers fled the city and took to the hills above Sarajevo. It was there the Serbs began their sporadic mortar shelling and sniper fire at the city of Sarajevo, just to show Izetbegović who was the boss. When the shelling began the speaker of the Parliament, a Serb, asked for a meeting with Izetbegović; before the conflict they had almost become friends.

The speaker, Momčilo Krajišnik, said, "I arrived first and it was already dark. I saw Izetbegović's guards, they had machine guns with silencers and I said 'Is that what you call a gun?' We Serbs are better equipped. That was just a joke that went down like a lead weight. When Izetbegović arrived we sat together in Parliament, it was just like old times. I told Izetbegović we Serbs had always planned to divide Sarajevo. The Muslims would get their part and we Serbs would get ours. I told Izetbegović you couldn't avoid a partition of our city. To stop the further bloodshed, I was hoping to strike a deal over Sarajevo. But Izetbegović would not agree to my plan. As we left the abandoned Parliament building I said goodbye to Izetbegović, and gave him my pen for a souvenir."

After the secret meeting between Izetbegović and Krajišnik, the Serbs hesitated before launching an assault on Sarajevo. Their first objective was to take those parts of Bosnia closest to Serbia itself, no matter who lived there. On television Karadžić said, "We Bosnian Serbs must have independence. The fact that the Muslims are in the majority makes no difference. They will not decide our fate. That is our right."

In the territories where Serbs were the majority it did not take them long to take control, but between Serbia and the Serb areas of Bosnia lay a region where most of the people were Muslim.

In each of the principal towns of Foca, Gorazde, Srebrenica and Zvornik the local Serb leader gave an order to the Muslim Mayor to disarm the town's police forces and surrender. Zvornik in particular, since it was the crossing point with road and rail links between Bosnia and Serbia.

The Serb party leader in Zvornik said, "There is no reason to run away from Zvornik, everybody knows our Serb party cares about the people."

Zvornik's Muslim Mayor, Abdulah Pašić, was called to a meeting regarding the disarming of his police force, the Mayor said, "I had no choice in the matter, when you consider that I was told, there would be no chance of an attack on Zvornik from Serb or Croat if we disarmed our police and surrendered. In that way we can all live in peace together."

However, Mayor Pašić was not aware that the Federal Army tanks and the Bosnian Serb Army had already surrounded Zvornik. Serb paramilitary commander, Vojislav Šešelj, said, "Milošević was in total control, and the operation was planned in Belgrade. The Bosnian Serbs did take part but the best combat units came from Serbia. These were special police Commandos called the Red Berets. They were from the Secret Service of Serbia, and my forces took part as did others."

Šešelj briefed Serb forces in a nearby hotel which, according to the UN War Crimes Commission, was where he read out the names of the leading Muslims in Zvornik to be killed.

The Serbs then launched their attack of Zvornik. Most of Zvornik had been disarmed before the attack began, but what few of Zvornik defenders were left had been driven out of town within a day. Those that stayed, at their own peril, were taken prisoner. One such prisoner said, "They think we are the Green Berets Muslim commandos. Look at us! None of us has a Green Beret. In fact I wish we were Green Berets, we are the only defence left in Zvornik."

That same day a UN official for a refugee agency in Yugoslavia, José María Mendiluce, was driving from Serbia to Bosnia. He was stopped just outside Zvornik where the Red Cross told him not to go any further as everyone in the area had *gone crazy*. A paramilitary commander, proud of his work, gave his permission to let in a news crew to witness his regime of terror being established.

The Serb paramilitaries were mopping up house after house.

A soldier shouted, "Hey. Come on out!" to someone hiding. The soldier shouted again, "Nobody is going to hurt you."

Another soldier shouted, "Bring him here. I said get over here!"

The soldiers kept their weapons trained on this very frightened man. When the man came over to the Soldiers, they asked the man, "Who was shooting at us?"

The man answered, "I swear by my children, I don't know."

The fate of this man, and many more like him, I will leave to the imagination since to know the truth could have chilling consequences.

The Serbs had prepared for this operation carefully and everything went exactly to plan. The UN Official, José María Mendiluce, recalled, "As the Military Police were trying to identify the Muslims, the tension was absolutely terrifying. On one bend my jeep skidded on the blood in the road. At the same time the artillery were firing from the Serb side of the river. I could see the flashes and smoke from their big guns. After the paramilitaries had finished their so-called mop up I saw lorries full of corpses. I witnessed soldiers dumping dead women, children and old people onto the lorries. I saw four or five lorries full of corpses."

Some 2,000 people in Zvornik were unaccounted for, and nobody truly knows how many were executed on the spot, or how many were sent to concentration camps where the murder continued.

The rest of the Muslims were expelled from Zvornik. Over forty-nine thousand had lived there, after five centuries of Islamic life none remained and their culture had been erased.

This was what ethnic cleansing was all about.

This action became common routine as the Serbs took control of three quarters of Bosnian territory. In lieu of worldwide condemnation, the Serbs soon learnt to keep the cameras out of their ethnic cleansing, but the practice continued throughout Bosnia. Commander Vojislav Šešelj said, "I cannot deny this took place, mostly it was organised in Belgrade. Milošević himself asked me to send my fighters in."

In reply to the comments made by Šešelj, President Milošević said, "There is no one who can believe what is mentioned as organised genocide from Belgrade, or that I was responsible for such an act, it is really out of all consideration."

The Foreign Minister for Bosnia, Haris Silajdžić, said, "Considering the tragic situation in Bosnia, we have no choice, and our Presidency had no choice but to appeal for military intervention in Bosnia/Herzegovina."

Instead of military intervention the international community sent a peace envoy; and once again the job was given to Lord Carrington. He put forward a proposal to President Izetbegović, requesting they partition Bosnia into ethnic provinces. Lord Carrington said, "It was very clear to me that he was far from happy with my proposal, the Bosnian President wanted a unitary state. It was even more clear to me the overwhelming military superiority favoured the Serbs. He was in a very difficult position."

President Izetbegović said, "Lord Carrington asked me, 'What will I do?' I told him that we would fight. Carrington paused, looked me straight in the eye and said, 'How do you expect to fight back?' He also said, 'Mr Izetbegović, you don't know what you are facing. They have thousands of tanks, hundreds of planes, three to four thousand artillery pieces and a mountain of ammunition. Don't you know that you cannot resist such force?' I replied, 'We have no choice, if we surrendered we will be murdered'."

Two weeks later, on the 2nd May 1992, the Serbs finally launched an assault on Sarajevo, after a handful of UN peacekeepers had just opened an office in the city. On the day of the attack, the UN general, Lewis Mackenzie, was expecting a package. He sent his administrator clerk down town to find the post office and collect the package. The clerk returned one hour later and told General Mackenzie that he had *some good news and some bad news...*

General Mackenzie asked, "What's the good news?"

To which the Clerk replied, "I found the post office."

The General said, "Great, what's the bad news?"

The Clerk said, "The bad news is, it's not there anymore. Serb saboteurs destroyed the Sarajevo Central Post Office, and your package."

The Serb attack had also knocked out the city's phone lines, including those of the Bosnian Presidency and the defence headquarters. From three directions the Serb forces, backed up by tanks and air strikes, closed in on the heart of Sarajevo.

The city's defenders included local criminal gangs; even a few Serbs willing to fight for a multi-ethnic Bosnia. One such man was General Jovan Divjak, a Serb that believed Bosnia belonged to Muslim, Serb, and Croat and there should be no discrimination either way. He said, "Our worst moment came when the Serb Army crossed the bridge into the city centre. They were within fifty metres of the presidency building." Bosnian Vice President, Ejup Ganić, a Muslim, said, "There was shooting all around the presidency building. My bodyguard said he would be more useful outside, it was then I realised they might take the Presidency."

Sarajevo's narrow streets gave the defenders the edge; anti-tank missiles stopped the Serb armour in its tracks. Then the Bosnians turned the tables on the Serbs, encircling the Federal Army Headquarters in the city centre.

Federal Army Commander General Kukanjac said, "It was a life and death struggle. There were about 270 of us in the entire command. It seemed like a thousand Muslims were firing at us. At times they were only a few metres away, firing at us at point blank range and these were fanatics who were not afraid to die."

The two sides had fought to a standstill, but the General and his men were still surrounded in the Federal Army building. Within hours the Serbs would get a chance to finish off Bosnia with a single clean blow to the head.

The EC had summoned the Bosnian President, Alija Izetbegović, to peace talks and as usual his daughter was by his side. Upon returning to Sarajevo, the pilot checked for clearence to land; travelling with the President was Bosnian delegate, Zlatko Lagumdžija, he said, "We were a few minutes from Sarajevo when the pilot walked into our cabin to tell us that Sarajevo Airport was closed."

The Federal Army had seized the airport and it was now under direct control of Belgrade, who would decide if the President's plane should be given clearance to land at Sarajevo. Due to the volatile situation in Sarajevo, the President had arranged for UN protection on his return.

UN officer General Mackenzie was informed that President Izetbegović's aircraft was on route to Sarajevo, and given an estimated time of arrival. The General was unaware that the President's plane had not yet been given clearance to land at Sarajevo, so sent an officer to escort him through the airport. The officer waited for one and a half hours after the scheduled arrival time, and still there was no sign of the President. When he made some enquiries regarding the President's arrival no one was forthcoming with information about his arrival, or whether the President had even left the Netherlands to return to Sarajevo. Thinking there must have been an unforeseen delay, or even a change of plan due to the situation at the airport, the UN officer left the airport.

With General Mackenzie now out of the picture the President's plane was given clearance to land, but the pilot was told it would be *at your own risk*. The President was informed of the risk but, after a short pause, he ordered the pilot to land unaware that there was no UN protection waiting to escort him. When President Izetbegović and his delegation got off the plane they were instead met and escorted by a Federal Army major.

President Izetbegović said, "Where is my UN guard?"

The major replied, "He has not arrived yet."

Unfortunately the President's pilot had landed them straight into a trap. He was now in the hands of the Federal Army. The President was now prisoner to a man his own forces had surrounded, General Kukanjac, and nobody hated the President as much as he did.

Kukanjac knew he could not liquidate Izetbegović, so decided to call his chief in Serbia for advice. He was ordered to treat the President well, and not to let him go. His chief was going to report to the superior on the State Council, hoping for some guidance in this very *delicate* situation.

The new Chairman of the State Council, Montenegro's Branko Kostić, said, "That was unexpected news, but I can't deny I was pleased to hear it. This situation had all kinds of implications."

President Izetbegović was a very important figurehead, he alone held the government in Sarajevo together. At this point his ministers were unaware the Federal Army had seized him.

Earlier that day a group of children had been evacuated from Sarajevo Airport. A worried mother concerned about her child had managed to find a working phone and contacted the Airport for peace of mind. One of the President's delegates, Zlatko Lagumdžija, recalled what happened next, "God knows how she got through to the Airport manager. He was telling the worried mother not to worry, your child got off allright and there is no cause for alarm."

President Izetbegović stood up as he approached the manager and said, "Excuse me, may I have the telephone?"

Izetbegović took the telephone and said, "Good Evening madam, I am Alija Izetbegović, President of the republic of Bosnia Herzegovina."

There was a brief pause before she answered, "Sorry. What? Who?"

The President said, "Yes. Yes. That is correct, I am Alija Izetbegović the President on the line. Madam, I wonder if you could do me a favour? I am sitting here at the Airport, would you be so kind as to call the Presidency. Please tell them you spoke to me, and that I am at the Airport. If you can't get the Presidency please call a TV station and tell them that I am at the Airport, and that the Federal Army will not let me leave. I am told it's an order from General Kukanjac. Yes, Madam, General Kukanjac."

The woman could not believe what she was hearing. She was repeating everything the President was saying over and over again. The President said, "Thank you very much, yes, yes, thank you, yes madam."

As the woman got on the phone to the television station, the President was about to be moved to an Army base in Serb-controlled territory. The television evening news staff started to make enquiries into the President's whereabouts. The President's close aide, Ejup Ganić, said, "My bodyguard answered the phone and said that the President is in trouble. Sarajevo television wants to speak to you. They told me, 'We have President Alija Izetbegović on the line'. The television reporter asked the President, 'Why are you at the Federal Army Base?' The President replied, 'Effectively I am a prisoner'.".

The television station set up a four-way telephone link live on air between the President, a TV reporter, Ejup Ganić, and the Army base commander. The following conversation took place between the four participants.

The commander told the reporter, "The President is not a prisoner."

Ganić asked the President, "If that is so, why don't you return to the Presidency?"

The President replied, "Because they won't let me go."

Ganić was close to losing his temper, and with rage he said, "That is ridiculous!"

After a slight breakdown in communications, the President could be heard saying, "Hello? Hello? It's true, what line are we on?"

Ganić replied, "Most of the phone lines are down, President I don't understand."

The television station had a radio line in operation. Whilst this conversation went on, the citizens of Sarajevo watched their televisions in amazement as they witnessed the President appoint Ejup Ganić as his deputy in case he was killed. Ganić suddenly felt he was under an enormous burden, he was getting more frustrated as the conversation went on. With a raised voice Ganić said, "Alija the world is watching this broadcast, you are the President of a sovereign state. The Army cannot arrest you. Belgrade will not get away with this, Mr President they must release you! You have a right to return to the presidential office."

The reporter asked, "What does the Commander have to say?"

The base commander said, "The President was at the base and I demand a fair exchange for him. Our troops must be allowed to leave Sarajevo."

The reporter asked, "Will the Bosnian presidency guarantee their safe passage?"

The commander said, "They don't have enough authority to make that offer."

Ejup Ganić said, "Our Bosnian forces will obey our orders."

President Izetbegović said, "Listen, and give the orders to our defence forces."

Ejup Ganić said, "We will do that Mr President."

The President finished the four-way live link on television and said, "Don't worry about me, my nerves will hold out," but really he was more worried about his daughter than himself.

The President went on to say, "For the first and only time in my life, I did not sleep a wink. There was a big clock on the wall; I watched the hands go around, one a.m., two a.m., three a.m., and so on. They had taken my daughter away and I feared for her safety. I was sick with worry."

Ejup Ganić telephoned General Kukanjac, who was holding President Izetbegović at the Federal Army base and told him, "General, you do know we have got you surrounded? A bird could not get out of your base without detection. We have mined the sewers. You are dicing with death."

General Kukanjac said, "Back down off your high horse, or I won't answer for the consequences."

Ganić said, "Take good care of the President, we will let you go and your men can follow later. But if you screw up we will blow your arse go the top of Mount Trebevic."

They agreed to a meeting at first light between Ejup Ganić and General Aksetijević in the UN Headquarters. UN General Mackenzie would chair the meeting. The meeting started with fierce exchanges from both sides. General Mackenzie was to have his work cut out if he meant to keep the proceedings calm and constructive. Ganić said, "General, no army has the right to arrest a democratically elected President of a sovereign state. What kind of army kidnaps the head of state?"

General Aksetijevic said, "But your President ordered an attack on the Federal Army base commanded by General Kukanjac. Our general and his men must be allowed to leave the army base safely."

Ganić roared, "No! No! No! No deal until the President is released!'

General Mackenzie suggested that exchanging their general for the President would be the best way out of this stalemate. Ganić finally agreed that General Kukanjac could leave with a few aides, but insisted rest of the General's men were to be a separate issue to be negotiated after the President was released. All parties agreed and reported to their respective commands.

General Mackenzie was the go-between, there to make sure the two sides honoured their agreement. Ganić was not at ease with the situation, as he returned to the Bosnian headquarters he worried that he might not be able to keep his side of the agreement; some of his forces were out of control and lacked military discipline. General Mackenzie proceeded to the Federal Army base to collect President Izetbegović, and General Kukanjac plus his aides. However, when Mackenzie arrived at the Army base he found that the goalposts had been moved.

The Army raised their demand and insisted their entire staff be given safe passage out of the city centre. General Mackenzie was not happy with the Army's fresh demands. His main concern was that he only had enough staff to deal with a small escort party, not a large convoy of vehicles, which is what it would take to evacuate the entire army staff. It was clear to Mackenzie the army was not going to take no for an answer.

The army staff had already started to load their equipment onto vehicles and was expecting to leave. President Izetbegović could see that General Mackenzie had been put into an awkward position. Eventually the President intervened, giving his personal guarantee of a safe passage for all the army staff and their convoy.

Mackenzie had no choice but to accept the President's guarantee. He knew the guarantee would count for nothing once the President was sitting in an armoured personnel carrier. Ejup Ganić, his deputy, was in charge and he had not been informed about the change of plans brought about by the Army's sudden demands. The General was anticipating it was going to lead to sheer chaos.

Mackenzie's plan was to escort the President, and General Kukanjac and his men through the Bosnian forces that had surrounded the Federal Army base. They proceeded in a convoy to the front line where the General and the President would be received by their respective forces; the President would also be reunited with his daughter there at the front line.

The convoy set off through the streets, which had seen vicious fighting the day before. As the convoy crawled through the streets laden with burnt-out tanks and cars, debris littered the streets with dead bodies that from far away looked like they were sunbathing. It was a very nasty scene; throughout the convoy nerves were at a fever pitch, like they were carrying volatile explosives through fire, and word soon got out that Kukanjac's men had been allowed to leave the Army base.

Deputy President, Ejup Ganić, said, "None of us agreed at the meeting that the weapons, files and troops could leave with General Kukanjac. That was still up for discussion."

General Mackenzie's white UN armoured personnel carrier led the convoy; they could see the streets around them filling up with Bosnian forces eager for revenge. It had only been the day before that General Kukanjac and his men had ordered the shelling of Sarajevo. The Bosnian forces and the civilians acted under their own volition as a vehicle came out of a crossroad and split the convoy in two.

Suddenly rapid gunfire could be heard. Kukanjac cowered in the corner of the personnel carrier for protection while President Izetbegović peered out to see his Bosnian people ambush the section of convoy carrying General Kukanjac's men. As each vehicle showed no sign of resistance, the Bosnian forces siezed the Army's equipment, the President spotted one of his generals commanding his men to hold their fire, but could still see that civilians and soldiers from both sides being killed. General Divjak edged through the now stationary convoy, and with a loudhailer he ordered that his Bosnian forces hold their fire. The President wanted this major problem resolved before the situation turned into a bloodbath, and as the sound of gunfire echoed in the streets the President shouted, "Don't shoot. Don't shoot!" appealing to his people to stop firing, but without any sign of panic.

General Divjak and the President managed to calm some of the fighters, but General Kukanjac did not look happy. With his pistol tucked in his belt he was getting ready to kill the President, and himself, if the Bosnian forces attacked the personnel carrier. The President and General Divjak decided to radio Bosnian Army HQ to stop the mutinous forces who continued laying siege to the convoy, despite the President's demands. General Divjak spoke to an officer at HQ, who would not identify himself, telling the man, "We have already negotiated the safe passage of the General's men."

The officer at HQ spat, "What the hell is this? Fuck You, and fuck the President. Nobody is leaving the town."

General Divjak order the officer, "Identify yourself! I am ordering you to let the President and the convoy through."

The President took the radio receiver from General Divjak and appealed to the officer for restraint. After a brief pause the officer said, "I am prepared to let the President and General Kukanjac through, but they will have to negotiate for the rest of the convoy."

At this point Bosnian Army commander, General Sefer Halilović, took charge of the radio receiver, and the situation that had developed. He apologized to the President saying, "The orders did not reach every individual officer because our army was not properly organised."

A local Bosnian officer went back through the convoy with General Divjak to calm his forces down. After nearly one hour silence prevailed over the sound of gunfire and, slowly, they withdrew. General Mackenzie likened the situation to the film *Zulu*, he said, "One minute all hell had broken loose, surrounded by Bosnian forces, and the next minute they all disappeared."

The President was reunited with his daughter, and they returned home; as did General Kukanjac.

Unfortunately the General lost a few of his men, but I guess there will always be a price to pay for freedom...

The Serbs who nearly extinguished the President and his state set siege on the President's capital, Sarajevo. Bosnia became a member of the United Nations; but nobody would help Bosnia control her own territory. US Secretary of State, James Baker, made it quite clear in a statement to the media, in May 1992, when he said, "There will be no unilateral use of

United States force in Yugoslavia. As we have said before, we are not and cannot be the World's police force."

Mr Baker would be made to eat those words within ten years of having made that statement – how world politics change in such a very short time.

In the meantime, Milošević sent the Bosnian Serbs a new commander-in-chief: the infamous General Mladić. When it came to terrorising innocent civilians, Mladić was in a class of his own. This is what this butcher ordered for the people of Sarajevo when speaking to his artillery officer on a radio receiver, "I want you to shell the Presidency and the Parliament, fire at slow intervals until I order you to stop. Then target Muslim neighbourhoods, not many Serbs live there. Look at all that smoke. Shell them till they are on the edge of madness."

CHAPTER FIVE

The Phantom Peace Road

The war in Yugoslavia brought about regular news coverage centring on the ethnic cleansing. Europe could no longer stand back and let this evil activity take place, especially not on its doorstep. With the leaders in Bosnia appealing for help, the United Nations passed a resolution to send a peacekeeping force to protect the civilian population in Bosnia. The UN requested the warring parties to treat certain towns as safe areas for civilians.

On the 17th April 1993, the UN Commanders in Bosnia summoned the Serb commander-in-chief, General Mladić, to a meeting. The UN presented a *resolution* to General Mladić, but he immediately got on his high horse saying, "I am the Serb Army. You cannot treat me like this. *I* will lay down our terms for not running the safe towns under this so-called UN resolution. If the UN wants these towns to be designated safe areas for civilians, then the UN must persuade the Muslims to surrender their weapons."

Mladić went on to play argumentative ping-pong with the French UN colonel, Jean Le Morillon. With a face like a bull's backside and his fists clenched, Mladić retired to a small room to allow Colonel Morillon to ask General Halilović, commander of the Bosnian Army, to accept Mladic's terms, or Srebrenica and other safe area towns would be doomed. For the sake of innocent civilians caught up in a vicious feud, General Halilović accepted Colonel Morillon's recommendation.

The UN claimed a physiological victory; they had halted the Serbian Army's advance into Srebrenica, although General Mladić knew he could take the town whenever he wanted. In exchange for allowing the UN assigning a few Canadian peacekeepers into Srebrenica, the town's Muslim army had to disarm in order for it to be made into a *safe area* under the UN resolution.

Unfortunately, a piece of paper could not protect civilians against a Serb army who had no respect for human rights under the Geneva Convention. The Bosnian Serbs had plans to turn Srebrenica into a concentration camp, and they were not prepared to let the UN stand in their way. Mladić would not rest until he had assumed control in Srebrenica.

It was no coincidence when, on the 22nd April 1993, America's President Clinton opened a Holocaust museum in Washington, in memory of Jews who had suffered under the Nazi regime. The problems in Srebrenica served only to remind everyone at the ceremony in Washington the parallels between the Serb ethnic cleansing, and the Nazi genocide during World War II. Auschwitz survivor, Elie Wiesel, addressed the ceremony and said, 'I have been to the former Yugoslavia and, Mr President I must tell you, we must do something to stop the bloodshed in that country."

It became national news in America, even being discussed on *The Phil Donahue Show*, where they debated the issue of ethnic cleansing. Donahue opened the debate saying, "Ethnic cleansing, what does that remind us of? And what is our responsibility in this world of ours? It was not that long ago the Jews suffered persecution and genocide under the Nazi regime, whilst the world stood by and did nothing. Are we to bury our heads in the sand again, when we boast of a much more civilized world since the end of World War II?'

To deal with such questions the international community offered the Vance-Owen plan, devised by two ex-foreign ministers. Lord Owen even appeared on *The Phil Donahue*

Show to explain their peace plan. The first part of the plan was to get the three ethnic parties together and encourage them all to share the country. As such Bosnia would remain one country with ten provinces; but each having control over their own transport, education and police forces. The plan would allow the Serb local control over much of the territory they now held; however the provinces were so arranged that it would have been impossible for them to form one unified Serb state in the country. The plan seemed to be idealistic; attempting to roll back the victorious Serb Army by 27th March 1993

On the 24th April 1993, Lord Owen arrived in Belgrade to meet Serbia's President Milošević. The United Nations had given Lord Owen a new weapon to bargain with: the threat of crippling sanctions on Serbia, and their ally Montenegro, if they refused to back the Vance-Owen peace proposal. When the media in Belgrade asked Lord Owen about issues surround the Vance-Owen plan he replied, "What is the issue, are the Serbs in Bosnia Herzegovina, Serbia, and Montenegro prepared to take on the world?"

President Milošević said, "Our bottom line was equal treatment for all ethnic groups. The Vance-Owen plan gave us that, but I am concerned that the interim presidency in Bosnia could still use their Muslim majority over the Serbs and in certain areas the Croats."

The Croatians seemed to be the floating voters between the Serbs and Muslims in Bosnia. Most of the Croats seem to back the Muslims, but ill winds change people's outlook as easily as they change the weather. Lord Owen reassured the leaders in Serbia and Montenegro that the provinces would have the power to self-rule. With that in mind, Milošević and Bulatović embraced the Vance-Owen Peace Plan. For the first time since the troubles in Yugoslavia began Milošević had backed a peace plan, and he was confident it could work; but deep down he knew he could have problems selling it to his ministers, not to mention the power-hungry Serb army commanders.

Lord Owen summoned all the parties to a hastily arranged conference at the Astir Palace Hotel in Athens, on 1st May 1993. The Bosnian President, Alija Izetbegović, and the Croatian President, Franjo Tuđman, had already agreed to the Vance-Owen Plan; only the Bosnian Serbs remained. Lord Owen was confident President Milošević, as their financial and military overlord, could make the Bosnian Serbs sign the peace plan. The leader of the Bosnian Serbs, Radovan Karadžić, told Milošević, "If we sign this peace plan huge members of UN troops will be deployed here, and we will be isolated."

Greek Prime Minister, Konstantinos Mitsotakis, opened the conference and said, "I pray that we will achieve success here in Athens. We must bring joy to the suffering people of Bosnia."

As soon as the formalities were over Milošević took the Bosnian Serbs up to their hotel suite to discuss the peace plan, wanting to assure them that, by backing the plan, he was not betraying them. Milošević told the Bosnian Serbs, "The Vance-Owen plan will never work. They will never be able to implement it."

Karadžić did not understand the benefits of the plan, he was too obsessed with the issue of territory. Milošević commented, "I asked him, 'Are you blind? Radovan can't you see we are saying the same thing? Are we really that stupid?'"

Karadžić said, "It was far too risky for me. The west only had to deploy 10,000 troops split between two most vulnerable points and we Serbs would be finished, but everybody was urging us to accept. Even the waiters bringing the coffee asked, *Are you going to sign?*"

Serb Minister, Dobrica Ćosić, said, "We had not convinced the Bosnian Serbs throughout the night-time session."

The meeting continued into the morning, by one o'clock in the afternoon Milošević said to Karadžić, "Time's up Radovan."

Karadžić gritted his teeth as he picked up his pen and signed the Vance-Owen Peace Plan. Lord Owen said, "This is a happy day for the people in the Balkans, a day in Athens with the sunshine. Let us hope this wonderful day and this moment marks an irreversible peace process in Bosnia Herzegovina." On Serb television the newsreader started his broadcast with his head down as if he were writing; he then put his pen down and pulled out a revolver from underneath his desk. Upon cocking the revolver he placed the barrel to his temple, the screen went blank just as the revolver was fired.

Within a few seconds the newsreader reappeared smiling with some fake blood smeared on his temple and said, "We may have signed the Vance-Owen Peace Plan but we have not committed suicide. Quite the opposite, we have shown the world that this is our territory and that our republic of Srpska will survive. Our Serbian Assembly has the final say regarding the acceptance of the Vance-Owen Peace Plan."

At the Serbian Assembly on the 5th May 1993, Radovan Karadžić was hoping that his attendance would be his escape clause for accepting the Vance-Owen Peace Plan. Karadžić signature in Athens was on condition of the Assembly's ratification of the Vance-Owen Peace Plan. The members gathered, at the self-proclaimed Bosnian Serb capital of Pala, in a former Olympic ski resort, with the Greek Prime Minister, Konstantinos Mitsotakis, accompanied the Serbian President Slobodan Milošević. The Serbs laid on a military parade for the Greek Prime Minister, in a show of their military prowess, and the men inspected the troops before they entered the Assembly. To the Serbs it was very important to have the Greek Prime Minister at their Assembly. It was a message to the rest of the world that the Serbs existed as a State.

In the Assembly Karadžić explained his reluctance in accepting the Vance-Owen Peace Plan, he said, "You know the plan, it would be catastrophic, but since I have signed it I must back it. The terms of the peace plan are hard to swallow, but to keep on fighting would be worse."

One by one the visiting leaders drove home their reasons for accepting the peace plan. Dobrica Ćosić told the assembly, "It is just a temporary solution, a Muslim Bosnia will not happen."

The President of Montenegro, Momir Bulatović, told the assembly, "Only our enemies, like Turkey, want us to vote against the Vance-Owen Peace Plan."

The Greek Prime Minister, Konstantinos Mitsotkis, told the assembly, 'If this Assembly does not accept the Vance-Owen Peace Plan it will be political suicide. It will be the Bosnian Serbs' very own Napoleon, and *he* made grave mistakes that cost France a lot of pain and hardship."

Whilst the Assembly was in session General Mladić, who had now been branded as a war criminal by the world's media, was held up by a rock fall on the road en route to the Assembly. When a news team from CNN gave him a hand to clear the rocks off the road Mladić joked, "CNN! That's the first help I have ever had from CNN."

When General Mladić finally arrived at the Assembly he got his aides to erect a map that showed the front line. When Milošević and Bulatović saw the maps they were stunned.

They could not work out what Mladić was playing at. Mladić, pointing at areas on the maps with a stick, said, "Only we soldiers can see the situation clearly. The first map shows our victories to date, and the territories we have gained. The second map shows how much territory we Serbs had to give up under the Vance-Owen Peace Plan."

The delegates didn't have to think about their decision, despite most of the speakers having recommended accepting, but Mladić had succeeded in raising doubts about the Peace Plan.

Milošević sensed the feeling of rejection throughout the Assembly. He leaned over to Karadžić and whispered, "Why don't you speak again?"

Karadžić replied, "What shall I say?"

Milošević said, "Tell them to vote in favour of the Peace Plan."

Karadžić replied, "But I am not convinced it is in our best interest to accept this plan."

Milošević found himself being snubbed by Karadžić, the leader *he* had put into power in Bosnia.

Milošević had no choice but to address the assembly again if he were to consolidate support for the Peace Plan. Milošević rose to speak, and said, "I believe there is no alternative but to accept this Peace Plan. We have to go for peace or we will be isolated. Dr Karadžić signed the Vance-Owen Peace Plan in Athens. It's a good plan. It's in the interest of all the Serbs in Bosnia, and the Serbs in other provinces. One can sacrifice everything for your nation. If you don't accept this plan, you will sacrifice the Serb people."

The deputy Bosnia/Serb leader, Nikola Koljević, said, "Milošević tried to win back support for the Peace Plan."

Momir Bulatović said, "If the vote had been called for then, I think the Peace Plan would have been accepted, Milošević did start to win back support but they called for a break. In open defiance of Milošević, the Serb Assembly went into closed session."

Milošević and Bulatović realised that they were fighting a lost cause. Their exclusion from the closed session could only mean one outcome to the Vance-Owen Peace Plan. The Bosnian Serbs rejected the Peace Plan.

Milošević left the assembly a very unhappy man. For the first time in his political career Milošević showed some common sense. The Vance-Owen Peace Plan was now dead, and with it the last chance of a united multi-ethnic Bosnia. Many more innocent civilian lives would be lost following this failure.

The Serbs would now continue to build their independent state, at the expense of the human rights of other ethnic groups. In the south of Bosnia the Croats, who had been Muslim allies, started to carve out their own state. The President of Bosnia, Alija Izetbegović, said, "Our front line with the Serbs was a nightmare at least a thousand kilometres long. I did everything to prevent a second front line with the Croats."

President Izetbegović was desperate to hold on to his ally. He travelled through Serb lines under heavy guard to meet the Bosnian Croat army commander, General Slobodan Praljak, in Mostar. President Izetbegović said, "We talked about the unsettled situation in the south of Bosnia Herzegovina. My army were having problems there with the Bosnian Croat forces. I knew the Bosnian Croats wanted to provoke war. They wanted to make Southern Bosnia part of Croatia, and they make their plan pretty obvious."

General Praljak said, "I agreed to meet President Izetbegović one morning in a private flat. We began with a coffee, made no secret of the fact that the Croats in Southern Bosnia would be happy if they were part of Croatia."

There was good reason for President Izetbegović to be concerned. The leaders in Croatia and Serbia had long toyed with the idea of carving up Bosnia between them.

On the 6th May 1992, at Graz airport in Austria, a television crew had a tip-off that the Bosnian Serb leader, Radovan Karadžić, had arrived in Austria for a secret meeting with the leader of the Bosnian Croats, Mate Boban. Karadžić said, "It was a very good meeting. The Croats wanted their part of Bosnia. We did have some territorial disputes with the Croats, but we agreed our young soldiers should not die over these disputes. We knew neither of us would get exactly what we wanted."

Boban said, "The idea of a Croat state in Bosnia had been around for several years. At the meeting in Austria the Serbs even mapped out a border between us in the South of Bosnia."

Almost a year after that meeting in Austria the Bosnian Croats turned on their former Muslim allies. The battle was orchestrated by the commander-in-chief of all Croat forces, President Franjo Tuđman, who said, "I ordered my army units not to advance into the heart of Bosnia. I just sent them to protect the parts of Bosnia that are Croat."

If Tuđman's forces went into Bosnia to protect the Croat population, why did the Muslim villages that stood in their way feel the onslaught of the Croat Army?

On the 17th April 1993, the Muslim village Ahmići was one of many Muslim villages to feel the onslaught of Tuđman's Croat Army; and as always the civilian population were not given any protection.

The brave soldiers, *or should I say the Croat bastards*, started to follow in the footsteps of the bloodthirsty Serbs who'd come before them – with no respect for the innocent civilian population.

Tuđman's Croat butchers left a trail of burning houses and dead people laying in the streets of any villages that dared stand in his way. The Muslims had bolstered the Croat Army for years, now the Croats had interned their former comrades. General Praljak said, "We had to put prisoners somewhere, so we set up camps. I told our Defence Minister, 'Be careful, don't do anything we will be ashamed of.' Some of our boys had been massacred. That is why this mistake happened. At such moments the blood boils, and you go mad. Later you're ashamed of your action as a man, and a Croat."

At a military camp near Mostar a Muslim journalist, Armin Pohara, talked his way into one of the internment camps. He said "The people were being held in underground tanks, where they had stored fuel at one time. Before the war the camp had been an Army barracks. These fuel tanks were half buried into the ground. It was unbearably hot. They had a tiny hole to breathe through. People were dying, and the prisoners were just skin and bone."

The responsibility for the camps went right to the top of the Croat Government. Croat Parliament Speaker, Stipe Mesić said, "President Tuđman must have known about the camps. I asked the President who had organised the prisoner camps?"

Tuđman said, "We Croats should not blame ourselves, there may well be camps but the Serbs and Muslims have them also."

Mesić said, "Tuđman answered my question with a very poor excuse why the camps exist throughout Bosnia."

The Muslim army was driven on by the fear of total annihilation. The lightly armed Muslims fought back with a determination that the Croats could not match, and eventually the Croat advance was broken. In retaliation the Croats shelled the Mostar Bridge. The Muslims had built this beautiful bridge 400 years ago and within seconds it crumbled into the river that had separated the Croats and Muslims. On that day it was four years to the day that the Berlin Wall had come down ushering in the new world order but, in the case of Bosnia, it was a return to the Old World conflicts. Two American administrations had stood by leaving the Europeans to police their own continent.

In May 1992 US Secretary of State, James Baker, made it clear that the United States would not get involved with the conflict in Yugoslavia, his counterpart and predecessor, Warren Christopher, endorsed the same opinion in January 1994. However, eventually through public and European pressure, the Americans decided to weigh in. Their strategy was to isolate the Serbs by settling the war between the Muslims and Croats. The US Special Envoy, Charles Redman, said, "If you line up all the territorial issues that were on the table and then ask yourself how many of those issues could be solved if we had a Muslim/Croat federation in Bosnia, supported by Croatia. A huge proportion of the territorial issues would disappear without any of the problems they face now."

On the 17th February 1993 in the Croatian capital Zagreb, the Americans used some strong arm tactics at a meeting with President Tuđman. He was warned that if he continued his war with the Muslims, Croatia would face the same UN sanctions as Serbia, which would have left Croatia isolated in the Balkans along with Serbia. That did not seem to be a particularly desirable long-term outcome for a country like Croatia, with ambitions of becoming part of the European Community.

The Americans knew that Tuđman wanted to take back the territories that Croatia had lost to Serbia and to achieve this Tuđman would require American support. The US Ambassador in Croatia, Peter Galbaith, said, "President Tuđman risked having no support from the international community just to regain the 27% of Croatia that was under Serbian occupation. So he had no choice but to accept the American mandate."

Tuđman said, "I realised that, in Bosnia, we must prevent a conflict between western and Islamic civilisations. That is why they proposed this agreement with the Muslims."

Tuđman's comments just showed how much he was prepared to camouflage his climb down over his campaign against the Muslims in Bosnia. Within weeks President Clinton presided over a diplomatic triumph, when Tuđman and Izetbegović signed an alliance to end one of Bosnia's wars. They shook hands with cold faces that barely looked at each other, and the world was soon reminded about *the other war in Yugoslavia.*

On the 5th February 1994, in a Sarajevo market place, an explosion killed sixty-eight people.

On the 6th February 1994, in Washington, President Clinton said, "I have just completed a meeting with advisors; we discussed the terrible and outrageous incident in Sarajevo yesterday. But the authority under which air-strikes can proceed requires the common agreement of our NATO allies."

Following President Clinton's press statement he sent his envoys to London, on the 8th February 1994, to try and muster support for air strikes against Serbia; unfortunately Britain became a stumbling block. The British Foreign Secretary at that time was Douglas Hurd who faced an emergency cabinet meeting to discuss the problem in Yugoslavia. Key members of the cabinet were opposed to any action that could draw Britain into conflict with Serbia.

Douglas Hurd said, "We are not just dealing with the Atlantic alliance, we are dealing with a very difficult situation in the former Yugoslavia. Having said that, there comes a point if we are to keep the alliance together, we must be prepared to accept situations that we believe to be risky."

With that in mind the British supported the American plan for action against Serbia. NATO issued an ultimatum to the Serbs, they had ten days to withdraw their heavy weapons from the hills of Sarajevo or they would face air strikes against their heavy weapons. The Serbian commander–in–chief, General Mladić, said, "Ultimatum? We Serbs have never accepted any ultimatum and we never will."

Radovan Karadžić said, "I reject the ultimatum. Giving in would lead to more NATO ultimatums."

With four days of the ultimatum to run, the British Prime Minister, John Major, arrived in Moscow for a previously arranged summit. The Russians were furious about the NATO threat against their allied Serbs. The Russian special envoy, Vitaly Churkin, said, "When the NATO ultimatum came we were very worried that the place would be blown apart. We were not given any prior notice of this proposed action against Serbia."

The President of Russia, Boris Yeltsin, said, "Some people are trying to solve the problems in Bosnia, without any Russian involvement. That will not succeed. We will not allow that to happen."

Douglas Hurd told the Russian leaders that, "NATO was not trying to keep the Russians out of this problem, and in fact the West would like to invite Russia to help resolve the problems in Bosnia."

Boris Yeltsin accepted this challenge, but he did not tell NATO what he had planned.

On the 17th February 1994, Vitaly Churkin travelled to Sarajevo with a letter from the Russian President for the Serb leaders. The letter contained a request that the Bosnian Serbs do the right thing, by not going into a confrontation with NATO, and withdrawing their heavy weapons from the hills overlooking Sarajevo. If they accepted the Russian's advice, in return Russia would deploy troops to the area.

The Bosnian Serb leader, Radovan Karadžić, said, "We quickly agreed to Russia's request. I thought it was vital that Yeltsin got involved, and that Russian troops came in."

On the last day of NATO's ultimatum, columns of Russian tanks and military vehicles moved troops in and around the hills of Sarajevo. Their presence made a NATO air strike all but impossible. The Serbs now complied with Russia's request and withdrew their heavy weapons from the hills of Sarajevo.

For the first time in eighteen months the people of Sarajevo could safely walk their streets without fear of shelling and sniper fire from the Serbian-held hills around the city. The Serbs had been bullied into peace, in Sarajevo at least.

On the 29th March 1994 the US Ambassador to the United Nations, Madeleine Albright, was in Sarajevo to dedicate the new site for an American embassy. She used the occasion to quote the last line of President J. F. Kennedy's speech in Berlin thirty years ago when the Berlin Wall had been removed. President Kennedy ended his speech in German saying, "I am a Berliner." Madeleine Albright ended her speech in Yugoslavian saying, "I am a Sarajevoan", but Sarajevo was not anything like Berlin.

When the Serbs tested the UN resolve, the UN was fully stretched to breaking point due to the lack of peacekeeping troops in Bosnia. The Bosnian Serbs wanted to show the outside world, in particular the Americans, that they were superior and could crush the Muslim army. The place they chose to demonstrate the might of Serbia was one of the most important Muslims enclaves in eastern Bosnia, Gorazde; which, like Srebrenica, had been designated a UN safe area.

The UN commander in Bosnia, General Michael Rose, was awoken up at four a.m. to be informed that Serbian tanks were shelling Gorazde, and the town was now in flames. The report was exaggerated but nevertheless Serb shells were landing in the town. The hospital had been hit. Three patients were killed and many more were wounded, yet General Rose decided no military action was required.

The UN Security Council resolution requires the UN commanders to deter attacks in safe areas. The trouble was with the actual wording of the UN resolution, *to deter attacks and defend or protect against attacks*, mean two different things. The senior military officers were not happy with the way the resolution was worded. They did not have a clear mandate to take action against any side that violated the UN safe areas. They were also concerned about the vulnerability of the small contingent of UN peacekeepers should an air strike take place against the violators of the UN resolution.

When two Serb tanks reached the town of Gorazde, General Rose felt the time had come to request an air strike to protect the UN safe areas. The first NATO air strike in its entire history hit a tent, which was being used as a Serb command post. The Serbs were not deterred for long, after the air strike they retaliated when their commander-in-chief, General Mladić, and a contingent of the Bosnian Serb army surrounded 150 United Nations personnel. They became his hostages to stop further air strikes.

General Mladić contacted General Rose and, in a rage, threatened him. If there were any more air strikes directed towards Mladić's army, he would make sure the UN personnel would not leave there alive. This situation brought home how vulnerable and exposed UN ground forces would be after an air strike.

On the 15th April 1994 in the Bosnian Serb capital Pala, the UN sent a high level delegation to negotiate the release of the UN personnel being held hostage surrounded by the Bosnian Serbs. Radovan Karadžić said, "We had come to an agreement, and were about to settle down to our aperitifs, when the head of the UN delegation Mr Yasushi Akashi was wanted on the telephone."

General Rose had to use open radio to contact the delegation in Pala. General Rose told Mr. Akashi, "While you have been sipping your wine with the Bosnian Serb leaders, the UN peacekeeping forces are being fired on by Serb gunners. The situation here had deteriorated very rapidly. We need air support now."

Mr Akashi suggested to General Rose that he ask Dr Karadžić to order an immediate ceasefire. General Rose replied, "Sir by the time the order for a ceasefire reaches the Bosnian Serb Army, the UN personnel here will be dead or captured."

Karadžić was furious with his commander-in-chief. He contacted General Mladić and demanded, "Mladić, what are you up to?"

General Mladić insisted his guns were firing on the town, and not on General Rose and his men. If the UN was being shelled it was their own fault for being in the wrong place. Karadžić returned to Mr Akashi and insisted General Rose tell the truth about his position. Did General Rose and his men try and find a way out of their hostage situation only to find they had moved into a more perilous one? Whatever way you cut the cloth, the United Nations admitted their troops were in the wrong place. They had no choice but to call off the air strike.

The UN sent a helicopter to pick up a dying British soldier, but the Bosnian Serb offensive on Gorazde continued. The Bosnian Government summoned Mr Akashi and General Rose to explain themselves. Bosnian Prime Minister, Haris Silajdžić, told Mr Akashi and General Rose, "We have been warning you for weeks that the Serbs were planning this offensive, this situation has become a laughing stock. That was the moment those yobs in the Bosnian Serb army realised they could stand up to the United Nations, and knew no one would do anything."

The Americans were determined to reassert their credibility. In a statement to the press, President Clinton said, "The Bosnian Serbs shelled a hospital and the United Nations headquarters. We warned them if they ever threaten our people we would use air power against them. They are the aggressors and wrong doers."

Following this press statement, President Clinton demanded a NATO air strike immediately. At NATO Headquarters the Americans forced through an ultimatum giving the Serbs twelve hours to pull back from their offensive, if the threatened air strikes went ahead.

NATO planned to attack a wide area across the Bosnia/Serb front line. Only one man was prepared to carry on negotiating with the Bosnian Serbs and that was the UN special envoy, Yasushi Akashi. He felt the United Nations had to avoid air strikes, as such action would push peacekeeping efforts in Bosnia over the edge. Two hundred Adriatic NATO planes had been armed and were waiting for the green light. In Belgrade, Mr Akashi emerged with Milošević and Karadžić to announce another ceasefire. President Milošević comment, "I can honestly say this was s successful meeting."

For two weeks the Serbs had defied the United Nations and NATO, and in that time they had learned not to fear the international community. On the 17th May 1995, they had captured and handcuffed UN peacekeepers to posts.

On The 10th July 1995, the Bosnian Serbs cleared Srebrenica of Muslims.

On August 1st 1995 the Bosnian Serbs took Žepa.

The Vice President of Bosnia, Ejup Ganić, said, "We were so happy when the UN peacekeepers arrived, but 10,000 civilians have been killed in Sarajevo alone. In Srebrenica we all thought we were under the protection of the UN forces, but the UN stood by and watched as civilians were attacked, how ironic."

Three months after the fall of Srebrenica, NATO launched a huge air strike against the Bosnian Serbs, and a new peace process began.

CHAPTER 6

The Volunteer

It almost becomes a regular practise to hear news of conflicts in some part of the world we live in.

In March 1993, I came home from work as usual, prepared a meal and sat down to watch the news on the TV. All hell was breaking loose in Yugoslavia. The reports and pictures of ethnic cleansing left me feeling numb with disbelief. I could not believe or understand how any human being could inflict such cruelty on so many innocent victims of war.

We have all read and witnessed the suffering caused to so many innocent people in past conflicts. In fact, I thought World War II was the war to end all wars but, with the pictures that we were now seeing on our TVs, it seemed we never learned from the mistakes of our past. Perhaps we all have a self-destruct button in our lives.

Over the next few weeks the news from Yugoslavia seemed to be getting worse. After watching several more reports I felt I could no longer sit back in my comfortable life style and say "It's not my problem."

Although what could I do to help in Yugoslavia? I am just one man, how can I change or even stop the terrible events that I was seeing on my television screen.

I have done charity events to raise money in the past, which included walking from Exeter to Plymouth for the *Save the Children* charity, running the Plymouth Marathon for children in Africa and a parachute jump for a burns unit in Derriford Hospital in Plymouth.

I felt my heart telling me it was not enough to raise money for these poor victims of war. I needed to somehow be there to help these people, in person.

Over the next week or so I spent some time in battle with my conscience. I could hear my critics saying, "George charity begins at home."

I would say to those critics, "I believe that we all share this planet that God entrusted in our care, when any nation, and their people, fall on hard times albeit their own fault at times, we should help those innocent victims of war who are homeless, and face starvation no matter what the colour of their skin, religions, or culture."

I guess the bottom line is, Would these charity-begins–a-home critics have the same view if they had a conflict on their own doorstep? If they needed help from another country so that their own families might have a chance to live? That's enough of my soapbox speech of the rights and wrongs of our society.

So with my mind made up to somehow try and help in a country, which is now being called on the news *the former Yugoslavia* due to the break-up of their federation. On the news I noticed some Red Cross vehicles. I decided to phone the British Red Cross in Plymouth for advice. They advised me to phone the British Red Cross HQ in London with my enquiry for overseas service with the International Committee Red Cross, known as the (ICRC).

I spoke to the overseas officer, Ann Kerr, and explained my reasons to volunteer for a mission in the former Yugoslavia. I also explained that I was employed as an HGV driver with Crown Berger Paints. Ann asked me to send her my CV and a couple of weeks later I received an ICRC information pack, and a letter explaining to me that at the moment the ICRC did not have any vacancies, but they would keep my details on record in case a vacancy came up.

This gave me some breathing space to think a little more about my decision to volunteer for missions overseas. Not that I was getting cold feet but, as the old saying goes, *fools* generally *rush in*! Over the next few weeks I read all the very large ICRC information pack I had been sent. Then I remembered that I had volunteered for an overseas mission without asking my current employer Crown Berger Paints if they would be willing to give me unpaid leave for this mission. Then, if I had unpaid leave how, would I pay for all my financial commitments, like my mortgage? Would I receive any payment from the Red Cross to cover these expenses? The information pack did not mention any payment, but all these questions plus many more were to be answered in the coming weeks. It also allowed me some time to search my soul about the right, or wrong, reasons for volunteering and undertaking such a dangerous endeavour overseas.

Was I running away? Was I ashamed of my failures from a twenty-four-year marriage that had ended two years previously? Or was it because of the heartache my current partner had caused me over the last few months, when she decided to have an abortion without any consideration for my views, or feelings? Was I looking for an easy way out to put so many failures behind me? Only God can answer why we make certain decisions in our lives that leads us on a journey to our destiny.

With all these doubts and questions in mind, I suddenly remembered all those dreadful pictures and stories of the innocent victims of war on TV. I came back to earth with a big bump. Whatever my past failures and heartaches, it was nothing compared with the problems the people in the former Yugoslavia faced every day. I guess it's true, there's always someone somewhere worse off than you.

The weeks went by and still no news from the British Red Cross.

Had I been forgotten?

Was my CV not good enough?

Then one day, near the end of May, I came home from work to find a message from Ann Kerr on my answering machine asking me to give her a call.

On returning Ann's call, she asked me if I was still interested in an overseas mission in the Former Yugoslavia, if so could I come to the British Red Cross HQ in London? I told Ann that I was still interested, and we arranged an interview for the following week. Before I travelled to London for the interview, I obtained permission from my employer Crown Berger Paints that, if I was accepted for an overseas mission, could I have three months' unpaid leave?

Whilst I was waiting for my interview in London, I got talking to a guy called Terry Gibson. He was from Rugby, and was also waiting for an interview regarding an overseas mission. I told Terry that the company I worked for was based in Rugby. He was unemployed, and needed this job. After talking to Terry it was so clear that the people who volunteer for these overseas missions all share the same common goal, and determination to help people less fortunate than ourselves.

Terry and I both did well at our interviews. However, we were told that the British Red Cross responded to requests from the ICRC in Geneva regarding the installation of overseas personnel from the UK, commonly known as expats. We were also told no such requests had been received yet, but they were expecting a request in July for new UK personnel to replace the volunteers that would be completing their current missions in the former Yugoslavia. In all likelihood we would be next in line to begin our service.

Ann explained that throughout June we would have to return to London for a Red Cross induction course; and a medical, which would include a chest X-Ray. Ann explained to us that the Red Cross were waiting for the completion of two armour-plated Land Rovers, from Rolls Royce in Coventry, and it was likely that Terry and I would be asked to collect these Land Rovers sometime in July. We would then convey them through Europe on route to Zagreb in Croatia. The excitement of this challenge filled us both with such anticipation.

Ann was also able to ease our financial worries, including life insurance cover of £500,000. Very nice I thought, although if something happened to me I wouldn't have been here to enjoy the cash windfall; but at least my family will be financially secure.

Now that all my early worries had been put to rest, I could concentrate on the preparation that would herald the adventure of my life. Before leaving the Red Cross HQ in London, I asked Ann if there was any chance of giving my employers a little notice of when the Red Cross might want me to start my mission as they would be very grateful and it would give them time to replace me whilst I was away.

Ann said, 'You'll be given a week's notice."

I thanked her and returned to Plymouth.

In Plymouth I started to prepare a route through Europe to Croatia. We would board the ferry at Felixstowe to Zeebrugge in Belgium, and then travel through France, Luxemburg, Germany, Austria, Slovenia and finally to Zagreb in Croatia. In the meantime Terry and I kept in touch by phone just to give each other a little reassurance, while we wondered if we were ever going to get the green light.

On Friday 25th June 1993, we both received a letter asking us to attend the Red Cross HQ in London for our briefing induction schedule, and a medical on the 1st and 2nd July 1993. On the 31st June 1993 I once again boarded a bus from Plymouth to London. The following morning Terry and I attended the briefing induction. Every time the Geneva Convention was mentioned, my thoughts strayed to a scene from a prisoner of war movie: when the British commanding officer complains to his German counterpart about the treatment of his men and that they should be treated better under the Geneva Convention, and that his men had not received their Red Cross Parcels.

In the months that lay ahead of us, we would soon find out the reality of the war in the Former Yugoslavia. From what history had taught us about World War II, very much the same was happening fifty years later in the former Yugoslavia.

In war, earthquake, flood, famine, or any disaster, the ICRC is always alert to respond to a call from a *sister society*. When catastrophes occur overseas the ICRC mobilizes all its resources to give aid wherever needed. This can be in a form of money, mupplies, or personnel.

The Red Cross or Red Crescent Society of the disaster-struck country, asks for their most needed requirement as their highest priority. Close links with overseas societies ensures that aid of a kind most needed reaches those in need without delay. In addition to the emergency disaster relief the ICRC is increasingly providing help to overseas societies on a more long term basis, aiming at prevention, and development wherever possible.

CHAPTER SEVEN

The Birth of the Red Cross

In 1859 Henry Dunant was travelling across the war-ravaged plains of Lombardy. He arrived in the vicinity of Solferino just after a terrible battle, and was horrified to see thousands of wounded soldiers abandoned, without any care, and facing certain death. The idea of the Red Cross was born from this dreadful sight.

After organizing relief activities on the spot, improvising them with the means at hand, Henry Dunant undertook to tell the world what he had seen by writing *A Memory of Solferino*; a book which was to stir the soul of Europe. In this story, which foreshadowed the age of modern news reporting, he proposed a remedy to the deficiencies of army medical services by training voluntary relief workers in peacetime and securing for them a *neutral status*, even on the battlefield.

Four citizens of Geneva, Gustave Moynier, General Guillaume Henri Dufour, Dr Louis Appia and Dr Théodore Maunoir, joined Henry Dunant in setting up the *International Standing Committee for the Aid to Wounded Soldiers*, which subsequently became the International Committee of the Red Cross (ICRC). With enthusiasm and perseverance, they succeeded in 1864 in persuading the Swiss Government to convene an international conference in which the representatives of twelve European states participated. A tangible result was the signing, in that same year, of the *Geneva Convention: for the Amelioration of the Condition of the Wounded in Armies in the Field.*

From then on wounded and sick soldiers were rescued and cared for, with no adverse discrimination based upon the side to which they belonged. Medical personnel, equipment and installations were to be respected. They were to be identified by a distinctive emblem: a *Red Cross* on a white background was created, with a specific purpose of insuring the protection of those wounded in war, and those who cared for them. Any misuse of this sign instituted by the Geneva Convention of 1864 – for example, transporting armed troops in an ambulance, or flying a Red Cross flag over a munitions dump – was not only in breach of International Law, but also threatened the very notion of protection granted by the emblem itself.

To prevent such breaches states party to the Geneva Convention were issued strict regulations on the use of the emblem. *It may only be displayed on vehicles, aircraft, ships, buildings and installations assigned to the transport and shelter of the wounded and worn only by the personnel caring for them. It is forbidden to use the emblem for commercial, or publicity, purposes.*

National Red Cross and Red Crescent Societies are also allowed to use the emblem to identify their premises, vehicles and equipment, as well as their staff, who often wear a uniform or badge. In this case the emblem must be small, so as not to be confused with the wartime protective sign.

The 1864 Convention mentioned only the Red Cross, but a second emblem made its appearance a few years later, and is still in use, *the Red Crescent.* The Red Cross had been adopted as a tribute to Switzerland, and was not been intended to have any religious significance. However in 1876, during the Russo-Turkish war, the Ottoman society for relief to the wounded replaced the Red Cross with a Red Crescent. This emblem has since been adopted by a number of countries in the Islamic world. It is recognized as having an equal status with the Red Cross, as such is mentioned in the *1949 Geneva Conventions and Additional Protocols*.

Originally created for service in time of war to help army medical personnel care for the wounded and sick, the national Red Cross and Red Crescent societies today carry out a wide range of activities in both war and peace.

The first Geneva Convention signed in 1864 marked the beginning of International Humanitarian Law. In 1899, at The Hague, another convention was signed adapting the principles of the Geneva Convention to warfare at sea. In 1906, the provisions of the 1864 convention were improved and supplemented. In 1907, the fourth Hague Convention defined the categories of combatants entitled to the status of *prisoner of war* when captured, and to a specified treatment during the whole period of their captivity. These three conventions were reaffirmed and further developed in 1929. In 1949, the Four Geneva Conventions, which are at present in force, were adopted.

The diplomatic conference of 1949 was of vital importance for more than one reason. It not only adopted the *Geneva Convention Relative to the Protection of Civilian Persons in a Time of War*, but also carried out a revision of the three earlier Conventions bringing each of their diplomatic texts into harmony. The four 1949 Geneva Conventions, containing some 400 articles, constitute a legal achievement of historic importance, which for more than thirty years has afforded protection for the countless victims of armed conflicts.

In 1859, on the battlefield at Solferino, human suffering was met with care and compassion and without distinction of nationality. The work of the International Red Cross and Red Crescent movement has expanded steadily ever since, and now takes the form of a wide range of activities. Many of them bear the fruit of long experience, while others are improvised on the spot to meet emergencies of all kinds, but all are grounded in certain humanitarian values.

In the early years of their existence, unity of thought was essentially maintained by the unity of common endeavour. Without being set out in any written agreement, specific humanitarian values rapidly come to light as constituent elements of the movement. As early as 1875, Gustave Maynier spoke of four basic working principles that the movement Societies must observe:

Foresight, which means that preparations should be made in advance, during peacetime, to provide assistance should war break out;

Solidarity, whereby the societies undertake to establish mutual ties, and to help each other in times of hardship;

Centralisation, which implies that there is only one society in each country, but whose activities extend throughout the entire national territory;

And, *Mutuality*, in the sense that care is given to all wounded and sick, irrespective of their nationality.

It was not until 1921 that the fundamental principles of *Impartiality*, *Political*, *Religious* and *Economic Independence*, and the Universality of the movement and equality of its members were formally put in writing. That was when they were incorporated into the revised statutes of the International Committee of the Red Cross (ICRC), the movement's founding body.

After the Second World War, the nineteenth session of the League's Board of Governors met in Oxford and adopted a declaration confirming the four principles established in 1921. Supplementing these further were another thirteen principles and six rules of application. The eighteenth International Conference of the Red Cross in Toronto, 1952, reaffirmed the Oxford principles.

Those principles were not, however, the subject of a systematic treatise until 1955, when Jean Pictet, in his book on the Red Cross principles, defined all the values which guide the work of the movement. He thus listed seventeen principles divided into two categories. On the one hand there were the *Fundamental Principles*, which express the very reason for the movement's existence and influence everything it does; and on the other hand there were the *Organic Principles*, which concerned the movement's structure and how it worked.

On the basis of this in-depth study the movement's seven *Fundamental Principles*, as they stand today, were unanimously adopted in 1965 by the twentieth International Conference of the Red Cross, which also decided that the principles should also be solemnly read out at the opening of every international conference.

The twenty-fifth International Conference of the Red Cross in Geneva, 1986, reaffirmed the importance of the principles by including them in the preamble to the movement's statutes. The responsibility of the national statutes to respect and disseminate knowledge of the principles was underscored in the new statutory provisions, and the states were called upon to be, at all times, adherent to all the components of the movement and its fundamental principles.

Of course the world did not wait for the Red Cross to come to the rescue of suffering people. Feelings and gestures of *Solidarity*, *Compassion*, and *Selflessness* are to be found in all cultures. Our concern, however, is somewhat different from this fundamental observation. We wish to consider various aspects of the specific nature of the Red Cross and Red Crescent work to alleviate human suffering. This specificity illustrates especially well, in the words of the movement's principles, the first which reads:

Humanity, the International Red Cross and Red Crescent movement born of the desire to bring assistance without discrimination to the wounded on the battlefield, endeavours in its International and National capacity, to prevent and alleviate human suffering wherever it may be found. Its purpose is to protect life and health and to ensure respect for the human being. It promotes *Mutual Understanding*, *Friendship*, *Co-operation* and lasting *Peace* amongst all peoples.

The universality of the Red Cross and the Red Crescent has its roots in the universality of suffering, and it is thus that the principle of humanity must be understood. Indeed, the movement has no *dogma*, no special philosophy; it is attentive to human misery.

Caught up in war or stricken by natural disasters, often struggling to survive, countless human beings suffer from man's inhumanity to the civilian population and non-combatants in conflicts. The cries of distress heard throughout the modern world cannot, and must not, be met with indifference, they must instead foster activity to hear one's fellow man. To recognize his, or her, suffering is to feel a call to service. Therein lies the movement's sense of purpose.

Is the principle of humanity, as some suggest, too vague, too general to serve as a basis for the movement's work? We think not. The words used in the text to prevent, to alleviate, to protect, to ensure respect, require very concrete efforts. *Then is the undertaking not too ambitious*? Not at all! There are at least two reasons why not:

The principle of humanity implies that no service whatsoever for the benefit of a suffering human being is to be dismissed out of hand, it is a reminder of how important it is to seize the opportunity for humanitarian action, of how important the Red Cross and Red Crescent spirit of initiative are.

The principle of humanity is only the first in a declaration of seven principles which must be read as a whole. The principles of *Impartiality*, *Neutrality*, and *Independence* in particular are indicative of how clearly the movement has determined both the framework and the means for attaining its objectives.

The Red Cross and Red Crescent endeavour to prevent and alleviate human suffering, *but what kind of suffering*? Throughout its existence the movement has gradually broadened the scope of its activities to reach new categories of victims; both in the time of war and in peacetime, but its components do not seek to do everything and anything. Their priority is to act in situations where no one else can, or will. They work as auxiliaries to the public authorities; they do not wish to replace them, but to make their own unique and unbiased contribution in situations which are often totally unforeseen.

The principle of humanity embodies one especially important idea: to protect. This is a very tangible concern. At the root of the word lies the idea of shelter from the elements. The notion of protection suggests a screen or shield placed between a person or thing and the danger they face. o protect means: to help someone by sheltering him or her from attack, ill-treatment, etc; to frustrate efforts to destroy, or make persons disappear; to meet a person's need for security; to help a person to survive; to act in a person's defence. Protection may therefore take many forms, depending on the situation of the victims.

In peacetime, protection of life and health consists primarily in *Sickness*, *Disasters*, and *Accidents*, or reducing their effects by saving lives. A first aider in a national society, who cares for the injured and saves them from an otherwise certain death, has engaged in a fundamental form of protection. Protection in this sense can also mean, as it does for some national societies, efforts to maintain a healthy environment.

It is the function of International Humanitarian Law to protect the victims of armed conflict and to ensure that their lives are as normal as possible under the circumstances. The provisions of the law are not however always applied. It is up to the ICRC in particular to make sure the rules of humanitarian law are applied, and to assist those persons protected by law to make sure they do not die of hunger, are not ill-treated, do not disappear, and are not attacked.

There are some points of convergence between humanitarian interest, which require that prisoners be treated humanely, that the wounded be cared for, and civilians be spared, and that there are clearly defined no political interests from the ICRC. Compliance with humanitarian rules in war and protection for the victims can, in the medium and long term, encourage a resumption of dialogue between adversaries, eventual reconciliation, and finally the restoration of peace.

Protection goes hand in hand with prevention and alleviation of suffering. The Red Cross and Red Crescent are sometimes reproached for not doing enough for prevention and concentrating albeit very effective at the alleviation of suffering, but the reproach is not entirely well founded.

Is it the doctor's fault, if one patient has a fever, he should leave a patient's bedside to vaccinate everyone in the village? Probably not, but we are well aware that relief, which does no more than help the beneficiaries to subsist, is at best a limited, short-term measure. At worst it may even exacerbate the negative effects (*Passivity, Dependence*, etc.) of present or future disasters. We must therefore reconsider the meaning and scope of our humanitarian activities.

This opens whole new horizons to the movement. It must of course always help those who suffer, but it can also act to prevent their suffering. It must provide relief in an emergency, but it can also help reconstruct and indeed assist in the development process. *In this contest, how do the Red Cross and Red Crescent contribute to peace?*

The movement has always been active in two domains concerned with the prevention of cruelty and other forms of abuse, which are so widespread in armed conflicts. The first and most essential lies in the development and extension of International Humanitarian Law: to ensure compliance with and extend the scope of the law's protective rules. This is an absolutely essential undertaking, which helps promote respect for life and human dignity. Then, as a corollary, the movement promotes the dissemination of humanitarian law; spreading knowledge of the basic rules protecting victims and non-combatants is another vital task.

The overall work of the Red Cross and Red Crescent, their teaching of solidarity between people and nations, the multitude of practical and selfless acts they perform, their activities in the midst of strife can all help bring about a spirit of peace that, as we have said, can facilitate the reconciliation of adversaries. In view of the political hazards involved, the question of the prevention of armed conflicts is, however, one the movement has thus far approached only with great caution.

The Red Cross and Red Crescent base their activities on behalf of suffering humanity, on what Jean Pictet once called an *optimistic philosophy* – the refusal to despair of mankind. Yet this optimism in no way detracts from the philosophy's realism. It is aware that humanitarian work is difficult. Its greatest enemies may well be neither weapons nor disaster, but selfishness, indifference and discouragement. It is for this reason that the movement has not based its activities on dry principles, but on service to suffering humanity, and to life, often fragile and vulnerable. This is how we understand the principle of humanity.

. The principle of *Impartiality* thus represents the very essence of the Red Cross and Red Crescent thought. It inspired Henry Dunant at Solferino, it has been cited at every stage of formulation of the principles and it is, moreover, inherent to the Geneva Conventions. The text of the principle of Impartiality is worded as follows:

The International Red Cross and Red Crescent movements make no discrimination as to *Nationality*, *Race*, *Religious Beliefs*, *Class* or *Political* opinions. It endeavours to relieve the suffering of individuals, being guided solely by their needs, and give priority to the most urgent of distress.

The preliminary condition for non-discrimination was embodied from the outset in the Geneva Conventions. According to the initial 1864 Convention any soldier no longer able to fight, by reason of wound or sickness, was to be collected and cared for, no matter what his nationality. That Convention, which was revised in 1906 and 1929, explicitly prohibited discrimination only between nationalities, whereas the 1949 Geneva Conventions state that adverse distinctions based on *Sex*, *Race*, *Religion*, *Political Opinions* or any other similar criteria, are also forbidden. The final words indicate that all types of discrimination are prohibited and that those listed are given merely as examples. This basic prohibition is also contained in the *Additional Protocols* of 1977, with a more detailed, though not exhaustive, list of the criteria on which it is prohibited to have discrimination.

As one of the principles of international law, non-discrimination is above all an imperative rule governing the work of the movement, whose concern reaches out to all those in need regardless of any factors that are not humanitarian.

Theoretically, non-discrimination is the refusal to apply distinctions of an adverse nature to human beings simply because they belong to a specific category. In the context of humanitarian ethics, non-discrimination requires that all objective distinctions among individuals be ignored, so that the aid given transcends the most virulent antagonisms, in time of armed conflict or internal disturbances, friend and foe will be assisted in the same way, likewise those in need will be secured at all times; whoever they may be.

In practice all the components of the movement must strictly avoid any form of discrimination when providing material assistance or giving medical treatment. For example, in a hospital run by a national Red Cross society and treating numerous casualties, among them enemy wounded, it would be incompatible with the principle of non-discrimination to refuse to admit the latter so that the hospital could take in more wounded compatriots. The same would be true if the national Red Crescent society in a country torn by internal strife gave food aid to the victims of only one of the parties involved in the conflict, and made no attempt to bring relief to those whose ideas the society did not share.

The ICRC has the additional duty of opposing discrimination in connection with visits to persons detained as a result of a conflict or internal disturbances.

It requests the detaining authorities to give the same humane treatment to all such persons and ensures that none of them is placed at any kind of disadvantage for reasons of nationality of differing political convictions. Distinctions arising from humanitarian and national motives, however, are not incompatible with the rule of non-discrimination; for example requesting extra blankets for those less able to tolerate cold because of their origin, age or health.

The national societies are particularly concerned with the requirement of non-discrimination, which is in fact a condition for their recognition. They must be open to all who wish to become members and must permit all *Social*, *Political* and *Religious* groups to be represented. This representation is the guarantee of the societies' abilities to engage in exclusively humanitarian activities and resist all partisan considerations.

National societies must be open to all nationals of their respective countries who are willing and able to help them. Foreigners who wish to join should also be able to become members, although the societies would not be acting contrary to the principle of *Impartiality* by refusing to accept them, since the time of war, the national societies can operate as auxiliaries to the armed forces medical services and the volunteer workers assigned to this task are placed on the same footing as medical personnel in these national armed forces. This could lead to difficulties for resident foreigners recruited as volunteers.

Non-discrimination means that all those in need shall be helped, yet to treat everyone in the same way without taking into account how much they are suffering, or how urgent their needs are, would not be equitable. This means that, for the movement, the only priority that can be set in dealing with those who require help must be based on need, and the order in which available aid is shared out must correspond to the urgency of the distress it is intended to relieve.

International Humanitarian Law stipulates that preferential treatment must be given to certain especially vulnerable categories of protected persons, such as children and the elderly. It requires that the sick and wounded be treated with complete equality as regards care and protection and that *only urgent medical need* may justify an order of priority in the case provided. Therefore, when medical personnel are dealing with an influx of casualties, they must exercise a choice based on proportionality and treat first of all those whose condition requires immediate care.

The same holds true for all the components of the movement, they must ensure that the distribution of food or medicines corresponds to the most pressing needs. In other words, for equal suffering, the aid will be the same, while for unequal suffering, aid will be proportionate to the intensity of distress.

In practice the rule that relief must be proportionate to the need is not easy to follow. For example, it is sometimes difficult for the national society to collect funds for victims in countries other than its own, since everyone gives according to his affinities, and national self-centredness wants aid to improve the well-being of the local population before that of foreigners. Even when this kind of nationalism is surmounted, there is a greater willingness to help neighbouring countries, whose distress is more familiar and can be sympathized with more readily.

The magnificent wave of solidarity with Romania among European countries at the beginning of 1990 was such that at one point restraint had to be called for, since the gifts received far exceeded the immediate needs. Yet at the same time, in Africa and the Middle East, hundreds of thousands of displaced were barely surviving.

The ICRC for its part has great difficulty in getting the parties to a conflict to understand that the only thing it must grant equally to each is its willingness to serve, and that in other respects its activities are proportional to the needs, and consequently unequal when distress is greater on one side than on the other.

These few examples demonstrate how difficult it is to apply the principle of proportionality in the strictest sense; but the movement observes the principle as clearly as possible by taking the most urgent suffering as the sole criterion for priority in its work To illustrate the difference between the two notions, a national society that refuses to provide its services to a specific group of people, because of their ethnic origin, fails to observe the rule of non-discrimination, whereas a national society staff member who, in the exercise of his functions, favours a friend by giving him better treatment than given to others, contravenes the principle of *Impartiality*.

As shown above, *Impartiality* is expected of those called on to care for the less fortunate. It demands that an effort be made to overcome all prejudices, to reject the influence of personal factors, whether conscious or unconscious, and to make decisions on the basis of facts alone in order to act without bias. In other words, *Impartiality* implies the objective scrutiny of problems and the *depersonalization* of humanitarian work. Thus, while it is natural and human for volunteer workers of a national society to side emotionally with one of the parties to the conflict, they are nevertheless expected to disregard their feelings in the matter when distributing relief supplies, by making no adverse distinction regarding one of the parties to the conflict.

It appears, indeed that the principle of *Impartiality* thus defined is an ideal to be attained, an inner quality that is rarely born and often requiring one to overcome one's instincts. It demands from members of the Red Cross and Red Crescent Society an arduous and prolonged effort to overcome their own prejudices and preferences in order to be able to perform the purest act of *Impartiality*, which is to give more help to the adversary, who is the victim of great misfortune, than to a friend whose suffering is less severe; or to care for the more severely wounded, even if guilty, before the innocent whose injuries are slight. When confronted with distress the International Red Cross and Red Crescent movements respond by giving aid without distinction. Mindful of human suffering, it has established an ethical foundation which is embodied in the fundamental principles, and acts as a guideline for its work in the midst of conflicts and disasters for the victims it has pledged to assist. Each of the movements' components, in its own area of activity, and every one of its millions of members, are committed to implementing these fundamental principles and manifesting them in their work, so that the ideas of human solidarity and love upheld by the movement shall not be merely empty words.

Neutrality, the ultimate objective of which is action. It is often *Neutrality* that opens prison doors to delegates of the International Committee of the Red Cross, and allows relief convoys displaying one of the movement's emblems to enter conflict areas, and spares national society volunteers from attack in countries torn by international disturbances.

Paradoxically, however, *Neutrality* is not a well-loved principle. There are those who express indignation at the *Neutrality* of the Red Cross and Red Crescent, in the mistaken belief that *Neutrality* betokens lack of commitment and courage. Others point out that while the ICRC can remain neutral with relative ease, national societies may find it an impossible task..

In the following lines we look at the meaning of the principle of *Neutrality* and its relation to the other principles, to give some examples of the problems implicit in its application, and to show what ends it can serve. The meaning of the principle of *Neutrality* reads as follows: in order to continue to enjoy the confidence of all, the movement may not take sides in hostilities, or engage at anytime in controversies of the Political, Racial, Religious or Ideological nature. There are therefore two facts to *Neutrality*:

Military Neutrality, in a situation of a conflict, or unrest, *Neutrality* implies not acting in a way that could facilitate the conduct of hostilities by any of the parties involved. Thus, in an international armed conflict, national society volunteers working alongside official military or civilian medical services must not support, or hinder, military operations in any way. This *Neutrality* is the necessary counterpart to the respect due to the enemy's medical personnel, units and establishments.

There are many examples of violations of this *Neutrality* surrounding a military objective with medical units, so that it will not be targeted . The ICRC will not tolerate hiding weapons in a hospital, transporting able-bodied combatants in an ambulance, using an aircraft displaying the Red Cross emblem for military, or reconnaissance missions, all have three things in common: they seriously weaken the system of protection embodied in the International Humanitarian Law; they divert people and objects displaying the Red Cross or Red Crescent from their humanitarian purpose; and they put lives in danger by fostering mistrust.

Ideological Neutrality, implies standing apart at all times from *Political, Religious* or any other controversies in which the Red Cross or Red Crescent, were it to take a position, would lose the trust of one segment of the population, and thus be unable to continue its activities. If the national society branch expresses sympathy for a movement, a cause or a political figure, for example by permitting the latter to take advantage of Red Cross or Red Crescent membership for electoral purposes, many volunteers may cancel their membership. If a dispensary run by a national society also displays a religious affiliation in a country in which there is tension between the members of different faiths many patients will no longer wish or dare to come for treatment. In other words, *Neutrality* is a state of mind, an attitude that must guide every step taken by the movement's components.

Neutrality of the ICRC. For the ICRC *Neutrality* has a specific meaning, as indicated in the movement's Statutes. To discharge the mandate conferred on it by the states party to the Geneva Convention, and to take the humanitarian initiatives that are part of its role as a neutral intermediary, the ICRC must remain independent. With this view, it has adopted a special structure which allows it to resist political, economic and other pressures and maintain its credibility in the eyes of all governments for its activities. The ICRC members are co-opted from all nationals of the same country whose permanent *Neutrality* is internationally recognized.

The ICRC may have a *Neutrality* of its own, but every national society, while acting as a auxiliary to the public authorities in the humanitarian field, must be ready to do relief work in the event of a conflict, and must therefore fully comply with the principle of *Neutrality*, even in peacetime. In addition, as a member of the movement, each national society must ensure that nothing it says or does could be detrimental to the activities of the movement's other components.

Neutrality, is closely related to the other fundamental principles. Thus, a national society which limits some of its services to a specific ethnic, or other group, thereby violating the principle of *Impartiality*, would soon be perceived as to be lacking in *Neutrality*. A national society whose leaders are for the most part designated by their government, and which has thus lost its independence, would find it very difficult to observe the principle of *Neutrality*. On the other hand, a national society open to all, with members from all walks of life, all ethnic groups, all ideological tendencies, one that clearly adheres to the principle of *Unity*, will be better able to resist pressure to take initiatives, and to preserve some freedom of judgment and behaviour, in order to conduct its activities in accordance with all the movement's core principles.

It is admittedly not always an easy task to apply the principle of *Neutrality*, not least because everyone has personal convictions. When tension mounts and passions are aroused, every member of the Red Cross or Red Crescent is called upon to exercise great self-control, and refrain from expressing his or her opinions in the discharge of their duties. Volunteers are not asked to be neutral; everyone is entitled to have an opinion, but to behave *neutrally*. That is an important distinction.

The next difficulty is the fact that the parties to the conflict often take a dim view of *neutral behaviour*. In countries where an internal conflict is taking place, the armed forces fail to understand why their national society does not condemn the activities of those they regard as *bandits*, much less why it wants to provide assistance to any of their number no longer able to fight. As for the opposition, they are critical of the society's connections with authorities.

Anyone trying to work on both sides to help non-combatants is considered at best naïve, at worst a traitor. The extremely polarized nature of many struggles is such that not taking a stand is a hostile act in itself. This is why the Red Cross and Red Crescents *Neutrality* and *Impartiality* must be explained. As one national society member put it, "The best argument I have, is to tell one of the parties to the conflict that if I take its side and ignore victims on the other side, I will never again be able to bring help to its own wounded."

In any conflict situation, by definition highly politicized, another problem is that the national society is judged not only by its public statements, but also by its every act, the underlying humanitarian motivation of which is not always understood. Therefore, bringing food to the displaced, destitute people assembled by the government in camps can be construed as support for a policy of emptying a territory of its civilians, the better to crush the combatants. Giving cooking utensils to peasants whose dwellings have been burned down by a guerrilla army is sometimes considered by that army as tantamount to supporting people who, to its way of thinking, received the punishment they deserved for collaborating with the authorities. Treating wounded individuals who come to the national society in the mistaken belief that they will benefit from some form of immunity, can give rise to mistrust on the part of those looking for them, who will feel that the national society, in agreeing to care for them, has demonstrated where its sympathies lay.

Another problem is determining which controversies the Red Cross and Red Crescent must avoid.

Can a National Society lobby for ratification of the protocols additional to the 1949 Geneva Convention if those protocols are a bone of public contention?

Can it take a stand against Capital Punishment, if the death penalty is a topic of heated debate in the country?

What should be the attitude of its member volunteers towards hunger strikers trying to force the authorities to give ground?

The questions are countless and bear testimony to the wide variety of ethical problems that the application of the principle of *Neutrality* can create. Everyone must find ways of applying the principle that are in keeping with the dictates of their own conscience.

It is only by consistently applying the principle of *Neutrality*, in spite of all the difficulties involved, that the International Red Cross and Red Crescent movement will continue to enjoy widespread confidence. Standing apart from issues at stake so as to be able to conduct relief activities is not easy in conflict situations, where suspicions run rife on all sides. It is not much easier in peacetime, in countries where freedom of opinion and general security permit every individual to defend their ideas, or even to put pressure on the national society to support a current of opinion, with all the weight of its moral authority. To make matters more difficult the spokesmen of other charities do not hesitate to take militant positions, or denounce publicly those responsible for injustices, or inhuman acts.

As for the ICRC, it rarely waives its policy of discretion. Only when it observes grave and repeated breaches of International Humanitarian Law, when its confidential representations have been in vain, and it considers that the only means of helping the victims of a conflict, or disaster, is to ask for the support of the international community, does it make public representations. This sometimes takes the form of an appeal to the state's party to the Geneva Conventions, whose responsibility it is to respect, and ensure respect for International Humanitarian Law. Such initiatives are nevertheless the exception, rather than the rule.

The Red Cross and Red Crescent have only one cause that of people who are suffering today, or will be suffering tomorrow, and only one means of defending it: persuasion. Red Cross and Red Crescent leaders must be willing to talk, even to corrupt officials who are responsible for violations of human rights, about International Humanitarian Law. They cannot pass judgement on them publicly, but must speak to them on behalf of those to whom speech is denied and who have no one else to turn to. They often do so at considerable risk to their own personal safety, and their words may fall on deaf ears; but if this policy of refraining from public denunciation makes it possible to alleviate the suffering of just one man, woman, or child, that is ample recompense.

Independence, the movement is independent. The national societies, while auxiliaries in the humanitarian services of their governments, and subject to the laws of their respective countries, must always maintain their autonomy so that they may be able at all times to act in accordance with the principles of the movement.

In its present wording the principle of *Independence*, which dates back to the very foundation of the movement, comprises three elements which we will examine here, a general statement of *Independence* as one of the movement's principles, the role of national societies as auxiliaries to the public authorities in humanitarian matters, and finally, the need for national societies to remain autonomous in order to be able to take action at all times in accordance with the fundamental principles.

The general meaning of the principle of *Independence*, means that the Red Cross and Red Crescent institutions must resist any interference, whether *Political*, *Ideological* or *Economic* capable of diverting them from the course of action laid down by the requirements of *Humanity*, *Impartiality* and *Neutrality*. No national Red Cross or Red Crescent society could accept financial contributions from any source that are granted only on condition that they be used for a specific category of persons chosen according to *Political*, *Ethnic* or *Religious* criteria, to the exclusion of any other group of people whose needs might be more imperative.

Similarly, in order to merit the trust of all and to enjoy the credibility essential to carrying out their mission, Red Cross and Red Crescent institutions must on no account appear to be instruments of Government policy.

In addition to resisting pressure of a political or economic nature, the movement must demonstrate its independence to public opinion. In a world increasingly influenced by the media, and where competition between humanitarian organizations grows steadily keener, the speed and visibility of the Red Cross and Red Crescent actions may indeed have a considerable impact, not only on the image and credibility of the movement, but also in financial terms. Nevertheless it is indispensable for the movement to know how to stay aloof from media pressure, since the scale or duration of the needs are not measured solely by the volume of newspaper articles, or the level of popular reaction.

For instance, a national society that undertakes a relief operation under pressure from public opinion, and in so doing ignores one of its own criteria for taking action, such as the preliminary assessment of needs, would run the risk of supplying aid that was completely inappropriate, or even harmful. To plunge blindly into the race to provide humanitarian aid may, moreover, resulting in subsequent criticism from that same public, which might reproach the Red Cross and Red Crescent institutions for a lack of responsibility and consistency in their work.

Officially recognized by their governments as auxiliary to the public authorities in humanitarian matters, in particular in the event of armed conflict (Article 26, First Geneva Convention of 1949), the national societies must nevertheless enjoy an autonomy that enables them at all times to observe the Fundamental Principles. The requirement of government recognition is also one of the ten conditions which all national societies must fulfil in order to be admitted within the movement, and to continue to be a valid part of it (article 4, paragraph 3, of the movement's Statutes).

A decree granting official recognition to the national society is essential, since the society is thereby distinguished from other charitable organizations in the country and entitled, in the event of armed conflict, to the protection of the Geneva Conventions and, if relevant, the additional protocols, as well as to the use of the Red Cross and Red Crescent emblem.

Although the content of the decree of recognition may vary from one country to another, it must at least include the characteristic of voluntary service, co-operation with the authorities in humanitarian matters, and a reference to the Geneva Conventions.

To provide the national society with a sound legal basis for its subsequent development and activities, the decree of recognition, or equivalent text should explicitly specify that the national society is the country's only Red Cross, or Red Crescent, organization and that it is autonomous in relation to the state, that it performs its activities in conformity with the Fundamental Principles, and the conditions governing the use of the emblem.

Initially conceived as officially recognized auxiliaries to the armed forces, and medical services, the national societies have progressively diversified their peacetime activities, and are today responsible for numerous medical and social welfare programmes which, to name just a few, include: Health Education, Blood Banks, Hospital Management, Aid to Refugees, etc. In carrying out these functions, the national societies act as auxiliaries to the public authorities, either by reason of an express mandate, and sometimes even a national monopoly, or by having spontaneously undertaken work that relieves the official bodies of duties that they themselves would otherwise have to assume.

In view of the extent and importance of the national societies activities, these should evidently be incorporated into the overall framework of existing national programs. However, this does not mean that the authorities are able to do as they like with the National Red Cross and Red Crescent societies, which must enjoy genuine autonomy in relation to their governments.

Autonomy, the National Red Cross and Red Crescent societies must play their part as auxiliaries to the public authorities, without in any way abandoning their freedom of decision, which alone enables them to remain faithful to their ideals of Humanity, Impartiality, and *Neutrality*. This condition is moreover laid down (in Article 4, paragraph 4) of the movement's Statutes. The degree of autonomy necessary to a national society cannot be defined uniformly and absolutely, since it depends partly on the political, economic and social conditions in the country. In time of civil war, for example, it is obviously essential for the national society not to appear to be a tool of the government, since it will be unable to carry out all its duties if it does not possess the trust of all parties.

This requirement is of a different kind in peacetime when what matters, above all, is for the national society to be free to decide which areas of activity to engage in, and the form its activities should take. Thus, the national society must show itself sufficiently willing to support the public authorities, yet without the state being able to compel it to accept a mandate that the society might consider as inappropriate to actual needs, or incompatible with fundamental principles. At the same time, it must be free to relinquish certain tasks, or to change its priorities in accordance with the material and human resources at its disposal. The role of auxiliary to the public authorities does not in the least prevent a national society from freely choosing the activities it carries out completely independently of the state. For example, a national society may decide to undertake social welfare activities in favour of especially vulnerable groups among the population, such as: Refugees, Released Prisoners, Drug Addicts etc, even if the state does not request it to take action in these areas.

Although the state undertakes to respect the principle of *Independence*, it is sometimes greatly tempted to interfere in the life and work of a national society, for instance by assuming a certain right to monitor its activities in return for state subsidies and other facilities.

Often the state is represented in the governing bodies of the national society. This can be useful in itself. The need for proper co-ordination with the public authorities can, in fact, justify representatives of the ministries concerned with the Red Cross or Red Crescent activities e.g. the ministries of Health, Education, and Defence, etc, taking part in decision making within the societies, active members remain in a large majority in the society's governing bodies.

The national societies can offer effective resistance to interference, or attempts at control only if they adopt specific structural and operational rules. In this context the importance of the government recognition, which lays the basis for co-operation between the state and the national society, must be re-emphasized a good declaration of recognition is in fact the first guarantee of *Independence*.

Another equally important guarantee is for the national society to be run democratically. It will safeguard its *Independence* still further by recruiting volunteer workers from all social, cultural and economic sectors of the population, and by giving them the opportunity to take part in important decisions, and to be elected to leading positions.

This incidentally is why the league Board of Governors, meeting in Oxford in 1946, and Stockholm in 1948, requested that each society should be organized on a truly democratic basis. This directive was confirmed by the 18th International Conference of the Red Cross, and remains wholly valid.

Other measures, which cannot all be enumerated, likewise contribute to the national society's *Independence*. It must for example provide its own financing from regular and other sources, and take care not to depend totally on income from the public services it performs.

It must also diversify its activities so that if it relinquishes certain duties, it must maintain its image and credibility in the eyes of the general public, so that if ever its independence is threatened it will be able to count on public support.

Finally, there is a close link between development and respect for the fundamental principles. A national society whose administrative and financial structure is inadequate is less well equipped to uphold its *Independence* compared with the authorities than if its structure is sound, and can rally the support of well trained, and motivated volunteers,

It is therefore essential that solidarity within the movement be expressed by strengthening the least developed national societies. This undoubtedly helps to increase knowledge of, and respect for the fundamental principles in the national society concerned.

Voluntary Service, for the International Red Cross and Red Crescent movement, voluntary service is the unselfish gift of oneself, in most cases anonymously, to carry out a specific task for someone else in a spirit of human fraternity. Whether it is without pay, or with some form of acknowledgement, or even modest remuneration; it is not inspired by the desire for financial gain but by individual commitment and devotion to a humanitarian purpose, freely chosen or accepted as part of the service that the Red Cross and Red Crescent render to the community. The quintessence of voluntary service is unpaid service to others, the most direct expression of the humanity which is the first of the movement's principles.

The origin of *Voluntary Service* was on the battlefields of Solferino that Henry Dunant, struck by the insufficiency of medical services, the great number of soldiers who died for lack of care, and the vast suffering that could have been avoided, conceived the great project of forming relief societies for the purpose of having care given to the wounded in wartime by zealous, devoted, and thoroughly qualified volunteers.

Henry Dunant's idea made headway. To overcome the misgivings voiced by many senior military officers, who were concerned about civilians being given access to the battlefield, it was decided that voluntary medical personnel would be placed under military command (resolution 6 of the 1863 Geneva International Conference). As they were then acting under military discipline, and were placed on the same footing as military medical services, it was secondary whether or not they kept their status as civilians, being officially authorized they were entitled to the same protection as military medical personnel.

Although the first Red Cross volunteers worked on or close to the battlefields, they are now also present at the scene of natural disasters and everyday life, performing a host of medical and social welfare tasks. This was a natural development, stemming from the history of the movement and its tradition of pioneering in the humanitarian field.

Why is the International Red Cross a voluntary relief movement not prompted in any manner by desire for gain, as stated in principle of voluntary service? There are three factors which explain the importance attached to this principle.

The human dimension of voluntary service. It is thanks to the many volunteers who have offered their help that the movement has been able to undertake its task, as defined in the principle of Humanity, to prevent and alleviate human suffering wherever it may be found.

Let us take an example to illustrate the link between the two principles. Some people may doubt the usefulness of volunteers, either in countries where health and well-being of the public are largely or entirely provided for by the state, or in countries whose national societies are prosperous and have large, well-trained and competent salaried staffs. *Would it be possible under these circumstances to get along without volunteers*? We think not!

First of all, however competent and devoted public health workers may be, there is always suffering that the public authorities overlook, that only volunteers familiar with local conditions can detect.

In addition, the very fact that the Red Cross and Red Crescent volunteers are not public employees working under orders, that they do not represent authorities who may be feared or perhaps even contested, is likely to gain for them the confidence of the men, women and children they seek to help. Especially in the case of unpaid volunteers, the selflessness of this gesture without any thought of recompense gives it particularly human dimension.

Finally, the national society itself, if it fails to recognize the value of the voluntary services, is in danger of becoming bureaucratic, thus losing touch with a vital source of motivation, inspiration and initiative, and of cutting off the roots which maintain its contact with human needs, and enable it to meet them, with the authorities' agreement and often with their active support. Voluntary service is token to and testimony of the *Independence* of these national societies.

Another reason why voluntary service is and must remain one of the pillars of the movement derives from the other Fundamental Principles of the Red Cross and Red Crescent. What better security do national societies have against the many pressures, to which they are exposed, than their nature as private institutions, based on voluntary service without any desire for gain? A national society's independence is especially important in the event of civil war, and internal disturbances and tension, when a country is divided between rival factions. The national society could not gain the confidence of all parties in the conflict, indispensable for access to all the victims, if it did not remain free to act in accordance with the principles it has adopted, and if it did not have the support of volunteers from every quarter, *Political*, *Religious*, and *Social.*

Voluntary service is also a source of economy, to consider more prosaic matters. Yet let us just imagine how much suffering would have to be neglected for lack of means, if all the work done by volunteers had to be paid for. It is sometimes sufficient to have a relatively small, but motivated support staff with the necessary minimum of financial resources, to enable volunteers to render community services whose cost could never be borne, either by the national society or by the state.

Challenges posed by the principle of Voluntary Service, voluntary service within the movement is going through a period of crisis, according to some people who are concerned about the difficulty of recruiting volunteers, and ensuring that their motivation does not flag. Other people argue that the humanitarian involvement of young volunteer workers, in countries in the throes of political transformation, may give new life to national societies which are at times themselves disconcerted by the rapidity of change, or seeking to gain greater credibility with the general public. Although everyone agrees that voluntary service is one of the mainstays of the Red Cross and Red Crescent's work, the problems encountered by national societies vary considerably depending on their level of development, and the political situation within their country. *What are the challenges which this principle poses*?

Voluntary service during armed conflicts, the Red Cross and Red Crescent volunteers may act as auxiliaries to official military and civilian medical services. Many have given their lives courageously evacuating the injured, treating the wounded, tending the sick, or retrieving mortal remains in places no one else dared to approach. In countries ravaged by conflict, Henry Dunant's humanitarian ideas have more than proved their merit.

Despite this, many national societies beset by other problems do not realize the need to prepare themselves for situations of conflict, to define the activities incumbent upon them in such a case, in co-operation with the civilian and military authorities, and to train volunteers to undertake such activities. In other countries, the official medical services are so fully developed that the authorities see no need for volunteer help should a conflict arise. Admittedly, assistance to the victims of conflict is primarily the duty of the state, but experience has shown that forward-looking national societies which, for example, have stockpiled emergency supplies, trained volunteers in first aid and established the necessary contacts, can do invaluable work once a volatile political situation flares up in violent clashes. Furthermore, it should not be over-optimistically assumed that the official medical services are capable of handling every contingency.

The recruitment of volunteers: competition among humanitarian, sporting, cultural and political organizations to attract volunteers has become more and more intense in certain countries. People looking for something to do, be they members of the working population with limited free time, or young, or retired people, are all spoilt for choice. There are now countless institutions for voluntary welfare work, even in the humanitarian sphere.

In this connection, the qualities from which the Red Cross and Red Crescent Societies derive their strength can play against them. They are generally well structured, to such an extent that some particularly young people could perceive them as being too rigidly bureaucratic, and they are governed by principles, such as neutrality, whose justification is not always understood.

In today's world, where the perpetrators and the victims of violence, as well as those who alleviate the suffering it causes, are very frequently adolescents, the movement must pay heed to the aspirations of young people, because the hope for a more peaceful and more united society depends on their energy, their enthusiasm and vitality. It is therefore of paramount importance that they should be fully integrated in the life of the national society, that they should participate in decision making and be able to benefit from the experience of their elders. Their supervision and guidance should be flexible enough not to discourage spontaneous initiative, but close enough to ensure efficiency. Needless to say, all volunteers have to be given a clear understanding of the significance of the Fundamental Principles in their day-to-day work.

The motivation of volunteers: to sustain their motivation the national society must endeavour to entrust volunteers with tasks in line with their abilities, to ensure from the start that they understand their rights and duties which, in some societies, are laid down in a working agreement and to give them satisfactory working conditions. For example, in certain countries this can mean providing appropriate accident insurance.

Properly trained volunteers, whose work is appreciated and who are aware of this fact and whose relations at the professional level are facilitated by having clearly defined responsibilities, should be able to find personal fulfilment in the task assigned to them. Irrespective of how long they work for the movement, for the rest of their lives they will help to enhance the reputation of the Red Cross and Red Crescent.

Voluntary work is an expression of solidarity; many individuals are imbued with desire to help others. Whether it is within the family, the clan, the community, the local club, the religious community or the national society, every time suffering is alleviated by a selfless gesture, the spirit of humanity triumphs over poverty, illness, the violence of man, or the forces of nature. Whenever such a gesture is performed somewhere in the world within the International Red Cross and Red Crescent movement, it is yet another expression of the universal solidarity that bonds the movement together.

Unity is the oldest of the seven fundamental principles. As early as 1875 Gustave Moynier spoke of the principle of what he called *Centralization*, whose content was essentially the same the same as that of the current principle of *Unity*.There can be only one Red Cross or Red Crescent society in any one country. It must be open to all. It must carry on its humanitarian work throughout its territory.

The principle of *Unity* specifically relates to the institutional structure of the national societies. Indeed, the three elements which are mentioned in the principle correspond to three conditions National societies must meet in order to be recognized, the society must be the sole institution with that status, it must show non-discrimination in recruitment of members and it must cover the whole national territory.

Being the sole national society in the country, a governmental decree constituting state recognition of a national society, usually stipulates that it is the only National Red Cross or Red Crescent society which can carry out its activities on the national territory. This uniqueness of the national society is also one of the conditions for its recognition by the ICRC, under Article 4, paragraph 2, of the movement's Statutes. It is important for the society's credibility that there should not be within one country several rival organizations, all claiming to belong to the same body, pursuing similar objectives and carrying out the same activities independently of each other. Apart from the risk of confusion in the public mind, there is a inconsiderable risk that each of these associations would come to represent different communities within the country.

Uniqueness necessarily implies *Unity* of administration. From the internal view point only a central body can have an overall view, to ensure harmonious co-ordination of the human and material resources available and evaluate the priorities for action. As for external relations are concerned, if the national society is to participate in international conferences and meetings, it must obviously have a central body qualified to represent it among the other members of the movement.

In practise, it sometimes happens that another society is set up in a country where there is already a national society, without the latter having the means to prevent it.

CHAPTER EIGHT

The Long Goodbyes

After spending the first day of our induction course on the history and principles of the Red Cross, which I found very interesting, Terry and myself left the British Red Cross HQ in London and made our way to the nearby hotel for a well earned meal, a couple of beers and a chat about our pasts.

The next day, after breakfast, we made our way back to the British Red Cross HQ to be given instructions and to attend the X-Ray Department at 25 Wimpole Street in London, just a short bus ride from HQ. When we returned from our X-rays, we attended a briefing from Pierre Townsend, the officer for Eastern Europe. Pierre showed us on a map the possible areas in the former Yugoslavia that we could be working in, and what to expect in a country torn apart by war and ethnic cleansing. It appears we would be based in either Zagreb, or Split, in Croatia. From either of these two bases we would be joining convoys of four to twelve trucks supplying food, blankets, cooking equipment and medical supplies, wherever they were needed throughout the territories.

Pierre explained one day we could be conveying supplies in Serbian-held territory, the next day supplies to Bosnia, or Croatian-held territories. We were also warned about the dangers of possible sniper fire, and the need for some of the convoy's to travel through heavily *mine-fielded* areas. We both knew what the dangers could be: it would be no picnic.

After lunch our next appointment was an informal chat with Ann Kerr, the Overseas Personnel Officer, and a short quiz on how much we had learnt over the last couple of days. Terry won the quiz with a score of 88% and I came second with a score of 81%. Or should say I came last since only two of us took part in the quiz!

Ann kept a photo file of all the British personnel serving overseas on a large noticeboard in her office. By the time she had given us a personal account of each one serving in Croatia, I felt a strange feeling that I knew them all, before even meeting them. Ann dug deep into our thoughts wanting to know how we felt about the forthcoming mission to the former Yugoslavia. Ann explored our fears, doubts and our families' opinions on the matter. Ann told us that most of the British Red Cross volunteers she had interviewed for a mission in the former Yugoslavia seemed to sing from the same hymn sheet – fearless, and full of good intentions and enthusiasm. Yet when they returned from their mission and attended their mission debrief at the London HQ, Ann noticed a marked change in their personalities. She mentioned most of them were not so forward in talking about their experiences and just a little quieter in general.

Only to find there was no self-righteousness in war, no glory for people who might think and feel a brave attitude towards their duty. Albeit very commendable, to witness any suffering or hardship in a war zone must affect even the most hardened person. Change their personality in a way no one could imagine possible. For the lucky ones, who return home a different person, their message is very clear, *Life is for living*, not for destroying just because they have a different race/class, political opinion, or religious belief. We have no right to take the lives of the innocent just to endorse our own beliefs, and further our own cause.

Having said all that, I fully understand the need to defend your country against unlawful aggression, and to fight at all times for the freedom and justice for all human beings in a free and democratic society.

After lunch Ann introduced us to Denise Meredith, the Press Officer for the British Red Cross. Denise wanted our permission to approach the local press in our respective areas, in order to highlight our forthcoming mission to the former Yugoslavia. Denise explained the exercise was not meant to boost our egos, or make us into some superhero, but to highlight the work the British Red Cross was undertaking with our help in the former Yugoslavia. Terry and I had no objection to the request that Denise had made. Denise indicated that the local press and radio stations in our areas should be in touch in the next few weeks following her approach to them.

We ended our two-day induction course with a medical. The doctor advised us to make an appointment to see our own doctor, and to make sure we had the necessary injections he recommended, before embarking on our mission. Apart from waiting for the chest X-ray results, which should not have revealed any problems, we were both given a clean bill of health.

Before leaving the Red Cross HQ Terry and myself were asked to see Ann Kerr again. Ann informed us that she had just received a fax from Rolls Royce in Coventry, confirming that the two armour-plated Land Rovers would be ready for collection on Tuesday 20th July.

Ann also informed the ICRC in Geneva that the vehicles they ordered would ready on the collection date, and that she had received a fax from ICRC in Geneva requesting two drivers to collect the vehicles on the date stipulated. They would then board a ferry from Felixstowe to Zeebrugge in Belgium, and convey the vehicles through Europe to Zagreb. The two drivers would then be required to replace two drivers who had completed their missions in the former Yugoslavia. There was an air of excitement coming from Terry and myself for our adventure was soon to begin; but for me, the journey had begun back in March 1993, with the TV pictures of the victims of war. Now there we were four months later with chance to help those unfortunate souls, just how we imagined the scenario would be.

Ann seemed to share our joy. After all, four months waiting for this mission might not be long to some people, but it felt like a year. Ann gave us each a folder full of documentation, a first aid kit, and a list recommending what could be taken on the mission. Ann requested that we report to HQ eleven a.m. on Monday 19th July to collect our ferry tickets, money to purchase fuel, and our own expenses for food and accommodation; plus all other necessary paperwork for this mission.

Terry mentioned to Ann that he only lived twenty miles away from where the vehicles had to be collected at in Coventry, and offered to put me up at his place on the night before we were due to collect the vehicles. Ann thought that was a great idea and thanked Terry. We said our farewells to Ann, and told her that we looked forward to seeing her in just over two weeks' time. Before Terry returned home to Rugby, I showed him the route I had prepared for our journey across Europe. He seemed quite happy with the route, commenting, "I will let you take the lead when we get over there."

Terry returned home to Rugby, and I returned home to Plymouth with just over two weeks to prepare for the long awaited mission. Plenty of time I thought, but how quickly the next seventeen days would go, but I had a few promises to carry out before I left.

My wife Anita had just moved house and, although we had been separated for two years, after twenty-three years of marriage we remained good friends. I had promised to help her with some decorating and fitting a new kitchen and bedroom units. Due to the short time I had left, I managed to get a couple of days paid leave from my employer in order to finish the promised work for Anita before leaving for my mission.

After some very long days and nights, all the work I had promised to do for Anita was finished. I also managed to fit in time for an appointment to see my doctor in order to get the necessary injections that the doctor in London had recommended. I even found time to be interviewed on local radio, and a reporter wrote a piece in the local newspaper highlighting the Red Cross work in the former Yugoslavia, and my mission to help them.

All this in two weeks! I was feeling quite tired by that point and needed the last few days for a little relaxation to prepare myself mentally for the mission I had volunteered for. I am not a great lover of goodbyes, but I could not leave without them.

At that time I was running a local football team called AFC Rangers. So there were a lot of goodbyes to be had there. My son, Martin, and two committee members were going to look after the team and club affairs while I was away.

Both my sons worked in Plymouth, Martin as a sixth form Maths teacher and my other son, Lee, worked for the Audit Commission. Anita and I are very proud of our sons and what they have achieved through their education and careers. They have never been in any trouble. I know most parents can sing the praises of their sons or daughters but, hand on my heart, they have been model sons to Anita and I – but enough of our admiration!

After my wife and I had separated in February 1991, I met Sandy in the July of the same year. A few months later we were in a relationship. In March 1992 Sandy announced she was pregnant, and told me she was going to have an abortion. I begged Sandy not to go through with this abortion. I will never forget what Sandy said to me that day, she said: 'It's my body, and it's up to me what I do with my body, and its nothing to do with you."

I walked away from Sandy that day, feeling completely hurt, helpless and rejected. I did not see Sandy for a couple months until, one day, she was waiting outside my workplace. I told her that we could never have a future together after what she had done. So we remained good friends frequently speaking on the phone together. In June 1993, I told her that I had volunteered for a mission overseas with Red Cross. Sandy got very upset and asked if she could write to me, and would I let her know the date I was due to go. I took her out for a meal three days before my departure, gave her all the details, and then said my goodbyes to Sandy.

The weekend before my departure I said fond goodbyes to my sister, Shirley, and my brother-in-law, Peter. I also took my father out for our usual Sunday lunch. Dad was very sad when I said my loving farewells, but I guess that was understandable.

Sunday evening I was just finishing some last minute packing before my son Lee, and his fiancée, Tessa, came to my apartment. You know every parent hopes and prays your son or daughter will find a good partner and true love in their life. When Lee found Tessa, he found that pot of gold at the end of the rainbow. Tessa is truly a lovely girl, and they make such a perfect couple. After a chat, the goodbyes to Lee and Tessa turned out to be a particularly emotional farewell. Lee is very much like me, not afraid to show his true feelings and emotions. We all said goodbyes with tears in our eyes.

Family and friends wanted to throw a farewell party, but I did not want to make too much of a song and dance about my mission. I was worried my emotions would just run out of control! Some of my family and friends felt I was too old to embark on such an adventure. Forty-six, that's not too old, I wasn't ready for pipe and slippers yet! My sons' concerns played more on my emotions; how would I manage if I witnessed my family getting hurt in a war zone? I will admit that could have been my Achilles heel. If I watch a movie where children get hurt, my emotions take over, but I was determined to see this mission through no matter what circumstances I would have to face!

Monday 19th July, Martin arrived at eight a.m. to take me to the bus station. Whilst waiting for the bus, we passed the time away with a lot of unimportant small talk. I guess we were both lost for the right words to say. When the bus arrived Martin helped me with my luggage. I turned to Martin to give him a hug, only to see Sandy standing there in the distance behind him. For a brief moment we just stood and looked at each other. We both walked towards each other before we embraced, she whispered *I will write to you*, and I said my second goodbyes to Sandy and Martin before getting on the bus. I waved to them both before they disappeared in the distance, I could not help wondering if I would ever see them, again.

I arrived in London just a little bit later than planned. Terry was already there waiting patiently. After all my emotional goodbyes behind me now, I felt no regret or lack of conviction to the task that lay ahead of me. At the British Red Cross HQ, Ann Kerr gave Terry and myself a last-minute briefing. Ann said the only change of plan from the last time she saw us was that, after we had collected the Land Rovers from Coventry, we will have to go to the British Red Cross warehouse in North London, to collect first aid and medical supplies. Ann gave us all the necessary documentation for our journey, which included the address of the British Red Cross warehouse, the ferry tickets, our British Red Cross IDs, plus travellers' cheques and some cash to cover accommodation, food, fuel and toll charges in Europe. Ann kindly wished us a safe journey and a successful mission, before we got a taxi to Euston Station to board a train to Rugby.

When we arrived in Rugby Terry's family gave me a warm welcome and had arranged a bit of a farewell party that evening at Terry's local pub. Terry seemed to be soaking up and enjoying all the adoration paid to our mission by his family and friends nearly as much as all the beer we were drinking. Okay, it was a nice to have a good send off and I really enjoyed myself, but after a while I found the acclaim was getting a little over the top. They were making us into some sort of superheroes and, although well intended, it just endorsed my decision not to have a farewell party back in Plymouth. After a very good night's sleep, and surprisingly no fat head after all that drink, Terry's daughter prepared a wonderful breakfast for us both. To give Terry a little bit of space to say his fond goodbyes to his family, I drank my tea in the garden. It was a lovely warm summer's morning with blue sky as far as the eye could see. I thanked all of Terry's family for their very kind and warm hospitality. Terry's daughter kindly gave us a lift to the Rolls Royce factory in Coventry. The workshop manager went through the necessary documentation with us, and took us to the vehicles for us to give them a thorough inspection.

We made sure we had a spare wheel and wheel brace, in case of a puncture en route. Overall we found the Land Rovers to be quite basic. Due to the armoured plating none of the windows could be opened, but luckily we had air conditioning. If you have ever had to drive a Land Rover you will know what I mean when I say: not the most comfortable ride on long journeys, and did we have a long journey ahead of us!

I had just finished checking tyres, water, oil, fuel and hydraulic levels when Terry called me over to his Land Rover. Terry had been trying to adjust the seat to accommodate his rather large frame, but the seat would not go back any further. When Terry sat behind the wheel, his stomach was touching the steering wheel. After a good laugh at Terry's expense, I told him, "There's only one thing you can do." Sounding very hopeful that I had found a solution to his problem, Terry said, "What's that?"

I told him, "Every time you need to turn the steering wheel, just breath in." Terry, rightly so, was not too impressed with my wit; but all joking aside, it looked like Terry was going to have a much more uncomfortable drive than I was!

We loaded our luggage onto our vehicles and left Rolls Royce in Coventry at ten a.m., en route to the M6, then onto the M1 to London to collect the first aid and medical supplies for Zagreb.

We arrived at the British Red Cross warehouse in north London just before midday without any problems. Not that we were expecting any; but after waiting so long for this mission the last thing either of us wanted was for something to go wrong that could delay or jeopardize our mission. When we saw how much first aid and medical supplies we had to load, we had to juggle our luggage around to accommodate the amounts we had to load. There was not a lot of space in the back of the Land Rovers to carry the amount of goods we had. It was like trying to fit a square peg in a round hole. We manage to find space for most of our luggage on the front passenger seat and on the floor. With all the supplies loaded, from the top to the bottom of the vehicles, with no room to spare, we just about managed to get all the supplies on board. Terry was a bit concerned about the security of the supplies, when leaving the vehicles unattended to sleep at night. I told him, "It's a chance we have to take, so long as we secure the vehicles in good light we should be okay.'

We left the warehouse in London at two p.m. and made our way on to the M25, then onto the A12 to Ipswich. Before we left the warehouse, I mentioned to Terry that if we had time before booking in at the ferry at seven thirty p.m., I would like call in to see my relatives in Ipswich. Terry said, "George we should have plenty of time to do that."

I estimated that if there was no traffic delay, we should be in Ipswich between four p.m. and five p.m. We should have at least two hours to spare before booking in at the ferry desk, which was a twenty-minute drive from Ipswich. My relatives would not have forgiven me if I had passed their door, so to speak, and gone to the former Yugoslavia without saying goodbye to them.

On the way up the A12 to Ipswich, memories swam of times I had spent with Aunt Dot and Uncle Cyril, and my dear cousins Sherry, Dawn and Lesley who, from the age of ten years old, had all played a big part in my life. I remember how excited I use to get when my parents planned to have a holiday with Aunt Dot and Uncle Cyril, and the girls in Great Yarmouth. We would travel to Ipswich by car to meet them, before setting off on holiday for two weeks in Great Yarmouth. Like every child would say *such happy days*.

As a child I was a very shy lad and would run a mile if any girl tried talked to me. Sherry, Dawn and Lesley managed to bring me out of my shell. I soon realized that girls were not so bad after all, and yes they can be fun. No, not in that way; don't forget I am talking about me when I was ten years old, but I guess today that would be acceptable. I will admit to carrying a torch for my cousin Lesley. You could say she was my first love but, although the flame still flickers for Lesley, dreams are replaced with reality, though I guess the warmth of your first love never dies. To this day I never know if she ever felt the same way; but I will cherish the moments in time that we all shared together for the rest of my life.

We arrived in Ipswich at four twenty p.m., just when you thought you had said the last of your goodbyes in Plymouth, and to Terry's Family in Rugby, here we were again with more goodbyes in Ipswich. I introduced Terry to my aunty and uncle.

After all the hugs and kisses, Aunt Dot and Uncle Cyril could not understand why I would volunteer to work in a war zone. I fully understand their concerns, Aunt Dot lost her brother Leslie at the D-Day landings on the 6th June 1944. He volunteered for a special mission in the glider landings. Her daughter Lesley was named after him, but let's take a reality check here: we cannot compare our mission in the former Yugoslavia to the heroics that was shown by the brave soldiers who gave their lives on D-Day, to free Europe of a sadistic dictator.

Yes there are always risks working in a war zone, but there is always a risk every time we get behind the wheel of our car. We can all sit back in our comfortable lifestyles and say what is happening in the former Yugoslavia is not my problem. But is that really what life is all about? If we all sat back, like America did at the start of World War Two, where would we be today? I feel, no matter what the situation, if there are people suffering, let us ease the pain. Where there is hunger, let there be nourishment, where there is despair, let there be hope, where there sadness, let there be joy, where there war, let there be peace, where there is hate, let there be love.

When we came to Ipswich and Great Yarmouth for holidays, I use to love to listen to my father and Uncle Cyril talk about all their wartime experiences. They both must have witnessed the horrors of war at some time or other, but all their stories where about fun and happy times. Like the time they met by chance in Dunkirk and came back to England with their tunics stuffed with cigarettes and booze. Perhaps that is their way to forget the horrors of war? That's fine. But let's not forget those who cry for help today.

Within fifteen minutes of our arrival, my dear cousins Sherry, Dawn and Lesley walked in. It was so nice to see them all again. Once again introductions were made between Terry and my cousins. Time was moving fast towards the final goodbyes to my Ipswich family. I did not want to drag out these goodbyes any longer. It was now five thirty p.m. I thought it would be best to get this over now. After yet more hugs, kisses, and tears we said are goodbyes and they all wished us a save return from our mission. From Ipswich we joined the east carriageway of the A14 to Felixstowe and arrived in Felixstowe at six p.m. We were both feeling hungry so,,with a hour to spare, we found a fish and chip shop near the sea front. After we stuffed our faces, we made our way to the ferry port to book in, and then joined a large queue of vehicles that were waiting to board the ferry, *The Pride of Suffolk*. I can now say all the goodbyes were behind us.

CHAPTER NINE

The Journey

Once on board our ferry the *Pride of Suffolk* we secured the vehicles and located our cabins, to put our overnight bags in, before going on deck to take our last look at England for a few months. At two thirty p.m., the *Pride of Suffolk* slowly moved away from the dockside; the pessimistic side of my nature wondered if that would be the last time I'd see England? Then Terry came out with a comment that went down like a lead balloon! He said, "Let's hope they have remembered to close the cargo doors!"

He had been hoping to get a laugh, but got a look of disgust instead from fellow passengers on deck. Which was quite understandable since it had been less than one year since a ferry leaving Zeeburgee sank, killing over 100 passengers – due to the cargo doors not having been shut properly...

With that in mind, I turned to Terry, and said, "Come on let's find the bar before we get thrown overboard!" We were both feeling a bit tired so, after a couple of drinks, we decided to get our heads down for a good night's sleep in preparation for our long drive tomorrow.

After a fairly good night's sleep and some breakfast, the ferry docked in Zeeburgee at six fifteen a.m. on Thursday 22nd July 1993. We checked our vehicles and disembarked from the *Pride of Suffolk* at seven a.m. No problem going through customs, but perhaps the Red Cross on our vehicles helped us there. From the route I had made out a few weeks ago, we soon found the E40 sign to Bruxelles well signposted from Zeebrugge, and thereafter the E411 to Luxembourg, E25 to

Merzig. During our lunch break and refuel we decided to head for Stuttgart for our overnight stop.

We joined the E29 to Saarbrucken, then the A10/A8 at Pirmasens, and then the A65 at Karlsruhe to Stuttgart. We drove into Stuttgart while looking for accommodation where the vehicles could be parked securely, without much success. We passed some buildings that still had the scars from the intense RAF bombing raids there. We found a safe place to park to discuss our next move.

Terry said that he had noticed signs for the airport just before we came off the highway into Stuttgart and we should find a hotel there. I agreed. So we got back on the highway and followed the signs for the airport well outside Stuttgart, which proved to be a successful move. Ten kilometres from the airport we found a very good hotel, with secure parking facilities. Perhaps it was a little bit sophisticated for us but we were both tired and felt the need to be spoilt.

The rooms reminded me of those Hollywood movie hotels, which included a luxury bathroom, minibar, TV and video, phone, laundry service and room service. I had never stayed in a hotel like that before! But most important of all, we had separate rooms. I think we both needed our own space after travelling together over the last four days. It was nice to spend nearly an hour in the shower, not that I have a problem in the smelly department, it was just my way of chilling out after such a long journey. I arranged to meet Terry at the hotel restaurant at seven thirty p.m., for an evening meal. After dinner we discussed our plans for tomorrow's drive. Terry was not keen on having another long drive like we had today. He made it clear that he found the vehicle was uncomfortable, and he felt the air con was not working properly, because he was sweating so much: it was like being in a sauna, he said. You could not open any windows, they were all sealed units due to the nature of what the vehicles were going to be used for, hence the use of air-con units. Last but not least, Terry moaned that every time he went over a bump, his stomach hit the steering wheel. I was trying so very hard not to laugh.

After listening to Terry's agony hour, I had indigestion and felt depressed. I was ready to end it all. But no, I be must strong and face the storm of Terry's wrath. All joking aside, Terry had a point, I agreed with most of his comments, and to be honest it was getting warmer by the hour, due to heading in a southerly direction. So I suggested we have look at the map, over a couple of more beers, and decide our destination for tomorrow, and from there it would give us a steady drive on the following day to Zagreb.

On our first day's drive we had covered 430 miles. We had roughly another 550 miles to travel from Stuttgart to Zagreb. I suggested to Terry that if we make Salzburg in Austria our next stop tomorrow, that would not be far off the halfway point from Stuttgart to Zagreb. Terry welcomed the idea of dropping our daily mileage from 430 miles to 275 miles. I know that's not far to travel for a day's work, but these Land Rovers were not designed for a comfortable long journey. Plus, as I have already mentioned, the further south we travelled the hotter it became in those vehicles.

While we finished our beers, before retiring for the night, I could not help feeling a bit guilty, suggesting to Terry that we stayed in Salzburg tomorrow night. Was I considering an easy drive that we would both have tomorrow, or was it my selfish motive and obsession to visit Salzburg? Because one of the greatest musicals of all time was made in Salzburg, *The Sound of Music*, and I have always held a deep affection for the movie.

Best sleep on it, and I would tell Terry in the morning why I suggested staying in Salzburg.

Friday 23rd July 1993. Over breakfast I told Terry my reason for wanting to visit Salzburg. It was now Terry's turn to have a good laugh at my expense. But when we were checking out of the hotel, Terry's laughter soon disappeared, when his bill was about thirty Deutschemarks more than my bill. Thinking there must be some sort of mistake, Terry confronted the hotel receptionist to query why his bill was more than mine. With embarrassment the receptionist explained that he had been watching the adult channel on the television, and that he had incurred extra expense for this service. Red-faced Terry picked up his bags to go out and check his vehicle. Apparently Terry had been watching *blue* movies until one a.m. After the long drive we had yesterday I thought Terry would have welcomed the sleep, rather than waste his time on blue movies! Perhaps it was not a good idea after all to have an easy drive today?

I just hoped Terry was not going to moan about how tired he was throughout the day.

We checked the vehicles, before rejoining the E52 to München and Salzburg. During our drive through Europe we encountered numerous toll charges, mainly on the borders of each country we had travelled through. Apart from the toll charges on bridges and ferries in the UK, we don't have border charges to go to Scotland or Wales. Just as well, the knock-on effect on transport cost would be quite considerable, especially on heavy goods vehicles!

We stopped for lunch and refuelled near München just before the Austrian border. After lunch we crossed the German/Austria border on a very warm sunny day, the scenery all around us breathtaking. The sight of beautiful chalets perched on the sides of hills and mountains had us stopping in lay-bys to take photos. You would think we were on holiday instead of a mission, but it was good to get out of our vehicles and smell the fresh mountain air.

We finally arrived in Salzburg at two fifteen p.m., and we had no problem finding a very good hotel with a secure parking lot for our vehicles. We had plenty of time before our evening meal, so we decided to have a quick wash, change and headed for the town to do a bit of sightseeing, while singing *The Hills are Alive with the Sound of Music, Climb every Mountain* and many more from that great movie. I think I might have gone over the top; Terry started calling me *Captain von Trap*. When we arrived in the town we were fortunate to find the Salzburg Music Festival was in full swing in the main square. I have never seen so many marching bands displaying various Austrian folk costumes. It was truly a colourful spectacle – and for all the classical lovers out there, who would know Salzburg was also the birth place of the great composer, Mozart?

I found Salzburg absolutely fascinating, and one of the most enchanting and romantic cites I have ever been to. And with all due respect to Terry, it would have been far more enjoyable with a beautiful lady at my side, to share the romantic atmosphere. During the afternoon's sightseeing in Salzburg we were both clicking away with our cameras and soon used up all the films that would hold some wonderful memories of our brief visit to the beautiful town of Salzburg.

On our way back to the hotel in the taxi the driver, who spoke very good English, gave us a brief but interesting history lesson on Salzburg. He explained how Salzburg got its name from salt mining activity in the area, and that they have the old part of the town on one side of the river, and the new part of the town on the other side of the river. Back at the hotel we decided to have a quick nightcap, before having a fairly early night, in preparation for the last part of our journey to Zagreb, tomorrow.

Saturday 24th July 1993. Following another good night's sleep we had our usual continental breakfast, but could not stop talking about the good old English breakfast. Surely we are not getting homesick already, how are we going to survive in the months that lay ahead of us? I thought. I guess that old saying would come into practice, *Where there's a will, there is a way.*

We paid our bill. Terry must have been tired last night, because he never incurred any extra charges on his bill.

We gave the vehicles their usual early morning check before joining the E55 to Villach. En route we encountered two small tunnels at Golling and Eisriesenwelt, plus two very long tunnels at Zederhaus and St Michael, near Katachberg. All these tunnels were situated at the foot of mountains. Approaching these tunnels from a distance you could see two black holes, like eye sockets, at the foot of these mountains.

Although they were a fascinating work of engineering, I would not recommend these formidable structures to those who have a claustrophobic nature.

At Villach we joined the E61 to Ljubljana before crossing the border into Slovenia. We decided to have lunch, and refuel, in case we had a problem getting fuel in Slovenia, due the conflict being so close now. It was in Slovenia where the conflict started, which brought about the break-up of the federation known as Yugoslavia. Which included Slovenia, Croatia, Serbia/Kosovo, Bosnia, Herzegovina and Montenegro. When President Tito was alive he kept tight reins on the brotherhood of the Federation, and its different cultures in Yugoslavia. Although it meant the people did not enjoy the democratic freedoms that we take for granted in the West, Tito stopped them killing one another.

Slovenia declared itself independent from Yugoslavia and escaped the bloodbath that followed between the remaining states. We can only hope, and respect Slovenia's decision to withdraw from the federation that made up the states of the former Yugoslavia. I believe Slovenia wanted to create a more democratic society that would bring them closer to the European Union. Slovenia would find it difficult to achieve that status if they remained in the federation of Yugoslavia. It's not for me to question or judge the rights or wrongs of any conflict that explodes in our world. But how many times do we have to witness the needless lost of life, and suffering, inflicted on the innocent victims that get caught in the crossfire of the power game of politics, religions, race, class, ideals and the difference of opinions?

In the innocence of my childhood war and conflict was only a game you played in the playground, copying a war movie that you had seen. It was only acting. I have already told you how much I enjoyed listening to the World War Two stories and experiences from my father and Uncle Cyril. I always found their conversations fascinating, but my father said to me one day, "Son I hope and pray you will never have to fight, witness or experience the suffering that war can cause."

These words remained with me throughout my childhood, and installed a fear within me about war, and the hope that I would never be involved in one. Over the next few months, all my father's hopes and prayers would disappear, along with my own fears of war. We can only pray to God that all the nations in our world, and their leaders, will start to value life, a lot more than they did at the present – but enough of my dreams of a perfect world.

We crossed the boarder into Slovenia, and stopped in Ljubljana to make a phone call to ICRC delegation in Zagreb. Terry informed them that ETA in Zagreb was expected to be four thirty p.m. The duty delegate asked us to locate the Intercontinental Hotel in Zagreb and wait in the car park, and he would arrange for the Transport Workshop Manager, Eddie Heywood, to meet us in the hotel car park. From there he would escort us to the ICRC's workshops.

From Ljubljana we joined the E70 for Zagreb and cross the border into Croatia without any problems. One hour later I could see, in the distance, a large sign. It said *Welcome to Zagreb*. The Intercontinental Hotel was very well signposted so we were able to locate it without to much trouble. On arrival at the hotel at four forty p.m., just a little later than our estimated ETA. We both felt a sense of achievement, and elation, that we had arrived here in one piece, without any problems whatsoever.

While waiting for the workshop manager to meet us we had just enough time to reflect on our journey through Europe, and wonder what adventures the next few months would bring. Why is it human nature to try and draw a picture in your mind of the person you are going to meet for the first time? I was no exception to the rule, that most people get it wrong. The workshop manager arrived in smart casuals, wearing a cowboy hat, apparently a gift from one of the Australian drivers. Eddie welcomed us to Zagreb and then introduced us to his wife, Anita, and their baby son, Leon.

Eddie was a jovial character from London, and his pretty petite wife was from Grimsby. They both made us feel so welcome. Anita said, "I understand that it's not easy for some blokes to be away from home, and their loved ones, if ever you need someone to talk to. Eddie and I will be here to listen to your problems."

With that thoughtful gesture, we could not have had a more sincere welcome.

CHAPTER TEN

Zagreb

From the Intercontinental Hotel we followed Eddie's vehicle to the ICRC workshops in Zagreb. Eddie informed us that the Land Rovers we brought over would be serviced before being sent to Sarajevo, and put into service in and around the notorious snipers alley in Sarajevo. Hence the reason for the armoured plating. The medical supplies we brought over would remain in the vehicle until Monday, in order for a nurse to decide what supplies would remain on the Land Rovers for Sarajevo, and what supplies would be unloaded for Zagreb. There was a touch of sadness leaving the vehicles that had played a big part in our journey to Zagreb over the past five days. Albeit an uncomfortable journey, they never let us down. I think even Terry got attached, if only through his stomach touching the steering wheel, for well over 1,000 miles.

Eddie, Anita and baby Leon then drove us to the ICRC delegation in Zagreb. Talking to us all the way there. If I could pay any compliment to the warmth of Eddie and Anita's personality, it would be how comfortable I felt being in their company, without any airs or graces. I felt that I had known them for years. At the delegation we thanked Eddie and Anita for making us so welcome, and for all their help. We told them that we would look forward to seeing them again, soon.

The Duty Transport Officer, Dennis Cretenet, informed us that until such time as an apartment becomes available, two rooms had been booked at the Dubrovnik Hotel in the city centre of Zagreb. Transport would pick us both up at eight a.m. on Monday 26th July 1993, for briefings to be held at nine a.m. at the delegation. Tomorrow, Sunday 25th July 1993, we'd have a day to rest and settle in after our long journey. We thanked Dennis for his help and boarded ICRC transport that dropped us off at the Dubrovnik Hotel.

The hotel was pleasant enough but certain aspects of the hotel were in desperate need of modernization. With it being so hot at that time of year in Zagreb the rooms were like greenhouses. Air conditioning would not have gone amiss. But eh, there was a war on. What did we expect, the *luxury* hotels we stayed in on our journey? Not Likely! We hoped we wouldn't have to wait to long for an apartment.

We decided to have a good wash and brush-up, and then have a look around town to see what Saturday night was like in Zagreb. Just a five-minute walk from the hotel brought us into the main square that was situated in the city centre. The square seemed to be a hub of activity. There were various bars where you could sit outside and the waiter would come to take your order – coffee or *Pivo* (beer).

We sat outside one of these bars drinking *Pivo* on a very warm evening. Not too far away in the square there was a Croatian folk festival. I was captivated listening to the folk music, and soaking up the atmosphere, while watching the dancers perform in their national costumes with such colourful splendour. In the background, trams rumbled in and out of the square in all directions of the city. Neon lights glowed like a firework display advertising various products. On one building the evening temperature would flash every ten minutes – sometimes up, sometimes down, I am not sure if Terry and I were getting bored with each other's company, but we started to have bets on which way it would go until we eventually got bored with that stupid game, too. We decided to have a walk around the city centre for some welcome exercise, and to stretch our legs after being cooped up in those Land Rovers for five days. After a good stroll around the city centre, we decided to call it day and returned to the hotel where we tried to get some sleep in that hot greenhouse.

Sunday 25th July 1993, after a restless night's sleep due to the heat, I had a nice cold shower before knocking on Terry's door to see if he was ready for breakfast. I thought I had a bad night's sleep, but when Terry opened the door he looked terrible. Apparently he hardly slept all night. We had breakfast before we decided to explore the Zagreb city centre in daylight. We found plenty of fashion shops, with merchandise imported from Italy, Austria and Germany, but some shelves were nearly empty and none of the clothes rails were full.

Zagreb had plenty of bars, some with light entertainment, pizza cafés and you would not have any trouble finding nice restaurants. There didn't seem to be any shortage of food, for those who could afford to buy it. Just off the square there was a large daily market where food was readily available, with a great section of fruit, meats, dairy produce, clothes and souvenirs from Zagreb. There was also a number small grocery shops. For the young at heart there were the usual discos and for those a little older, Jazz clubs, if you liked that type of entertainment. If none of that floated your boat, then you could always go to the cinema in Zagreb.

The conflict in the former Yugoslavia did not show any signs of destruction in Zagreb, at the least I could not find any to talk about. All in all, despite the conflict that Croatia was involved in, it seemed like business as usual in Zagreb. Yet to say the people of Zagreb were unaffected by the conflict and the trauma that comes with war would be a very unfair misconceived statement. After all, who am I to perceive that the people of Zagreb were not affected by the conflict; especially when I had only been there for less than a day?

The only visual indication that Croatia was at war with its neighbours was the sight of uniformed soldiers, either on leave or waiting for transport to join their units. With two grown-up sons of my own, my thoughts were with the mothers, fathers, wives, brothers, sisters and children, saying goodbye to their loved ones who were leaving to fight in the war. Worrying and always wondering if they would ever see them again. All too common a price so many have to pay in war, which can only bring heartache at a measure too great to bear, or even thinking about it happening to you.

Terry and I only had a continental breakfast at the hotel and, after a good walk around Zagreb, we started to look for place to have lunch. We opted for a pizza café and a beer. After lunch Terry said he felt tired and was going back to the hotel to try and catch up the sleep he did not get the last night. I continued to explore Zagreb.

Worldwide nearly every city has its fair share of beggars on the streets. Most of which are also known to be homeless. Zagreb was no exception to that fact. Walking the streets of Zagreb I passed a few women sat on the pavement, begging for money while breast-feeding their babies. In my heart I asked myself why any baby should have to start its life in that way? The mothers obviously cared for them, but in this *caring* society we live in, who cared for these poor women? So desperate yet forced to take measures like that to live.

While sat outside a cafeteria, occasionally children as young as seven to twelve years old would approach you begging for money. Apart from the obvious reasons that these children were putting themselves at risk, all the money they were lucky to get was then handed to their pimps. So you can use your own discretion for how much money the children got at the end of the day. I have never witnessed so many vulnerable women and children begging on the streets before. I could not say the problem was any worse in Zagreb than anywhere else in the world. Poverty hits so many vulnerable people, and it is beyond their control, but you cannot stop yourself from getting emotionally concerned about the women and children you see in that way. I felt that I had seen enough of Zagreb for the day and decided to go back to my hotel to write some letters home.

I did not want to disturb Terry in case he was asleep. After I finished writing letters, I lay on my bed thinking about the sad faces of those women and children begging for money.

While I was searching my soul looking for answers to so many questions, I must have nodded off to sleep: only to be woken by someone knocking on my door. Upon opening the door there was Terry looking fresh as daisy and saying, "Come George, let's go for a *Pivo* and something to eat." When I looked at my watch it was seven p.m. I had been asleep for roughly one hour. Terry, give me ten minutes to freshen up and change. Nearby the church bell rang, calling Christians to God for evening Mass. Was that the answer to all the problems we faced in our troubled world, I thought, still obsessing over the women and children begging in the streets? Perhaps we should follow the teachings of the Bible in the New Testament? I am no different to other people who want to live their life to please God, only to find yourself going in the opposite direction at times to what God might of wanted you to do? We can only pray that God's wisdom and light will shine in us all, and guide us through these troubled waters, to make us more aware of other people's needs before our own. "Where has the day gone?" I thought as I joined Terry for a bite to eat and, of course, a couple of *Pivos*.

Monday 26th July 1993, six a.m. and another restless night. A cold shower would do the trick, then to make sure Terry was awake to go down and have some breakfast, while we waited for the ICRC transport to arrive to take us to the delegation. Terry seemed to be more with it, most likely because of a better night's sleep. Transport arrived on time and made its way through heavy traffic to the delegation. Our first appointment at the delegation was with the Personnel Officer, Sophie Matkovic, in the aptly named *Welcome Office*. You could not wish to be welcomed to the delegation, on the first day of you mission, by a more beautiful and charming lady. As Terry and I gazed at Sophie, like a couple of lovesick teenagers, she explained the terms of our contract with the ICRC. After we signed all the necessary documents, Sophie informed us that our ICRC IDs would be available at the end of the week, and that they would be required on convoys to insure we got through the checkpoints. First, we were required to complete our briefings on a two-day induction course and a two-day driver training programme. At that point, Terry and I looked at each other in disbelief and lost our lovesick gazes at Sophie. Terry was thinking exactly what I was thinking. Another induction course? Stuck in a classroom after driving over a 1,000 miles across Europe, we would now be trained again to make sure we were up to the task and capable of driving on the right-hand side of the road!

The only way to explain our disappointment: we did not expect to be spending most our first week in courses and driver training. We both expected to be on convoys within a day or so, after waiting so long for our mission to help those suffering in the conflict. I know it sounds a virtuous comment to make, but we had months to think about and mentally prepare ourselves to be in the thick of things within a short time of our arrival. We were obviously disappointed not be part of the mission we had volunteered for sooner rather than later.

In the next few days we would soon find out why the ICRC were justified in giving us this necessary extra training – that would prove to benefit and enhance our missions. Our righteous, selfish egos would soon diminish; with good reason. Sophie with an air of grace and reassurance concluded our appointment by telling us that, if we had any problems, we were not to hesitate in coming back to her for help and advice.

Our next appointment was with Sonja Stipic who was a local girl, employed by the ICRC to work in the accounts office. There was not a lot to say about our financial arrangements, but Sonja did the best she could by explaining how much money we could draw each month, to pay for food and telephone expenses if you had a telephone in your apartment. When we were allocated an apartment the ICRC accounts department would pay the rent directly to the landlord, or landlady. The ICRC would also employ a housekeeper to clean our apartment, laundry and iron our clothes. Until an apartment became available, we would need to stay at the Dubrovnik Hotel. The ICRC would cover the cost of our stay there. That was Sonja's closing comments on our financial arrangements during our mission in the former Yugoslavia. You could say Sonja's briefing was short, sweet and to the point.

We then made our way to the lecture room and were introduced to the medical coordinator from Switzerland, Louisa Chan, also joining the lecture was fellow Swiss colleague and a new administrator, Marysa Gay. Louisa made sure that we were all given the necessary injections before leaving the UK and Switzerland. No matter where we were working in the former Yugoslavia, Louisa advised us to boil the water before drinking, or to use purifying tablets (if supplied). Any fruit or vegetables purchased must not be eaten, unless washed thoroughly in preboiled water.

It was not pleasant to be working with someone who has not been looking after themselves in the hygiene department, so every effort must be made maintain one's own personal hygiene. Louisa not only looked after the medical welfare of the ICRC staff. She helped to coordinate the nursing staff in various areas throughout the former Yugoslavia, including visits to prisoner of war camps. In war-torn countries we only tend to think of horrific injuries inflicted on soldiers and civilians alike, but war does not stop people becoming ill, some with serious diseases, with no medical help on hand.

The ICRC would do everything in its power to help people who fell into that category. Another side of Louisa's department was coordinating medical supplies sending relief operations into much needed areas. As we were speaking Louisa's colleague was at the ICRC workshops sorting out the medical supplies, which Terry and I had brought over from the UK.

The ICRC provides war surgery medicines and first aid supplies to hospitals, health centres and first aid stations, throughout the former Yugoslavia. All sides involved in the conflict get exactly the same treatment, under the adopted principles of the Red Cross and Red Crescent. The demand was always increasing for medical supplies, which included:

anaesthetics, sterilization equipment, laboratory and blood bank facilities, infusion materials and sutures, antibiotics, and many more emergency medicines. Louisa completed her briefing with some advice for us, to relax on our days off from relief convoys and to avoid any stress.

Any medical problems would be treated by Louisa's department. We thanked Louisa for her lecture and advice. Before our next briefing there was a welcome twenty minutes' coffee break.

On returning to the lecture room, Swiss nationals Claudia Rizzo and Martin Damary were waiting to give a briefing on our own personal safety, in what could be called a dangerous situation.

Present-day warfare, which in many instances has become indiscriminate by its methods and means, for example the use of landmines, booby traps and indiscriminate bombings, has increased the risks run by relief workers in carrying out their mission. The following recommendations, which correspond largely with the ICRC internal safety instructions, are intended to draw the attention of the national society personnel to some simple, practical safety measures that can contribute to the reduction of risk connected with relief work in the field, in times of conflict.

Personal factors: in addition to the observance of practical measures, it was clear that relief workers' safety depended also on their attitude when confronted with situations involving danger. That attitude was primarily a part of their personality, but could also be related to a possible weakening of stamina, as a result of the circumstances they face.

Personality, maturity and self-control, the capacity to evaluate a situation in the heat of the moment, an ability to assess the danger and determination are some of the qualities that are required of a good relief worker. The recruitment process does not always allow for an in-depth evaluation of such qualities, and the relief worker must make, in all honesty, their own assessment in that respect. There was no reason to be ashamed of giving up. On the contrary, the reasonableness of those who have done so, considering that they did not have the qualities required, has always been appreciated. For lack of experience, however, the attitude one would have in the face of danger is not always known to the individual and it may happen that, in the course of a mission, one may discover that one is absolutely not made for the job. True courage lies in knowing when to give up.

Weakening of endurance: different factors can undermine the most secure personality. Among those that particularly come to mind are stress fatigue, the medical and psychological syndrome of war fatigue, apathy, indifference to danger, automatic behaviour is well known, signs of Automatic Behaviour is the excessive consumption of alcohol, or medications, strained relations within a team, a feeling of powerlessness regarding the enormity of the task. Relief workers should always be aware of these. It is essential, for them in the long term, to keep in good physical condition, even at the expense, sometimes of tasks which appear to be urgent. It is clear that there are periods during which the workload is heavier than at others. That must be taken into account, but it is absolutely essential to try to spare some time for relaxation, which will allow for the recharging of body and mind.

Fear, the natural reaction to danger, is a normal feeling which should be admitted, both in oneself and in others. It can even play a positive role of regulator, or protective mechanism signalling danger. What should be avoided is the excess that leads either to panic or to temerity. Panic is the result of uncontrolled fear; it can be contagious and lead to mishaps. It is therefore necessary in all circumstances to endeavour to give at least an appearance of calm and confidence which, by easing the tension, often makes it possible to overcome the most dangerous situations.

The majority of accidents however arise from absence of fear and recklessness. In all circumstances, therefore, the relief worker should seek to control their impulses, not, for example, to leap unthinkingly to the rescue of victims falling near them, but to evaluate the situation calmly, to be wounded yourself is not the best way for a relief worker to assist a another wounded individual.

Other factors; relief workers should also be on their guard against such feelings as fatalism, a presentiment of death or, at the other extreme, a sensation of euphoria, or a feeling of invulnerability. It is essential in such cases that the person expresses their feelings and confides in his superiors, or colleagues, there is no shame in that. Thus a frank and open discussion must in all circumstances be the rule within a relief team.

The first pillar of safety is information. Everything depends on its quality, abundance and reliability. It is essential that it be gathered, synthesized and transmitted rapidly and completely at every level. Decisions concerning safety can only be taken on the basis of a very good knowledge of events. The relief worker should endeavour to keep his superiors, and colleagues, fully informed about the situation and developments to be expected in any area. Headquarters, through the team leader, would provide the relief worker with more general information concerning points relevant to safety. Furthermore, all authorities concerned should be fully informed of where, when and how the relief action takes place. In addition to that, dissemination of the Red Cross and Red Crescent and general humanitarian principles should be made at all levels, and at all times.

Action principles: no action should be undertaken within a territory against the will of the authorities.

No action should be undertaken without taking every precaution to ensure the safety of the participants.

In principle, the Red Cross and Red Crescent would neither request, nor accept a military escort.

In principle, all Red Cross and Red Crescent vehicles involved in the field should be clearly marked with the corresponding emblem. No armed persons, whether military or civilian, should be allowed aboard such vehicles.

In no case should Red Cross or Red Crescent personnel be armed.

Assigning others to a dangerous mission. Never assign anyone exposed to danger, the danger must not be greater than that to which it would be acceptable to submit to oneself.

The subcontracting parties who take a risk, must only do so in full knowledge of the facts.

No pressure must be brought to bear on anyone to carry out a dangerous mission.

Wearing of emblem in general: on mission the relief worker would be identified in the course of their work by means of a distinctive emblem. According to the circumstances, the emblem may be a badge, an armband, a tabard with the emblem on the back and front, a helmet with the emblem on the back and front, a flag, or a combination of any of these.

Documents: the relief worker should always be able to identify themselves as a member of the national society. In addition to that, they should be in possession of the necessary ICRC ID and other established documents, required by the authorities.

Field missions: before undertaking a difficult mission, the itinerary to be followed should be fixed and left in writing at the base, in case of repeated missions, a regular timetable is a safety factor.

During a mission, the established itinerary should always be adhered to.

At the end of each mission, the actual return should be made known to the base.

Photographic equipment or video recorders were not recommended as they could jeopardize a relief worker's safety, or even the whole operation.

Activity at night: relief action should not take place in the field at night, except by special decision of those in charge.

An evacuation plan, both individual and collective in case of accident, illness or military action should be drawn up and made known to all personnel in every team, where an emergency might be necessary.

Other safety measures: with regard to the marking of the vehicles, it must not be forgotten that the most important factor was its visibility, the protective sign of the Red Cross and Red Crescent on a white background must be as large as possible, visible from all directions, particularly from the rear of the vehicle and illuminated if necessary.

Additional recommendations regarding vehicles: two vehicles was the minimum requirement for any undertaking in danger zones. The number of persons per convoy in danger zones shall, as a rule, be restricted to a strict minimum. The vehicles would always be parked in the direction of departure during missions in the field, to allow for a quick and safe evacuation from the location, in the event of a dangerous situation. If the vehicles were equipped with radios, a liaison check would be made at the time of each departure and arrival, other checks were to be carried out along the way whenever possible. The standard daily checks on the vehicles included: oil, water, lights, signals, brakes, tyres, etc. and were to be carried out by the driver before any journey without fail. This was to make sure the vehicle was in a roadworthy condition, thus avoiding needless breakdowns, which in turn could jeopardize the safety and success of the relief convoy.

Recommendations related to the danger of mines, experience have clearly demonstrated that passive protection measures for vehicles such as armour plating are not advisable. Relief workers should therefore not have been assigned to missions into areas where any presence of mines was suspected.[1]

---

[1] Footnote. During the course of my future mission, and in reference to the last sentence, and its recommendations relating to mines. On some convoys I would find myself in minefield areas and would not be adhering to the recommendations. Of which I had no objection to carrying out, if victims of war required medical supplies and food. That had to be done to save lives!

Checkpoints and barriers: always stop, if requested to do so. No objection should ever be raised to an identity check, or the search of all luggage within the vehicle, including the cargo in transit.

Cease-fire and truce: orders and timetables in force should be scrupulously respected. Our comprehensive briefing on safety and protection, concluded with some personal advice – to wear plain sweat shirts or T-shirts, because some garments with prints and slogans on them could be offensive in some cultures in the former Yugoslavia. Quite often the slogan on a garment could lead to a serious misunderstanding.

We were under no illusions when we were told that our own safety and lives could be at risk. During some relief operations, I believe any volunteer who thought it might be a holiday was obviously not living in the real world. After our longest briefing that morning, it was time for lunch and a bit of fresh air.

Our last briefing of the day, on relief distribution, was given by Feena May from Ireland. Feena helped to coordinate supplies in too many needed areas. Sometimes Feena's work turned into a logistic nightmare trying to prioritise requests for supplies, coupled with the demand for urgent life-saving supplies, or straightforward replenishment of stocks. Feena could only operate the demand and supply with the vehicles she had at her disposal. At times it was like trying to put a square peg in a round hole.

But Feena somehow got by, as we all must endeavour to do when life throws you these challenges. Regular convoys would be sent to: Banja Luka, Vojnić, Velika Kladuša, Bihać, Cazin and Knin. The vehicles would carry up to twenty tonnes, consisting of complete or mixed loads of: medical

---

Recommendations connected with the local situation. It was essential for all relief workers to be acquainted with the general situation, so that all the laws in forced in the country, whether written or unwritten, are respected. Special attention must be paid to the following: curfew. It should be strictly observed, and the instructions of the civil or military authorities should be followed.

supplies, flour, rice, sugar, cooking oil, tinned proteins and individual food parcels. Additional supplies would include: blankets, clothes, plastic sheeting and cooking stoves. Sanitation and public health would also be a priority, ICRC engineers provided technical assistance for water supply systems, and the convoys would convoy spare parts, chemicals and purification systems, to insure that the population had access to clean water.

The ICRC regularly supplies 1,250 patients treated in Cazin and Bihać hospitals. More than 1,000 million tonnes of food and nonfood articles were directly distributed by the ICRC during the first six months of 1993.

We have already covered the principles of the Red Cross and Red Crescent. And all the principles were very much in practise in the former Yugoslavia. Regarding the principle of *Impartiality*, the relief operation bears no discrimination; supplies are evenly distributed to all sides in a conflict, with a priority to ease suffering and give relief supplies to those in urgent need. With the severe winter only a few months away, the demand for life-saving supplies would increase with each day that went by.

On a much lighter note, we had previously been told about Feena's hidden talent, and were shown some great photos of Feena performing her act. In Feena's limited spare time, our little Irish lady from Dublin would put on heavy make-up, a red wig, colourful baggy pants and big, top-boots.

Any guesses what Feena's talent might be?

Feena loved that special outfit, because it turned sad faces into happy faces. Feena had a very good reason to get dressed up for that special occasion. No, not a fancy dress party or a girl's night out. To give the game away on Feena's *hidden* talent, Feena would make sure the red nose she put on was redder than the Red Cross itself. Yes you got it! Feena dressed up as a clown. She would then visit sick children in hospital and try to bring some laughter into their very sad and heartbreaking lives.

Tell me, what child does not have a good laugh at a clown!? Feena also extended her talents visiting orphanages scattered around the former Yugoslavia. I guess the bottom line to that wonderful story would be: behind every dark cloud, there is always the warmth of the sun that will bring you a silver lining and happier times. Feena was certainly playing her part to give joy where there was sadness, and to give love where there was so much hate. God bless you, Feena!

Feena concluded our last briefing for the day by inviting us to a drink, and that we might catch some of the drivers and delegates at a couple of nearby bars. After a day of trying to take in so much information, Terry and I decided to accept Feena kind invitation and check these bars out. If only to switch off for a while and meet some new faces. Not that I was tired of Terry's company, but a change was as good as a rest, they say!

On a beautiful sunny day we made our way to one the small bars just three minutes' walk from the delegation. At the bar we had the great pleasure of meeting Eddie, Anita and baby Leon again, Eddie introduced us to David Tarttelin, nicknamed Dave T from Eastbourne, UK. I remember Ann Kerr mentioned Dave T back in London, telling us he was a great cook, and cooked meals for the drivers and delegates. Must make him my best friend, I thought!

Dave, introduced us to a couple Australian drivers, Stuart Downes (nickname Skippy) from Wellington Point, Queensland and Anthony O'Connor, from Melbourne. With a name like O'Connor you would think Tony might be Irish, but Tony's links with Ireland goes back to a great-grandfather. In fact, before immigrating to Australia over twenty years previously, Tony lived and worked in Cardiff, South Wales, with his wife Queenie. In the time Tony spent in Australia, he lost his Welsh accent and sounded more like a native Aussie by then. It was beginning to sound like a scene from the soap opera *Neighbours* at the bar. I was just about to mention one of England's greatest cricketers, Ian Botham, when in walked another driver who was introduce to us as Frank O'Neele from Dublin, Ireland. Frank immediately made us welcome, while cracking jokes in the manner of the favourite Irish comedian Frank Carson. We had a good couple of hours getting to know some of the drivers and delegates who really made us both feel so welcome. Terry, suggested we return to the hotel, to get something to eat, only he was feeling a bit hungry. I must admit I was feeling a bit peckish myself. Most of the drivers had to be up early tomorrow morning for their convoys, so we all decided to call it a day. We thanked everyone for making us feel so welcome and wished them a safe return from their convoy tomorrow, but we were a bit envious not to be going on convoy with them.

Back at the hotel we had a good meal and decided to write a few more letters home before trying to get some sleep. I found it to be a very restless night. I was not worried about anything, but it was just so hot and stuffy. I had a continuous sweat and tried to keep cool with a cold water flannel. Before the alarm went off I think I managed a couple of hours. I would need matchsticks to keep my eyes open in the classroom! After breakfast, we boarded the ICRC transport to take us to the delegation.

Tuesday 27th July 1993. At the delegation, our first briefing on day two was on general information regarding security, given by Jette Soerensen from Denmark. Before departing on convoy, or as the only vehicle in transit, check you have the 'Green Light' from the militaries, the opposition and the delegation.

We had already been briefed on checking our vehicles regarding safety, but it also came under the umbrella of security. Apart from the obvious checks one would associate with the vehicle, Jette brought to our attention that many people would forget to check to see if they had a spare wheel before setting off on a journey. Or that they had the tools to change the wheel if required to do so. The vehicle you take out on convoy should have been refuelled at the end of the day it was last used, or when it was necessary. Before departing on your journey never take that rule for granted! Always check you have a full tank of fuel before embarking on your mission. Don't rely on thefuel gauge in the cab. Diesel vehicles, not petrol vehicles, should be used for cross-line activities. Diesel doesn't explode, as petrol does, when a bullet hits the fuel tank! In case one of the vehicles in the convoy should break down, check that one or more vehicles in a convoy are carrying a tow bar, or tow chains so that, if required, recovery could be on hand to tow the vehicle out of a possibly dangerous area. Don't use ropes to tow heavy vehicles. The use of a rope is okay for light vehicles, but it will break easily if attempted to tow vehicles laden with up to twenty tonnes of cargo. Final checks, radios: ensure VHF and HF are working. Take portable VHF if indicated. Check medical kit and equipment. When necessary always ensure you have a field officer translator.

Jette advised us to think, look, listen and smell on our missions in the field. Think, before making a hasty reckless decision, always evaluate a difficult situation. Look, for anything unusual. Be prepared for the unexpected and be alert. Listen, gunfire can be heard miles away. When you have located the gunfire or shelling, you don't want the convoy to be caught in any crossfire. Smell: can detect the presence of many dangerous substances. Gas, fuel and burning material, to name just a few that could mean your life may be in danger. We must never rule out the use of chemical and biological warfare. It was a sad fact of life that, in modern warfare, governments and political leaders of certain countries do not show enough concern towards the civilian population. With the use of any mass destructive weapon, you cannot select your enemy from amongst the innocent civilian population. Chemical and biological warfare is no exception to that rule. Its use is one of the cruel methods of mass destruction in modern conflicts. Unfortunately detecting its use could also mean you are already infected and, without the proper protection, or urgent treatment, you could face a long period of suffering that could eventually lead to death.

At checkpoints, when communicating with the police or guard, always open the vehicle window wide. If you are wearing sunglasses, take them off before you get to the checkpoint, to avoid that suspicious look. If you need to get out of the vehicle, greet the police or guard in their local language, or as per local custom, smile, make friends, shake hands, or hand on your heart for females in a Muslim country. Always be courteous, talk about their welfare, sport and music, help them to feel at ease, ask if there was anything to be concerned about in the area. In future convoys they would get to know you and trust you.

Dissemination material: offering bandages, pens, cigarettes, sweets, or ICRC leaflets etc, are good, but should not become a habit; they might expect something from you every time you see them. Or it could also be misconceived and taken as a bribe.

More than likely you would meet the same checkpoint guards from one day to the next. Try to work towards a good working practise of trust. Someone who knows you would think twice before shooting at you. Respect everyone, be courteous to everyone. Remember the spotty teenager is more likely to take a shot at you than a commander. Keep calm: you loose respect if you start shouting at people. If threatened, give them what they ask for, vehicle keys, medicines, money, watch, cigarettes etc. Do not antagonize or resist a volatile situation with armed people.

At checkpoints, when asked the nature of the convoy, explain what you are doing and what is in the vehicle, or what you are carrying in your bag, etc. Only by being open and honest with the checkpoint guards will you allow them to have confidence in you. At the checkpoints, remind your field officer/translator to ask about recent fighting, shelling, security, strange movements, noises, etc. It may be necessary to ask the same questions to two or three people to get a more accurate idea of the true situation. Sometimes the answers you get to your questions are tailored to appease you.

If you might be entering an area where there has been a report of shelling, or gunfire. You might need to evacuate your vehicle in a hurry, to take cover. Therefore never lock the doors on your vehicle, or wear a seat belt. Have both side windows slightly open, in case a shell explodes near the vehicle, this will allow the shock waves from the blast to go through the vehicle and not blow a smashed window into your body. Having your window slightly open also helps you to hear in which direction the firing was coming from, in order to take cover in the opposite direction and, of course, any orders to stop the vehicle!

While in the field, look at the military positions. Have they changed from before? Have the number of soldiers in the area increased? How are they holding their guns (ready to fire, or stand down)? Observe the soldiers, have they taken cover and seem to be ready with their guns to fight? All that might sound a bit undercover spy-behind-enemy-lines stuff, but the main reason for these observations was purely to protect the safety and security of you, and your fellow workers, involved in relief work in a dangerous area.

Watch for civilian traffic and ask the drivers about the situation ahead. The movement of civilian traffic was not necessarily a sign of no fighting ahead. In some countries delegates have witnessed a game of Russian roulette played with local buses, taxis and civilian vehicles. Always be alert for the unusual signs, even if you don't understand them immediately. It was better to stop and reconsider the situation! You cannot be alert if you are overtired, or suffering from a hangover from the night before. It's dangerous! If shelling or gunfire is going on in the area ahead you, stop! Turn back to a safe area, at least one mile away from the dangerous area. Try to get further information if possible, from anyone who might have just through the volatile area, etc. Always remember to contact the delegation by radio and inform the delegate in charge of the security situation you are in, giving the delegate your location and what is happening, and what action you are planning to carry out. If you are not sure what to do, ask for advice, or instructions on what your delegation wishes you to do. Keep the relief workers in convoy fully informed.

If you have to take cover, while in the field, remember the road verges may be mined. Look for areas which seemed to have been well used, trodden paths, etc. Man-made ditches and shelters are often around for the protection of soldiers and civilians. Check them out on calm days, so you know where to run when the bullets fly. Look for wires, or soft freshly disturbed soil, large stones, etc. across the road or footpath, could be a sign of a booby trap, the area could be an unmarked minefield. Check it out before proceeding. However much you, or your field officer likes to listen to music on the radio or cassette, or DVDs in volatile situations, these practises must cease, because the noise in the vehicle could obliterate the noise from outside the vehicle, i.e. shouts to stop, the direction of gunfire, etc. cannot be heard if you are listening to loud music. If during the fighting, if you are told there are wounded people, don't rush in to grab the wounded: ask if they are receiving medical treatment. If you can't give them medical treatment, or get them to someone who can, ask, if it's possible for them to be brought to you. Give stretchers if necessary, in order for your instructions to be carried out. Tell them you would wait for them to return at X spot, until Y time, evaluate the situation and allow enough time for them to return. In the long run, you would save more lives by being patient. If necessary wait longer in a safe area, until you are sure you can safely proceed after making contact with all parties involved in the military action, or the delegation has given you the all clear its safe to proceed with the convoy. If necessary wait longer if you are not in danger. Remember there are many dead heroes who can't tell you their story. Always balance the risks taken with the possible end results of your actions.

Only in exceptional circumstances was a relative, or friend, allowed to accompany a patient in a Red Cross or Red Crescent Vehicle (e.g. an injured child, a patient seriously wounded and liable to die, or a seriously injured patient unable to do basic care for him- or herself, etc).

The accompanying person must not be involved with the military and must be unarmed. An evacuation book should be kept with all the names of those who have been evacuated. That was important for when you had to return the patient to where they came from. It is also important also to record if a relative or friend accompanied the patient that had been evacuated. When carrying opposition patients through so-called *enemy areas* (if there were any) it is important to lock the back door of your vehicle. No one was allowed to enter the vehicle. At check points, when asked, only the name and father's name of the patients you are carrying was allowed to be given, no further information should be given, (e.g. where have you come from, how many people died, etc).

In Muslim areas the field officer was a martyr if he dies while working with the ICRC, or fighting in a conflict. Such people are prepared to die for the cause they believe in. The truth was they would gain nothing for their cause if they were wounded or killed. In fact, the whole ICRC operation would be negatively affected and the relief work may have to stop, pending an enquiry to the incident. Who would help the wounded and hungry, then?

Jette then showed us a security film which covered all the issues in our lecture. After a few minutes watching the film, all the actors and actresses seemed very familiar to all present. Then the penny dropped: the full cast of the film was the delegates and local staff, employed by the ICRC in Zagreb. Some of them were drivers who had been our taxi service to and from the hotel.

Of course the drivers played the bad guys and the delegates were the good guys, but they have all been given a chance to rise to stardom, and become movie stars, with Hollywood very much in their minds. The cast acted out many situations that we might experience during the course of our mission. First they showed the wrong way to deal with a hostile situation, then the right way on how to deal with the same situation. At that stage, I thought it would be apt for me to play the part of a film critic. I found the film very enlightening, well directed, and produced. Each scene was well acted, and made to look truly realistic in every situation. No expense was spared in the special effects department and it was clear to me, by the use of a blood substitute, that there was no shortage of tomato sauce in Zagreb. All the cast did their own stunts, which I found very commendable. Over the next few weeks I would certainly be collecting some autographs in my book. However, I am sorry to say the film did not get a nomination for a Oscar, but bravo to all concerned who were responsible for the production of that film, and all the performers in scenes played their part in making that film truly realistic. All joking aside, the film really prepared us all, and gave us an excellent insight in what we might have to face during our mission in the former Yugoslavia.

Jette concluded her briefing and offered everyone some sound advice, "Do not hesitate to turn back if the situation ahead of you does not feel right. Even when there are no obvious signs of fighting. Never forget that you also need a good sense of humour for field work. On your days off, try to find time for relaxation, and be happy, and smile."

After a short coffee break, we returned to the lecture room for our next briefing which would be given by Michael Tatti and Daniel Sardonini, both from Switzerland. Michael and Daniel were employed by the ICRC as tracing delegates. The ICRC Tracing Agency endeavours to re-establish family contact. In order to restore communications, the ICRC arranges with the help of the local Red Cross, the exchange of Red Cross messages between detainees, their families and between family members separated by the conflict in Bosnia, Croatia and Serbia.

In April 1992 the ICRC opened a subdelegation in Bihać and, later in the year, an office in Velika Kladuša. The main activities of these offices were to re-establish family contact through the Red Cross Message Service and the distribution of medical and relief supplies. Their work also includes important visits to persons who have been detained as a result of the conflict in the former Yugoslavia. Three expatriates, two delegates, one nurse, and ten local staff work in these offices to carry out the essential ICRC tasks throughout the Bihać pocket. In the Bihać area alone, there are over 4,000 Red Cross messages collected and distributed every week. Throughout the former Yugoslavia the ICRC handle a staggering 50,000 messages per week.

Family reunion, on a case by case basis, the ICRC reunites children under sixteen years old, elderly people over sixty years old, forheir relatives who are living abroad. Following the release under ICRC auspices of some 5,540 detainees, the ICRC also works with UNHCR, and the International Organisation for the Migration, in order to reunite ex-detainees already resettled in third countries with their families.

During the period from November 1992 to June 1993, over 500 family reunions took place from the Bihać area, 950 family reunions took place in Bosnia-Herzegovina. Also in that same period, persons reunited through the ex-detainees programme amounted to 148 in the Bihać area and over 300 from Bosnia-Herzegovina.

Children and elderly people were being transported by ICRC staff to Zagreb, where they were reunited with their relatives. Family members reunited through the ex-detainees programme were being transported by the ICRC staff to the Karlovac Centre, where UNHCR and the International Organisation for Migration took care of them, and organized their onward flights to their country of resettlement.

Tracing relatives in a country divided by conflict and ethnic cultures can be a long and arduous task. Visits to places of detention can result in success or failure and, of course, in many cases sadness. A specific task of the ICRC was visits to places of detention to hold interviews, without witnesses, with all the detainees and check the condition of their detention. That task was conducted all around the world according to the same criteria: registration of all detainees, with repeat visits and interviews without witnesses. In the Bihać area of the former Yugoslavia, the ICRC delegates regularly visit persons detained as a consequence of the conflict, and regularly observes three places of detention, Bihać Prison, Bihać Military Prison and Kladuša Prison. Releases under ICRC monitoring from detention places in the Bihać area, started on the 3rd November 1992, with twenty-eight Serbian detainees released and transferred under the ICRC auspices to the Federal Republic of Yugoslavia. In October 1992 and March 1993, the ICRC Headquarters in Geneva. Organized meetings with representatives of all three parties involved in the conflict in Bosnia Herzegovina, in order to set up the unconditional and unilateral release of all persons detained due to the conflict. As a result, the ICRC monitored the release of 5,540 detainees between October and December 1992. However, despite numerous appeals further releases were refused. The failure to obtain the release of detainees in December 1992, increased the daily mountain of letters and Red Cross messages sent to the ICRC from relatives, who were trying to locate their loved ones. To enable the ICRC staff in locating relatives torn apart by conflict, all the letters and Red Cross messages must be read to gather the necessary information, in order to find their relatives. But with any war there was always the sad and heartbreaking news that no relative wants to hear. It was therefore very easy to understand that the ICRC staff working in the tracing department can carry a very heavy burden, leaving many of the staff emotionally drained by the contents of all the letters they have read during the course of a day's work. And with the day's work done, some sense of achievement. The tracing staff can find it very difficult to put their work behind them, when you consider the amount of heartache conflicts can cause.

That briefing really stirred up the emotions and deepest thoughts within us all. Can we imagine the anxiety relatives go through, not knowing if your loved ones were safe, in a hostile area of conflict and vast destruction and, on top of that, the worry of ethnic cleansing, sometimes waiting for months to hear good or bad news? Only those who have been in that position can relate to that very heartbreaking and emotional experience.

Which brings us back to the question we all ask, because of a person's culture, religion or political views, why should that motivate a person to take the life of another person, who believes in a different way of living their life? Just because you don't agree with another person's ideals. That does not give anyone the right to force him and his family to leave the area, or worse still, cause him and his family serious harm, with fatal consequences at times? No! That was not the way to conduct disagreements with fellow human beings, no matter what their culture, religion or political views. Why can't we show more tolerance to other people's way of life, without forcing our own way of life on them? What makes us right, and other people we don't agree with wrong? Would it be a better world, if we could all just agree to disagree at times? I would always fight for that person to have an opinion without any malice, in a free democratic society. Let's not forget the men and women who gave their lives for the ideals of freedom that most of us enjoy today. We must endeavour to honour their sacrifice by living together in peace and goodwill, and trying to solve the problems we face in our world together. Remember that we all live and share this world, and it was only the people on this earth that can make our lives a cruel living hell, or a beautiful place to live in harmony. Please don't misunderstand me, I don't have any sympathy or condone the work of terrorists, murderers or soldiers who murder innocent civilians in their evil ethnic cleansing campaign. They must all be brought to justice and be punished for their crimes against humanity.

There are so many questions we could ask about this troubled world, and why we take the self-destruct route to show the dark side of our lives. No doubt all these questions would have us going around in circles. I hope and pray the day will come when we will find all the answers, that would result in the nations of our world living in Peace, Love and Understanding. Together we will endure against any evil temptations that could destroy humanity. The bottom line is, for the sake of future generations, we must all work harder, to make this world a better place to live and create caring society.

Michael and Daniel concluded their joint lecture by wishing us all a safe and successful mission in the former Yugoslavia. We thanked them for their lecture and their good wishes. And retired for lunch, to reflect on the morning's lectures so far. We all thought the morning seem to have flown by.

After lunch we returned to the lecture room for our penultimate briefing on the ICRC telecommunications that comprehensive briefing was presented by Mirko Kustan, the senior radio operator at the ICRC delegation in Zagreb.

The ICRC radio was an autonomous communication system. Nevertheless the ICRC required the agreement on installing parts and using it in the former Yugoslavia.

The ICRC radio must be used for transmitting short information about: Position, Security, Departures / Arrivals and Incidents. It must not be used for: long conversations, requests implying a long occupation of the radio, and for whatever reasons for private communication.

The HF radio was not a confidential transmission system. Everybody can copy what was being transmitted. The HF radio was a long-distance communication system. Its working range was within thirty kilometres and 900 kilometres. But because of its transmission operation regarding atmospheric rebound, the reception quality was constantly changing. You can start your communication with an excellent quality reception and finish your communication with a very bad quality reception, and of course vice versa.

The ICRC use mainly Channel 5 on VHF, in the former YugoslaLike HF, VHF Radio was not a confidential communication system either. Always remember that on both these HF and VHF everybody can copy what was transmitted. VHF has a shorter range than HF, with a working range within fifty kilometres, depending on the physical conditions and the position of the transmitter. On the other hand, the quality of transmission was much better than HF.

From 1990 the ICRC used the satellite communication system. It's not completely autonomous as the HF Radio. It depends on the Inmarsat satellite network. The ICRC pay a fee to Inmarsat for owning and using two satellite telecommunication systems. Although it was not completely confidential, the degree of confidentiality was quite higher than the HF and VHF radios.

Most of the ICRC delegations are equipped with Standard C, also known as the Blue Box, to send telex messages via satellite. Yet this is not a real-time transmission system, i.e. you could not talk, or hold a conversation with your contact.

Belgrade, Zenica, Mostar and Banja Luka are equipped with the Standard A, also called the Big Umbrella. This system was a fax and telephone via satellite. For security reasons cars and trucks in the field limit their AMTOR contact duration according to a radio contact timetable, in order to free the frequency for emergency calls.

All field trips would be made with one vehicle equipped with both HF and VHF radio.

As mobile stations – cars and trucks to the layman – we'd fill in the *Field Trip Form* before every field trip and give a copy to the radio room. As a rule, a radio contact must be made at a field trip departure, before passing the border, or entering an unsafe zone, also after entering an unsafe zone, and when leaving an area to return to base. Upon return to your base station, you must also notify the radio operator of your safe return. Failure to do so would alert concern for the safety of you and your colleagues in the convoy. Always check that your radio equipment was working properly, and keep your radio on all through the field trip, even if the noise was bothering you.

When passing through checkpoints, lower the volume on your HF radio. On convoy, only the Convoy Leader would establish all the HF radio contacts, for all the vehicles in the convoy. Drivers can keep in contact among themselves with VHF radios. We were reminded that Channel 16 could work better than Channel 12. If you switch to Channel 16, you also change your Blue Antenna, for the Orange Antenna. After every field trip, we have to insure we switched off both HF and VHF radios, and removed the antennaes from the vehicle.

Mirko concluded his briefing on the ICRC telecommunications by wishing us all a trouble-free mission and that he would look forward to hearing from us on radio transmission.

We all had time for a quick cup of coffee, before returning to the lecture room for our last briefing with the Head of Transport in Zagreb, Laurent Tosoni from Switzerland.

Laurent's job was to ensure the smooth running of the transport and logistics operations in Zagreb. Also under his umbrella was the ICRC transport workshops. They were under constant pressure to service and repair vehicles urgently required on relief convoys. He explained that the supply operation for relief could not be held up, because vehicles were off the road for long periods at a time. When a vehicle went in for its service, the service was usually completed within four hours, and the vehicle would then be returned to the warehouse parking lot, in order for the vehicle to be loaded for a convoy on the following day. Sometimes there could be a short delay getting spare parts for the vehicles from nearby countries, Austria, Germany, Hungary, etc. as the vehicle cannot afford to be off the road while waiting for spare parts. Whenever possible, it has been known for some of the local mechanics employed with ICRC to make a spare parts for vehicles on the workshop lathe, in order to get the vehicle back on the road for urgent relief work.

Most convoys departed from the ICRC Velika Gorica warehouse, which was located near Zagreb Airport, following signs to Sisak. Drivers were picked up from their apartments, or hotels, and were required to be at the warehouse at 0530 hours. This gave you plenty of time to check your vehicle and carry out a radio check. The convoys departed at 0600 hours in the running order that the Convoy Leader had requested. Your Convoy Leader would inform the Zagreb radio room that he, or she, was departing Zagreb with X numbers of trucks and the convoy's destination. When the convoy was in a built-up area, or town, we'd always try to keep the trucks close together to avoid becoming separated. In the event that happened, because of traffic lights or heavy traffic, it was important not to panic. Your Convoy Leader would slow the convoy down to allow you to catch up. Once out of the towns, you'd allow a distance of fifty to 100 metres between the trucks ahead of you. Your Convoy Leader would keep all the drivers informed by radio, of any problems on the road ahead, (i.e. check point, rocks in the road, people in the road, etc.) so always make sure your radio was left on after you did your radio check before departure from the warehouse. The last truck in the convoy (known as *Tail-end Charlie*) always informed the Convoy Leader that he, or she, had cleared the check point, or any obstruction that your Convoy Leader radioed to the convoy. When the convoy was just a few minutes away from their destination, your Convoy Leader would inform the destination radio room that he, or she, was arriving with X number of trucks. Upon return to the warehouse in Zagreb, your Convoy Leader would inform the radio room that the convoy retuned safely with X number of trucks.

On return to the warehouse the last duty every driver must carry out, without any exception, was to refuel the truck and report any defects to the workshop, in order for the truck to be used on the following day's relief convoy. All the trucks would then be loaded in the evening by the local ICRC warehouse staff, ready for tomorrow's convoy – apart from convoys on more than one day trips – that was the daily routine practise for convoy drivers and the warehouse staff.

Laurent introduced us to his right hand man and Transport Manager, Beat Mosimann from Switzerland. Beat's job was to formalate all the convoys from Zagreb. There could be as many three or four convoys leaving Zagreb every day, all going in different directions. So Beat would juggle the urgent relief demands with the trucks and drivers at his disposal. Every Saturday morning Beat would hold a meeting with the drivers, to notify them of their convoy duties for the coming week. Beat would also deal with any problems or complaints drivers might have. Beat then introduced us to, would you believe it, yet another Beat, this time the driving instructor Beat Trinkler, and he was also from Switzerland.

After all, the Swiss did form the Red Cross, it was their baby all right. And of course the Swiss are famous for cheese and chocolate; although I'm not sure about the Swiss Roll (joke).

Apparently Beat was a Swiss version of the British name, Bert, I hope that's all clear for you now. There was no need for Marysa, a trainee administrator, to attend the last briefing. Beat Trinkler was only there for Terry and me, and took over the briefing after Marysa, Laurent and Beat Mosimann left the lecture room. Leaving us at the mercy of Beat Trinkler.

We did tell Beat that we were a bit surprised for the need for driver training, after we had driven through Europe to get to Zagreb, and we both held HGV-1 licences in the UK. Beat just looked at us with a smile, as if to say *But that's my job, you wouldn't want to see me out of work, would you?* Perhaps the Swiss felt us Brits' driving skills were not very good when it came to driving on the right-hand side of the road! First Beat showed us some short films on the *Hazards of driving Articulated Trucks*, Rigid and Truck/Drags in various terrains, (i.e. snow, mountains, etc). Beat insisted and emphasized that, at all costs, select a low gear and use the exhaust brake – not the footbrake! – when negotiating the descent of very steep hills and mountain terrains. Failure to use a low gear and engage the use of your exhaust brake on long steep roads would result in brake fade. Prolonged and continued use of your footbrake on very long and steep hills would cause the brake drum to overheat and expand. Thus your brake shoes would lose contact with the brake drum, leaving you with no brakes. A second hazard for truck drivers, when they continuously pump the footbrake to slow down, was to release air from the air tank that operates the brakes. Resulting in no air and brake fade, if you were driving down a mountain road or track, and couldn't control the speed of your vehicle. There was a risk of you coming off the road or, worse still, going over a sheer drop to the bottom of the mountain or hill.

At that point Beat's lecture made a lot of sense, because the terrain we would be driving on in the former Yugoslavia would be nothing like UK roads. Beat then covered the hazards of driving in snow and icy conditions. In the former Yugoslavia, winter temperatures can fall below minus twenty degrees, with a chance of one to two metres of snow. These harsh winters usually Start around October, and lasted until March the following year.

These severe winters cause a list of problems, some of which you would not have experienced in the UK. For example, brake fluid frozen solid in the pipes. The use of snow chains on the wheels keeps the relief convoys on the road, supplying much needed medical supplies, food, blankets, etc. Beat enjoyed a joke at our expense by telling us whenever a truck got stuck in the snow on the convoys, you could guarantee it was a Brit driving the truck. Beat could see that we were not laughing and decided to call it a day. He told us to be at the delegation at 0830 hours tomorrow morning and, from there, he would take us to the ICRC warehouse for some driver training over the next two days. We thanked Beat and made our way to one of the bars near the delegation for a well-earned *pivo*. The bar was practically empty, just a couple of locals. The drivers were not back from their convoys yet. We hoped everything was okay with the guys on the convoys, so we stayed there for about an hour until a couple of delegates walked in and told us it was normal for some convoys to get back a little later, they might have had a delay on check points. Terry's stomach started rumbling, so we decided to go back to the hotel for a bite to eat. After a shower and something to eat, Terry said he was knackered, because all that classroom work had stewed his brain. While Terry went to his room to get some rest, I decided to write a couple more letters home. When you're writing to your father, ex-wife, sons, sister and friends, it was a job to find the time to write to them all, so I did the best I could, while I had some spare time, before going to bed.

Wednesday 28th July 1993. With a bit of luck, Terry and I would be back on the road. We had not been behind the wheel of a truck, since the last Saturday. Better make sure Terry was awake and get some breakfast, before the transport arrived to pick us up at 0800 hours to take us to the delegation.

Beat was waiting to take us to the warehouse. Weather was a bit overcast, with bouts of fine drizzle. At the ICRC warehouse, Beat went through the daily vehicle checks. Once again Terry and I looked at each other, as if to say, "Beat, between us we've been driving trucks for over forty years, in that time do you not think we have never checked a vehicle before taking it out on the road?" But the best was yet to come, when Beat went on to cover the laws regarding the use of tachographs. I could not believe what I was hearing from Beat! For those of you who might not be familiar with the tachographs, it's a paper disc that you load behind your speedo dial; the disc would record your speed, how many times you stopped to unload, or load, and record your rest times (i.e. dinner breaks).

You were supposed to have a forty-five-minute dinner break, or rest, after four and a half hours' continuous driving. While taking a dinner break you were not supposed to be behind the wheel of the truck, or attempt to move the truck. That law was fine on the peaceful roads in the UK, but come on, this was a war zone! Was Beat really saying that we must use tachographs in a war zone? Can you imagine the convoy on a dinner break, then suddenly it comes under attack with gunfire and shelling? Then the Convoy Leader says, "Oh dear lads, we are under attack! Better finish our din-dins before we move the vehicles to cover!" Two words, "Sod off!' … putting it politely! Quite honestly I thought *Swiss Bert's* idea of using tachographs in a war zone was the most stupid thing I had heard in a long time.

We finally got on the road with a couple of old trucks to demonstrate our driving skills. Beat sat in with me first, while Terry followed behind in another truck.

After about an hour Beat sat in with Terry while I followed Terry's truck. Beat took us on these narrow country roads, about ten kilometres outside Zagreb. I had been following Terry's truck for about forty-five minutes when I noticed an old clapped-out farm truck in my rear-view mirror. The driver was continuously swaying from one side of the road to the other, looking for room to overtake. There was no problem with oncoming traffic, the road, if you could call it a road, was deserted and hardly ever used. The problem the driver was having was *how* to overtake, when the road was clearly not wide enough for two trucks to pass alongside each other. But no matter what, that idiot was determined to overtake me on that secondary road! Terry's truck was about 150 metres ahead of mine. So I decide to radio Beat and tell him that I was looking for a safe place to pull over, in order to let that impatient driver behind me pass. That driver must have had an appointment with death! No sooner had I replaced the radio receiver than I noticed that bloody farm truck had decided to overtake. We were now side by side, with no more than inches between our vehicles. It was like a scene from the movie *Ben Hur*, where you had a couple of chariot drivers fighting for what little track was left in the arena. If anything, the road was getting narrower as both trucks approached a narrow left-hand bend. On the bend I felt my truck starting to slide to the right, upon which I started to lose control of the steering. I wanted to go left, but my truck had other ideas and was now sliding to the right. I was no longer in control of the truck as it went into skid for about fifty metres, at the same time slowly tilting to the right, until the truck stopped at a forty-five degree angle in a ditch. When I got out I noticed the edge of the road that I was on had collapsed. The farm truck carried on regardless without stopping. Beat and Terry reversed their truck back to mine and made sure I was okay. I was fine: I'd had a lot worse than that before! Beat radioed the delegation requesting the assistance of a recovery truck to tow my truck out of the ditch. When the recovery team arrived, they were concerned that the truck was fully loaded with twenty tonnes of food parcels, which was destined for Banja Luka on tomorrow's convoy. Any attempt to tow the truck out of the ditch could result in tipping the truck completely on its side.

They radioed for more help from the warehouse staff to unload half of the food parcels that were making the vehicle top heavy. When all the warehouse staff arrived, we all rolled up our sleeves and set about the task of unloading the top-heavy food parcels on my sorry-looking truck. After the unloading was complete we secured the tow cable to my truck and, with the cable taut, slowly and successfully the recovery vehicle towed my truck out the ditch. Surprisingly there was no damage to the truck. So the truck would be checked over at the workshop that afternoon and hopefully resume its place on the convoy to Banja Luka the next morning. What a day! From the time we'd arrived at the warehouse at 0900 hours, we had spent over an hour on vehicle checks and tachographs, with only one and three-quarter hours' actual driving time.

Another one hour we spent waiting for the recovery truck and the warehouse staff, one and a quarter hours unloading the food parcels onto another truck and fifteen minutes towing the truck out the ditch. It was now 1415 hours. Beat, Terry and yours truly had just about had enough and decided to call it a day. We thought it best to end it on a high note. So on arrival at the ICRC delegation, we wasted no time in heading for the nearby bar and enjoyed the company of some drivers and delegation staff, and of course over a few *pivos*. We all had a good laugh at my expense following my mishap with the ditch.

Thursday 29th July 1993: when the alarm went off, I just hoped and prayed that this day would be a more successful than the day before. But hey, yesterday was now history. Let's think positive! Usual routine, shower and breakfast, before the transport arrives to take us to the delegation to meet Beat. On arrival at the delegation, Beat told us that he had been instructed to take only one driver out at a time. From the way Beat spoke, I think Beat had his wrist slapped yesterday for taking two drivers out at the same time. I was lucky to be going out on driver training in the morning, poor Terry had to come back to the delegation that afternoon. Twenty kilometres from Zagreb, Beat had me driving up and down mountain tracks with hairpin bends, gear changing and exhaust brake all morning. I reckon Beat had it in for me after the circus with the farm truck. In the near future that training was going to be so invaluable and help me tackle the hard mountain terrains of Bosnia. It was a beautiful sunny day, perhaps a little on the warm side, but everything was going well. Beat decided that my driving was up to scratch and instructed me to go back to the ICRC warehouse. En route we travelled through the rural outskirts of Zagreb. Suddenly I felt this very sharp stinging pain in the middle of my back! Beat noticed that I was in some sort of distress and asked me if I was okay. I told him that something big flew in the open window, falling inside the back of my shirt, and stung me. I have been stung before, but never felt pain like that before from an insect, which continued its attack on me. I pulled the truck over to the side of the road and got out of truck as quickly as I could to take my shirt off and get rid of that parasite that was trying to eat me alive! I was hopping around the side of the road like a demented frog before it flew off. It was huge, with a long body like a hornet.

Two ladies who had seen me in some discomfort appeared from a nearby house. One of the ladies went back into her house and returned with a bottle of brandy and some cotton wool. She bathed the bites on my back for a few minutes, while Beat was shaking his head in disbelief. I guess the last two days had been too much for poor Beat, he looked close to a nervous breakdown. After I had a swig of brandy, I thanked the two wonderful ladies for their kindness and resumed our journey back to the ICRC warehouse; with Beat crossing his fingers. He breathed a sigh of relief when we arrived without any further incident. Beat must have been so relieved to see the back of me! But our paths would cross again at a later date, when Beat's driving skills would only come second to a Brit.

Back at the delegation Terry had left for his afternoon driver training with Bert. I went to see the transport manager, Beat Mosimann, and he informed me that I would be on the convoy to Banja Luka tomorrow as a passenger; to get experience in convoy procedure. This was because the next week I would be driving on convoys myself. I thought, at last I would be doing the job I had volunteered for! After I had a sandwich and coffee, I arranged to meet Terry at the bar near the delegation. While waiting for Terry at the bar, I met a couple more drivers, who would be on the Banja Luka convoy the next day too: Frank Karlsen and Kent Furuly from Norway, and Ross Burborough from Australia. When Terry walked into the bar he was not looking too happy. Apparently the driver training went okay, but Terry was informed at the delegation that tomorrow he would be taken to Split on the Adriatic coast of Croatia. There he would take up driving duties on convoys from Split. That evening we had a couple of farewell drinks with the other drivers, before returning to the hotel.

CHAPTER ELEVEN

The Convoy Diaries

Friday 30ᵗʰ July 1993. The alarm woke me at 0445 hours to give me a time for a shower and shave before Dave T picked me up in an ICRC Land Cruiser at 0515 hours. En route to the ICRC warehouse Dave T also picked up Australians, Stuart Downes and Tony O'Connor, and a Swiss guy, Jean-Marie Bosson. We arrived at the warehouse where Dave T introduced me to the other drivers on his convoy: Peter Milne, from Scotland; Frank Karlsen and Kent Furuly from the bar; another Norwegian known only has Knuit; and last but not least, the guy I would be travelling with, Australian Ross Burborough.

With great respect to Ross, he reminded me of the type of guy you might meet at the Glastonbury Festival. I had already met some of the guys in the bar; nevertheless they all made me feel very welcomed on their convoy. With all the trucks and loads checked, all the drivers responded to Dave T's radio check and confirmed they were ready to roll. After they had positioned their trucks behind the Convoy Leader, Dave T radioed the ICRC delegation to report that he was about to depart Zagreb with nine trucks en route to Banja Luka. In the radio room at the ICRC delegation was a local lady called Vanja, she replied, "Okay, Dave T, message received, I wish you all a good and a safe journey."

The convoy departed the warehouse on time at 0600 hours. At first the convoy made their way through the urban areas of Zagreb. We encountered several traffic lights that split the convoy. In that situation it was important for the last truck in the convoy, which was Tony O'Connor (our *Tail-end Charlie*), to keep in radio contact with his Convoy Leader, in order to inform him that he had just passed a certain landmark that would be known to the Convoy Leader. That would give the Convoy Leader some indication on how far the last truck in the convoy was behind him. The Convoy Leader would then regulate the speed of the convoy, until all the trucks had rejoined the convoy.

The same procedure would apply whenever the convoy became split going through checkpoints, towns, etc. Any situation that could cause the convoy to be separated could endanger individuals in the convoy. It was not before we joined the E 70 highway travelling south-east towards Beograd that the convoy had chance to regroup, with the last truck informing the Convoy Leader he was on the highway. Dave T dropped his speed until the convoy was together. Ross and I talked about a wide range of subjects, from girls, Australia and the UK, etc.

The convoy travelled through a toll booth, charges for which the ICRC was exempt. All the road signs were riddled with bullet holes, the crash barriers were all mangled and twisted. The highway was once a busy road, but now we were the only vehicles to be seen on it. Ross's truck was sixth in the convoy. All of a sudden the truck in front of us broke from convoy and turned into a disused service station before then rejoining the convoy without stopping. The driver was Peter Milne. Ross told me that Peter and Dave T had a history, something to do with a grenade, but he didn't know the full story, just gossip among drivers. Yet the bottom line was they didn't get on, too well.

Peter had broken from the convoy to annoy the Convoy Leader, Dave T. *How childish*, I thought. The convoy passed through a couple of checkpoints without any problems. After

140 kilometres we turned right off the highway, heading south on a rough dirt track, because the bridges ahead of us were destroyed. When we managed to get back on a minor road to Banja Luka, it was then that I first witnessed the signs of the war here. Houses riddled with bullets, roofs missing and burnt out.

It was hard to believe, or imagine, families once lived in these houses. Dave T radioed our Serbian Red Cross escort, called Vanja, to let her know the convoy's ETA would be in about twenty minutes. Vanja was waiting at Gradiska Bridge with her driver, called Branco, to escort the convoy to Banja Luka. Vanja was employed by the ICRC as an interpreter, which was essential on checkpoints if the guards did not speak English. That was the first time I heard Vanja's voice and it was not going to be the last time. Little did I know just how much Vanja would play a big part in my future mission. Before we arrived at Gradiska Bridge, I witnessed even more signs of the devastation that had ripped this beautiful country apart. More houses, schools, shops, factories were gutted and burnt out. This, once a thriving community where men, women and children had lived together in peace, was now left shamefully deserted.

The convoy arrived at Gradiska Bridge at 0845 hours and parked at the side of the road, while all the necessary documentation was checked by the Serbian checkpoint guards. Dave T introduced me to the beautiful and charming Vanja and Branco; he could not speak any English, but cracked jokes with the drivers with the help of his interpreter, the enchanting Vanja. They would be our Serbian Red Cross escort to Banja Luka.

Vanja and Branco were summoned to the Serbian checkpoint, to be informed that the convoy papers were not in order. Before any convoy movement across the borders of the former Yugoslavia, the ICRC was required to give prior notification to all the relevant authorities in the conflict. In that notification the ICRC had to submit how many trucks would be used, including the trucks registration numbers, the

172

cargo they were carrying, the convoy's destination, etc. Last, but not least, the names and IDs of all the drivers or personnel on the convoy. Taking into account the latter requirement, you would not need three guesses to work out whose name the the ICRC delegation in Zagreb had forgotten to include on the convoy. Yes, it was mine! The bad luck that I had experienced on Wednesday and Thursday had now followed me on my first convoy.

They say bad luck happens in threes, first the farm truck, second the insect bite, and now this! What a bloody nightmare. Was someone up there trying to tell me something, like you are not meant to be here on this mission? Dave T radioed the ICRC delegation in Zagreb to inform them about the problem at Gradiska Bridge. Meanwhile Vanja and Branco tried to sort out the problem with the Serbian guards at the checkpoint. After about forty-five minutes Vanja and Branco returned with the news that the convoy would be allowed to continue to Banja Luka. That was after Vanja and Branco had returned from taking me back to the UN checkpoint near Novska, approximately thirty-five kilometres from the Bridge.

From there the ICRC delegation in Zagreb would send transport to pick me up and take me back. For the sake of the convoy, it was the only sensible solution to the problem. I wished all the lads a safe journey and told them that if they were not too late back, I would see them in the bar. The convoy would have wait for just over an hour, for Vanja and Branco to return before they could proceed to Banja Luka. On the way back to the UN checkpoint, Vanja was telling me how she was a little worried about the outcome regarding my unofficial presence on the convoy. She said, "They might have thought you were a spy and arrested you, or accused you of anything."

I started to laugh, hoping Vanja was joking... I was happy when she changed the subject and asked me about England and my family. Vanja told me about her family, her father was a doctor and, before the war, he was hoping Vanja would follow in his footsteps. She was told me how hard it was to study to be a doctor, but she had an ambition to qualify as a nurse and maybe one day she would achieve all her dreams in England. I have already mentioned that Branco did not speak any English, but with Vanja's help Branco managed a few jokes with me.

We arrived at the UN checkpoint near Novska on the highway, where I was put in the hands of the Jordanian Army for safe keeping. I thanked Vanja and Branco for their kindness and understanding, and that I was sorry to have caused them the inconvenience. Vanja replied, "It is not your fault, the delegation in Zagreb is to blame, George, we hope to see you again soon but until then *dovidjenja* [goodbye]."

So after I had said my farewells to Vanja and Branco, I found my new guardians were very hospitable towards me. I talked to a Jordanian major about his duties in the former Yugoslavia, while enjoying a much welcomed cup of coffee. He then showed me some photos of his wife and children. I guess that's the sort of thing guys do in war zones. The major kindly offered me one of his cigarettes, I politely refused, but offered him one of my miniature cigars, he accepted the cigar but looked at it in a strange way. I think he must have thought it was a UK brand of cigarette. Upon lighting the cigar, and taking a long drag, he started coughing and spluttering, when he finally caught his breath, he said, "What the fucking hell is this?" I explained to him that it was not a cigarette, it was a cigar, and if you are not used to cigars it would be better not to take the drag back. I talked about my family for a while and told him why I was in the former Yugoslavia.

The major again offered me a cigarette, as if say we smoke these, not them bloody cigars. For the sake of international relations I accepted the cigarette, but did not enjoy it; he certainly got his own back. The ICRC transport arrived at 1400 hours to take me back to Zagreb. I thanked the major and his men for their hospitality. On the way back to Zagreb, the Croatian Red Cross driver did not seem very talkative. I think he only had a limited knowledge of English, or he might have heard that I had become a bit of a jinx and was afraid I would bring him bad luck.

The silence, gave me time to reflect on my first week's mission with the ICRC in the former Yugoslavia. I felt that I had more than my fair share of bad luck and that I had not achieved anywhere near my full potential. One thing I was not going to do was feel sorry for myself. When you feel you have reached the bottom, there was only one way to go from there and that was UP! And with God's help, I prayed that my mission would take on a much more rewarding feeling. When I got back to the delegation in Zagreb, Beat Mosimann apologized for the error, and assured me that after tomorrow's drivers meeting I would feel a lot happier. Can't wait, I thought, but I wonder what he was going to say to make me feel happy? I went to the nearby bar get a sandwich and *pivo*, and wait to see if the Banja Luka drivers get back okay. Eddie, Anita and baby Leon were there enjoy a late afternoon drink. They had a good laugh listening to my adventures on the first week here. They inquired where Terry was. I told them Terry was sent to work on convoys in Split that morning. I think they thought I might be lonely without him. No chance! It was nice to get some peace and quiet. When all the drivers walked in, we all had a good night before calling it a day.

Saturday 31st July 1993. Did not need the alarm that morning but, due to the heat, still woke up early 0500 hours, I spent one hour in a cold shower to cool down. While I was having breakfast, there was an area screened off from the other hotel guest. Behind the screens were refugees. UNHCR had supplied overnight accommodation for some of the refugees, awaiting distribution into safe areas, or waiting to joining relatives in another country. All of them were families with children that were in danger in the area they once lived, in harmony and peace. Before I left the UK, my sister Shirley gave me bags of sweets and chocolates to give to the children who were victims of war. I went back to my room to get all the sweets and the chocolates from the coolest place, the bathroom. Went back downstairs and put all the sweets and chocolates on the tables where the children were sat. Just to see their faces light up brought a lump in my throat.

Thank you, Shirley.

Transport arrived to take me to the delegation for my first Convoy Operations Meeting for the drivers at 1000 hours. En route I was thinking Terry must be settled in Split by now, I wonder how he is getting on? At the delegation I met some drivers that I had not met before and they duly introduced themselves. From Switzerland, Raoul David and his little Yorkshire terrier called Goliath. Yes, I love that connection – David and Goliath – very good Raoul! Also from Switzerland, Vincent Feux; then we had the French drivers, Didier Blanc, Jean Claude Chesaux and Johnny Heritier, communication with the French drivers was difficult because they spoke very little English. From Iceland, Diego Thorkeelsson; from Ireland, Martin Vaughan, Mark Keating and Frank O'Neele; and from Italy, Carlos Melara. Apparently most of these drivers had been on other convoys to Knin and Bihać. The rest of the drivers at the meeting were all on yesterday's convoy to Banja Luka. In total twenty drivers, including myself, attended the meeting. Beat Mosimann (the Transport Manager) opened the meeting, and distributed leaflets with the details of the forthcoming week's relief convoys, with the names of the drivers allocated to the convoys. Wow! Yesterday Beat said I would be happy: today, I was on convoys to Banja Luka Monday, Tuesday and Wednesday, Knin on Thursday with a overnight stay in Knin, return to Zagreb on Friday. Beat asked if anyone had any problems? I think the drivers were keen to enjoy their weekend off and not spend to long at that meeting, so there were no problems to disgust. After the meeting, with a smile on his face, Beat asked me to go down to the Welcome Office to see Sophie Matkovic before I left the delegation.

Even more good news for me, Sophie dealt with the accommodation for ICRC staff and gave me authorisation to check out of the Dubrovnik Hotel to move into an apartment. No. 10 Boškovićeva, which was close to the hotel, in the city centre. I would be sharing the apartment with the Australian, Ross Burborough and Frank O'Neele from Ireland. I felt like it was my birthday, and Beat knew what presents I would be getting – convoys the next week and getting out of that greenhouse of a hotel! Hopefully I would get a good night's sleep that night. Sophie asked me to read the apartment documents and sign them, and also sign for the keys. I thanked Sophie and joined the lads at Metor's Bar for just a couple of *pivos*, before going to the hotel to check out.

After booking out of the hotel it was only a ten-minute walk to No. 10 Boškovićeva. Ross and Frank were still out, still at the bar I guessed. I was pleasantly surprised how big the apartment was. The kitchen was well stocked with utensils, a fridge, washing machine, cooker, etc. a shower over a bath and I had the biggest bedroom. Before unpacking my bags, I thought it would be best to get a bit of shopping (food, tea, coffee, milk, etc). I was not too sure what time the shops and market closed on Saturday. I managed to get most of the things I needed for the time being, but I'd probably get some more shopping tomorrow. I remembered the last Sunday there were shops open.

With all the unpacking done, I chilled out on my bed with my thoughts. To be honest, I was so happy that I'd be on convoys all the next week. At last I was getting the chance to help innocent victims of war, even if it was only a small contribution, to relieve any suffering. Perhaps, in time, that would help to dry the tears in my eyes; but to eliminate such emotions would not be easy. None of us know what joys or heartaches lay ahead of us. Just look at those refugees in the hotel that morning. If you had asked them two years ago, "Do you think you might have leave your home because of war and become a refugee?" I am sure all of them would have laughed at you. All of this started five months ago, with those terrible pictures and reports on our TV screens in the UK. From that day until now, I felt it had been on one of the longest journeys of my life. Little did I know that that mission was going to make me into an even more sensitive person, on my return to the UK.

I must have nodded off for a about an hour or so, only to be disturbed with a noise in the lounge. Better go and investigate. It turned out to be Ross and Frank, having just a little bit too much to drink. "Hi George all... settled... in... matey?" was the slurred welcome. "Hi lads, had a good time?" was my reply. After trying to hold a conversation with a couple of guys who were not sure what day it was, I was relieved when they decided to go to bed and sleep it off. Bless them! I was not too far behind them. I found the apartment a lot cooler and with a bit of luck I would catch up with my sleep.

Sunday 1st August 1993. It was the best night's sleep I had ever had in Zagreb. Although I still woke up early, just this time it was not because of the heat! I think over the years of getting out of bed at five or six a.m. for work, your body clock automatically wakes you up. The lads were still asleep – a good time to get in the bathroom. After two weeks of hotel life, it seemed strange preparing my own breakfast and a pot of tea. I guessed the holiday was over. While I was having my breakfast, Ross staggered in looking worse for ware. I know the feeling, mate! Ross said he was spending the day with his lady friend.

Frank was still in bed when I left to get a bit more shopping. On return, Frank was up and seemed a little worried about something. Over a cup of coffee Frank was telling me that he had some problems at home. I told him how sorry I was to hear that. That was not the best place to be, if you have problems at home. You are isolated from dealing with family issues. Frank was going to phone his wife later on in the day, after he'd had more time to think.

I decided to explore more of Zagreb. I found a lovely place that was similar to a McDonalds, if anything it was better. While I was having my Sunday lunch there, I was shocked to see twelve- to thirteen-year-olds smoking openly in front of adults. I know cigarettes were very cheap there, but that was ridiculous! On a lovely fine summer's afternoon in Zagreb, I explored the old part of that beautiful city. I must have walked miles, while thinking about my family back home and if they were enjoying their Sunday afternoon as much as I was. Thinking about families, I thought I'd better get back and write a couple more letters. I had bought some postcards to write and send home. I got back to an empty apartment. Just as I was about finished with the postcards, Frank walked in seeming a little happier. I prepared my gear for the next day's convoy.

Monday 2nd August 1993. Despite all that exercise yesterday afternoon, I didn't sleep to well last night. To be honest, I could not stop thinking about the day's convoy. I was not afraid, but I just hoped nothing went wrong and the delegation would remember to include my name on the convoy. Ross was also on the convoy, after a cup of tea we were both ready and waiting for Dave T, leaving Frank to enjoy his day off in bed.

As per last Friday Dave T was on the dot. And picked us up at 0515 hours, then went on to pick up Ross's fellow Australians, Tony O'Connor and Stuart Downes. At the ICRC warehouse we joined the other drivers on that convoy, Norwegians Frank Karlsen, Kent Furuly and Knuit, and last but not least the Swiss guy Jean Marie Bosson. Much to the joy of Dave T, I had replaced the Scot Peter Milne on that convoy. So it was as we were last Friday, minus Peter.

After I checked my old Mercedes truck, I informed Dave T. He told me to position my truck fifth in the convoy. I hoped that was a good omen, five is my lucky number. Then I heard Dave T inform the radio room at the delegation that he was about to leave Zagreb with nine trucks, en route to Banja Luka. As we encountered last Friday's route and checkpoints, the closer we got to Gradiska Bridge the more nervous I got. Dave T kept a radio check on me from time to time, doing his best to reassure me. When we were about twenty kilometres away from Gradiska Bridge, Dave T contacted Vanja our

Serbian escort to Banja Luka. It was nice to hear her voice again, I was hoping that was not going to be a case of déjà vu.

We arrived at Gradiska Bridge at 0815 hours and parked on the left hand side of the road, while we waited thirty agonizing minutes for the papers to be checked. I kept everything crossed during that time. Then over the radio I heard Dave T say, 'Okay, lads, *Ida Mo*!' Which means, *Let's go!* The feeling of relief and joy could not be hidden as I followed the trucks in front of me over Gradiska Bridge. The convoy twisted its way over Gradiska Bridge like a snake, through a chicane of large concrete blocks and railway lines welded together in a cross, all covered in barbed wire and positioned to stop any vehicle travelling over the bridge at speed. Those who tried would easily be shot.

Vanja and Branco were waiting on the other side of Gradiska Bridge for the last vehicle to cross the bridge. As my truck passed Vanja and Branco, they both gave me a thumbs up and a beaming smile, as if to say *George, you made it without any problems*. I now felt part of team that was giving so much needed relief to innocent victims of war. About one kilometre after the bridge, Dave T was parked on the left-hand side of the road waiting for the last truck (Frank Karlsen's) to radio through that he had cleared Gradiska Bridge. At the same time Vanja and Branco's Land Cruiser would pass the convoy, to take the lead and escort the convoy to Banja Luka. Before we got to Banja Luka we passed through a couple of small towns called Laktasi and Klasnice, they seem to be quite intact, with no immediate signs of destruction. We arrived at the ICRC warehouses in Banja Luka at 0930 hours and were directed were to park our trucks to enable the local ICRC warehouse staff to unload the trucks which contained: medical supplies, food parcels, blankets, flour and stoves. To unload nine trucks would take four to five hours. These supplies would then delivered into much needed areas of Serbia by their own Serbian ICRC staff in Red Cross vehicles. While waiting for their trucks to be unloaded the drivers could prepare a breakfast, or dinner, play cards, relax or catch up with some sleep.

At 1415 hours all the trucks had been unloaded and the convoy was ready to depart. Dave T informed the Banja Luka delegation of nine trucks departing Banja Luka en route to Zagreb, with Vanja and Branco's Land Cruiser escorting the convoy back to Gradiska Bridge. As each truck passed Vanja and Branco's Land Cruiser at Gradiska Bridge, all the drivers thanked them for their help and said goodbye for now, see you tomorrow. Vanja would reply, '*Dovidjenja* [Goodbye], my knights of the road'. I replied, '*Hvala* [Thank you] Vanja and Branco.'

With Vanja's cute giggle she said, "George, you say *hvala* like a true Bosnian."

About forty kilometres from Zagreb the convoy stopped for a little refreshment, at one of the few cafés that was still in business on the highway. On return to the ICRC warehouse in Zagreb at 1650 hours, all the trucks were refuelled, so they would be ready for the next day's convoy to Banja Luka, once the warehouse staff had loaded all the trucks tonight. With all the duties finished, most of the drivers made their way back to Metor's bar near the delegation.

After a few *pivos* and a good relaxing chat with my colleagues, we all went to our respective apartments to prepare for tomorrow's convoy. Back at the apartment Ross and I were enjoying soft drink and sandwiches when Frank O'Neele walked in with the news that he was being transferred to Split in the morning. Frank seemed quite happy about joining convoys in Split. Apparently the accommodation in Split was a lot better than here. Frank was telling us his apartment was right on the sea front facing the Adriatic. Sounded really nice, we wished him well before turning in for the night.

Tuesday 3rd August 1993: the convoy to Banja Luka was as successful as yesterday, no incidents, or problems to report.

Wednesday 4th August 1993. The convoy to Banja Luke was again successful, no incidents, or problems to report. I received my first mail from home, letters from my ex-girlfriend, Sandy, and my Brother-in-Law, Peter, who kindly included some newspapers from home.

Thursday 5th August 1993. The bedside alarm, awakened me to face yet another new challenge today, a long eight-hour drive to a place called Knin, about eighty kilometres from split. The last forty kilometres would be made over a rough mountain terrain, followed by a twenty-five-minute descent from a mountain road leading to Knin, which lies in a basin surrounded by mountains.

Ross was on the Banja Luka convoy today, and would be picked up by Dave T. At Metor's Bar last night the Norwegians, Frank Karlsen, Kent Furuly and Knui, who are on that convoy, offered to pick me up at 0515 hours. Also on the convoy were Australian, Tony O'Connor, and as Convoy Leader the Swiss Raoul David and his little dog, Goliath. At the ICRC warehouse, just before I was going out to check my truck as I was sat in the armchair, Goliath jumped on my lap and, with his front paws on my chest, started to lick my face. Perhaps Goliath thought I needed waking up, or I had not washed at 0530 in the morning. Not the greatest experience at that time of the morning. With all the vehicles and radio checks confirmed, Raoul radioed the ICRC delegation to confirm six trucks departing Zagreb en route to Knin.

After the convoy had negotiated the urban district of Zagreb at the E70 highway, the convoy headed west to M11, E65/71 to Karlovac and then to the first checkpoint at Tusilovic, once like so many picturesque villages you would find in the UK. Now the houses were peppered with bullet holes, some burnt out and gutted, with roofs missing.

While the convoy papers were checked at the Tusilovic checkpoint, I was parked outside a school. As I looked to the right, not even the school had escaped the carnage of war, such mindless destruction in what should have been a safe place for children to learn. I looked further to the right to see the empty playground, where children once played between their lessons, but now it was covered in debris. Tusilovic was now a heavily mined area, making Tusilovic completely uninhabitable. I felt so sad to see what was once a lovely place to live in, turned into a desolate scrapheap. The convoy moved steadily through Tusilovic, en route to Vojnić where Diego Thorkeelsson from Iceland, was waiting with his translator, Gordana, to escort the convoy to Knin.

The convoy passed through the town of Slunj, before stopping for some light refreshment at a lay-by in a national park, near Plitvice. After a short break the convoy continued en route through the towns of Rakovica, Titova Korenica, Pacane, Udbina, Gracac and Srnopas, some of these towns bearing the scars and devastation of the conflict. The convoy also negotiated a couple of checkpoints en route. When the convoy reached Obrovac, we turned south-east onto a mountain track for approximately forty kilometres to avoid fighting and shelling reported in the south-west. After one and a half hours of mountain terrain, in the distance you could see Knin surrounded by mountain ranges.

Our Convoy Leader instructed the drivers to engage in a low gear and apply the exhaust brake, on the decent to Knin. The descent was going to take the convoy twenty-five minutes, requiring little use of your foot-brake during that time, because; (a) excessive use of your foot-brake would result in brake fade, (i.e. no brakes); (b) continuous pumping of the foot-brake during a long descent will extinguish all the air in the truck's air tanks. With its hairpin bends, the convoy twisted its way down the mountain track. Because Knin was sat in the pocket of these mountains it was nearly 100 degrees, very hot, but a marvellous sight to behold. In a small way it felt like we were in an aircraft, coming into land, with ears popping all the way down. The convoy arrived in Knin at 1445 hours. Diego went to the delegation in Knin, to organise the unloading and distribution of the relief convoy.

Diego returned to inform us that five trucks would go to the main ICRC warehouse, and unloading would start that afternoon. It would be completed early the next morning. The truck carrying bags of flour, my truck, would be unloaded at a different warehouse early in the morning, but the local authorities needed to arrange labour to unload my truck by hand. All the trucks were secured at the ICRC warehouse in Knin; three had been unloaded that afternoon. The other three would be unloaded early tomorrow morning. The delegation transport took us to our apartments, which are solely for convoy drivers and ICRC delegates visiting Knin. The landlady of these apartments kindly supplied a bottle of Slivovitz, to drink with our meal. That was my first taste of Slivovitz, it's a brandy made with plums, with a kick and a punch that hits your throat. Its warmth is felt all the way to your stomach. After the first one, the second don't taste so bad. We finished the evening playing cards, before turning in for an early night, making sure we would be up early in the morning to insure the three remaining trucks were unloaded by 1000 hours, in order for the convoy to return to Zagreb by the next night.

Friday 6th August 1993. In the morning we wasted no time in preparing the three remaining trucks for unloading. At 0700 hours I drove my truck to a small warehouse close to the town centre. At 0725 hours six guys arrived to unload my truck, or should I say five guys, one seem to be watching over the other five doing all the work. I then discovered that the five guys were prisoners of war. The guy that was watching over them was not even armed. I guess the ICRC must have insisted that if you are to use prisoners of war to unload an ICRC vehicle, on no account must firearms to be used to guard them. I suspect armed guards were not that far away in case of any trouble with these prisoners.

After one hour the guys were taken away, my truck was only half unloaded, and it was now 0830 hours with no sign of labour to carry the remaining ten tonnes of flour into the warehouse. Having a little concern for the convoy's deadlines to leave Knin on time, in order to clear the necessary checkpoints and return to Zagreb before dark,. I started to look around for someone to help with that unloading. I found that guy working in the warehouse, who spoke excellent English, and I explained my situation to him. He told me, from 0730 to 0830 was the first prison work party, and from 0900 to 1000 the second prison work party would arrive to finished the unloading in time for you to leave Knin by 1000 hours. I thanked him for that information, and remarked how good his English was. I was then in for a shock! That guy was English, and came from Brighton. Apparently he was a mercenary; he joined the Croatian Army to fight the Serbs. He was taken prisoner. When the Serbs found out he was English fighting for the Croats, they put a rope around his neck and were about to hang him, when that Serbian officer intervened. I told him that if you wanted to help out in the former Yugoslavia, why didn't you volunteer to work for the Red Cross and help victims of war on all sides, rather than take sides in a war you might not understand what your fighting for? He replied, "With hindsight I would not have done that, but when I came out of the Army, I could not find work in the UK. So I came here to do the only job I knew, 'Fight!'"

He also told me the *Daily Mirror* newspaper was campaigning for his release. I wished him well and a safe return to the UK. I went back to my truck, to find the second prison work party had arrived to complete the unloading on time at 0955 hours.

The convoy regrouped to departed Knin at 1005 hours and then started the long climb up the mountain roads. Since the trucks were empty, the convoy reached the top of the mountain in fifteen minutes. The convoy did not encounter any problems on the journey back to Zagreb, and arrived there at 1755 hours.

The last five days on convoy had gone so quickly, but it's been a good experience, and an eye-opener. From Banja Luka to Knin, there was no comparison between them. Each convoy brought new challenges. And on reflection of the last five days, I felt sure there would be much bigger challenges that lay ahead of my mission in the former Yugoslavia. I now looked forward to the next day's drivers' meeting to see what convoys I would be on the next week. With that in mind I only had a couple of *pivos* with the lads before going back to my apartment. Ross was out, with his girlfriend no doubt? But I heard a noise coming from what was Frank O'Neele's room. Surely he was not back from Split?

I shouted "Hello!" and in walked Austin McEvoy, a new driver from Ireland. He'd arrived on Wednesday with fellow Irishman, Tony Kehoe. They'd spent the first two days in the Dubrovnik Hotel. Tony Kehoe was sharing an apartment with Swiss and French guys.

Austin could not believe how hot it was in the Dubrovnik Hotel. I told Austin he was lucky to get out of the Dubrovnik in just two days; I was in that greenhouse of a hotel for a week! It was getting late so we decided to talk more tomorrow.

Saturday 7th August 1993. Over a very enjoyable breakfast, Austin and I picked up where we had left off the last night, continuing the conversation. Austin, in a nice way, was certainly a comical character full of the renowned Irish wit. Finally, Ross climbed out of his pit to join us for breakfast.

We arrived at the delegation for the drivers' meeting; once again I was pleased to see that I had been allocated the following convoys: Monday and Tuesday, two convoys to Banja Luka; Wednesday, convoy to Bihać and Velika Kladuša; Thursday and Friday, off; Saturday, Sunday and Monday, convoy to Split. Hopefully I'd get a chance to see my old friends, Terry and Frank O'Neele. Drivers voiced their concerns to Beat Mosimann after the decision was made to send Tony Kehoe home to Ireland, since his driving did not come up to the standard required by ICRC. Austin was obviously upset, having arrived here in Zagreb from Ireland with Tony. Beat said there was nothing he could do, because the decision had been made by a higher authority.

After the meeting Ross, Austin and I joined most of drivers for a customary Saturday *pivo* at Metor's Bar, that also gave me a chance to introduce Austin to the other drivers he had not had a chance to meet. Austin was wondering what he was going to do with all his spare time in the coming week. His only convoys that week were Bihać and Velika Kladuša on Wednesday, with Kent Furuly, Frank Karlsen and me. Then Split on Saturday, Sunday and Monday with Tony O'Connor and me. Austin had Monday Tuesday, Thursday and Friday off. We all told Austin to make the most of it, because you could find yourself on convoys week after week, with no time off.

Dave T was telling us that some of the girls in the delegation were going to Maribor for a barbecue tomorrow. The drivers were welcome to join them if they wished. A few of us who didn't have much on the next day and accepted Dave T's kind offer; including Austin and myself. Dave T suggested we meet at the delegation no later than 1000 hours. I needed to get a little shopping before the shops closed and Austin wanted to get home to write a letter to his wife. So we said our farewells to the lads. When I got back from the shops, Austin had just finished writing his letter, and was on his way down to the post office to find out the opening times.

When Austin got back, I asked him how he got on at the post office. Austin told me, he spoke to the manager of the post office, asking him about the opening times. The Manager told Austin we are open seven days a week, nine to five. In true Irish wit, Austin replied does that include Sundays. Only an Irishman could get away with such a comment. I asked him, "What did the manager say to your comment?" Austin replied nothing, but he gave me a strange look. Saturday evening we decided to go out for a meal and a few *pivos*. Austin got quite upset to see children, the same age has his own children, begging for money on the street. Apart from the children begging, we had a good night out, and returned to our apartment. When we arrived, Ross seem to have had a good evening. He was swaying around like a tree in the wind, and his speech was slurred. I thought Ross had been drinking until he offered me a reefer! I declined, never had the stuff in my life. The Aussie was high on wacky backy,

Sunday 8th August 1993. That was a good night last night. Ross and Austin had me crying with laughter. It does you good to find some sort of enjoyment, to relieve the tension of convoys, and the very depressing sights you see in that beautiful country. Hopefully we would charge our batteries further with a day out in Maribor.

At the delegation the two Land Cruisers were loaded with food for the barbecue, and of course the boys and girls to eat it. So off we went, the journey to Maribor gave the lads a chance to get acquainted with the girls from the delegation. After some ninety kilometres we arrived at the national park in Maribor. My first impression was, Wow! It was breathtakingly beautiful, the lakes shimmered in the warm sunshine. Close by, overlooking the lakes was a picturesque castle that had recently been restored to its former glory. After seeing so much destruction over the last week, the sight of Maribor Nation Park would lift the spirits of us all.

While the food was being cooked Dave T got out easel, stool and canvas, and sat there like a true artist capturing the beauty before him on canvas. Those who felt brave enough were few, but some us did have a swim in the crisp icy lake before dinner. But first in were the Australians Tony, Stuart and Ross, followed by Austin and me. It sure was cold; when I came out, I had goosepimples stacked on top of one another. Not surprising really, the water in these lakes comes from the snow-covered mountains that slowly thaw in the summer. We all had a cracking day, great company and wonderful food. Who could ask for anything more?

Back at the apartment, it was time to prepare for tomorrow's convoy to Banja Luka. Poor Austin was wondering what he was going to do over the next couple of days. His first convoy was not until Wednesday to Bihać and Velika Kladuša. I thought shopping and writing letters would be the order for the next two days.

Monday 9th August 1993. Convoy to Banja Luka. The Norwegians, Frank, Kent and Knuit picked me up the usual time, and we made our way to the ICRC warehouse in Zagreb.

Today the Convoy Leader was Raoul David, and his second in command the Yorkshire terrier, Goliath. A few more changes to drivers that were on last week's convoy. No Australians today, or Jean Marie Bosson from Switzerland. In their place came two French drivers, Didier Blanc and Johnny Heritier, giving us a seven truck convoy. When we arrived at Gradiska Bridge it was nice to hear Vanja's voice again and see her beaming smile that could light up the darkest room in your house. The convoy did not encounter any problems, and with only seven trucks to unload in Banja Luka, the convoy returned to Zagreb a little earlier at 1615 hours, without any problems to report.

Austin, Ross and Tony, who had the day off, were already at Metor's Bar with Eddie, Anita and little Leon. We had a good conversation with a local guy called Goran. Over the coming weeks the drivers seemed to adopt him as a local guide. Next door to Metor's Bar was a little shop where they would make you salad roll with the ingredients of your choice. Frank, Austin and myself went in there to order a sandwich to eat with our *pivo*, it was there I was fortunate to meet Andréa, Nina and a wonderful girl called Dragica, whom I still keep in touch with to this day. They were all beautiful girls, and Frank and Dragica already had eyes for each other, I thought they made a lovely couple. After a bit of fun with the girls, we returned to Metor's Bar to eat our sandwich with our *pivos*. When the girls finished in the shop, they joined us for a drink.

Tuesday 10th August 1993. Convoy to Banja Luka, with the same drivers has yesterday. Everything went well, no problems, or incidents to report. That was apart from a slight problem from my good friend and colleague from Norway, Frank Karlsen; Frank was telling me how much he liked Dragica.

I told Frank that Dragica's body language towards him indicated that she liked him also, and he had nothing to lose by asking her out for a meal, or maybe a drink? Frank then told me he was engaged to a girl in Norway. I advised Frank that, if he had really fallen for Dragica in a big way, he needed to be honest with Dragica, his fiancé in Norway and himself. "For the time being why don't you just see how it goes for a couple of weeks, before making up your mind?"

Away from the real world, and your loved ones you have at home, it was so easy to get lonely in a war zone. Working in a war zone was not without its dangers, some guys might think that if they should die tomorrow, then they would like to have the company of a woman before that happens. Some of the girls here are so friendly, they suffered financial hardship due to that conflict. When they see guys like us, with money in our wallets, they're not always being friendly for the right reasons, or because you might think look like a famous film star. Having said all that, all the girls we got to know at Metor's Bar were great company, and they never asked you for money. In some ways they were like us, wanting a good time, and to forget the daily heartache of that conflict. I guess the bottom line was that, in a war zone, your feelings are all over the place.

The recipe of love and war don't mix, but it can be a comfort at a time of stress and heartache. After a good night with the lads and the local girls, we all called it a night. Just for the record, the girls went to their homes, not our apartments!

Wednesday 11th August 1993. Convoy to Velika Kladuša and Bihać and Austin's first. Norwegians, Frank and Kent, picked Austin and myself up at 0515 hours and then picked up Aussie, Tony. At the ICRC warehouse in Zagreb we met our Convoy Leader, Diego Thorkelsson. Diego was accompanied by his translator Tanya and would lead the five relief trucks in his Land Cruiser. With all the necessary vehicle and radio checks completed, Diego informed the ICRC delegation in Zagreb of our departure.

From Zagreb the convoy headed south west on the M11, E65/71 to Karlovac. We passed our first checkpoint at Tusilovic, and then proceeded to Velika Kladuša passing through the small towns of Vojnić, Miholjska and Maljevac, and a couple more checkpoints. After 100 kilometres the convoy arrived at Velika Kladuša at 0815 hours, unloading four pallets from Kent's truck. We had a short coffee break and a chance to meet some of the local staff at the ICRC subdelegation. Once again the delegation was full of beautiful girls. The convoy departed Velika Kladuša 0915 hours to proceed to Bihać. En route the convoy passed through some more small towns of Krakaca, Coralici, Cazin and Ostrožac, and yet again a couple of more checkpoints. After sixty kilometres the convoy arrived in Bihać at 1000 hours while the trucks were being unloaded, Tony carried out his favourite pastime, sleeping!

Diego went to the Bihać delegation. Outside the ICRC warehouse in the sun, Austin, Kent, Frank and I stayed near our trucks and played this silly Norwegian card game. When all the trucks had been unloaded, all the lads joined Diego at the Bihać delegation for lunch. We all had the pleasure of meeting the head of the delegation in Bihać, a local lady called Dika Dulic, and more beautiful girls.

After lunch, we said our goodbyes to Dika and the girls and made our way back to our trucks for the return journey to Zagreb. Departing Bihać at 1400 hours, we did not encounter any problems or incidents and arrived at the ICRC warehouse in Zagreb 1615 hours. We refuelled the trucks and made our way to Metor's Bar for our daily refreshment. Austin was pleased to get his first convoy trip under his belt, and I fully understood how he felt. Frank's face lit up when Dragica and the girls joined us for a drink. Austin, Tony and I had Thursday and Friday off, but because our next convoy to Split meant we would working the weekend. I suggested to Austin, if he was up to it, we should find a place to swim. Goran, the young local lad at the bar who had been adopted by the drivers as their tour guide, suggest to Austin and me that we try the Salata Sports Complex, about one kilometre north of the city centre. So with that sorted, we finished a very enjoyable and accomplished day, with a sandwich and just one more *pivo*.

Thursday 12th August 1993 After breakfast Austin and I found our swimming trunks, towels and suntan lotions and set off to find the Salata Sports Complex. No trouble finding the this. On arrival at the entrance, we felt compelled to read the plagues, and information board on the history of the Salata Sports Complex, of which we both found so fascinating. Apparently that Salata Sports Complex was built by the people of Zagreb in the nineteen fifties. Most of the people were volunteers, on display were some old photos showing the people of Zagreb digging and using building tools. Some of them were women. That complex boasts of tennis courts, gymnasium, basketball courts and football pitches, with changing rooms and showers, a swimming pool with a full range of high diving boards and plenty of poolside shower points to use before, and after swimming-pool use, plus there was also ample room to sunbathe between your dips. It was by far the best outdoor swimming pool I have ever seen. In many ways, Zagreb was turning out to be a surprise package. After a wonderful day at the Salata Sports Complex, we decided to come back here again tomorrow. But our throats were getting a bit dry, from swallowing too much chloride, no doubt.

Well, we had to make some excuse to head for Metor's Bar!

When we got to Metor's Bar, most of the lads were already on their second *pivo*. Before we finished for the evening, the Norwegian lads, Frank, Kent and Knuit, invited Austin and I to join them for a meal tomorrow night. We gratefully accepted, but would live to regret accepting the invitation by the early hours of Saturday morning.

Friday 13th August 1993. I guess for all those who are superstitious, there was one place you don't want to be on Friday 13th! Yes it's a war zone, but lucky for Austin and me, it was our day off. Not that I am superstitious anyway. If I see a ladder leaning across my path, I would walk under it to prove to myself, *I am not superstitious*. Austin had to post a letter and get some shopping before going to the Salata Sports Complex. I started to wash up a few breakfast dishes, when I heard the front door close. I thought, "That was quick,

Austin!" Only to hear a lady's voice say, "You should let me wash those dishes for you, it's my job."

It was our housekeeper. She introduced herself as Edit. After all the formal introductions, Edit continued to clean the apartment while I finished what I had started. Before Edit caught me doing her job, but I did explain to Edit that I don't mind doing odd jobs on my days off. Austin got back and, before we went to the Salata Sports Complex, we had a cup of coffee and a chat with Edit while she did the ironing.

Austin and I found Edit so easy to talk to; in fact, you would have thought we had known her for some time. Edit was so relaxed and happy to talk to us both. It was not to long before Edit opened her heart, to tell us how much her family had suffered when the Serbian Army took control of her home town of Petrinja. Edit, her family and her friends had all experienced the savages of war. Edit's account on how the conflict had affected her community and turned their world into a living nightmare could happen to any peace-loving community in this crazy world we live in. At the end of the book I will attempt to tell Edit's story in detail. I pray my words will give justice to her heartbreaking story. In the meantime, we thought it best to let Edit get on with her work.

At the Salata Sports Complex we were approached by a couple of Canadian peporters that were sat near us; they heard our accents and it was obvious to them we were not locals. With the Red Cross logo on our bags, they had already assumed we were working for the Red Cross and asked us about our work. They told us they had been in Sarajevo for a month, reporting on the events in *Sniper's Alley*. They went on to tell us how they had witnessed people being shot there. In particular they told us that one guy had been shot and slid down with his back to the wall, until he was sat on the pavement and there he sat for days, because people were afraid to retrieve his body in case they suffered the same fate.

There was also the story of a couple very much in love. She was Serbian and he was a Croatian. She was going to met him and was shot in *Sniper's Alley* just a short distance from were he was waiting for her. When he saw her fall he went to her aid by running to points of cover. He finally managed to get to her and held her in his arms. Within minutes he fell beside her and lay dying while holding her in his arms. They, too, both lay there for days before their bodies were recovered.

After the Canadians had left us with these heartbreaking stories we both felt a little withdrawn and just lay there in the sun for a moment of quiet. The conflict must have been full of heartbreaking stories like that. Today was a day of mixed feelings with the joy of a nice sunny day by the swimming pool, but on the other hand the sad stories from Sarajevo.

Late afternoon we called it a day and went back to our apartment, to get ready to meet the Norwegians, Frank, Kent and Knuit for a few *pivos* and a meal. We all met up at Metor's bar for a drink before going on to that nice restaurant. The food and company were great, and the *pivo* flowed one after the other. To be honest, we all found it hard to keep up with Knuit. He was a big burly guy that looked like the old Viking warriors that use to invade the UK shores, and drank like them too! On the other hand Kent was the technical type of guy, always using the phase *I have idea* and would talk about computers long before they were as popular as they are today. And Frank was a young good-looking guy with no hair, apparently the hairloss was brought on by a suicide; this guy purposely drove his car into the bus that Frank was driving in Norway. That terrible experience, and his flashbacks, brought on the hairloss for Frank. Over the coming months Frank would be like an adopted son to me, and Frank used to pay me the compliment of saying I was half Norwegian. We really had a good night with our Norwegian hosts, but that night out was a big mistake. Austin and I had to be up at 0400 hours in the morning. Aussie Tony was picking us up 0430 hours. We left our hosts around midnight a bit worse for wear and finally managed to get to bed about one a.m.

Saturday 14th August 1993, 0400 hours, 'OMG! My head!'

I staggered out of bed to wake Austin. His response in a slurred mumble, 'Ugh! It can't be time to get up, I have only just got into bed!'

To wake up, I had a cold shower. Tony arrived to pick us up at 0430 hours. As we clambered into Tony's Land Cruiser, Austin was still trying to come back to the land of the living. By the time we reached the ICRC warehouse in Zagreb, I felt a little better, but Austin still looked like death warmed up. After making the necessary vehicle and radio checks, Tony informed the ICRC delegation that we were departing Zagreb en route to Split with three Land Cruisers. The purpose of the trip was; to convoy three Land Cruisers to Split and return to Zagreb with three ten-tonne trucks.

With the sun rising ahead of us, Tony took the lead, followed by Austin. I took the *Tail-end Charlie* spot. We headed south west on the M11, and the E65/71 highway to Karlovac, and then joined the roads 11/13 to the checkpoint at Tusilovic. From Tusilovic we joined the E59 passing through the checkpoints of Krnjak and Slunj. When we reached Titova Korenica, we headed south west on a mountain track to Bunic. Joining road 6 at Licki Oslk to Gospić. At the town of Karlobag on the Adriatic coast we queued to embark on the ferry to Pag. I was so pleased to have a short break on the ferry, just to get away from watching the brake lights on Austin's vehicle, flashing on and off. Austin said he was so tired and worried about falling asleep behind the wheel, he kept touching the footbrake to keep him awake. At Pag we disembarked from the ferry on to a minor island road with sea either side of us. That sixty-kilometres rocky island, that was shaped like a long stick, was joined to the mainland at the narrow straights in Ranzac. Back on the mainland we joined the E65 to Zadar and Šibenik, and our destination Split. The road from Zadar to Split was mainly a coastal road on cliffs facing the Adriatic Sea, with lots of tight bends.

Every four or five metres, small stone markers were embedded on the edge of the coastal road. These stones were no bigger than a breeze block; the stones were all that separated your vehicle from a sheer drop below. Poor Austin got really nervous again, to keep his vehicle away from the edge of that cliff road he started driving near the centre of the road. And once again his brake lights were flashing on and off like a Christmas tree! I was concerned Austin might hit oncoming traffic, so I decided to radio Tony and ask him to find a place to stop for a rest. When Tony found a rest area, I explained to Austin my concerns. Austin said, "Did you see how high these cliffs were? And with a sheer drop into sea, those bloody stones would not stop your vehicle from going over the cliff edge."

I told Austin if you hit any oncoming traffic that could also push you over the edge. Tony suggested we should try to get some sleep for the next hour, after that he would slow his speed down to help Austin cope with the driving conditions on the road. After a rest, we resumed our journey at a slower speed and Austin was coping a lot better now. We arrived in Split at 1500 hours covering 430 kilometres. The ICRC delegation in Split arranged transport to take us to our apartments. In the evening we found a very nice restaurant; looking at the menu, I said to the lads, "The prawn dish looks nice."

Austin said, "Yes, I fancy that."

Austin ordered the prawn dish, Tony and I each ordered steak with all the trimmings. When Austin's prawn dish was served with the heads and shells still on.

Austin said, "Shit what's this?"

Tony and I could not stop laughing as Austin got himself into a right mess, trying to eat his prawns!

Sunday 15th August 1993. After a good night's sleep and a hearty breakfast, Tony left us to call the ICRC delegation in Split to arrange the collection of the trucks to be taken back to Zagreb. Austin was still trying to get over the meal he had had last night, telling me what made it worse was that my and Tony's steaks had looked really nice. In Dublin he was used to prawns having already been shelled before you eat them. Tony joined us with a smile on his face and said, "Well lads I know you are not going to like this. But today is your day off, to enjoy the sun on the Adriatic Coast of Split."

Tony went on to explain that one of the trucks was still being repaired at the ICRC workshops in Split and would not be ready for collection until midafternoon. The ICRC delegation in Split told Tony that departing Split for Zagreb midafternoon would be too late for the three trucks to arrive back in Zagreb before dark fell. For our own personal safety the delegation suggested we leave Split, early Monday morning, and of course Tony agreed!

We decided to find the guys who were transferred from Zagreb to Split. Namely, Terry Gibson, who I'd travelled with from the UK and Frank O'Neele, who I'd shared an apartment with Ross briefly before Austin had arrived a few days later. I expected Austin and Frank, both from Dublin, would be glad of a bit of Irish blarney between them. We found the guys okay, enjoying the sun outside their apartments. Wow! No wonder Frank was happy to be transferred to Split. Their apartments were right on the seafront, facing the Adriatic Sea, some fifty metres away from the water's edge. The type of place you would look for in a holiday brochure.

Terry seemed a little distant. After a short conversation, he went and sat outside his apartment on his own. Frank was telling us that Terry was not all that popular with the lads down there, because he was always full of himself and not interested to know about the guys he was working with. I was so surprised to hear that because Terry never seemed that way with me; yes, Terry could be a little opinionated, but we could all be a little bit like that at times. Frank was also telling us that their housekeeper cooked for them. So apart from the dangerous convoys down in Split, the rest of the time was spent in luxury, not bad, eh?

With the conversation exhausted, the Adriatic Sea was inviting me to try its warm waters. Lucky enough, I always carried swimming trunks and a spare towel in my bag.

The water was beautiful and I started to swim about 150 metres from the shore when the lads shouted, "George, don't swim out to far, there was sharks out there early this morning!"

I am not a fast swimmer by any means, but somehow I swam back to the pier like an Olympic swimming champion with the thought of being attacked by a shark! Scared the shit out of me, much more than being attacked on convoy duty.

Tony, Austin and I really enjoyed the unexpected day off; it also helped Austin and me recharge our batteries after a foolish night out with the Norwegians on Friday. With the sun about to set, it was time for wash and brush-up before Tony, Austin and I returned to the last night's restaurant for our evening meal. That time Austin played it safe with a delicious beefsteak with French fries, mushrooms and side salad. Not forgetting a couple of *pivos*. Austin was not a big guy, but he certainly enjoyed his food. So much so, over the coming weeks, I would find out Austin might even consider killing for food. With a long journey ahead of us we decided to have a reasonably early night, rather than Austin having to face the traumas of the day before's drive to Split.

Monday 16th August 1993. Really had a good night's sleep, followed by a nice breakfast that would prepare us for the journey back to Zagreb. The ICRC delegation transport picked us up at 0700 hours, taking us on to the ICRC workshops in order to collect the three trucks. Austin was worried about driving on those cliff roads in a much bigger vehicle. That was until I explained to him that, on the return journey to Zagreb, he would be driving on the right-hand side of the road, away from the edge of the cliffs. Austin's reaction to my comment could be compared with a doctor telling his patient that his life was no longer in danger.

With the necessary vehicle and radio checks completed, Tony informed the ICRC delegation in Split of our departure to Zagreb at 0745 hours. The return journey to Zagreb was much more enjoyable. Austin's brake lights only came on when it was really necessary. We were making good time, and at the national park near Plitvice we pulled in a rest area for refreshment. We resumed our journey and arrived in Zagreb at

1700 hours, Tony informed the delegation accordingly, and managed to acquire transport to take us to the delegation in Zagreb. Due to our trip to Split, we had missed the drivers' meeting on Saturday. Beat Mosimann was at the delegation to give us our convoy duties for the rest of the week. My duties were as follows: Tuesday, collect the BBC team and their equipment from the Intercontinental Hotel in Zagreb, and proceed to Karlovac, Velika Kladuša, with an overnight stay in Bihać. Wednesday, return at p.m. with the BBC team and equipment convey to Zagreb Airport. Thursday, day off. Friday, convoy to Banja Luka.

Checked my mailbox, had another letter from Sandy and my brother-in-law, Peter. I was disappointed not to receive letters from my sons, Martin and Lee, or their mother, Anita. I joined the rest of the lads and the girls at Metor's Bar for a quick *pivo*, before going to the apartment to get some rest. Checking the next day's job sheet to Velika Kladuša and Bihać and the authorization document, which contained the names of the BBC team I had to collect from the Intercontinental Hotel, I noticed one of the names was Simon Bates. Surely not *the* Simon Bates? Was this the Simon Bates I'd listened to on Radio One, between ten a.m. and midday, while on my multidrop deliveries in Devon and Cornwall?

It was only a month ago that I had been working in Cornwall, listening to one of Simon's renowned *Our Tune* slots that he presented at eleven a.m. The *Our Tune* slots used to tell a sad story, sometimes with happy endings. The stories were mainly about love and relationships, followed by a meaningful song. The old saying *It's a small world* came to mind. How could I ever imagine while listening to Simon Bates show in the UK that, in a month's time, I would be taking him and his BBC team into a war zone? Two Land Cruisers would be required for the mission. Travelling in one Land Cruiser would be the Zagreb delegation staff, Jette Soerensen and Christine Boar, from Denmark, Annie Sewell, from the UK and the local Bihać delegate, Dika Dulic. Passengers in my Land Cruiser would be the BBC staff,

Simon Bates, Denise Laver and their equipment, plus the Director General of the British Red Cross, Michael Whitlam. In the morning I would be required to collect my Land Cruiser by 0700 hours at the ICRC delegation in Zagreb.

Tuesday 17th August 1993. I arrived at the ICRC delegation in Zagreb. Checked my Land Cruiser and followed the other Land Cruiser, driven by field nurse Annie Sewell, to the Intercontinental Hotel to collect the BBC staff and their equipment.

At the hotel I was introduced to Radio One presenter, Simon Bates and his producer, Denise Laver, also the Director General of the British Red Cross, Michael Whitlam.

We loaded all the BBC equipment in the Land Cruisers and at 0810 hours informed the ICRC delegation of our departure from Zagreb, en route to Velika Kladuša and Bihać. We followed the usual route to Karlovac, continuing to the first checkpoint in Tusilovic. Simon's eyes were opened to the destruction in Tusilovic, and that that conflict was a serious matter for the rest of the world to be concerned about.

En route Simon was interested to know why I decided to work for the Red Cross in the former Yugoslavia. When we stopped in Vojnić, Simon asked me if I would mind being interviewed live, on Radio One, via satellite dish in Velika Kladuša? I had no objection, so long as he cleared it with the delegation staff travelling with us. Simon mentioned my proposed interview to Michael Whitlam; he thought it was a good idea, because it would highlight the work of the British Red Cross in the former Yugoslavia. While we were at the Vojnić delegation we enjoyed a coffee and visited an old school, where, up to ten families lived in each classroom, fed under the protection of the ICRC. Before leaving the school, a teenage lad who spoke good English noticed a couple of bottles of water in my Land Cruiser, so he asked if he could have a bottle of water. I left a bottle of water purposely by the back wheel of my Land Cruiser when we drove off. I looked in my mirror at the children waving us goodbye, and the teenager with the bottle of water in one hand and his thumb up on the other.

On arrival in Velika Kladuša, Simon and Christine required time to set up their BBC satellite dish, to work off the battery of my Land Cruiser that would enable Simon to report live on air to the Radio One studio in London, and broadcast any interviews. My interview resulted in Radio One contacting my employer, who then gave me an extra three months on my mission, Mr Whitlam and the delegation staff seemed pleased with the way I answered all Simon's questions, live on Radio One.

This was my short climb to fame and glory on Radio one. When we listen to local children singing, I asked Dika what they were singing about. Dika told me, "It's a sad song about children not wanting their father to go to war, and that they are afraid they might not see their daddy again." The song was beautifully sung, with words I did not understand, but with Dika's help I understood the children's heartache and fear. The memory of those children singing to us would live in my heart forever. We then left the children of Velika Kladuša and made our way to Bihać Hospital. All the windows of that hospital were boarded up to protect the patients against day and night shelling. The sight of all those sick children, and the children that had been abandoned by their parents, was far to much for me to handle; with tears in my eyes, I wondered why that world was so cruel? Simon carried out more recorded interviews with Annie Sewell, our field nurse, and with the hospital medical staff, including the doctor in charge at Bihać Hospital. In the evening we enjoyed the hospitality given at Dika's family Home. We all sat around a campfire, drinking home-made soup with home-made bread. Dika's sister stared at me all night. Dika told me her sister was fascinated with people from other countries.

It was not long before the Slivovitz (plum brandy) appeared. We were waiting for Simon to join us. Apparently a Bosnian commander placed Simon Bates under house arrest, until he promised to tell the UK about the Bosnian struggle in that conflict. Eventually the ICRC negotiated Simon's release, and he joined us far from happy with the situation he had found himself in. Simon kept telling that Bosnian commander that he was under contract to be in New York next week. It just was not Simon's day. He went to sit down on a chair by the campfire, which collapsed into a broken heap with Simon sat among the debris on the ground, whilst we were all trying not to laugh. Dika's brother was with us on army sick leave. He was telling us he had been shot in the leg. Dika then told us her brother had been shot on six different occasions, each time in the leg. I didn't know if her brother was lucky or unlucky, but just in case I moved away from Dika's brother, and sat with her grandmother; she could not speak English, but with Dika's help we managed to have a conversation. Her grandmother asked me about my mother. I told her that my mother was called Jenny Irene, but died in 1984, and that I miss her so much. At that point Dika's grandmother put her arms around me and gave me a big hug. I felt quite moved by that gesture, because it was the sort of thing my mother would have done. My mother was the most wonderful caring mother and friend a son, or daughter, could have ever wished for. We thanked Dika and her lovely family for a most pleasant evening, and returned to our hotel in Bihać, to get some sleep.

Wednesday 18th August 1993. Slept well, after breakfast we visited families with sick and handicapped children. I returned to the hotel in order for Simon to link his live report to London. Simon seemed to be a bit stressed out that morning. He got upset with his producer Christine. To give Simon a chance to calm down, I took Christine down to the river in Bihać. While having a paddle in the freezing cold river, Christine was telling me that Simon had a go at her when he got out of bed, because he could not find his toothbrush. I told Christine that perhaps Simon's house arrest yesterday frightened him a bit, and that's why he was so stressed out today. Simon came across has a guy that needed to be waited on. You know we all listen and watch our favourite celebreties on radio and TV. But do we ever wonder what are so-called stars of radio or TV really like? I found Simon Bates arrogant, at times rude, and disorganized. Simon was also a bit accident prone. He dropped and broke his very expensive camera, so I let Simon borrow my camera; I had already taken twelve snaps on the film in the camera, which left him with twenty-four snaps on the film. After he used the rest of the film, Simon returned my camera, got my address and promised to send me the twelve prints I had used on the film. I never got to see those prints. Even months later, when I got back to the UK I tried to obtain my twelve prints; I left a message, and my phone number at the radio station. I guess the lesson I learnt was the person you hear on the radio, was not always what that person was truly like.

Christine and I went back to the hotel, to prepare for our journey back to Zagreb. With all the BBC equipment checked and loaded on the Land Cruisers, we thanked Dika for all her help and said our farewells. We arrived back in Zagreb at 1520 hours and informed the ICRC delegation accordingly. I made my way to Zagreb Airport in order for the BBC team to catch their flight back to London. Christine, Michael and Simon thanked me for everything, wishing me a safe mission, and we said our goodbyes.

Thursday 19th August 1993. Austin and I had a day off. Arranged to go to the Salata for a swim that afternoon with Austin, but first I needed to get a haircut and some shopping. I remembered seeing that barber's shop near the Dubrovnik Hotel.

Very impressed with the hairdressers in Zagreb, they certainly know how to give you a decent haircut and the service I received was excellent. I sat in the Park for a quite moment, and for a silent prayer to remember my mother, who died nine years ago today, on Sunday 19th August 1984.

When I finished shopping, I got back to the apartment to find Austin, with a bag in his hand, waiting like an eagerly excited schoolboy to go swimming. I asked him if he had been a good boy. He looked at me strangely. The Irish only get their own jokes! Once again we had a fantastic afternoon by the Salata swimming pool, and with a suntan to prove it! We also decided to have a meal at the Salata restaurant. It was there, that I first tried a side dish, called *kymack*, I can only describe its taste being similar to a cottage cheese, but in my opinion far better. We also had an interesting conversation with the restaurant waiter, who was once on Red Star Belgrade books, and had a promising football career ahead of him, until he picked up a serious injury that put an end his football career.

We finished the day having a few *pivos* at Metor's Bar with the Lads and the growing female company. Austin and I were both on the Banja Luka convoy tomorrow. Dave T said he would pick us up at the usual time, tomorrow morning.

Friday 20th August 1993, convoy duties to Banja Luka, in total eight trucks. The mission to Banja Luka, was accomplished, without any problems or incidents.

Saturday 21st August 1993, a drivers' meeting. While waiting for Beat Mosimann, some of us were looking out the window. We noticed a couple of new faces walking towards the delegation.

Dave T said, "They must be new drivers, I bet they are British."

Austin said, "How can you tell they are British, Dave?"

Dave T replied, "Austin, they are carrying Tesco and Sainsbury's carrier bags, you plonker!"

The new drivers were: Robert Fenwick from Romford, England; Thomas Handley, from Caerphilly, Wales; and Patrick Davis, from Bristol, England. All the drivers made them feel welcome.

Beat Mosimann arrived to issue our convoy duties for the following week. My duties were as follows: Monday, Banja Luka with a nine-truck convoy; Tuesday, Bihać with two Land Cruisers, one minibus and a twenty-six seater bus followed by an overnight stay in Bihać; Wednesday, evacuate refugees from Bihać area to the Zagreb delegation; Thursday and Friday, Knin with a seven-truck convoy and an overnight stay in Knin.

Beat informed us that the ICRC had been given an old bus that was currently having a comprehensive overhaul, and service, at the workshops. The Australian, Ross Burborough, was assigned to be the main driver of the bus, and the bus would be used for the first time on Wednesday in the Bihać area in order to evacuate refugees to Zagreb. With the meeting now closed, all the drivers retired to Metor's Bar, to officially welcome the new drivers.

Sunday 22nd August 1993. Seems we might have a problem with the boiler in our apartment. Only cold shower that morning, had to boil the kettle to get a hot wet shave. We went to the delegation to report the defect. The delegation were having difficulties contacting the landlord, it was looking like the boiler would not be repaired for some time. After two hours they decided to move us to alternative apartments. Austin and Ross moved to apartment 33b at 8 Vrbik, I moved just across the road to apartment 7a at Boškovićeva, I shared that lovely apartment with Australians, Tony O'Connor and his wife, Queenie. Yes! You could have your wife with you, but you would have to support her, out of your single ICRC allowance. But we all know that it was just as cheap to feed two as it was one. The move to share that apartment with Queenie and Tony would prove to have considerable benefits to me. Tony was a trained chef, and cooked some gorgeous meals. Having Tony and Queenie around was like having a mum and dad with me. Every time I was going out, they would ask me if I had everything, and what time would I be home. But I drew the line when Queenie said, "George, have you got a clean shirt on?" It was a standing joke that they were my adopted parents, and I was their adopted son!

After I had unpacked everything, there was a handy writing desk in my bedroom. So I decided to have a quiet afternoon, and evening writing a couple of letters, followed by an early night in preparation for tomorrow's convoy to Banja Luka.

Monday 23rd August 1993, convoy duties to Banja L The mission to Banja Luka was accomplished without any problems, or incidents. Usual night at Metor's Bar, Frank Karlsen and Dragica seem to be getting very close. Dragica introduced me to her beautiful sister, Zana. I had a very pleasant evening.

Tuesday 24th August 1993. Due to couple technical problems with the new bus, we had a much later start today for the trip to Bihać. The drivers met at 0800 hours in the ICRC delegation, Zagreb, and waited for Ross Burborough to arrive with his new toy: the bus. Our mission was to evacuate refugees from the Bihać area tomorrow morning, and convey them to the ICRC delegation in Zagreb. Convoy Leader Diego Thorkelsson (Iceland), followed by Ross Burborough (Aussie) driving the twenty-six seater bus. Austin McEvoy (Ireland) drove the twelve-seater minibus and I took a Land Cruiser which had an eight-seat capacity.

Ross finally arrived at the delegation at 0945 hours. Ross gives us all a good laugh; the bus had been christened with the name 'Reg' professionally hand-painted on the front of the bus. Of course, the bus had been named after Reg Varney from the comedy TV show of the 70s *On the Buses*. Ross said it was his favourite TV show in Australia. Last night Ross went to the workshop to paint the Reg on the front of the bus.

With the four-vehicle convoy ready to roll at 1015 hours, Diego informed the ICRC radio room accordingly. Much like me, you should be getting used to the route by now? Via Karlovac, to our first checkpoint in Tusilovic. We had lunch in Vojnić, and picked up Dika, before arriving at our hotel in Bihać at 1400 hours. The hotel had a secure area for us to park our vehicles. After a wash and brush-up, we joined the rest of the crew for evening dinner, and a night cap, before we settled down for the night.

Wednesday 25th August 1993. At 0800 hours I had a light breakfast before going out to check the vehicles. I had just finished checking my Land Cruiser when Austin appeared in some sort of distress, looking as white as a sheet. I ask him what was wrong. He said, "George I have lost the keys to the minibus." I told him to calm down! And think when and where you last had the keys? Austin's reply was he could not remember. I told him, "They must be in your room somewhere." We both made our way to his room to look for these keys. Austin was saying, "George if we can't find these keys, how am I going to help these refugees get out of that life threatening situation?" I told him we would cross that bridge if, or when, we reach that situation. When we walked into Austin's room, the first thing I noticed was his bag and jacket on the bed. I said to Austin, "Have you checked your jacket pockets?"

"Yes!" he replied.

Within one minute of being in Austin's room, I lifted his jacket off the bed, and there underneath the jacket were the minibus keys staring me in the face. Austin's sigh of relief was followed by a comment of:

"Thank God! And thank you George, I owe a couple of *pivos* tonight."

Dika had organized the pick-up point for us to go in, and get the refugees out. I have never seen such a sorry-looking group of women and children, plus a few elderly people. They soon boarded our vehicles. In case of situations like that, I carried a bag of sweets with me, and duly started handing out the sweets to the children. Dika travelled in my Land Cruiser with seven refugees. An old lady was sat beside me in the passenger's seat looking at my bag of sweets. I offered her and the rest of our refugees some sweets. The small convoy of refugees left the Bihać area 1010 hours. After about five kilometres the old lady who sat beside me pointed in the direction of an old farm. She was trying tell me something, but because she didn't speak English, I could not understand what she was trying to tell me, Dika came to my rescue, and told me, the old lady was telling me that she was born in that farm eighty-one years ago. That was the first time, in her whole life, that she has ever left the area of Bihać. I found that so sad, that poor old lady was brought up on that farm, and when she was old enough, she worked on the farm, alongside the rest of her family, until that conflict forced her to leave the only life she has ever known. Dika told me that all these refugees' lives would be in danger if they stayed in the Bihać area.

When we arrived at the Tusilovic checkpoint, the guards thoroughly checked the ICRC paperwork and purposely delayed the continuation to Zagreb. I asked the guards if it was okay for the refugees to get out of the vehicles, to stretch their legs. These refugees were packed like sardines in a tin, and it was very hot in these vehicles. I was also concerned about the children and the elderly. But the guards would not let them get out, not even to go to the toilet; they kept those poor refugees in the vehicles for over an hour, in over 100 degrees of sweltering heat. Finally, with most of the bottles of water now empty, we were given the all clear to continue our journey to Zagreb. At the ICRC delegation in Zagreb, some of the refugees had relatives waiting for them. The sight of all the hugs, and tears, brought a lump to my throat. In total we evacuated forty-five refugees.

Thinking about today's mission left me with mixed feelings of sadness, joy, failure, and success. To elaborate my feelings, I found that relocating refugees from their homes they don't want to leave brings the feeling of sadness and failure. On the other hand, their lives were at risk if they stayed. So a safe evacuation brings the feeling of joy and success.

Thursday 26th August 1993: convoy duties to Knin. In total six trucks. The ICRC delegation in Knin prepared a very tasty evening meal for the drivers, and the delegation staff. A good evening was had by all.

Friday 27th August 1993. The mission to Knin was accomplished without any problems or incidents and we arrived back in Zagreb at 1640 hours. Drivers Peter Milne from Scotland and Jean Claude Chesaux from Switzerland went home and Dave T would go on a week's leave to the UK the next day. Dave asked me what I missed most from back home. I told him, "Sunday roast beef, fish and chips, and a good old English breakfast."

Dave said, "I will see what I can do!"

I wondered what he meant by that..?

Saturday 28th August 1993. I attended drivers' meeting at the ICRC delegation, Zagreb. Beat Mosimann introduced two new drivers from Holland, Erik Gerrit-Hengstman and Walter Weerhiem, and then continued to issue next week's convoy duties to all the drivers. My convoy duties were: Banja Luka on Monday; Tuesday, Wednesday and Thursday, Dvor; Friday, Plaški. With no major issues brought up at the meeting, Beat thank us all for all the hard work over the past week, and wished us all a good weekend.

You can probably guess where all the drivers were headed after the meeting? Spoton: Metor's Bar to officially welcome our Dutch drivers, Erik and Walter. Not that we needed any excuse to go to Metor's Bar, it was part of our programme of relaxation and building the camaraderie that helped the drivers feel they belonged to a family, and that we all shared a common goal to help one another through difficult missions. I think the rule of thumb was that we all worked hard, and risked our lives on these missions. It was important to switch off from the stresses that could confront you on some missions. The worst thing you could do in a war zone was become a loner. Yes, we all needed our own space at times to write letters to our loved ones at home, or get our shopping, but it's not a good idea to spend to much time alone with your thoughts when you're not required on convoys. Frank the Norwegian and Dragica were now in a serious relationship. They kindly invited me to join them at the local cinema tomorrow afternoon, to see the movie *Sister Act*, I thanked them, but told them two's company and three's a crowd. I had to explain to Frank and Dragica what that meant, but Frank insisted that I joined them, and would not take no for an answer, telling me he had already bought the tickets. Apparently when you go to the cinema in Zagreb, you buy tickets a day or so before you go. I reluctantly accepted Frank and Dragica's invitation, but was not looking forward to playing my new role, has a gooseberry. No I didn't explain the meaning of a gooseberry to Frank and Dragica; I didn't want to confuse them anymore than I had already.

Sunday 29th August 1993. That morning, weekly shop done, I wrote a letter back home. Time for Sunday lunch before meeting Frank and Dragica near the cinema. Was I in for pleasant surprise at the cinema? I would not be playing gooseberry after all. Dragica's sister Zana joined us, and I was asked to escort Zana to the movie. Of course I was very flattered because Zana was a beautiful young lady. I had a really nice time with them.

Monday 30th August 1993, convoy duties to Banja Luka. nine trucks in total. When the convoy got on the road the Swiss French and French drivers spoke their own language over the radio, which was against ICRC policy. The ICRC always required all their personnel to speak English only on the radio during convoy missions. That policy would allow all the personnel on the convoy to be aware of any important information, or if there was any danger ahead. The certain personnel who decided use their own native tongue made the other drivers feel they were driving at night, without lights. Despite feeling like an alien on that convoy we managed to arrive safely in Banja Luka. Tony O'Connor and myself did manage to converse with English-speaking Norwegians. The convoy returned to Zagreb without any incident, and we all enjoyed a well-earned beer at Metor's Bar.

Tuesday 31st August 1993, convoy duties to Banja Luka with the same drivers as the previous day; apart from one extra truck driven by my drinking partner, Austin McEvoy: ten trucks in total. I was surprised at the decision from our Convoy Leader, Raoul, to put Austin at the rear of the convoy as tail-end Charlie. Although Austin had been to Banja Luka a couple of times, should he become separated from the convoy I'm not sure if Austin was fully familiar with the route.

The convoy departed Zagreb. While en route to the main highway several trucks became separated at traffic lights and junctions. When Raoul reached the main highway to Banja Luka, he slowed down all the trucks behind him to allow the convoy to regroup. After some twenty minutes on the highway, nine trucks had now regrouped, and we were travelling at a speed of twenty mph, waiting for Austin in the last truck to rejoin the convoy. The radio conversation between Austin and Raoul was hilarious:

Austin: "I am trying to catch you up, Raoul, where are you?"

Raoul: "I have slowed the convoy down to enable you to rejoin us, where are you Austin? Are you on the highway yet?"

Austin: "Yes I am on the highway, but I can't see the convoy yet."

Raoul: "I have now parked the convoy at the *péage*. We will wait for you there, Austin."

Austin: "Okay, Raoul."

Five minutes later, Raoul: "Where are you now Austin?"

Austin: "On the highway, Raoul!"

Raoul: "… But you should have been with us by now, Austin. When you reached the highway did you take the left or the right lane to join the highway?"

Austin: "I took the left lane Raoul."

Raoul: "Austin you are going the wrong way, you should have taken the right-hand lane. At the next exit leave the highway and rejoin the highway to travel in the opposite direction."

Austin: "Shit!"

Thirty-five minutes later, a little embarrassed, Austin finally rejoined the convoy. Realising his mistake, Raoul asked Austin to rejoin the middle of convoy in fifth position. Frank Karlsen took over as his tail-end Charlie. Apart from Austin we all saw the funny side of that cock-up. Meanwhile at Gradiska Bridge, Vanja and Branco were getting a little worried due to the convoy being some forty minutes late.

Vanja sounded relieved when Raoul established radio contact to confirm our ETA. The rest of that mission to Banja Luka was completed without any incident, and we all returned safely to enjoy a *pivo* at Metor's Bar, and of course we all had a good laugh at poor Austin's expense.

Wednesday 1st September 1993, convoy duties to Banja Luka. The following drivers: (Convoy Leader) Raoul David (Swiss), Didier Blanc (France), Jean Marie Bosson (Swiss), Kent Furuly and Frank Karlsen (Nor), Tony O'Connor (Aussie), and me (Eng): in total seven trucks. The convoy mission to Banja Luka was carried out without any incidents.

Thursday 2nd September 1993, convoy duties to Plaški. in total six trucks. Just heard some bad news about Norwegian driver Knuit who was suppose to be on that convoy. Apparently he went out last night and got drunk. But worst still, got behind the wheel of an ICRC Land Cruiser, which collided with a tram in Zagreb city centre. Knuit was okay, but he has now been supended of duties by the ICRC delegation. His fellow Norwegians Kent and Frank told us he would probably be sent home for that. Knuit would find out his fate later today, Carlos Melara (Ita), took Knuit's place on today's convoy.

The convoy departed Zagreb heading west on the highway E65/71 to Karlovac and the checkpoint at Tusilovic. From there the convoy made its way the ICRC delegation in Vojnić to collect a local ICRC translator called Gordna. After a quick coffee break the convoy continued through small towns of Krniak, Tobollc and Plavca. En route the convoy negotiated some rough moutain terrain before reaching our destination in Plaški. That journey not only brought some fresh challenges, but a few drivers including myself on that convoy were now on unfamiliar ground.

The trucks were unloaded by hand at Plaški. After the trucks were unloaded, some locals then escorted us to a farm for refreshment. On arrival at the farm we found a sheep had been killed for us, and was being spit roasted on an open fire with a large pole going through its arse and coming back out of its mouth. Very kind of these people to show us such wonderful hospitality, but I guess I was not used to that type of roast back home in the UK. While we all sat down on a log to eat the food, a guy handed me a glass of Slivovitz. I have already mentioned Slivovitz on a mission to Knin, and that that plum brandy was very strong. Every time I took a sip of Slivovitz, a young lad about ten years old sat near me kept topping my glass with more Slivovitz. Was that young lad trying to get me drunk? It got to the stage where I was getting a bit apprehensive to take a sip from my glass.

With all the drivers fed and watered with Slivovitz, we thanked our hosts for their kindness and made our way back to Zagreb. When the convoy reached the summit of that mountain we had to drive down that rough track with many hairpin bends. At the front of the convoy went Diego and Stuart, where I was sure they were racing each other because we seemed to be going very fast down the mountain track. I was beginning to feel like I was in some sort of rally. One thing was for sure, none of us would have driven our vehicles in that way without the input of Slivovitz. Having said that, none of us were that intoxicated with Slivovitz that we should not be driving these trucks. My thoughts strayed to the incident involving Knuit last night, and wondering if he would still be with us on our return to Zagreb. The convoy arrived safely back in Zagreb were we refuelled our trucks for tomorrow's mission to Dvor. When we arrived at Metor's Bar, Knuit was there to give us all the bad news that he would be sent home to Norway tomorrow morning. Knuit did not seem to be too bothered about his dismissal. In fact he seemec quite happy. We all drank to Knuit's health, and said our goodbyes to him.

Friday 3rd September 1993, convoy duties to Dvor. in total, six trucks.

The convoy departed Zagreb heading west on highway E65/71 to Karlovac and the checkpoint at Tusilovic. Once again the convoy made its way to the ICRC delegation in Vojnić to collect the local ICRC translator called Gordano. No time for a coffee today. From Vojnić the convoy headed south-east, travelling through the small towns of Vrginmost, Prnjavor, Ćemernica, Glina, Dragotina, G. Klasnić, Žirovac, Gvozdansko and Medju Majdan. Just as yesterday the convoy negotiated some rough terrain en route without any problems, and all the relief supplies were delivered to Dvor before returning to Zagreb without any incidents.

Saturday 4th September 1993: drivers' meeting at the ICRC delegation in Zagreb. Beat Mosimann informed me that I would be taking over Knuit's truck and, because I was moving from driving a rigid truck to a semi-trailer, I would have to undergo another driver training programme with Beat Trinkler that coming Monday and Tuesday. I did say our paths would cross again in Chapter 10. My duties for the rest of the week would be: Wednesday and Thursday, convoy to Banja Luka, Friday, meet field nurse Rachel Lavy here at the ICRC delegation, and transport Rachel to Lipovac Bridge, collect an orphaned child and return Rachel and the child to Zagreb.

Beat also confirmed the delivery of fourteen rigid Scania trucks which were a gift from the Swedish government. These fourteen trucks would be used on relief convoys from Zagreb to Zenica, via Banja Luka. Due to military action en route from Split to Zenica, convoys in Split were unable to continue relief convoys to Zenica. Beat continued with the announcement that the ICRC had recruited a further five drivers and they were due to arrive in Zagreb over the next two days. Plus six more drivers would be transferred from Split to Zagreb; that would give a total of twenty-eight drivers in the Zagreb transport pool. That pool of drivers would cover regular convoys to Zenica, Banja Luka, Knin and Bihać, plus other convoys' destinations as and when they arose. With this Beat closed the drivers' meeting.

It was good to see Dave T back from his week's leave, and he did not come back empty-handed. Apparently he managed to get some British roast beef joints and bacon through customs, and invited Austin McEvoy, Tony O'Connor, Robert Fenwick and myself to a good British roast dinner on Sunday. With the bacon he bought in the UK, DaveT was planning to cook a full English breakfast for all the lads on Wednesday morning's convoy, and Dave T was making sure I didn't miss the breakfast treat. Thank you mate! Some drivers did not like Dave T because he seemed to spend a lot of his spare time with the Swiss delegates, but I found Dave T To be very decent guy, plus he helped me a lot to settle in to the convoy tasks.

Dave T had another surprise for us. Dave knew that some of lads had been looking for a decent football to have a kick around. So he bought a good football in the UK for us. Instead of going to the bar after the meeting, most of the drivers made their way to a nearby park for some much needed exercise. But after two hours of running around like headless chickens, we all crawled back to Metor's Bar for some light refreshment. In the evening I had a meal with Frank, Dragica, Zana, Kent, Goran, Austin and Robert Fenwick. Robert had too much to drink, and collapsed in his soup.

Sunday 5th September 1993. Field nurse Annie Sewell and Dave T were perfect host, making their guest proud by cooking the most mouth-watering roast beef, with all the trimings, for a party of sixteen. It was a very pleasant occasion, and a good time was had by all. Late afternoon returned to my appartment fat and full, to write a couple of letters home.

Monday 6th September 1993. Transport arrived to take me to the ICRC delegation in Zagreb to meet Beat Trinkler for two days driver training. Beat greeted me with a big smile on his face, as if to say *Welcome back to my torture chamber*. Before going to the warehouse to pick up Knuit's truck, Beat showed me films on semi-trailers driving in normal weather conditions, then in hazardous conditions. After a morning coffee we made our way the warehouse to check Knuit's old truck that would be my second home for the next few months. I say second home because of its double bunk sleeper cab. After all the necessary vehicle checks, we finally got on the road. After a couple of hours driving around Zagreb, we headed out of town towards the nearby moutains. I knew what was coming up next, up and down mountain tracks with hairpin bends, lots of gear changing, and the use of the exhaust break coming down the mountain. But before entering that driver training exercise, we stopped for some light refreshment. After lunch I spent the rest of the afternoon sweating my balls off going up and down that bloody mountain on a very hot day. I am sure Beat has a sadistic nature, because he always had a smirky smile on his face when I was working like Trojan. On returning to the warehouse I refuelled the truck ready for tomorrow's final day of driver training. Back at the delegation I checked my mail box – to my delight I had letters from my sons Martin and Lee, my girlfriend Sandy and my brother-in-law Peter, who had also sent me some UK papers to catch up with the news from home and abroad. After a sweaty day's driving, my poor dehydrated body needed some fluid. So off I went to Metor's Bar to read my letters and papers, while waiting for the lads to get back from their relief convoys. When the lads arrived we exchanged the day's news before returning to our appartments for a good night's sleep.

Tuesday 7th September 1993. Transport to the delegation for my last day's driver training torture with Beat Trinkler. With the morning spent on that bloody mountain, we stopped for lunch, before heading for area for some semi-trailer manoeuvres. For the first time I rendered Beat speechless when I completed each manoeuvre that Beat gave me on the first attempt. Beat must have been getting a bit bored with my success when he asked me to sit in the passenger's seat while he did the semi-trailer manoeuvres. It was now my turn to have a smirky smile on my face, as Beat failed to negotiate all the manoeuvres that I had completed. Beat tried so hard to back the semi-trailer into a box. After many attempts he got out of the truck a defeated man, and hiding his embarrassment Beat asked me drive back to the warehouse. In a way I felt sorry for Beat; he was supposed to instruct me on the best way to carry out each semi-trailer manoeuvre, but on that occasion his pupil rose above his teacher's expectations, leaving Beat wishing he had never got behind the wheel. That would be my last encounter with Beat, apart from sharing a few and far between drinks with Beat at Metor's Bar.

That evening I met my fellow drivers at Metor's Bar. My adopted son Frank from Norway said, "George, you are now half Norwegian."

I replied, "Why's that, Frank?"

He answered, "George you're driving Knuit's truck with the Norwegian flag painted on the door." I felt honoured by Frank's comments.

Wednesday 8th September 1993, convoy to Banja Luka. eight trucks in total.

Vanja welcomed the convoy at Gradiska Bridge. Then over the radio I heard Vanja say, "Welcome back George, pleased to see you back on convoy duties." That resulted in a bit of ribbing from the other drivers; joking, they said I was Vanja's favourite. The convoy arrived in Banja Luka on time, and as Dave T disappeared into the kitchen I was now looking forward to his fried breakfast. Thirty minutes later the smell of bacon was coming from the kitchen, and that smell was making me very hungry. At last Dave T served up our lovely English breakfast. That breakfast made me think of a weekend in the UK. Thank you so much, Dave T. With all the trucks unloaded the convoy departed Banja Luka and returned to Zagreb to refuel the trucks without any incidents.

Thursday 9th September 1993, convoy to Banja Luka. six trucks in total. En route to Banja Luka Dave T noticed the last truck driven by Patrick Davis our so-called tail-end Charlie was not keeping up with the rest of the convoy. Dave T dropped his speed to fifty mph and asked Patrick over the radio if fifty mph was okay for him? When I looked in my wing mirror Patrick's truck was some 500 metres from the rest of the convoy. The normal distances between trucks should be 100 to 200 metres. Patrick did not answer Dave T's radio call. Having driven Patrick's truck, I knew that the governed speed of that truck was fifty mph, and that speed would be okay for him. Dave T asked Patrick again over the radio, "Patrick is fifty mph okay for you?"

Still no answer from Patrick, perhaps he forgot to switch his radio on? It was then I remembered that I gave the lads a good laugh in Metor's Bar by impersonating Patrick's voice.

For those who might remember the film star James Mason, Patrick's voice was very much like that. The lads seem to think that I had Patrick's voice spot on. So I thought I would put it to the test. I radioed Dave saying, "Patrick calling Dave T, over!"

Dave T answered, "Are you okay Patrick, over?"

I answered, "Yes Dave T, I forgot to switch my radio on, over!"

Dave T replied, "Okay Patrick, was that speed of fifty mph okay for you, over!"

I answered, "Yes Dave T that's fine, I can close the gap, and catch the convoy up when you get to the checkpoint, over!"

Dave T replied, "Okay Patrick over and out."

Dave T did not have a clue that he was talking to me instead of Patrick. But I let him and the lads know when we got to Banja Luka, and we all had a good laugh especially when we found out that Patrick had switched his radio on halfway through my conversation with Dave T.

Patrick said, "It was so funny, I didn't want to spoil the fun. Having said that George, I had to stand on that bloody accelerator to keep up with the convoy, and my leg was aching when we got to Banja Luka."

It was events like that, which took your mind off the dangers we all faced while working in a war zone. That was not to say that we where not focused and alert to the dangers we faced. Once all the trucks were unloaded the convoy departed Banja Luka, and returned to Zagreb without any further incidents. After we refuelled the trucks we all headed for Metor's Bar still laughing about Dave T falling for my impersonation of Patrick.

Friday 10th September 1993. Arrived at the ICRC delegation in Zagreb to collect a Land Cruiser and meet my passenger, field nurse Rachel Lavy. After all the necessary vehicle checks on the Land Cruiser, I went to meet Rachel and collect all the documentation required for that mission. With Rachel on board I notified the Zagreb radio room of our departure to Lipovac, and Bačka Palanka Bridge. En route Rachel and I conversed in the usual idle chat about families, friends and our mission here. Rachel was from Tunbridge Wells, starting her mission in the former Yugoslavia in March 1993, and was due to end her mission in November 1993. Like so many personnel working for ICRC here, Rachel had mixed feelings when I ask her if she was looking forward to going back home in November. Although we all missed our friends and families back home, the work here was so rewarding, it would hard to find the same job satisfaction back home. We successfully passed through several checkpoints on the E70 highway to Lipovac. At each checkpoint Rachel went a little quiet, and seemed to be a little nervous. Later Rachel asked me how I could be so calm and friendly with the checkpoint guards pointing guns at you. I told her you've got to show the checkpoint guards that you're a happy friendly person and that the guns don't frighten you, although deep down inside you are a little nervous, never show it, because they would think you are trying to hide something. If you smoke offer them a cigarette. Next time you go through their checkpoint they would greet you with a smile, and maybe a handshake. I think Rachel understood the reasons for my approach to negotiate checkpoints.

After three hours and 300 kilometres we reached Lipovac, and turned north-east on a regional connecting road Llok, and Bačka Palanka Bridge a further twenty kilometres. We established radio contact with our ICRC counterpart from Beograd. We were instructed that upon arrival at Bačka Palanka Bridge we were to wait at the south side of the bridge until further notice. We arrived at the bridge 1145 hours. One hour later we contacted the ICRC in Beograd, to make enquiries on the ETA of the child we had to escort back to Zagreb. We were informed there were some problems with the documentation at their end, and that would have to be sorted out before the authorities would release the child waiting at the other side of the bridge. I said to Rachel that reminds of a spy movie where the opposing sides exchange spies on a bridge. Rachel saw the funny side of my remark. Rachel was telling me that the child's mother and father were separated when war broke out between Serbia and Croatia. The child's mother was Croatian and the father, who had been killed, was Serbian. I just could not believe how anyone could be so pedantic over a child's welfare when that child had no living relatives in Beograd, and her mother was waiting for her child in Zagreb. That bloody war always hurts the innocent parties. Finally, forty-five minutes later the child, a little girl, was brought to our Land Cruiser. Rachel sat in the back with the child. With a lump in my throat, I handed Rachel a bag of sweets for the child, Rachel gave me a warm thank-you smile, and we made our way back to Zagreb where the child would safely be reunited with her mother. We arrived back in Zagreb at 1635 hours. Rachel paid me the best compliment I could have ever wish for when she said, "George if ever I have to go on another mission like that I would ask for you to escort me, that's if you don't mind George?"

I replied, "Rachel it would be my pleasure to work with you again."

Before we said our farewells we wished each other safe missions for the future, and a good weekend.

That evening at Metor's Bar the lads wanted to know why I was so quiet. I told them about today's mission, and I could not get that frightened child's face out of my mind. You start to wonder how many more children are in that position. How do you explain war to a child? How do you explain to a child that they would never see their mother or father again? How do you explain to a child that their home has been destroyed, and why some soldiers are being nasty to them? My thoughts also strayed to the poor children in Bihać Hospital. They were abandoned, and only had the overworked hospital staff to kiss away their tears, and give them a brief cuddle. The lads were very understanding to the way I was feeling. To be honest, I don't know how I would have got through that mission without them. But I guess it was the same for them, we all have feelings on the tragedies of war. Like a close family, we all supported one another through that moment in time of our lives, and when we could, it was so important for us to meet at Metor's Bar. Not just for the drink but to unwind the tension of the day's mission, and to feel the support from the rest of lads. Although we all came from many different countries and backgrounds, we all shared that one common goal, and were united to help all victims of war.

Saturday 11th September 1993, drivers' meeting at the ICRC delegation in Zagreb. Transport Manager Beat Mosimann opened the meeting by introducing the new drivers, Robin Creelman, Keith Descalchuk and Keith Marsden, all three from Canada, Barry Sadler from the UK, Vincent Negro, Heinz Schoeni, Antonneio De Gobi, Stephen Gillespie, Alain Porchet, all five from Switzerland, Michel Baud and Regis Pillet, two from France, and James Alexandersson from Iceland. Our meeting room was now looking quite full. Beat continued to hand out next week's relief convoy duties. My duties were as follows: Monday, Banja Luka; Tuesday, Banja Luka; Wednesday, Banja Luka; Thursday and Friday, Knin over two days with an overnight stop in Knin on Thursday night. Beat told us that Heinz Schoeni would be the Convoy Leader on all Zenica convoys. Heinz was transferred to Zagreb from Split, where he had carried out Convoy Leader duties to Zenica from Split. After all the matters arising and questions were dealt with, Beat closed the meeting, and wished everyone a good weekend.

Most of us decided to go to the nearby park for another game of football, that was apart from the Swiss and French drivers. They all seemed to disappear back to their apartments, or just do their own thing. To be honest, apart from a few, I found most of Swiss and French were inclined not to socialise with the other drivers. After our Saturday game of football, we went to Metor's Bar to replace the pounds lost during the football workout.

That evening most of the drivers were invited to a birthday party at Frank and Kent's apartment. The kind-hearted Norwegians with the help of Frank's girlfriend Dragica, had arrange that birthday party for a local girl called Irena, who worked at the delegation with Dragica. Irena thought she was going to met Dragica's boyfriend, but was so happy and surprised when we all greeted her. I also met Raoul's Swiss girlfriend, a beautiful blonde called Annie who worked in the delegation. Although everyone had a wonderful time, I can't help feeling sad while writing that paragraph. Little did we all know that that would be Irena's last birthday party? In January 1994, Dave T called me from Zagreb to inform that Irena had died in a swimming pool accident. Even to that day I have fond memories of that dear young girl, who used to call me 'Devil Eyes'.

R.I.P. Irena, x.

Sunday 12th September 1993. Went to a country club in Maribor with Frank, Kent, Bob, Patrick, Austin, Erik, Walter and our local guide Goran. Very hot indoor and outdoor spa baths. In mid September the air was cold when you got out of the baths, much like a hot tub in the winter, but much bigger. It felt strange diving into hot water. Had a good meal and met some ICRC drivers from Sarajevo and Beograd. The weekends always seem to go so quickly when you're enjoying yourself, but I guess that also applies at home in the UK. We all returned to Zagreb to prepare for the coming week's relief convoys.

Monday 13th September 1993, convoy to Banja Luka. in total eight trucks. The mission to Banja Luka was completed without any problems or incidents.

Tuesday 14th September 1993, convoy to Banja Luka with the same drivers has yesterday: eight trucks in total. The mission to Banja Luka was completed without any problems or incidents.

Wednesday 15th September 1993, convoy to Banja Luka. six trucks in total. The mission to Banja Luka was completed without any problems or incidents.

Thursday 16th September 1993, convoy to Knin. in total five trucks, plus one Land Cruiser. Arrived in Knin and unloaded the trucks without any problems or incidents. Enjoyed a great evening meal cooked by Raoul.

Friday 17th September 1993, convoy of five trucks and a Land Cruiser returned to ICRC Zagreb, without any problems or incidents.

That evening met all the lads at Metor's Bar. Whist enjoying a drink with the lads, Tony O'Connor was admiring the barmaid called Mirra. Tony had a wicked sense of humour, which reared its head when he suddenly asked the lads, "Do you think Mirra shaves her box?" Meaning does she shave her private parts.

We all nearly choked in our *pivos*. Tony continued to take bets off the lads, asking them how many thought that Mirra shaved her box. Only Tony could have come up with that stupid game.

I said, "Hang on a minute, Tony, how are you going to find out if Mirra does or doesn't, as you put it, 'shave her box'?"

Tony's answer shocked us all when he said, "I would go up and get the drinks, and ask her..." and once again we all nearly all choked in our *pivos*.

I said, "Tony you can't do that, you would get us all chucked out!" but Tony had the nerve of Old Nick.

As Tony walked to the bar, we all watched him, and waited for Mirra's reaction to his question. Mirra looked towards the direction that we were all sat. I don't know if I was imagining it, but Mirra with a glare in her eyes seem to be staring very much in my direction. When Tony returned to our table, collectively we asked Tony what he had said to Mirra, because she gave us all a dirty look.

Tony replied, "I just asked her that George wants to know if you shave your box."

With all the lads crying with laughter, and with embarrassment, I put my head in my hands. Frank asked Tony, "What was Mirra's reply?"

Tony said, "Mirra's reply was 'if George wants to know that, best he come up and find out for himself!'"

Tony had stitched me up good and proper; I was afraid to look at Mirra. Though even I could see the funny side of Tony's joke, albeit at my expense. At least I had two admirers: Dragica was telling me her sister, Zana, liked me, and Andréa, the girl who worked in the shop next door had eyes for me. I noticed that Andréa had started to come into the Metor's bar, and at times with a smile she was looking in my direction. Before we all left Metor's bar Tony spoke to Mirra, and explained that he was responsible for the joke, and George had nothing to do with it. As we left the bar, Mirra gave us all a smile, and wished us goodnight. Hopefully I was forgiven.

Saturday 18th September 1993, drivers' meeting at the ICRC delegation in Zagreb. Beat Mosimann opened the meeting, and handed the drivers their convoy duties for the coming week. My duties were as follows; Monday, Banja Luka, Tuesday, Banja Luka, Wednesday and Thursday, Zenica, with an overnight stop in Zenica on Wednesday night. Friday, day off.

Beat mentioned that after a few teething problems, the first Zenica convoy from Zagreb was a success last week, and the ICRC was hoping to run two relief convoys to Zenica every week. After all the matters arising were dealt with, Beat closed the drivers' meeting wishing us all a relaxing weekend.

All the energetic drivers among us made their way to the nearby park for their usual football workout, and of course we followed that workout by a little light refreshment at Metor's Bar. Where, I was glad to say, Mirra was still talking to me.

Today it was Goran's birthday. Goran, our local guide, had befriended all the drivers and had been good enough to show us around the best night clubs in Zagreb, and all the best places just outside Zagreb. Goran's brother had arranged a birthday party at his place tonight, and some of the drivers were invited. Frank and Dragica asked if I would escort Zana to the party. I told Frank and Dragica it would be my pleasure.

At the party I was sat in a chair having a drink and watching the guests dance. Zana was sat alongside me on the floor, with her arm resting on my knee. I said, "Zana, you don't have to stay here with me all night. Why don't you join your friends on the dance floor and have some fun?"

Zana replied, "George I came to that party with you, and I want to stay with you."

I said, "Zana, the girls and lads up there are the same age as you, and you're missing all the fun."

Zana replied, "How old are you George?"

I said, "Forty-six, old enough to be your father."

Zana replied, "George you are not old, I like being with you."

I should now point out that, although Zana looked a lot older than she was, she was still only sixteen years old. That situation made me very nervous. I decided to make an excuse to Frank, Dragica and Zana that I was not feeling very well, and I needed to go back to my apartment.

Sunday 19th September 1993. That morning Austin and I went to the Salata Sports Complex for a swim, before joining Tony and Queenie for lunch.

Monday 20th September 1993, convoy to Banja Luka. in total nine trucks. The mission to Banja Luka was completedwithout any problems or incidents.

At Metor's Bar that evening we all heard some bad news regarding a fellow colleague. Apparently while on a convoy to Knin, Swiss driver Roaul David had been caught with a camera in his truck at a checkpoint near Kladushka. We have all taken chances with cameras at some time or other but we all made sure they were well hidden. I put my camera among the electrical wiring under the dash. Roaul was caught with a camera in his bag, which he forgot to take out and hide, or leave at home. So unlucky, or maybe foolish, but the truth was that could have happened to any one us. The ICRC has strict rules which forbid any ICRC personnel carrying cameras while on convoy missions. The authorities that caught Roaul would now have to be appeased in order for future relief convoys to continue in the former Yugoslavia. Although it had not been decided what Roaul fate would be, most of us felt that it would result in the ICRC cancelling Roaul's contract and sending Roaul home to Switzerland. On that sad note we retired for the night hoping that the ICRC would find another way to appease the authorities, without sending Roaul home.

Tuesday 21st September 1993, convoy to Banja Luka. in total seven trucks. When the convoy reached Gradiska Bridge Vanja informed us that the convoy would be escorted to a nearby football stadium on the other side of Gradiska Bridge, and there the trucks would be given a thorough search. I was glad that I decided to leave my camera in my apartment, because the checkpoint guards went through each truck with a fine toothcomb. Not only did they search our cabs, but we had to open the canopies on the trailers in order for the cargo to be checked. The convoys to Banja Luka had never undergone such a thorough search as that before. Unfortunately that search was the fallout concerning Roaul David being caught with camera near Kladushka, yesterday. The Serbian authorities had informed all their checkpoints to be more diligent when searching vehicles. That was now going to be a regular practise on the Banja Luka convoys that would put an extra one and a half to two hours on the journey. Thankfully the checkpoint guards found nothing untoward on our trucks, and allowed the convoy to continue to Banja Luka where we arrived much later than usual. The rest of that mission to Banja Luka was completed without any further problems or incidents.

That evening at Metor's Bar, unfortunately, we all learnt that Roaul David would be sent home to Switzerland. The ICRC had to make an example to all their personnel that, by ignoring their rules, each and every one of us was endangering the programme of relief work in the former Yugoslavia, and that would not be tolerated by the ICRC. Some of the drivers who had the day off had gone to the delegation to plead for leniency in Roaul's case. Although the drivers' pleas were acknowledged by ICRC (albeit a big mistake on Roaul's part) he had to be dealt with to assure the Serbian authorities that the ICRC did not condone bad behaviour. The ICRC was also hoping their action would re-establish the credibility of the ICRC.

Austin and some of the other drivers were going to arrange a farewell party for Roaul. Roaul was a good Convoy Leader and a popular guy with the ladies. To be honest, with respect to Roaul, I was going to miss Roaul's little Yorkshire terrier, Goliath, the most.

Wednesday 22nd September 1993, convoy to Zenica. fourteen trucks in total.

Some of the drivers went white as sheet when we were all issued with flak jackets and helmets. After these fourteen brand new Scania trucks were checked by their drivers. Heinz our Convoy Leader positioned all the Swiss and French drivers directly behind his truck, with the Canadians, Irish and UK drivers following in the last seven trucks. Heinz notified the ICRC radio room in Zagreb that fourteen trucks were departing for Zenica, via Banja Luka.

To see that convoy of fourteen brand new *Scania* trucks shining in the sunrise must have been quite a sight from a distance. On route to Banja Luka, I heard Frank on the radio:

"Frank to George over."

I replied, "Hi Frank, how are you mate?"

Frank replied, "George why are you not with us today? You are half Norwegian, and you should be with us going to Knin."

Our brief radio conversion was then interrupted by Heinz. He said, "George, please don't talk to other drivers on another convoy."

With a deathly silence on the radio, apart from the bloody Swiss and French speaking their own native tongue (probably slagging us Brits off, no doubt) I thought, "Wow! That convoy is going to be fun." It was comforting to hear Vanja's voice waiting for the convoy at Gradiska Bridge.

After the convoy search and a short break in Banja Luka, the convoy headed south en route 16/5, for sixty kilometres that road ran parallel to the beautiful river called Borostica Jezero. The convoy travelled through the towns of Krupa Na Vrbasu, Crna Rijeka, and Barevo. Due to fighting ahead, the convoy was held up in Jajce for one and a half hours. To avoid the fighting, the UN arrived to escort the convoy onto a mountain track. As the convoy climbed that mountain track negotiating many hairpin bends, my thoughts strayed to that driver training exercise given by Beat Trinkler, and how much that driver training was helping me now to get up that mountain, and down the other side. Not everyone seemed to benefit from Beat's driver training. Poor old Austin kept on missing his gear change, causing him to stall and bringing his truck to a halt, along with the six trucks behind him – included me.

We certainly had some fun at Austin's expense. On that mountain track, the convoy continued through the small town Krezluk before joining E761 highway at again at Türbe. When the convoy arrived at Travnic, I would always remember the sight of these tall blocks of flats and buildings peppered with bullet holes. You start to wonder how many innocent people and children might have lost their lives in that hell hole. The convoy arrived in Zenica mid afternoon. Zenica was situated in the middle of the former Yugoslavia, and was in a Muslim pocket of Bosnia Herzegovina. Due to military action in the Zenica area, the relief convoys in the past few weeks have not been able to supply the area. So to many in Zenica that relief convoy was a welcome sight, especially with the harsh Balkan winters not to far way. With all the trucks unloaded, we were shown to our ICRC apartments for the night. We were also instructed not to venture out at night; because of Mujaheddin fanatics in Zenica, it was not a safe place to be at night. I shared an apartment with Bob, Austin and Tom. The other drivers were shown to other apartments in Zenica.

I was preparing some food that I had brought with me. I was surprised to see the other drivers had not brought much food with them; they seem to think food would be supplied for them by the ICRC in Zenica. I told them it's always best to bring some food with you, just in case. Fortunately I brought more food than I needed, and shared some of my food with my fellow drivers. Their faces lit up when I served some cooked chicken on their plates. What was it Bob said? "George, you're a diamond!" With the troops fed and settled and after quite a stressful day, we all turned in for the night.

Thursday 23rd September 1993. After a good night's rest the convoy departed Zenica at 0615 hours. By the time we climbed the mountain between Türbe and Jajce near Krezluk, the early morning mist was still very heavy. At the summit of the mountain the early morning mist covered all the land below, like a cotton-wool blanket. It was truly an amazing sight to behold. It made you feel like you were above the clouds flying to your destination. It also reminded me of that Hollywood musical, *Brigadoon*, staring Gene Kelly. The story was about a Scottish village that only appears through the mist every 100 years. Not that I was expecting that to happen here, but the sight of the dense blanket of mist just reminded of it.

The convoy stopped for a rest in Banja Luka, before continuing and returning to Zagreb. It was clear that some of these brand new trucks had now lost their pristine look; in fact some of the trucks had lost their mudguard marker lights on the narrow mountain track. May I add, not my truck! But my truck was looking a bit muddy, and very much used. On return to Zagreb, we all managed to give the trucks a wash down, and refuelled ready for the next convoy to Zenica.

I checked the mailbox at the delegation and there was another letter from Sandy. Just as I was about to leave the delegation, I saw Beat Mosimann was at the reception desk.

"Ah, George, how did the Zenica convoy go?"

I told Beat it was okay. Beat went on to say, "Tomorrow was your day off."

I replied, "That's right, Beat."

He went on, "George, I have a job for you tomorrow. I want you to take Dave T to Lipovac to collect a truck that needs to go to our workshop for repair. If you can meet Dave T here at the delegation at 0800 hours, pick up the keys to a Land Cruiser and proceed to Lipovac."

I accepted the task since, to be honest, I had not been looking forward to a day off knowing most of my drinking partners would be away on their convoy duties. Most of the drivers would have their days off on Saturday and Sunday. Bob, Austin and Tom joined me at Metor's Bar where we met Frank, Kent, Erik, Walter, Tony and Patrick. I think my adopted son Frank missed me. He said, "It was wrong to put me on the Zenica convoy, after you were supposed to be driving Knuit's truck."

I told Frank that I was happy to have the experience of the Zenica convoy, but I didn't want to work with Heinz on a regular basis. Heinz was not an easy guy to get on with, as we found out when he interrupted our radio conversation. I went on to tell Frank that we would just have to wait and see what convoys we would be on the next week. In a way it was nice of Frank to let me know that I was missed on the other convoys.

Friday 24th September 1993. Meet Dave T at the ICRC delegation in Zagreb, and pick up the keys to a Land Cruiser. After checking the Land Cruiser, I notified the radio room of our departure from Zagreb en route to Lipovac. At Lipovac we met another driver from Beograd. He told Dave T that the truck he would be taking back to Zagreb had a burnt-out clutch. With a bit of clunk and grind Dave T managed to get the truck back to Zagreb.

At Metor's that evening, Dave T was telling us that his arm was sore, due to the rattle and vibration from the gearstick, when he had to change gear. While I was at the bar getting drinks, Bob Fenwick and Tom Handley walked in.

There was something different about Tom's appearance. I looked at Bob he had a big grin on his face. Then I noticed Tom's grey hair had gone. That vain Welshman had dyed his hair jet black. Bob was telling us that Tom was trying to look younger because of all the attention that the drivers get from the young girls at Metor's Bar. Tom's transformation from grey to jet black was just too much, excuse the pun! But Tom did put his head on the chopping block, and he took a lot of stick that night, but it did give us all a big laugh.

Saturday 25th September 1993, drivers' meeting at the ICRC delegation in Zagreb. Beat Mosimann opened the meeting and issued the drivers with next week's convoy duties. My duties were as follows: Monday, Knin overnight stop; Tuesday, return to Zagreb; Wednesday, Bihać; Thursday, day off; Friday, Banja Luka; Saturday, Banja Luka. That coming week was about to bring an end to our regular weekends off. With the harsh Balkan winters just around the corner, the demand for supplies like blankets, stoves, food and medical supplies had increased. These supplies were required to get through whenever possible, even if it meant the interruption of your regular rest days.

After Beat closed the drivers' meeting, the usual bunch of drivers went to the nearby park for our normal Saturday football kick around. After the football match, and before we retired for our usual refreshment at Metor's Bar, we decided to give the football to the local youngsters that had joined us every Saturday. We told them that we might not be able to come every Saturday due our work. They seem disappointed, but happy to have a football to kick around. That evening most of the drivers attended a farewell party for Raoul, at Metor's Bar. A sad occasion, but we gave Raoul a good send-off.

Sunday 26th September 1993. Our local guide Goran offered to take us sightseeing on the outskirts of Zagreb. I was fascinated with our visit the birthplace of that great Yugoslav leader Tito. He was born in what we would call a bungalow, but very much smaller than the bungalows we were all use to in the UK. As a child Tito to had to share a very small room with his siblings. From that humble background, Tito grew up to be a born leader. His leadership came to the aid of the people in Yugoslavia during World War Two. Tito was a great ally to the UK, and to those who fought against Nazi Germany. History would tell us that Croatia supported Germany, and made several raids into the Yugoslav republic of Serbia. Tito and his partisans became a thorn in the side of the German Army. After World War Two, Tito became the Communist leader of Yugoslavia.

The Republics of Slovenia, Croatia, Bosnia, Macedonia, Montenegro and Serbia formed the Federation of Yugoslavia. Tito's strict leadership made sure that these republics stood together in a brotherhood. It was only after Tito's death that cracks started to appear in the Yugoslav brotherhood. First Slovenia wanted independence from Yugoslavia, followed by Croatia, and then Bosnia, that was the start of the conflict that brought that great country to its knees. Many mixed families would be torn apart: Serbs married to Croats, or Bosnians married to either. Goran was telling us that, as a student under Tito's regime, he had to tow the party line. Not many were allowed to have an opinion and it had not been advisable to speak out against the regime. Goran went on to say that Croatia might be at war, but we are fighting to have a little more freedom. So Croatia can decide the way we want to live without any oppression from Serbia.

After a very interesting morning, our stomachs were starting to tell us it was lunch time. Goran took us to a restaurant, and the food was very tasty. Sunday afternoon we visited a monument that was dedicated to the composer of the Yugoslavian national anthem. Throughout the day my camera was kept busy. Frank and Dragica seem to have their fair share of photo shots against the scenic countryside of Croatia. To be honest they looked so happy, and very much in love, that it did help to enhance every photo I took of them.

That was a truly lovely day out that helped us to forget the traumas of working in a war zone. In the evening I returned to my apartment to prepare myself for next week's relief convoys; and the reality of working in a war zone.

Monday 27th September 1993, convoy to Knin. in total, seven trucks.

We arrived in Knin without any problems or incidents. When all the trucks were unloaded, we all made our way to the Driver's Mansion for the night. Diego was required at the ICRC delegation in Knin for a short meeting. While waiting for Diego's return, we all sat down to play a game of cards. The landlady, who owned the mansion, supplied us with a bottle of Slivovitz.

Dave T was trying to think of a joke to play on Diego. He said, "I bet the first thing Diego does when he comes back, is go to his bunk for an hour's sleep. Diego always does that before we all sit down for something it eat." Dave's comment gave me an idea.

I said, "Dave where does Diego sleep?" After Dave had shown me where Diego usually slept, I started to remove some of the slats that held up the mattress. I then went back to my game of cards.

The guys knew what I had done, and while we waited for Diego to return, we all sat there like a bunch of giggling school kids; every time one of us thought about Diego falling through his bed, the giggles started, from one to the other. On hearing Diego's return we were all trying our best not to laugh before the event, that was until we heard a crash!

Diego screamed, in his Icelandic broken English, "You bastards!"

By that time some us were crying with laughter. We finally managed to prepare our evening meal, but the jokes were not over yet. While Diego poured some wine, I made a noise of wine being poured from a bottle, with my tonnegue and top lip. I stopped making the noise when Diego went to top up the next glass. He looked at the bottle before giving it a little shake. Diego soon rumbled that it was me making that stupid noise. It's moments like that that raises the morale of guys you work with.

Tuesday 28th September 1993. After a good night's sleep, the convoy departed Knin, and we returned to Zagreb without any problems or incidents. I think Diego might have been glad to see the back of me, but I guess there was one consolation. I would see Diego again tomorrow when our paths crossed on the convoy to Bihać. I don't think Diego knows that, yet.

Wednesday 29th September 1993, convoy to Bihać. in total five trucks.

En route to Bihać we were just going through the checkpoint at Tusilovic. Frank was our tail-end Charlie today. Frank informed Diego that the last truck had just cleared the checkpoint. Diego replied, "Thank you, Frank. Hey, you and Kent the only Norwegians left in Zagreb, over?"

Frank replied in his broken English/Norwegian tone, "No Diego that was not correct, we have three Norwegians in Zagreb, over."

Diego replied, "Frank who was the third Norwegian?"

Frank replied, "Diego, George was driving Knuit's truck, which now makes George half Norwegian."

That brought a hearty laugh over the radio from Diego, and a few wise cracks from us all. That might have been a tongue in cheek comment from Frank, but in a way I felt proud and honoured that Frank could even mention that I had been adopted as half Norwegian. In return Frank has been like a son to me, and we always looked out for one another, like a father and son would do. While the trucks were being unloaded at Bihać, we sat in the sun playing that stupid Norwegian card game. I thought that was asking too much of me, and my new half-Norwegian identity.

Once the trucks were unloaded, the convoy made its way back to Zagreb and arrived there without any problems or incidents. At the ICRC delegation in Zagreb, I checked my mail box. Wow! Someone loves me, letters from: my girlfriend Sandy, from my sons Martin and Lee and from my brother-in law Peter a letter and some UK newspapers. So it was off to Metor's Bar for a *pivo* and to read my letters, then catch up with the news from the UK and abroad.

Thursday 30th September 1993. Day off. Wrote a couple letters to my sons, Sandy, and Peter. Also done some shopping. That evening had a break from Metor's Bar and joined Tony at the Bar Caffe just across the road from our apartment. Had a very interesting chat with Zvonimir Papec, the owner of the Bar Caffe. Zvonimir was telling me about the history of Croatia thoughout the last 200 years. History was one of my favourite subjects at school, so was not at all bored, in fact, I could have listen to Zvonimir longer than the evening would allow. I would not bore you with the full history of Croatia, but briefly Zvonimir was telling me that Croatia and Serbia had been at each other's throats for over 200 years. Zvonimir also covered Croatia involment with Nazi Germany. It was getting late, and Tony and I were both on the Banja Luka convoy the next morning. So we thanked Zvonimir and his beautiful bar staff, Jadriawka and Jva, for a very pleasant evening, and we wished them all good night. The evening at Zvonimir's Bar Caffe made a lovely change from Metor's Bar, what was it they say? A change is as good as a rest.

Friday 1st October 1993, convoy to Banja Luka. in total eight trucks. The relief convoy to Banja Luka was completed without any problems or incidents.

Saturday 2nd October 1993, convoy to Banja Luka, with the same drivers as the previous day. While we were waiting for our trucks to be unloaded in Banja Luka, Dave T asked me if I would lead the convoy back to Zagreb once the unloading was completed?

I replied, "Me Dave, are you sure?"

Dave T answered, "Yes George I am sure. I just fancy a change from leading convoys. I will be your tail-end Charlie."

I replied, "Okay, Dave, I will lead."

Leading the convoy back to Zagreb felt a little strange. It was now up to me to notify the radio rooms in Banja Luka, and Zagreb of our departure and arrival respectively. I also had been given the responsibility to keep the convoy in order through checkpoints. I kept a good check on my mirrors to see the convoy was keeping the correct distance between each truck. I am glad to say the convoy arrived safely back in Zagreb without any problems or incidents. After the trucks were refuelled, we went to Beat's transport office to see what duties we were on next week. When I checked the Weekly Operations Board, my duties were as follows: Monday, Bihać; Tuesday and Wednesday, Banja Luka; Thursday, Vojnić; Friday, Banja Luka. Beat used to write the Convoy Leader name in red ink on the board.

I said to Dave T, "Dave, I think Beat has made a mistake, he has written my name in red."

Dave replied, "It's no mistake, George. It's been noticed that the guys have a lot of respect for you. Beat asked me to approach you. My way of doing that was to ask you take the convoy back from Banja Luka today. I called Beat from the Banja Luka delegation to let him know you were taking the convoy back to Zagreb. Beat told me he would pencil your name in for Convoy Leader duties next week."

Worried I replied, "Dave there are guys like Frank and Kent, who have been here a lot longer than me."

Dave replied, "These guys have been approached, George, and they don't want the responsibility that goes with being a Convoy Leader. A couple of weeks ago you escorted field nurse Rachel Lavy to Lipovac to collect a child. When Rachel returned, she told Beat that she had felt safe in your hands because you were so calm under pressure and that you never showed any fear. With Raoul being sent home, Beat needs a Convoy Leader to replace him."

I replied, "Okay Dave, I just hope I can do as good a job as Raoul did when he was here."

On reflection it proves that that no one there was indispensable. First I take over Knuit's truck after he was sent home, and now I take over the role as a Convoy Leader, after Raoul also gets sent home. They say things happen in threes. If that's the case what on earth was going to happen next? From my first convoy on the 2nd August it took nine weeks to reach that turning point in my mission.

That night at Metor's Bar it gave the guys an excuse to celebrate, and the usual harmless mickey-taking banter. Andréa stayed at my side for most of the night and asked me to take her home. I escorted Andréa home, but left her about 200 metres from her home. It felt like a bombshell had dropped when Andréa told me she was married. I wonder how I would feel if my wife was about to cheat on me? Andréa could see that her revelation had made me feel uneasy about the situation, and tried to justify her feelings for me when she told me that her husband was not good to her, and showed no love towards her. Andréa never explained in detail why she was so unhappy in her marriage. Maybe he ill-treated Andréa? Or was it the lack of money? I say that because the local girls were always hanging around us all at Metor's Bar, and I don't think it was because we all looked like handsome film stars. Perhaps I was being unkind to misjudge the local girls in that way. Maybe they just enjoyed our company, perhaps the attraction that there was never a dull moment around us, and we always had a good evening. To be honest times were hard for them. Their country was involved in a conflict, money was tight. So if they could have a good time with us, and take their minds off the hardship they faced, then so be it. I was not there, but was it not the same for the girls in the UK, during the Second World War?

Sunday 3rd October 1993. I could not get the events of yesterday out of my mind. First the responsibility of my new role as a Convoy Leader; second Andréa's revelation. I decided to write some unfinished letters home. Not sure if that was a good idea, because one of the letters was to Sandy my ex-girlfriend back home. With a part of me thinking about Andréa, I was feeling a bit guilty writing to Sandy. Without trying to justify my actions, Sandy and I had broken up a month or so before I came out here. I met Sandy two days before leaving the UK, to let her know that I was going to work for the Red Cross in the former Yugoslavia. She wanted to write to me, so I gave her the address in Zagreb. Technically we were not together when I left the UK.

I can hear everyone saying, "Typical man any excuse to make your actions right in your own eyes." The more I thought about Sandy and Andréa, the more confused I became. I decided to let life take its own course. Why worry? After all, I might die tomorrow. With all my letters finished and posted, I went for a long walk to clear my head. After all, next week brings another fresh challenge to my life, and my mission in the former Yugoslavia.

Monday 4th October 1993, Convoy Leader duties to Bihać. Th in total five trucks. On my first day as Convoy Leader, I notified the radio room in Zagreb of our departure to Bihać. The mission was completed without any problems or incidents.

Tuesday 5th October 1993, Convoy Leader duties to Banja Luka. : in total seven trucks. I notified the radio room in Zagreb of our departure. At Gradiska Bridge Vanja welcomed the convoy before escorting the convoy for a comprehensive vehicle search at the old football stadium. That search also included any personal baggage each driver might be carrying. I mentioned before that these now regular searches at the football stadium would prolong our daily trip to Banja Luka by up to two hours. After the vehicle search the convoy continued to Banja Luka. The mission to Banja Luka was completed without any problems or incidents, and the convoy returned to Zagreb at 1735 hours.

Wednesday 6th October 1993, Convoy Leader duties to Banja Luka. in total seven trucks. The mission to Banja Luka was completed without any problems or incidents.

Thursday 7th October 1993, Convoy Leader duties to Vojnić. in total five trucks. The mission to Vojnić was completed without any problems or incidents.

Friday 8th October 1993, Convoy Leader duties to Banja Luka. in total six trucks. The mission to Banja Luka was completed without any problems or incidents. With the first week accomplished in my new role, I could not have wished for it to have gone any better, I prayed that that success would continue for the rest of my mission.

238

Saturday 9th October 1993, drivers' meeting at the ICRC delegation in Zagreb. Due to fourteen drivers on a relief convoy to Zenica, the drivers attending today's meeting were looking more like the old days when I first came to Zagreb. Transport Manager Beat Mosimann opened the meeting. Before Beat issued the next week's convoy duties he informed us that, over the weekend, a group of drivers would be held on standby. These drivers would not be mentioned on relief convoys the next week, and would therefore be on standby over the weekend, and the drivers on standby must have an overnight bag packed and be ready to go at short notice.

Beat continued to tell us that he could not give us any details of that relief convoy, because as he spoke the ICRC were in negotiations with all the necessary authorities. All he could only tell us was that the area we would be going to had not had any relief convoys for over three months, and that the civilian population were desperate for food and medical supplies, plus stoves and blankets for the harsh winter. When Beat finally handed out the next week's convoy duties, the anticipation by each driver to see their duties was quite tense. The drivers on standby were: Carlos Melara (Ita), Diego Thorkelsson (Ice), Austin McEvoy and Mark Keating (Ire), Frank Karlsen and Kent Furuly (Nor), Robin Creelman, Keith Descalchuk and Keith Marsden (Can), and me: in total ten drivers on standby.

Before Beat closed the drivers' meeting, he asked the drivers on standby to keep him notified on their whereabouts, in order for him to keep us up to date on any progress with the authorities regarding the proposed relief convoy.

After the meeting the ten drivers went to their apartments to pack an overnight bag. We all agreed to meet in Metor's Bar with Beat at 1600 hours. Later at Metor's Bar, and full of apologies, Beat arrived at 1620 hours to tell us that nothing would happen today, and that we were all stood down. Beat continued to tell us that the ICRC would continue negotiations with the authorities tomorrow, and that we would all be back on standby from 0900 hours, tomorrow morning.

Tomorrow or whenever it might be, none of us knew where we would be sent. We could not even speculate. The former Yugoslavia was a big country, but what we did know was that wherever we had to go, it was not going to be easy, and that would be a fresh challenge for us all. For the rest of the evening we all relaxed with a few *pivos*, and put all our speculation to bed. Tomorrow would be with us soon, and hopefully we would have a clearer picture of what was planned for us.

Sunday 10th October 1993. I wrote a letter to Sandy and my sons that morning. After lunch with Austin we went to the ICRC delegation in Zagreb to see if Beat had any news. Beat had not heard anything yet. That was worse than being in a dentist's waiting room. We hung around the delegation drinking coffee for most of the afternoon. Finally boredom took over and we told Beat that we would be in Metor's Bar if he heard anything. Beat told us not to drink too much. It was now 1635 hours, and we were now thinking that nothing was going to happen now. That was until Beat walked in to Metor's Bar and asked us all to report to the delegation at 1700 hours. At the delegation we were told that, from here, we would all board a mini-bus and travel to Banja Luka, where we would stay the night.

"Tomorrow morning you will all attend a meeting in Banja Luka to find out details of the relief convoy. You will be using the trucks in the Banja Luka pool." The mystery continues! But at least we had a green light to go.

We boarded our transport and left Zagreb in darkness of early evening. Once again over the radio it was comforting to hear Vanja's voice greeting us at Gradiska Bridge. Vanja said, "George, would you like to ride with Branco and me?"

I replied, "Thanks for the offer, but I would stay with the lads."

Vanja's invite caused the lads to give me a bit of ribbing. Comments like "Vanja wants George's body!" began floating around, along with other jibes. There was nothing going on between Vanja and me. Maybe if the circumstances had been different, but out there you were not in the real world. Love and attractions in a war zone can easily be misinterpreted. Some might use the situation to try and forget the horrors of war, or use the attraction for some sort of gain for a better life. Having said all that, the respect and admiration I had for Vanja was immense.

We arrived at the Banja Luka delegation and were shown to our sleeping quarters. That was a large meeting room with camp beds already laid out to accommodate ten drivers. I told Diego that the last time I had slept in a billet like that was two years ago in France with the football team that I managed. I went on to tell Diego about the fun and games my football team got up to that night. We were all afraid to sleep that night because there was a bunch of practical jokers waiting to play some sort of trick on you – while I had been asleep all of my toenails were painted with a black permanent marker pen. One of the football team went to the bathroom to have a shave in the morning; when he looked in the mirror there was something different about his face but he could not work it out; he then realized he no longer had eyebrows – the guys had shaved them off while he had been asleep!

Similarly, when Diego noticed that his camp bed was next to mine, he moved it to the other side of the room. When we all turned in poor Diego was very nervous, any slight movement by any of the lads, Diego would sit up. When he laid down, he kept one forearm across his forehead. I guess that was to stop anyone shaving his eyebrows off.

Monday 11th October 1993. Diego looked rough, poor guy couldn't have slept too well. I wonder why? After a wash and shave we had coffee, and waited for the delegates to arrive with news of the destination for today's relief convoy.

At long last we were all summoned to another meeting room. Over the last forty-eight hours the suspense of not knowing where we were going was now about to be revealed. The head of the Banja Luka delegation Michel Minnig greeted us with a *Good morning* and welcome. Michel informed us in great depth about today's relief convoy. Our destination was a place called Žepče. Žepče was in the Muslim pocket of Bosnia, and was some 110 kilometres south-east of Banja Luka. Žepče and the surrounding area had had no relief supplies for over three months. Žepče was also surrounded by their enemy forces. The day's relief convoy would be required to negotiate Serbian and UN checkpoints. The area around Žepče was also a heavily mined. The ICRC had negotiated with all the necessary authorities, and has been given assurances by all the authorities to allow that relief convoy to reach its destination without any hindrance or harm. Michel also informed us that we would all be issued with flak jackets and helmets, and told us not to be alarmed, because that was just an extra safety precaution. We would drive the Banja Luka trucks that are normally used by their local ICRC Serbian drivers. The Serbian local drivers could not be used on that relief convoy, because it was required to go into a Muslim area. Now we were all fully briefed, we headed to the truck park to check our trucks.

These trucks were just the standard five-tonne Iveco. Not the most comfortable of rides, but if it gets the job done, then I guess that's the most important issue to consider.

The convoy departed Banja Luka at 0930 hours, and headed south-east on highway 4. Diego Thorkelsson led the convoy, while I followed at the rear as his tail-end Charlie. The convoy travelled through the small towns of Kotor Varoš, Borci, Maslovare and Klupe, negotiating various checkpoints and mined areas. Near the town of Teslić we travelled south on a mountain track for twenty-five kilometres, and arrived in Žepče at 1155 hours. Frank Karlsen felt a bit uneasy with prisoners of war being used to unload our trucks.

The unloading was completed by 1620 hours. Sunset was due at 1700 hours, and Diego was getting a bit concerned that the convoy would have to travel in the dark to get back to Banja Luka. When we departed Žepče at 1630 hours it was already looking very dark and overcast with rain clouds, which made the daylight very poor. Nevertheless we had to return to Banja Luka tonight. Within five minutes on the road, the heavens opened up with a cloudburst. When the convoy reached the mountain track it was already dark, and the rain was making the climb up the mountain track very difficult. It got so bad the trucks were losing traction, climbing the mountain track in the mud. Diego was driving the only four-wheel-drive truck, and his truck was now required to tow each truck up that steep mountain track. I would be the last truck to be towed up that track, while each driver was being towed. I listened to their radio conversation with Diego. I heard Diego say, "Watch out for that ditch on the left.

The driver replied, "Okay, Diego.. shit! I'm in the ditch. Sorry Diego I didn't see the ditch."

That happened three times with three different drivers. But the best radio conversation I heard was between Carlos Melara and Diego.

As Carlos was being towed up that mountain track, he was getting excited to reach the top when you heard him saying, "Diego, yes! Go Diego, Yes! Yes! Go, go, yes! Yes!' It sounded like Carlos was having an orgasm. I was getting hungry; I remembered I had a chicken leg in my bag. I was now alone with the last truck waiting for a tow. I had my cab light on while eating my chicken leg, when all of a sudden these soldiers appeared from nowhere. That major asked me to move my truck. I explained to him, that I was waiting to be towed up the mountain track. The major was waving his arms in the air saying you are endangering my operation. He left one of his soldiers with me. That soldier said to me, "You English?"

I replied, "Yes."

He then said, "Ha, Pet Shop Boys, I saw them in Zagreb."

I thought of all the groups he had to associate me being English with, it had to be the Pet Shop Boys! That young soldier could not have been any more than eighteen years old. He went on to tell me how many of his friends are now his enemies, and he did not want to fight them, because they went to school together. The soldier was then ordered to return to his unit.

I carried on eating my chicken leg, but I kept remembering what that major said to me when he said, "You are endangering my operation." I wondered what operation the major was on about. Then my vivid imagination took over. I thought *Shit! I could be in the middle of an ambush*, and caught in the crossfire. With that thought in my mind, I switched my cab light off and slid down my seat, until the top of my head was just below the dashboard.

Just when I was about to sing the Roy Orbison classic *Only the Lonely*, Diego finally arrived to tow my truck up that mountain. The convoy finally cleared the mountain track, and once on the highway, and somewhat relieved, we soon arrived back in Banja Luka.

Tuesday 12th October 1993. Was I missing the comfort of my bed in Zagreb, following sleepless night on the camp bed in Banja Luka! As I lay there thinking about the previous day's convoy, I wondered if that young soldier had managed to stay alive during the major's operation. So many young lives lost in that conflict. So many mothers, wives and sweethearts are left heartbroken. I wished I had the answers to give us all world peace. While we waited to find out the destination for the day's relief convoy, Vanja took us all out for breakfast; not bad, just a bit greasy for me.

On return to the delegation, Michel Minnig was waiting to give us a briefing on today's relief convoy. Michel thanked us all for yesterday's successful mission to Žepče. Michel continued to inform us that most of trucks we used yesterday had now been reloaded, and that remaining trucks should be finished within the next hour. Today's relief convoy was being sent to another Muslim town in the Bosnian Pocket called Tešanj. Tešanj was not far away from Žepče; like Žepče, the people of Tešanj were in a desperate situation for food and medical supplies, no relief convoys had made it through to Tešanj for over three months. Arrangements had been made for us to stay the night in Tešanj. On that convoy we must continue to wear our flak jackets and helmets. Michel wished us all a safe journey, there and back.

With all the trucks now loaded, we did our final vehicle checks. Led by Diego, we departed Banja Luka 1040 hours. On that convoy, I followed in the second truck, while Frank was our tail-end Charlie today. The convoy had taken the same route as yesterday, but instead of going south on the mountain range at Teslić, the convoy had continued east going through the small town of Stenjak. At a small town called Jelah, the convoy was held up for over an hour at a Serbian checkpoint. The track ahead was heavily mined. Finally, we were given the all clear to proceed; Diego decided that only one truck at a time should negotiate that heavily mined track.

As Diego's truck disappeared through the checkpoint and around a left-hand bend, I waited for him to contact me over the radio to give me the all clear to come through the minefield. You could feel the tension as each truck went through the checkpoint, and enter the minefield; one by one the drivers wished one another the best of luck. Thank God, all the trucks came through that ordeal without any incidents. With the convoy now regrouped, we continued the short journey from Jelah to Tešanj unaware of the reception that was awaiting us. As the convoy came into Tešanj the streets were lined with people and schoolchildren waving and cheering. I think I can speak for all the drivers when I say we did not expect such a wonderful welcome as that, and how overwhelmed we all were. When we reached the warehouse we all got out of our trucks with tears in our eyes and threw our arms around each other. People and children gathered outside the fence of the warehouse. I always had my big bag sweets with me; so I went outside the fence to give sweets to the children. Before returning to the warehouse I remember giving a big handful of sweets to one little boy. As I shut the gate behind me I noticed that little boy was sharing the sweets that I gave him with other children. I wondered if the children back home would share their sweets like that little boy did? In most cases I very much doubt it. The drivers were still feeling overwhelmed and speechless with the reception we all received from the people of Tešanj. Vanja said to me, "If only my family and friends could see that. I can't believe I am in the Muslim pocket of Bosnia." Vanja was Serbian; I was surprised the ICRC allowed her on the trip.

Vanja was a beautiful lady and she attracted the attention of some of the Muslim soldiers. One of them asked me if Vanja was from Bosnia. I told him she was from Bosnia but I did not know what part. I was worried that, if they found out she was Serbian, they might harm or even arrest her. From the warehouse the drivers were taken to an ICRC mansion for the night. As we climbed the stairs on each of the three floors, the drivers were given a room for the night – either two or three to a room. Somehow I ended up sharing a room and double bed with a big Canadian. I have never shared a bed with a guy before, and I was not looking forward to bedtime.

That evening one of the local ICRC workers entertained us playing his guitar. One by one he asked us our Christian names, and then started to sing a song involving an artist with the same Christian name. When he came to Austin and Walter, he was stumped, but that guy truly entertained us.

It was getting late, and the time came for us all to hit the sack. I told you that Canadian was a big-built guy. When he got into bed, he took up most of the bed. To avoid any bodily contact with him, I slept right on the edge. The only problem with that was trying to stay in the bed, because every time the Canadian turned over the bed rocked, and I had to hold on to the mattress to stop myself falling out of bed.

Wednesday 13th October 1993. It was a beautiful sunny, but chilly morning, and for obvious reasons I wasted no time in getting out of bed early. With a cup of coffee warming my hands I strolled around the gardens at the ICRC mansion. Frank and Kent joined me. I noticed some wild flowers, and started picking them. Frank said, "George what are you doing?" When I told him that I was picking flowers for Vanja, he broke to a Norwegian belly laugh. I gave the flowers to Vanja, and told her that these flowers were from all the drivers to thank her for all that she does for us. With a giggle, and beautiful smile that melts your heart, she thanked us all.

All the trucks had now been unloaded. Our departure from Tešanj was less dramatic than yesterday, but has we left Tešanj the convoy did get the odd wave or two from people and children we passed. The convoy successfully negotiated the mined area near Jelah, and returned to Banja Luka just after midday. At the delegation there was a great feeling of achievement from everyone who had been involved in the relief convoys to Žepče and Tešanj. From delegates to all the personnel on the relief convoy, we all played our part to help the victims of war in Žepče and Tešanj. One the delegates treated us all to a Banja Luka takeaway. It looked like a Cornish pasty, but once again very greasy. They certainly like their fatty foods in Banja Luka. All the drivers went to our Banja Luka billets to pack our bags in readiness for our transportation back to Zagreb. I had left my hi-tech running shoes under my camp bed, and they had now disappeared. I completed a twenty-six mile marathon in the UK, that was the only sentimental value I had with these running shoes. So I guess whoever took them, needed them more than I did.

Late afternoon we arrived back in Zagreb without any problems or incidents. The memories of the last few days would stay with us all. It did us all good to embark on new and fresh challenges that would test your resolved. If you were on the same convoy destination day after day, it would be so easy to complacent in your mission.

Thursday 14th October 1993. Day off, to do some shopping, and write some Letters. Boring compared to the last few days.

Friday 15th October 1993, Convoy Leader duties to Banja Luka. in total four trucks. The mission to Banja Luka was completed without any problems or incidents.

Saturday 16th October 1993, drivers' meeting at the ICRC delegation in Zagreb. Beat Mosimann opened the meeting, with a de-briefing on last weeks successful convoys to Tešanj, Žepče, and Zenica. He congratulated all concerned for helping the ICRC in its very important relief program. Beat then continued to issue next weeks convoy duties to the drivers.

My duties were; Monday, Dvor. Tuesday, Dvor. Wednesday, Banja Luka. Thursday, Banja Luka. Friday Knin overnight stop. Saturday return to Zagreb.

Beat closed the meeting, wishing us all a relaxing weekend and safe missions next week. Most of us retired to Metor's Bar, for some well-earned refreshment and arm exercise. It was no secret that our flying Dutchman Erik Gerrit Hengstman was carrying a torch for Tamera. When Erik asked us about the trip to Žepče, and Tešanj, we decided to have a bit of fun with Erik. I told Erik there was a shortage of sleeping bags in Tešanj. When Tamera found out that I did not have a sleeping bag, she asked me if I would like to share her sleeping bag tonight? I went on to tell Erik that Vanja kept me warm all night. The lads did well to keep a straight face, until they saw Erik's face looking like a smacked ass. Poor Erik's face was red and jealous with envy. Frank offered Erik a cigarette with Vanja's name written on it. Erik looked at the cigarette, and screwed it up in his hand. Erik had a very dry sense of humour, and struggled to understand the English banter between guys. Unlike his fellow countryman Walter Weerheim, Walter always greeted us with his impression of the Cockney accent saying, "It's a lovely day today."

Sunday 17th October 1993. Dragica's parents invited me for lunch at their house. Frank told me that Dragica and I were always talking about me, and her parents wanted to meet me. I just hoped they were saying nice things about me!

Dragica introduced me to her parents, Mr and Mrs Ivaucevic. They did not speak English. I therefore required Dragica to translate the limited conversation between Mr and Mrs Ivaucevic and me. I can only express how Mr and Mrs Ivaucevic made me feel at ease, and welcomed me into their home. Mrs Ivaucevic prepared a wonderful very tasty lunch, I helped myself to pork chops and vegetables until my plate was full... big mistake! It was customary to accept a second helping, to let your host know how much you enjoyed their food. Failure to accept the second helping would tell your host that you did not enjoy the food that they prepared for you.

Frank told me that when he first came to lunch, he made the same mistake. I wondered why Frank did not have much on his plate on the first helping. I wished he had told me about that before I started filling my plate on the first helping. I was so fat and full that I felt a little uncomfortable. With Dragica's help her mother was telling me about her work. After eating all that food, I was now feeling very guilty, when I found out that her mother gets paid in food, and not money. I know the outcome was the same; you need money to buy the food on the table. But I felt that I was eating the food she had worked so hard for. Thank you, and God bless you both, Mr and Mrs Ivaucevic.

Monday 18th October 1993, Convoy Leader duties to Dvor. in total five trucks. The mission to Dvor was completed without any problems or incidents.

Tuesday 19th October 1993, Convoy Leader duties to Dvor with the same drivers as the previous day: in total five trucks. The mission to Dvor was completed without any problems or incidents.

Wednesday 20th October 1993, Convoy Duties to Banja Luka. in total, four trucks.

That was Austin's last relief convoy. On Friday he would go home to his beloved family in Dublin, Ireland. We tried to get him to extend his contract and stay here for another three months, but Austin was missing his wife and children so much, he nearly went home before his contract ended on Friday. Austin was telling me that every week he spoke to his wife and children on the phone, they always cried. Rightly so Austin found it very upsetting. Unlike me, his children were still very young. Austin was a brave man to leave his family for three months. I am not sure I could have done that, if I had young children.

Throughout Austin's mission in the former Yugoslavia he has been a good friend. We had always shared problems, but most of the time we also had many, many laughs together. One particular time comes to mind, when about ten drivers went out for a meal one weekend. I have already mentioned that Austin loves his food. If it was a sport Austin would be a world champion. Many times I have seen Austin hovering over colleagues while they were eating their food, especialy when he was feeling hungry. Anyway back to that weekend: we all ordered our food and, while we were waiting, I went to the bar to get a round of drinks. At the same time I pointed out Austin to our waiter, and asked him to delay serving Austin's meal for five minutes after everyone had had their meal. I gave him an early tip, and reassured him it would be okay, and that he would not get into trouble. One by one everyone was served the meal they ordered. All except poor Austin, he kept looking to the kitchen doorway expecting the waiter to come through the door with his meal. Austin was now getting a little fidgety, true to form and Austin's hunger pains; he was out of his seat hovering behind the guys eating their meal. At the same time he was telling everyone that the waiter must have overlooked his order. The guys knew what I had done, and were trying so hard not to laugh. When Austin's meal was finally served, I told Austin what I had done, and it's not the waiters' fault. With a smile Austin's replied, "Bastards!"

I am honoured to have known Austin, and to have shared that moment in time with him. The mission to Banja Luka was completed without any problems or incidents.

Thursday 21st October 1993, convoy duties to Banja Luka. in total four trucks. The mission to Banja Luka was completed without any problems or incidents. In the evening most of the drivers were at Metor's Bar for Austin's last night in Zagreb. Austin said, "George I have a problem."

I said, "What's wrong, mate?"

Austin said, "My wife was meeting me at Dublin Airport."

I said, "That's good, what's wrong with that?"

Austin said, "Do I take my wife to a hotel to make up for lost time, or do we go to a bar so I can have a pint of Guinness?"

I said, "Austin you can't be serious, surely your wife comes before a pint of Guinness? Let me know the outcome, mate."

I know one thing for sure; I am going to miss Austin's Irish wit.

Farewell and God bless you, Austin.

Friday 22nd October 1993, convoy duties to Knin. in total six trucks. Arrived in Knin without any problems or incidents.

Saturday 23rd October 1993. All the trucks were unloaded, and the convoy departed Knin at 1000 hours. The convoy arrived back in Zagreb at 1710 hours, without any problems or incidents. We refuelled the trucks before going to the Transport Office to checked the relief Operations Board, and see what duties we were on next week. My duties were: Monday, Bugojno overnight stop in Zenica. Tuesday return to Zagreb. Wednesday day off. Thursday, overnight stop in Knin. Friday return to Zagreb.

Back to the apartment to freshen up before meeting the lads for our usual Saturday night binge at Metor's Bar. When I arrived, the party was in full swing with the local girls. Dragica was stood on a barstool dancing, the stool was rocking, and I was worried she was going to fall. I grabbed hold of the stool while she carried on wriggling her hips. I was afraid to look up, because she was wearing a miniskirt. Honest I did not look up... Andréa stayed at my side for most of the night. It felt strange not having Austin with us.

Sunday 24th October 1993. I wrote a couple of letters while Tony and Queenie prepared a Sunday roast; it was just like being home. Tony was an excellent cook. In the evening Tony and I went for a drink in the Bar Caffe across the road. I got talking to few of the locals. One of them was grinning at Tony and me when he reached inside his jacket, and placed a revolver on the bar. The bar owner Zvonimir Papec told us that the guy was a police detective. He liked to alarm people, especially foreigners, but he was really harmless.

Monday 25th October 1993, convoy duties to Bugojno via Zenica. in total, fourteen trucks.

Six trucks would contain relief supplies for Zenica and eight trucks would have relief supplies Bugojno. That was the second time I have been on a convoy with Heinz, and once again he positioned all the English-speaking drivers at the rear of the convoy. I did not have a problem with that, so long as the English-speaking drivers got important messages of any obstructions on the road. Not a chance: the bloody Swiss and French chatted away in their own language. The guys in the last five trucks did not know what the hell they were talking about. We were not informed of rocks in the road or to switch lights on unlit long tunnel ahead, or horse and cart in the road, or people in the road etc.

Tony O'Connor was not a happy bunny when we arrived in Zenica. Tony asked me why Heinz didn't warn us that the tunnel did not have lights. Apparently he nearly lost control going into that dark tunnel. I decided to have a quiet word with Heinz, to remind him that the ICRC expects all their drivers on convoy duties to speak English on the radio.

I asked Heinz if he had any objection to speaking English in order to inform the drivers of any obstructions ahead. Although Heinz seemed to take on board the points I made to him, I don't think he was too impressed with my comments, it was not meant as a criticism on his convoy leadership. We would just have to wait and see what happened from now on. Six trucks were unloaded in Zenica. the other eight trucks were unloaded in Bugojno

From Zenica, the convoy travelled south-west on a narrow mountain track for about thirty-five kilometres. We arrived in Bugojno without any problems or incidents. Before the cease fire, Bugojno was another town that had not received any relief aid for well over three months. It was just not safe for relief convoys to get through the battlefields and shelling.

On arrival in Bugojno the three trucks with medical supplies and blankets were unloaded at the Hospital, the remaining five trucks containing food parcels were unloaded at a church. My truck was carrying food parcels when we arrived at the church, a priest and two nuns welcomed us and, while the trucks were being unloaded, invited inside the church for some refreshment. We sat at a long wooden table; nuns served us food and drink. Because they have been so short of food for themselves I felt so guilty eating their food. But here we are eating what little food they had to give. I then looked over to the wall on my left, to see a large tapestry depicting *The Last Supper*.

I thought about Jesus sharing bread and wine with his disciples. I then looked over to the wall on my right, to see a large tapestry of Jesus on the cross. In my heart I felt God was talking to me, and he was telling me that the people of Bugojno want to share with you what little food they have. And they are prepared to make that sacrifice for you.

I came out of that church feeling very emotional, and humble towards the people of Bugojno. During your mission, it's hard to take on board some of the things you hear. Not far from Bugojno there were rumours of prison camps for children. That was very hard to comprehend. Surely in the eyes of most children you would see the innocent souls of our world? Most of us say, "When I meet God, I would ask him why he let so many people and children suffer in our world."

I am sure God would have many more questions for us all; especially in the way we treat each other, and innocent victims of conflicts.

The trucks were soon unloaded. While Tony O'Connor was checking his truck he found six stowaways in the back. These poor guys were so desparate to get out of Bugojno, they were all prepared to risk their lives. If our trucks had been searched at any of the checkpoints, and the guards found these stowaways, it would not only put their lives in danger, but our lives also. The guards would have every right to assume that we were trying to smuggle people out of an area of conflict. That would also endanger the ICRC relief program in the former Yugoslavia.

With all the trucks checked for unathorised passengers, the convoy departed Bugojno and returned to Zenica for the night. Zenica was not a safe place at night for foreign personnel to go out for a meal, or drink. While driving your truck through the streets of Zenica even by day it was easy to recognize the freedom fighters of the Mujaheddin with their green and yellow headbands. The Mujaheddin would shake your hand and, when you walked away, they would shoot you in the back.

Tuesday 26th October 1993. The convoy departed Zenica, en route to Zagreb via Banja Luka. At last! Heinz our Convoy Leader spoke English on the radio when he warned the drivers of any obstructions on the road ahead. Well done Heinz! After lunch in Banja Luka, we returned to Zagreb without any problems or incidents.

Wednesday 27th October 1993. Day fff. Shopping, and writing letters.

Thursday 28th October 1993, Convoy Leader duties to Banja Luka. in total six trucks.

The convoy arrived in Banja Luka without any problems or incidents. On the return journey to Zagreb, the convoy encountered very thick fog. In all of my twenty-seven years driving trucks, I have never driven in fog so thick as that. Visability was approximately twenty-five to fifty metres. the closer we got to Zagreb, the thicker the fog became. I told the drivers that I was slowing the convoy speed down forty mph, and to be alert for any vehicles going slower or parked on the highway without lights. Walter's was the second truck in the convoy.

Walter kept on asking me over the radio that he could not see the lights on the back of my truck. Walter also asked me how far ahead I was. In that thick fog could not see his headlights in my mirrors. I informed Walter that I had just passed a sign for Sisak and asked him to check his watch, to see how long it would take him to reach the same sign. Fifteen seconds later, Walter confirmed that he had just passed the

Sisak sign. I told Walter, "You are about 500 to 600 metres behind me."

Walter continued to tell me that he was afraid he would miss the exit junction for Zagreb. I told him not to worry, because when the convoy reached the *péage* (toll), we would try to keep the trucks closer together. I could understand Walters's concern; you could not see any road signs until you were right on top of them. Thankfully the convoy returned to Zagreb without any further problems or incidents. Although we all had eyes like piss holes in the snow, it was good to hear Walter's cockney impression of *It's a Lovely Day Today*.

Friday 29th October 1993, Convoy Leader duties to Banja Luka. The same drivers as the previous day: in total six trucks. The fog we encountered late yesterday afternoon had now lifted, and today's mission to Banja Luka was completed without any problems or incidents.

Saturday 30th September 1993, drivers' meeting at the ICRC delegation in Zagreb. Beat Mosimann opened the meeting by introducing the two new drivers: from Switzerland, Michel Braier, and from the UK Timothy Lynes. Beat issued next week's convoy duties. My duties were as follows: Monday, Banja Luka; Tuesday, Banja Luka; Wednesday, Bihać; Thursday, Knin with an overnight stop; Friday, return to Zagreb.

Beat informed us that due to renewed fighting south-east of Karlovac all relief convoys to Knin, Bihać and Vojnić must now take a route via Sisak, Petrinja and Glina. With no further issues to discuss, Beat closed the meeting by wishing us all a relaxing weekend.

The two new drivers joined the usual crowd at Metor's Bar. Over the last week the landlord Metor kept calling me Stef. I asked him, "Why are you calling me Stef?"

Metor replied, "Look at the statue of Prince Stefan in the square, he looks like you."

I did not know whether to feel honoured or insulted. Metor had a good heart, and he always looked after all the drivers. Let's be honest, nearly every night the drivers helped to fill his till.

Sunday 31st October 1993. Did a little shopping. In the afternoon met Dragica, Zana and Frank and went to see the movie *Somersby* staring Jodie Foster and Richard Gere. It was one of the most boring films I have ever seen, but the company was good.

Monday 1st November 1993, Convoy Leader duties to Banja Luka. The following drivers: Robin Creelman and Keith Descalchuk (Can), Tony O'Connor (Aussie), Michel Braier (Swiss), Frank Karlsen (Nor) and Robert Fenwick (UK): in total seven trucks. The mission to Banja Luka was completed without any problems or incidents.

Tuesday 2nd November 1993, Convoy Leader duties to Banja Luka. in total, eight trucks. The mission to Banja Luka was completed without any problems or incidents.

Wednesday 3rd November 1993, Convoy Leader duties to Bihać. in total six trucks. Little did I know that when I woke up that morning, my third challenge was about to unfold before my very eyes. I guess it must be true that everything happens in threes. I drew back the curtains in my bedroom to find a scene that you would expect to see on a Christmas card. While I was asleep, we had that much snow you could not see any individual cars that were parked outside. The snow had drifted onto the cars to make one large bank of snow about seven feet high, and the length of all the parked cars together. It resembled a skateboard park. The road itself was easily a foot deep. I have never seen snow like it, let alone driven in that amount of snow.

Since I have been in Zagreb I had not watched much TV, so I did not hear any weather reports. Over here they are not so obsessed with the weather as we are in the UK. I finished my cup of tea and then put on my brave face, and a warm coat, to face the elements outside. When I got outside, there was a lady who was frantically trying to find her car. I asked if she was okay. She replied, "I can't remember where I parked my car." There was nothing I could do for her. It was pointless me asking her the colour of her car, because all the cars were buried in the snow. Luckily, I remembered where I parked my Land Cruiser; it took me about twenty minutes to clear most of the snow off that. I picked up Tony O'Connor, and steadily made my way out to the ICRC warehouse.

Apart from our Norwegian Frank and our Icelandic escort Diego, who are both used to a lot worset conditions, the rest of us were all coming to terms with the driving conditions that we would all have to face on today's convoy. Michel was the biggest surprise to me. Coming from Switzerland, I expected Michel to be used to these adverse weather conditions. Michel was the fourth truck in the convoy, when the convoy was leaving Zagreb I glanced in my mirror, and noticed Michel's truck sliding from left to right.

I contacted Michel on the radio to ask him if he was okay. When Michel replied to my call he sounded very nervous, and his voice was all of a tremble when he said, "Don't like that much George."

I told him, "To try and avoid sharp or sudden braking. You will be okay when you get used the way your truck drives in the snow. Michel, let me know if you want me to slow down."

Not that I was driving fast; I was travelling at a speed of twenty-five mph (forty kph).

The convoy travelled south-east on highway 12/2 passing through the small towns of Buševec, Lekenik and Žažina, arriving at the UN checkpoint in Sisak, where Diego our Land Cruiser escort was waiting for us. The snowfall was not so bad at Sisak. The convoy continued on highway 4/3 passing through the small towns of Petrinja, Glina, Dragotina and G Klasnić, and negotiating checkpoints en route. Our tail-end Charlie Tony O'Connor contacted me on the radio asking me to stop the convoy. Michel's truck had tipped on its side. Apart from a few cuts and grazes, thankfully Michel was okay, but obviously shaken up a bit. Michel was very lucky, because the cab on the passenger's side was crushed.

The load of food parcels that Michel had been carrying was littered all over the accident scene. Diego informed Zagreb of the accident and returned to Zagreb with Michel in order to take him to hospital for a check-up. We remained at the accident scene waiting for the recovery team to arrive. Before the convoy could continue to Bihać, we had to wait for Diego our Land Cruiser escort to return. Meanwhile Eddy the Workshop Manager arrived with his team to assess the accident scene, and organize the recovery of the truck and the food parcels that could be saved. To establish the speed of Michel's truck at the time of the accident, Eddy checked the tachograph's reading on Michel's truck. Eddy felt that the road conditions, or his speed, had no bearing on the accident. His conclusion was that either the load had shifted when Michel came out of the bend or Michel overcompensated his steering coming out of the bend. He also thought it was possibly a mixture of both of his conclusions that caused Michel to loose control of his truck.

Diego returned, and the convoy continued on its mission to Bihać, passing through a couple of checkpoints and the small towns and of Žirovac, Gvozdansko, Medju Majdan and Dvor. When the convoy reached Bosan Novi we headed south-west on highway 14 once again, passing through a couple of checkpoints and the small towns of Otoka, Bos Krupe and Ostrožac before arriving in Bihać at 1400 hours without any futher problems or incidents. Using the route via Sisak to Bihać, instead of the usual route via Karlovac, added an extra sixty kilometres to the journey. On top of that we had lost two hours dealing with Michel's accident. The delays meant it was going to be difficult to get unloaded and return to Zagreb before nightfall. The ICRC delegation in Zagreb decided to make arrangements for the drivers to stay in Bihać overnight. The planned trip to Knin would now take place on Friday and Saturday.We spent most of the evening thinking about Michel's accident, and what a terrible experience it must have been for him. I kept thinking about how nervous he sounded when we left Zagreb, and did I do enough to eliviate Michel's fears?

Thursday 4th November 1993. Finished unloading trucks in Bihać, and returned to Zagreb without any problems or incidents. At the ICRC delegation I was pleased to hear that the hospital gave Michel the all clear.

Friday 5th November 1993, Convoy Leader duties to Knin. in total seven trucks. The convoy arrived in Knin without any problems or inidents, and unloaded three trucks.

Saturday 6th November 1993. Finished unloading the three remaining trucks, and returned to Zagreb without any problems or incidents. Refuelled trucks before checking next week's relief convoy rotas in the transport office. My duties were as follows: Monday, Cazin/Bihać; Tuesday, Wednesday and Thursday, Tešanj/Maglaj with an overnight stay in Banja Luka; Friday, day off; Saturday, Banja Luka.

Tony and I returned to our appartment for a bite to eat. Later that evening, I got ready to join Frank and Dragica to celebrate Zana's birthday at her parents' house. Zana's parents went to stay with relatives, and kindly let Zana have the house to herself. Not sure all the parents in the UK would be as trusting as that, but Zana was quite sensible for her age. I think the hardship of growing up in a war zone matures young people way beyond their age. Zana had plenty of her old schoolfriends at the party, and everyone seems to have a good time celebrating Zana's birthday that went on till the early hours of the morning. Sunday 7th November 1993. At 0130 hours, when all of Zana's friends had gone home, we talked for a little while; Zana had kindly prepared a bed in the spare room for me to crash out for the night. I think it was about two or three in the morning when I finally wished Zana a goodnight, and got to bed.

In the morning, Frank and Dragica were still asleep in bed, when Zana brought me in a cup of coffee. Zana sat on my bed, and we continued the conversation we were having from the early morning hours. We were still talking when her parents came home, and hearing Zana's voice in the spare room they came in to say hello! I thought, "Oh my God, I hope they don't think that Zana and I spent the night together in that bed!" Yet her parents were laughing and joking, not at all concerned to find Zana sat on my bed in the spare room. I asked Zana to tell them that we slept in separate rooms. They continued to laugh and joke with Zana, plus a wink from her father. Even Zana seem to be laughing at my embarrassment, I think they really knew that everything was above board, but took the opportunity to have a bit of fun with me.

Meanwhile my adopted Mum and Dad, namely Tony and Queenie, were a bit worried when I did not appear from my appartment bed that morning. And after finding my bed empty, they seem pleased to see me home safe and well. They made me feel like a teenager again. Once again Tony prepared a wonderful Sunday lunch.

In the evening Tony and I went across the road to the Bar Caffe. After a few *pivo*s, Tony was getting quite emotional talking about his dog in Australia that was being looked after by his relatives. Later Tony said, "George, thanks for listening to an old sentimental fool. You know I am on your convoy tomorrow, and if die tomorrow I could not die in better company." I think the drink might have opened Tony's heart. We just threw our arms around each other for a manly hug. Tony's comments might have been judged to be over the top, but I think his comments just illustrated the feeling of camaraderie that was felt by us all. Let's not forget we were all a long way from home. Out here we only had each other for support in a war zone, that many of us were experiencing a war zone for the first time. That was not the real world that we were all used to living in.

It was weekends like that that really lifted your resolve to face whatever challenges came your way over the forthcoming week's relief convoys.

Monday 8th November 1993, Convoy duties to Vojnić, Velika Kladuša, Cazin and Bihace in total seven trucks.

On route to Sisak, Dave T contacted me on the radio to inform me that he had a problem with his truck. I asked him, "What was the problem?"

Dave T replied, "The cab oil warning light was on, I am going back to Zagreb to get the truck checked out. Would you please take over?"

I replied, "Okay, Dave, take care, mate."

Diego overheard our brief radio conversation, and asked Dave T, "Is there any indication of the engine over heating?"

Dave T replied, "Not yet, Diego, but before I get too far away from Zagreb I think its best to go back to get that truck checked out."

Diego replied, "Okay Dave, best of luck."

The convoy arrived at Sisak to meet Diego our Land Cruiser escort, and continued to the ICRC warehouses in Vojnić, Velika Kladuša, Cazin and Bihać.

The convoy arrived at the ICRC warehouse in Vojnić, so Tony O'Connor and Michel Baud remained in Vojnić to unload their trucks. From Vojnić the rest of the convoy headed south on a minor road for twenty kilometres, passing through the small hamlets of Miholjsko and Maljevac. At the ICRC warehouse in Velika Kladuša, Patrick Davis remained to unload his truck. Diego continued to escort Frank and myself to Cazin and Bihać. We headed south on a minor road for twenty-five kilometres to Cazin. En route we passed through the hamlets of Krakaca and Coralici, and from Cazin to Bihać was a further twenty kilometres

Frank and I finished unloading part loads in Cazin and Bihać and returned to Velika Kladuša and Vojnić to rejoin the other members of our convoy. Apart from the withdrawal of Dave T truck from the convoy, the relief mission to Vojnić, Velika Kladuša, Cazin and Bihać, was completed without any further problems or incidents. On return to the ICRC delegation in Zagreb, we were all informed that, due to military action in the area, tomorrow's relief convoy to Tešanj and Maglai had been cancelled. Following that cancellation the ICRC delegation was hoping to re-arrange relief convoys to Banja Luka or Knin in order to fill the gaps in our rotas. In the meantime most of the drivers who were on the Tešanj and Maglai relief convoy would have a day off tomorrow (Tuesday).

Before leaving the ICRC delegation I checked my mailbox to find letters from my wife Anita, and my sons Martin and Lee. Although I was separated from my wife, we remained good friends. While I was on that mission in the former Yugoslavia, I let Anita have the use of my car. Unfortunately Anita's letter contained the news that she was involved in an accident with my car. Thankfully, she told me that she was not injured, but the car was a write-off. I was pleased to hear Anita was not injured in anyway, and to be honest I was not a bit upset about the car being a write-off. I think my reaction might have been a lot different if I had been home, but serving in a war zone had far more importance to me than my car. After all, cars can be replaced; human life can never be replaced. I phoned Anita to tell her not to worry, and that I would sort things out when I got home. Martin always addressed letters to me as Mr G. S. Budge (Del Boy). For those who are familiar with the scene on *Only Fools and Horses* when Del Boy falls through the bar. Then you would understand why Martin gave me that nickname, especially when I decided to lean on the bar at our local pub, and nearly fell through the raised bar hatch. I could have sworn the barmaid had put the hatch down after she collected empty glasses.

Tuesday 9th November 1993. Day off. Answered letters to Anita, Martin and Lee, and then attended the ICRC delegation in Zagreb to see if any relief convoys had been arranged for the rest of the week. After two hours of drinking coffee at the delegation, Beat finally had some good news for us. My re-arranged duties were as follows; Wednesday Banja Luka; Thursday Knin, an overnight stop; Friday return to Zagreb, and my original duty on Saturday to Banja Luka. Beat confirmed that I would be the only truck going to Banja Luka on Saturday, and asked me if I was okay with that

262

arrangement. I told him that was happy to be trusted to carry out the mission alone.

Wednesday 10th November 1993, Convoy duties to Banja Luka. in total seven trucks. The mission to Banja Luka was completed without any problems or incidents.

Thursday 11th November 1993, Convoy duties to Knin. in total eight trucks.

From Zagreb to Pacane the convoy encountered snow and icy conditions. From Gracac to Knin the road was clear, and we arrived in Knin at 1500 hours without any problems or incidents. We managed to get four trucks unloaded.

Friday 12th November 1993. Finished unloading the three remaining trucks, and departed Knin at 1020 hours, arriving in Zagreb at 1755 hours, without any problems or incidents. In the evening enjoyed a few *pivo*s with the lads. More Snow falling in Zagreb.

Saturday 13th November 1993. Today was going to be another fresh challenge. Not only was I travelling alone to Banja Luka, but I would have to drive in the most severe weather conditions that I have ever encountered in my life. My account of the day's events might be deemed to be far fetched by some but, with my hand on my heart, I can assure you all that it happened. Not in any way have I tried to dramatize that mission to Banja Luka.

Once again my day started by spending twenty minutes to clear the snow off my Land Cruiser. I arrived at the ICRC Warehouse at 0615 hours. Despite blowing the truck's air tanks when I returned from Knin last night, the air tank and some of the hydraulic pipes were frozen. I started the engine, hoping that eventually the heat from the engine would start to thaw the frozen components. At the same time I kept checking the truck's visual aids for any signs of the engine overheating, and the compression air tank gauge, which would indicate enough air for the use of my brakes. I informed the Zagreb radio room of my situation, and in order to inform Vanja and Branco who would be waiting for me at Gradiska Bridge at 0900 hours, I asked them to inform the Banja Luka delegation of my delayed departure. I told the radio room that I would be in touch when I was ready to depart.

At 0805 hours the air tanks finally start to fill with air. I informed the ICRC radio room that one truck was now ready to depart Zagreb en route to Banja Luka. The operator wished me a safe journey to Banja Luka, and a safe return to Zagreb. At the warehouse security gate, the security guard told me it was minus twenty degrees, and with the snow now coming down heavy he wished me luck on my mission. Everywhere I looked it was just a white blanket of snow.

On the highway there were no tyre tracks in the snow ahead of my truck. I was the only idiot foolish enough to be on the road. Each windscreen wiper had at least ten to twelve centimetres of snow clinging to its arm. I pulled over to clear the snow off the windscreen wipers. When I got out of the truck the snow was up to my knees. I thought, *What the bloody hell am I doing here?* But without sounding like a hero, my question was answered when I remembered that my truck was carrying medical supplies that could save someone's life. I continued my lonely journey through the snow; I was feeling like the only person alive in the world. Then I saw tyre tracks ahead, and from a distance there was another truck on the highway. I felt a bit relieved to see that I was not the only fool on the road. As I started to get closer to the truck ahead of me, I did not feel so alone. That was until I realized that that was not a truck, it was a snowplough! I would never forget the driver's face when I overtook his snowplough in my semi-trailer.

When I arrived at the checkpoints the guards give me that look of you-must-be-mad. I gave them my happy, determined look. After all Vanja and Branco were waiting for me at Gradiska Bridge, and I was running two hours late for our rendezvous. It was one of these situations that, once you have gone so far, you reached the point of no return, and I was never going to turn back. When I arrived at Okučani I contacted Vanja on my radio, to let her know that I would be at Gradiska Bridge in fifteen minutes. Vanja sounded relieved to hear my voice. They say only mad dogs and English men go out in the midday sun. Does that also apply to snow? I arrived at Gradiska Bridge at 1055 hours, where Vanja and Branco had been waiting for over an hour. I asked them if they got the message from Zagreb that I would be late, because of the adverse weather conditions. Vanja replied, "Yes George we got the message, but we wanted to get to Gradiska Bridge early, in case you got here before us." After the truck was searched, Vanja and Branco escorted me to Banja Luka, and we arrived there at 1145 hours.

Although the snow had now stopped Vanja and Branco wanted me to stay in Banja Luka for the night. I thanked them for the offer, but explained that I wanted to get back to Zagreb, because the lads would be waiting for me at Metor's Bar. Saturday night was the only night we could relax and have a drink without the worry of a convoy mission on the following morning. I asked Vanja to come back with me. With a sigh, Vanja said, "Oh, George, I wish I could." I could see Vanja was quite envious at the thought of enjoying a drink with the lads in Zagreb, and I would have loved to seen the lads' faces if I had walked in Metor's Bar with Vanja on my arm. Especially Erik!

The warehouse staff finished unloading my truck and I departed Banja Luka with my escort at 1410 hours. At Gradiska Bridge I thanked Vanja and Branco for their help, and continued my journey through the snow to Zagreb. When I reached the outskirts of Zagreb, I informed the ICRC radio room of my return. The operator replied, "Welcome back to Zagreb George." Never in my life have I felt such a sense of achievement as that.

I arrived back at the ICRC warehouse in Zagreb at 1750 hours. After I refuelled my truck and blew the air tanks on my truck, I went to the Transport Office to check next week's relief convoy rotas. My duties were as follows: Monday, day off; Tuesday, Banja Luka; Wednesday, Banja Luka; Thursday, Banja Luka; Friday, day off; Saturday, Bihać with an overnight stop; and Sunday return to Zagreb.

Although I had two days off next week, I would be on a relief convoy next weekend. It seemed that for most of the time now our regular weekends off were no longer going to be guaranteed. The severe Balkan winters had brought the need for relief convoys to operate whenever and wherever they could. Sometimes, to avoid military conflict areas, the weekends might be the only time relief convoys could safely operate in certain areas. The demand for food parcels, blankets, stoves and medical supplies were needed even more now, than before. It was not important what days you had off, even if we had to forgo our boozy weekends off, it was more important for the relief aid to get through to all the innocent victims of that terrible conflict.

I made my way back to my appartment to grab a bit to eat, and freshen up before meeting the lads and lasses at Metor's Bar.

I did not get to Metor's Bar until 2015, and by then the lads and lasses were all having a good time. Some of them were showing the worse for drink. Frank handed me a note from Andréa, it read: "Dear George! I am sorry about that night. I was here waiting for you; I was hoping that you would come. I had to go home early, just remember that I love you very much. I would call for you at your apartment on Sunday afternoon. I miss you, and love you very much. Andréa xxx"

Frank thought that I might have stayed in Banja Luka tonight. I did not want to use Andréa, she was a nice girl, but I am a bit of a coward when it comes to hurting a girl's feelings. Maybe the real reason and truth was that I was selfishly flattered, and enjoyed the adoration. Without making excuses to take advantage of any girl, but when you are in a war zone, you can't help living each day as if it was your last.

Sunday 14th November 1993. Tony and Queenie prepared lunch for Andréa and me. I spent the rest of the afternoon, and most of the evening, with Andréa.

Monday 15th November 1993. Felt guilty writing a letter home to Sandy, but I tried to condone my affair with Andréa by telling myself that, when I left the UK, Sandy and I were not an item. I spent some of the afternoon shopping, before meeting some of the lads at Metor's Bar. Heard news that UK driver, Timothy Lynes had to go back to the UK to sort out some domestic problems at home. I thought I was seeing things when my buddy Terry Gibson walked into Metor's Bar. You might remember Terry and I did our induction course together in London. We also drove through Europe together, in order to start our mission in the former Yugoslavia. Terry was telling me he had been transferred from Split to Zagreb. He was far from happy because he was settled in Split, plus it was a lot warmer in Split than in Zagreb. To be honest Terry was like a bear with a sore tooth. Not the happy-go-lucky guy I knew back in July and August. In some ways I suppose it was like a child starting at a new school. You don't know anyone, and you've got to start all over again making new friends. I tried to cheer Terry up, but not even my sick sense of humour seem to bring a smile to his face. With that battle lost, and before I lost the will to live, I made an excuse to return to my appartment.

Tuesday 16th November 1993, Convoy Leader duties to Banja Luka in total six trucks. The mission to Banja Luka was completed without any problems or incidents.

Wednesday 17th November 1993, Convoy duties to Banja Luka. in total eight trucks. The mission to Banja Luka was completed without any problems or incidents.

Thursday 18th November 1993, Convoy Leader duties to Banja Luka. in total seven trucks.

The convoy departed Banja Luka at 1425 hours to return to Zagreb. Ten kilometres outside Banja Luka in the town of Klasnice, some youngsters started throwing stones at the convoy. One stone broke the passenger's side window on Erik Gerrit Hengstman truck. My tail-end Charlie, Frank Karlsen, drove his truck into very large puddle spraying water over the youngsters that were throwing stones. With temperatures well below freezing, and driving a truck with no passenger's side window, that could not have happened at a worse time of the year. Between the drivers we were fortunate to find some blankets that enable Erik to keep warm and drive his truck back to Zagreb; by the time we got to Metor's Bar, Erik needed something a little stronger, and warmer, than our usual *pivos*.

Following that incident, the ICRC delegation in Banja Luka carried out an investigation. The outcome of the investigation led the ICRC to rumours from the local Serbian people in Klasnice; accusing the ICRC of supplying more relief aid to their enemies and not giving the same amount of relief aid to the Serbian people. When the youngsters heard their parents dicussing the lack of aid to Serbia, they decided to express their anger by throwing stones at our convoy. The ICRC delegation in Banja Luka held meetings with the local authorities, and visited local schools, to reassure them that all victims of war get treated equally. Irrespective of their nationality the ICRC would always remain neutral, and that the ICRC would never fail to remain impartial in all conflicts throughout the world.

Thursday 18th November 1993, Convoy Leader duties to Banja Luka. in total, six trucks. The mission to Banja Luka was completed without any problems or incidents.

Friday 19th November 1993, day off. Queenie was going back to Australia and, because Tony was on convoy duties in Knin, I went to the airport to see Queenie off. In three weeks' time Tony would finish his mission, and would be joining Queenie back in Australia. Although they were not much older than me, they had both been like a mother and father to me, and I was going to miss them both, especially Tony's cooking.

Saturday 20th November 1993, Convoy Leader duties to Bihać. in total seven trucks.

The convoy encountered heavy snow and icy conditions, snow chains were required. On the outskirts of Bihać the convoy successfully negotiated a minefield. We arrived in Bihać in the early afternoon, and were welcomed by a few children waving at the convoy. We manage to get all the trucks unloaded, and stayed the night at a French UN camp.

Before turning in for the night we had a few *pivo*s with our French hosts.

Sunday 21st November 1993. Overnight we had some heavy snowfalls. With all the trucks checked, we lined up, and were ready to roll as soon our Land Cruiser escort Diego Thorkelsson took his place at the head of our convoy. With Diego now in position, the convoy departed Bihać at 0800 hours.

Just outside Bihać the convoy approached a heavily mined area. Diego asked the checkpoint commander for assurances that all the mines had been uncovered from last night's snowfall, and were now visible to the drivers in the convoy. The commander reassured Diego that his men had uncovered all the mines, to allow the convoy to find a safe path through the minefield. Diego's Land Cruiser entered the minefield; I followed 100 metres behind him. I asked all the drivers to allow at least 100 metres between the trucks in the minefield. It was very clear to see the placement of the mines against the snow. They stood out like the proverbial sore thumb. Some of the mines in their rusty casings looked a bit past their sall-by dates. When driving through a minefield, you obviously feel so vulnerable. You could not drive your truck in a straight line through the minefield because, excuse my description, the mines were spread out like shit in a cow field. You had to zigzag through the minefield, with your head continually moving from left to right, checking both rear-view mirrors, as you observe the wheels of your trailer pass within fifty centimetres of the mines. The minefield was approximately 500 metres long, and my truck was just over half way through the minefield, when there was a loud *thud*! I felt my truck lift, my windsceen cracked in several places, the small window directly over my right shoulder had completely disappeared. Luckily my rear-view mirrors were intact, and the view I got of my trailer was not good. The canopy and some of the superstructure holding the canopy was missing; the back of the trailer resembled a scrap yard. From what I could see from my rear-view mirrors the wheels on my trailer were intact.

Aware that my truck had been in contact with a landmine, and I was now stationary, I gave myself a quick check to make sure I had no injuries. Vacuum from the blast of the explosion had turned my contact radio off. I switched my radio back on to inform Diego and the rest of lads that I was okay. I told Diego, "I have used my rear-view mirrors to carry out a visual check on the trailer, and wheels seem to be intact. Diego, rather than get out of my truck in the minefield, please continue through the minefield, hopefully I will drive the damaged trailer through the minefield. When we are safely out of the minefield we can then check the damage to the trailer."

Diego answered, "Okay George, best of luck!"

The convoy continued, and safely made it through the minefield. When we checked the damage to trailer, we found a large hole of about forty centimetres in the steel structure that went down the length of the trailer. The remaining superstructure that usually supports the canopy was tied and secured to the now flatbed trailer. Diego reported the incident to the ICRC delegation in Zagreb, and while we waited for their instructions, I lost count of the times someone said, "Are you all right George?"

They all meant well, and it was nice to know they were concerned. I think they were a bit surprised that I showed no signs of shock. The good news was that we all thought the trailer seemed roadworthy. The ICRC delegation in Zagreb instructed us to wait at the scene until the ICRC delegates from Bihać arrived, in order for them to make a report, and to take some photographs. While we waited I looked back over the minefield. In the distance, I could see the remains of the truck's canopy in the trees. When I hit the landmine Frank's truck was about 100 metres behind my truck. Frank said, "When I saw your trailer lift two metres in the air, I was so frighten you had been killed. I was relieved to hear your voice on the radio moments after you hit the mine."

I replied, "Frank, it was not my time to meet my maker."

The ICRC delegates from Bihać arrived and started taking notes, and taking some photos, and to that day I still have copies of all the photographs that were taken. We all stood by the wreckage having our picture taken, as if to say *Look what George done!* Diego went one better by having a picture of his head sticking through the hole in the steel structure. From that day on Diego had a new nickname for me – he always called me *The Bomber*.

The ICRC delegates from Bihać finished taking notes and photographs, and we got back on the road to return to Zagreb. En route through the small towns and checkpoints my truck attracted the look of dismay and astonishment from people and checkpoint guards. And when we arrived back in Zagreb my truck was the star attraction. Beat Mosimann and our Workshop Manager Eddie Heywood were soon on the scene to inspect my handiwork. Beat said, "George you were so lucky." Beat went to tell me that I had been taken off next week's convoy duties, to allow me to attend a medical, and to make out a report of the incident. Beat continued to assure me that in no way were they blaming me for that incident. That was just the ICRC standard procedure that follows incidents like that, your welfare was their main concern, not the damaged truck. My poor truck was now the tourist attraction of Zagreb.

That evening in Metor's Bar the attention I was receiving got a bit tiresome. Everyone wanted to know what it felt like to be blown up, and walk away without so much as a scratch on you. They could not understand how I could be so calm about it all. I tried to explain that we all deal with certain situations in different ways. I was not looking forward to being excluded from convoy duties next week.

Monday 22nd November 1993. Had a good night's sleep, no flashbacks or nightmares on yesterday's incident. Attended the ICRC delegation in Zagreb to make a statement, and was greeted by Diego who had just finished making his statement. Diego said, "Good Morning, Bomber."

I completed my statement with the emphasis that Diego had always ensured the safety of the convoy, especially when entering minefields.

Beat Mosimann informed me that on Wednesday I would be required to attend the ICRC delegation for a medical, and on Thursday you would be taken back to Bihać to meet the Bihać mililary commander. "He has requested to meet you."

I returned to my appartment to write some letters. Rather than writing the usual idle gossip, I guess I had a lot more exciting news to write about.

Tuesday 23rd November 1993. Had a haircut and went for a long walk around Zagreb.

Wednesday 24th November 1993. Attended the ICRC delegation in Zagreb for a medical. The doctor wanted to know if I was eating okay and asked me how much alcohol I consumed, and if I had been drinking more since the incident in Bihać on Sunday. I told him, "My appetite is fine, and my consumption of alcohol remained the same."

The doctor also asked me, if I was sleeping okay, and was I getting any disturbing flashbacks or nightmares following Sunday's incident in Bihać? I told him I was sleeping okay, but I was getting bored not being on convoy duties that week. After the doctor finished giving me a thorough medical, I had a meeting with a military expert. He showed me photographs of various landmines, and asked me to identify the landmines that I saw when going through the minefield in Bihać. The landmines I selected were old World War Two mines, and were very unpredictable, and unstable. It was possible that any large amounts of snow falling from the roof of the trailer's canopy would be enough to activate the landmine.

I spent the rest of the day shopping for souvenirs and presents to take home to my family when my mission ended in the later part of December.

Thursday 25th November 1993. Attended the ICRC delegation in Zagreb to meet Beat Mosimann and Diego Thorkelsson. Beat, Diego and I travelled to Bihać to attend a meeting with delegates, and a Bosnian military commander.

At the meeting in Bihać, the Bosnian general offered me his sincere apologies for the unfortunate incident with their landmine. I shook his hand, and thanked him for his concern and apology.

On the return journey to Zagreb, Beat asked me to attend another meeting tomorrow morning at 1000 hours in the ICRC delegation in Zagreb.

Friday 26th November 1993. Attended a meeting at the ICRC delegation in Zagreb. The enquiry report of that incident in Bihać stated: the landmines used by the Bosnian forces in Bihać were old and very unstable. For that reason, when the truck driven by Mr Budge activate the landmine, either by snow falling from the trailers canopy, or by the wheels of his truck coming into contact with a landmine that was not uncovered by the military authorities in Bihać. Either way, after the landmine was activated, there was a very slight delay in the landmine exploding. Which resulted in the landmine exploding in the centre of the forty-foot trailer, and not when either the wheels or snow had come into contact with the mine.

"It was possible that delayed explosion could have saved the life of Mr Budge. The fact that the trailer was not carrying any load helped the force of the explosion to continue on a vertical path. That could have also helped to save the life of Mr Budge. A loaded trailer could have had a much more destructive outcome, which would have resulted in the explosion spreading horizontal."

The ICRC delegates dealing with the landmine incident in Bihać recommended that I should have some leave. I replied to their recommendation stating that I had just less than a month to complete my mission in the former Yugoslavia, and I felt it was not practical for me to take leave and then return for two weeks to complete my mission. The delegates stated that I had taken part in over sixty relief convoys, they felt a short break would do me good, and offered to pay for a holiday, suggesting Italy, for an example.

I thanked them for their very kind offer, but explained that I was already having a break that week from the relief convoy work. And following the landmine incident in Bihać, I felt that I had not been affected with any health issues that could render me unfit to carry out my duties or otherwise continue my mission here with the ICRC.

The delegates looked at each other, and with a smile the head of the meeting said, "Okay George, considering the points that have brought to our attention, we feel you can return to convoy duties on Monday 29th November. We would like to wish you the best of luck for the remainder of your mission with us."

I was so delighted to be given the chance to finish my mission, and thanked the delegates for their kind understanding in that matter. Some of the lads who were not on convoy duties were waiting outside the meeting room when I came out. They seemed a bit anxious, looking at their faces anyone would think that I was about to face a firing squad. I took them out of their misery, and told them, "I'm sorry, but you'll have to put up with me on relief convoys for a little longer." The supid sods seemed quite pleased! To be honest it was going to be bad enough leaving these lads in just over three weeks' time. Taking leave, or any holiday that would shorten the time with the lads, would have been unthinkable. Not that we needed an excuse to attend Metor's Bar to celebrate, but that's where we ended up.

Saturday 27th November 1993, driver's meeting at the ICRC delegation in Zagreb. After Michel Brahier's accident, it was good to see him back from his sick leave break in Switzerland. You might remember that on the 3rd November, Michel turned his truck on its side while he was en route to Bihać, and escaped with a few cuts and bruises.

Following the landmine incident in Bihać last Sunday, it was sad to hear that Regis Pillet had decided to end his mission. Aparently that incident had affected Regis quite badly, he was getting all flashbacks and nightmares that I should have been getting. Regis told Beat that, when he volunteered for the mission in the former Yugoslavia, he did not expect to be driving through minefields, and could not face another experience like that again. I was a bit surprised, because Regis seemed okay on the day, he gave me plenty of moral support. Beat was telling me that sometimes you get a delayed stress reaction to any life-threatening situation, and that was why the delegates had requested you to take some leave.

Beat issued the relief convoy duties for next week. My duties were as follows: Monday, Banja Luka; Tuesday, Banja Luka; Wednesday, Bihać; Thursday, day off; Friday, day off; Saturday, Knin with an overnight stop; Sunday, return to Zagreb. The ICRC workshop had repaired my truck and, with a spare trailer, it was now ready for convoys. Beat closed the meeting in his usual jovial manner, wishing us all a relaxing weekend.

After a few *pivo*s at Metor's Bar, I went back to my apartment to get a bite to eat and get ready to join my other Norwegian friend Kent Furuly and Patrick Davis at the Astra Bars in the evening. That venue was a very popular night spot in Zagreb.

Later that evening at the Astra Bars, we got talking to some Russian girls. Kent was well aware of my love for rock'n'roll music, and set me up for a beauty when he told these Russian girls that I was a great rock'n'roll dancer. The next thing I knew that Russian girl grabbed my hand, pulling me onto the dance floor. She was a fantastic dancer; I came off that dance floor completely shattered, later to be told she was a professional dancer.

We continued to have a good evening with the Russian girls. I got on so well with one of the girls called Nadine, she was so beautiful and we seem to share a mutual attraction. Kent and Patrick also seemed to be enjoying the girls' company. All of a sudden Nadine went quiet; when I asked her if she was okay, she told me she did not feel very well. A few moments later she fainted. I went to the bar to get some ice wrapped in a napkin, and bathed her forehead. She opened her eyes, I told Nadine, "It's okay, don't worry you are safe. You just had a dizzy spell, and fainted." Nadine looked at me with a smile and said, "George, please take me home."

I told Nadine, "Sit down and sip that glass of water, while I arrange for a taxi to take you home." When the taxi arrived at Nadine's appartment, she asked me in for a coffee. We sat drinking coffee, and talked for a while, until Nadine said, "Excuse me George." I thought she needed to go to the bathroom. Yet five minutes later Nadine came back in the room wearing a see-through nightie, and said, "George you like? Please stay with me tonight."

I am no saint, after all we were both consenting adults. Jokingly, I felt I was playing my part for a closer diplomatic relationship with Russia. Nadine and I just enjoyed each other's company, and wanted to finish our evening on a high. In case you are wondering, no, I did not make Nadine faint when we made love.

Sunday 28th November 1993. For obvious reasons did not get a lot of sleep last night. Spent most of the day relaxing.

Monday 29th November 1993. After spending last week off convoy duties, it felt good to be back with the lads. Kent asked me if I enjoyed myself at the Astra Bar on Saturday night. Kent and the rest of the lads wanted to know all the sordid details between Nadine and me. Unfortunately for the lads, I am not the type of guy to talk about my sexual adventures. Convoy duties to Banja Luka, in total, eight trucks.

On arrival in Banja Luka, Vanja said, "I was so worried about you, when I heard about the landmine incident in Bihać, thank God you did not get hurt." I thanked Vanja for her concern, and told her not to worry, I was fine. I made a joke about it being the first time the earth has moved for me, since I have been on my mission. Vanja shyly giggled. The mission to Banja Luka was completed without any problems or incidents.

Tuesday 30th November 1993, Convoy duties to Banja Luka. in total seven trucks. The mission to Banja Luka was completed without any problems or incidents.

Wednesday 1st December 1993. Back on Convoy Leader duties to Banja Luka. in total seven trucks. The mission to Banja Luka was completed without any problems or incidents.

Thursday 2nd December 1993. Day off – I spent it shopping and writing letters.

Friday 3rd December 1993. Day off – finshed writing some letters, and went shopping for souvenirs and presents for my family back home.

Saturday 4th December 1993. The day's duty was to deliver a five-tonne truck to Knin. I was to meet my Land Cruiser escort, Diego Thorkelsson, at Sisak, and from there proceed to Knin.

About ten kilometres from Sisak, I picked up my radio microphone and said, "George to Diego, over."

Diego replied, "Good morning, Bomber, how are you today? Over."

I answered, "Hi, Diego, I am fine, how are you? Over."

Diego replied, "I am okay, Bomber, and happy we are not going through minefields today, over."

I answered, "Diego, don't you trust me going through minefields anymore? Over."

All I could hear was Diego laughing. I informed Diego that I was only ten minutes away from the rendezvous at the UN checkpoint in Sisak. Diego and I cleared the checkpoints at Sisak, the road ahead was very icy, and there were still large amounts of snow to negotiate en route.

When we reached Glina we heard gunfire. Diego slowed down, in case we came across any military action. Moments later we found out where the gunfire was coming from, as we joined the rear of a wedding convoy. They seem to have a wedding custom in the former Yugoslavia, whereby the entire wedding guest get into cars, blowing the horns, waving flags and firing guns into the air. Without the use of guns, I have seen the same noisy display in Zagreb. The convoy of flag-waving, horn-blowing cars drove around the streets of Zagreb for hours. After a while the monotonous noise gets on your nerves. The wedding party in Glina finally left the main road, which allowed Diego and me to continue our journey. Diego was certainly keeping a much faster paste than he normally would on convoy duties. At times I thought I was taking part in a rally, as my truck slid around corners.

When we reached Plitvice National Park, Diego's Land Cruiser hit a bank of ice and took off for a few metres before bouncing back on the road. I thought okay, Diego, whatever you can do I can do better. Upon hitting that ice bank my truck also took off, my truck bounced back on the road, and at the same time I was left bouncing on my seat. Bearing in mind I was driving a five-tonne truck in these icy conditions, it was easier for Diego in his Land Cruiser. Then I heard Diego laughing on the radio, he said, "Bravo Bomber! Bravo!" I know it sounds like we were driving like reckless idiots, but Diego and I would not have driven our trucks indiscriminately if there was any chance of meeting other road users on these roads. Because of the conflict in the former Yugoslavia the roads were virtually empty. You could drive for miles without seeing any traffic. People who were lucky enough to get fuel could only afford to buy fuel to use their vehicles in the towns. It was not safe for them to travel any distance from one town to another.

Considering the snow and icy conditions, we arrived in Knin in record time. Diego said, "Last week the same journey with six trucks in these conditions took us seven and a half hours. It took us six and a half hours." When I explained to Diego that where I lived in the south-west of England in a city called Plymouth, we very rarely get snow; and since it started snowing in the former Yugoslavia, that was the first time I had ever driven a truck in such severe weather conditions like that. Diego seemed astonished, and was full of admiration and praise regarding my driving ability in these conditions.

Diego and I had a pleasant surprise awaiting us in Knin. One of the Swiss delegates had finshed their mission, and was having a farewell party that evening in Knin. Diego and I arrived at the visitors' mansions. The mansion had a strong aroma of perfume. Some of the ICRC interpreter girls from

Vojnić and Kladuša were getting ready for the party. The smell of so many different perfumes was truly overpowering. With so many beautiful girls around you, it was difficult to know where to look next.

Many would have forgiven us for thinking we had died and gone to heaven. When I could finally get in the bathroom for a shower, and while in my birthday suit, one of the girls walked in on me. I don't know which one of us was more embarrassed. Diego and I were lucky enough to escort these young ladies to the party. I sat on that long sofa with some of the girls from Vojnić. Gordana said, "A couple of weeks ago I was in my parents' home when your convoy passed their house. When I saw the damage to your truck, I said to myself, *Oh my God*! Thankfully, you were so lucky not to get hurt."

I replied, "It's hard to explain why certain things happen in our lives, which results in the least likely outcome. Nevertheless, I am happy to be here to share that moment in time with you all." With the party in full swing, I thought I could dance; that was until Diego performed, and that guy could really dance. At one point Diego, while on his knees, slid from one side of the dance floor to the other, stopping at his dance partner's feet. It was like a scene from a movie. Bravo Diego! Bravo! We all had a good night, but it was time to escort the beautiful ladies back to our mansion. At the mansion we spent a little time talking to the girls, before we turned in for the night. Might I add, alone!

Sunday 5th November 1993. My eldest son's birthday, Martin was twenty-five.

Happy Birthday, son.

After I checked the truck that was exchanged for the truck I brought down yesterday, Diego and I departed Knin at 0830 hour, and arrived in Zagreb at 1550 hours, without any problems or incidents. I thanked Diego for a good weekend journey. After I refuelled the truck, I went to the Transport Office to check the rotas on next week's relief convoys.

My Duties were as follows: Monday, day off; Tuesday, Innsbruck, Austria to collect a Scania ten-tonne armour-plated truck, followed by an overnight stop in Innsbruck; Wednesday return to Zagreb with the Scania truck; Thursday, Banja Luka; Friday, Banja Luka; Saturday, convoy VIPs to Banja Luka with an overnight stop; Sunday, return to Zagreb with the VIPs.

What a mixed bag of work that was, at least I was getting a variety of duties next week. You could never get bored with your duties, here in Zagreb.

In the evening Tony and I went for a drink across the road from our apartment at the Bar Caffe. That was Tony's last week, his mission ended next Saturday. Over the last few months Tony and I have shared so many laughs. It's hard to see your mates leaving, especially when you have shared so much of the heartache of that conflict Tony helped me in so many ways, and it has been an honour to serve with him on my mission here.

Monday 6th December 1993. Day off. In order to purchase an engagement present for Frank and Dragica, the last couple weeks I have been collecting donations from the drivers, and ICRC staff. I managed to find a good jewellers and engravers, and ordered a silver plate to be engraved, *To Dragica and Frank Best Wishes on your Engagement. From All your Friends. Zagreb 1993*. I would collect that plate today, and we would present their engagement gift at the party in Metor's Bar that coming Friday night.

Tuesday 7th December 1993. My co-driver James Alexandersson and I departed the ICRC delegation in Zagreb at 0800 hours, en route in our Land Cruiser to Innsbruck to collect the Scania truck. Like Diego, James was from Iceland, he was a 6' 6" man mountain. Good guy to have around if there was any trouble.

That was the second mission in Zagreb for James; he was telling me that he was a Convoy Leader on his first mission. He sounded disappointed not to have that position on returning to Zagreb. I don't think James meant to drop hints that he should be a Convoy Leader instead of me. From Zagreb we headed north-west on highway E70 to Lubljana in Slovenia. Arriving at Lubljana we continued north-west on highway E61 to the Austrian boarder. At Villach we had a coffee break and, to give James a break from driving, I took my turn behind the wheel, and we continued north-west on highways E55 & E60. Arriving at Spittal we headed west on highway E66. At Seiaves we headed north on highways A22, A13, & E45, and arrived in Innsbruck at 1505 hours, covering 500 kilometres (312 miles). We located a company called Achleitner. The manager of Achleitner welcomed us and, before he gave us a guided tour of his factory, he booked James and me into a nearby hotel. Later that evening he arranged to take us out to dinner, that was followed by a short sightseeing tour of Innsbruck. It was a very pleasant evening; Innsbruck was truly beautiful town, also well known as a Winter Olympics venue.

Wednesday 8th December 1993. Wonderful breakfast at the hotel, it was just like being on holiday. Maybe that was a way the ICRC delegation in Zagreb got me to have a holiday break from convoy duties, who knows?

At Achleitner, James and I inspected the Scania that we were going to take back to Zagreb. The whole of the cab was armour-plated. The doors felt very heavy to open and shut. I guess that was to be expected, considering they were armour-plated. Before going into operation in Sarajevo, that truck would undergo a full service inspection in Zagreb. James and I decided that on the return journey to Zagreb, we would alternate our driving duties on the Scania and Land Cruiser that we drove here to Innsbruck. We thanked the manager for his very kind hospitality and departed Innsbruck at 0935 hours. Taking into account we now had to drive a brand new ten-tonne Scania truck, the journey back to Zagreb obviously took us a little longer.

I could not call that a mission, it was more like the type of work you might do in the UK. Let's just say the task to

Innsbruck was completed without any problems, and James and I arrived back in Zagreb at 1810 hours.

Thursday 9th December 1993, Convoy Leader duties to Banja Luka. The following drivers: Keith Descalchuk and Robin Creelman (Can), James Alexanderson (Ice), Michel Brahier (Swiss): in total five trucks. The mission to Banja Luka was completed without any problems or incidents.

Friday 10th December 1993, Convoy Leader duties to Banja Luka with the same drivers as the previous day: in total five trucks.

On the return journey to Zagreb the convoy was about to cross Gradiska Bridge when Vanja made radio contact, "Vanja to George, over."

I replied, "Receiving you Vanja, over."

Vanja replied, "George look to your left at the sunset, have you ever seen a better sunset? Over."

I replied, "Vanja it's beautiful, I am going to miss you all when I go home, over."

Vanja replied, "George please don't talk about going home. George, when the convoy clears Gradiska Bridge, please stop, over."

I replied, "Roger Vanja, out."

I got out of my truck to see what Vanja wanted. She said, "George, Branco and I wanted to thank you for everything you done for us, please accept that small gift from us."

Vanja and Branco had bought me a lighter in a soft leather case. I was so overwhelmed and speechless. All I could say was, "Thank you both so much, I would always treasure that lighter. It's been a real pleasure to know, and work, with you both, and from the bottom of my heart, I would miss you both so much."

I gave Vanja and Branco a big hug, and returned to my truck. And to that day twenty years later, I still have that lighter.

The mission to Banja Luka was completed without any problems or incidents.

That evening most of the drivers and ICRC delegates celebrated Dragica and Frank's engagement. Dragica and Frank were thrilled to bits with the silver plate we got them. Tomorrow Australian Tony O'Connor would go home. God, I hated these goodbyes, it's worse than saying goodbye to your own family. We had all shared a special moment in time, the experiences we had encountered on that mission in the former Yugoslavia, would live in our hearts until the day we died!

Saturday 11th December 1993. Arrived at the ICRC delegation in Zagreb to convey VIPs to Banja Luka. My passengers were: the head of delegation in Zagreb, Carlo Von Flue, administration delegate Jette Soerensen and field nurse Lisa Jones. Over the weekend, they would attend meetings and lectures in Banja Luka. They would also attend a public relations meeting with the authorities and citizens of Banja Luka.

We departed the ICRC delegation in Zagreb at 0700 hours, and arrived in the ICRC delegation in Banja Luka at 1015 hours, without any problems or incidents.

In the evening the Banja Luka delegation organized an informal party. I was talking to the Banja Luka workshop manager from Grimsby, Simon Baker. Across the other side of the room I saw Vanja talking to delegates. Vanja kept looking over and smiling. I went to buffet table to see what food was available. It was there Vanja joined me. She asked me if I was enjoying myself? I told her it was a pleasant evening. We chatted for a while. I enjoyed her company so much that I did not want to leave her side, but at functions like that you have got to circulate! When the guest had gone, Simon and I remained to have a drink and chat. I told him what I thought of Vanja, and what a remarkable lady she was. Simon told me everyone loves Vanja, she was a very popolar lady. After Simon and I finished drowning our sorrows, I wished him well and turned in for the night.

Sunday 12th December 1993. The delgates had more meetings today. Just before my VIPs were ready to return to Zagreb, I managed to see Vanja. I told her that I would see her next week on the convoys to Banja Luka. Luckily we exchanged addresses, unaware that would be the last time we would meet on my mission in the former Yugoslavia.

We departed Banja Luka at 1500 hours and arrived in Zagreb 1810 hours, without any problems or incidents.

At the ICRC delegation in Zagreb, Beat Mosimann informed the drivers that next week's relief convoys to Banja Luka, Knin and Bihać had been cancelled. All the drivers involved in these convoys were now on standby to take part in a prisoner of war evacuation near Split in Croatia. I felt sad that I might not see Vanja again.

In the evening at Metor's Bar Frank introduced me to Christian, from Switzerland. Christian had arrived yesterday to start his second mission in the former Yugoslavia. On Christian's first mission he was based in Zagreb as a Convoy Leader. He finished his last mission in July, as I was starting my mission. In an uncanny way our paths had crossed again.

Monday 13th December 1993. Attended the ICRC delegation in Zagreb, waiting to hear if the prisoner of war evacuation would take place near Split. Not the way I expected to spend my last week on my mission. Having said that, apart from the usual relief convoys to Banja Luka, Knin and Bihać, you could never guarantee or forecast what events came to light from one week to the next. Personally I found working for ICRC was varied and interesting, that was why you could never get bored on an overseas mission with the ICRC. While we were waiting, Frank introduced me to Alain Porchet, another driver from Switzerland. Alain had just come back from Split in order to take part in the prisoner of war evacuation.

No sooner than I was thinking how much more of coffee could I drink when, at mid-afternoon, we got the news: the prisoner of war evacuation was on. We were told that two convoys would be leaving for Split tomorrow morning, one at 0600 hours, and the other at 0630 hours.

I went back to my appartment to find I had new flatmate had moved into Tony's room. Australian Stuart Downes had returned to Zagreb for his second mission. Stuart and I had been on convoys together before he went back home. All these guys coming back to start their second missions. Word must have got around that I was going back home soon. Stuart had only just arrived, and would not be on tomorrow's convoy to Split.

Tuesday 14th December 1993. Two convoys were being sent to Split on a prisoner of war evacuation mission. The first convoy departed Zagreb at 0600 hours, and consisted of seven ten-tonne trucks.,

The second convoy departed Zagreb at 0630 hours, and consisted of seven thirty-tonne semi-trailers.

The second convoy met Diego, our Land Cruiser escort, at the UN checkpoint in Sisak. We headed south-west through Glina and Vojnić. At Krnjak we headed south through Slunj, Plitvice and Gospić. At Karlobag the convoy waited to board the ferry to Pag. Only four trucks boarded the first crossing to Pag, the four trucks waited in Pag until the remaining three trucks rejoined the convoy in Pag. When the convoy was complete we continued through Zadar, Šibenik, and arrived in Split at 1520 hours.

At the ICRC delegation in Split we were offered apartments. Christian told the delegate, "It's okay, we will sleep in our cabs." We all looked at each other with dismay; I could not stand by without addressing that issue. I told Christian that we did not mind sleeping in our cabs when the need required us to do so, but there was no need for us to sleep in our cabs tonight. "With respect, Christian, I think I speak for all the lads," I added, and told the delegate, "Thank you very much we will have an apartment." Christian was so stubborn, that night he decided to sleep in his cab, while the rest of us slept in a comfortable bed.

Wednesday 15th December 1993. The first convoy of seven ten-tonne rigid trucks departed Split at 0730 hours. We departed at 0800 hours in our seven thirty-tonne trucks. From Split we joined highway E65 on the south-east coastal road to Krilo, Omis, Brela and Baska Voda. At Makarska the convoy joined a minor road going through Kozica, Vrgorac, Ljubuški, Čitluk and Medjugorje.

At Kruševo, ten kilometres south-west of Mostar, the convoys encountered sniper fire, and was ordered to abort the mission. On return to Split the convoys stopped in Medjugorje for a break.

Medjugorje was delightful, picturesque town, so before returning to Split we decided to find a place for a coffee. I have never seen so many religious souvenir shops in one small town. After I found out why Medjugorje had so many religious souvenir shops, I could not leave that wonderful story out of my book: Medjugorje was a small mountain village located in the former Republic of Yugoslavia region of western Bosnia Herzegovina, twenty-five kilometres (sixteen miles) south-west of Mostar. That true story takes place in the Bijakovići section of Medjugorje.

On the afternoon of 24th June 1981 two girls, Ivanka Ivankovic, aged fifteen, and Mirjana Dragicevic aged sixteen, were returning home from a walk. Looking toward the hill called Crnica, Ivanka saw a bright silhouette of a woman.

Ivanka said to Mirjana, "It was the *Gospa*!' (*Our Lady*).

On the 25th June 1981 the two girls returned to the hill with four others. Their names are Vicka Ivankovic, aged sixteen, Ivan Dragivevic, aged sixteen, Maria Pavlovic, aged sixteen and Jakov Colo, aged ten. A figure in white was calling them to come up the hill. The children were somehow transported in some mysterious way to a beautiful lady who called herself, the Queen of Peace.

The Lady gives messages to all who see's her or the whole world. To date the Queen of Peace has left thousands of messages. At first the messages were almost daily. Now for the past several years they come on the 25th of each month. Though there are thousands of messages, there are six primary ones. The basic messages consist of, Conversion, Prayer, Fasting, Faith, Peace and Reconciliation.

The six childrenare also receiving ten secrets each. The secrets are of future chastisements because of sin. The visionaries know the day and time the messages would be revealed. The secrets would be released to the world one at a time through a priest, (now chosen.) Prior to each chastisement, the priest would receive a parchment. He would not be able to read the parchment except with much prayer, fasting and help from the Lady. The messages about chastisement would be announced to the world three days before the event was to take place.

Ivanka, Mirjana and Jokov have received all ten secrets, they no longer see the Lady except on special occasions. The remaining visionaries have each received nine of the ten secrets, and they still see the Lady almost every day. In an interview with Vicka on the 8th September 1988, she described the first apparitions of the Lady. Here is the interview:

The first day, Ivanka and Mirjana went for a walk because we sometimes went for walks on that road. In the afternoon, when I got up, I went and followed them. As I approached them Milka, sister of Mirjana, called to hurry.

I thought that they were looking at something on the road, maybe a snake. From a distance it seemed to me that they were looking on the road, not the hill, but when I came close they were saying, "*Ma Vicka, Gospa.*" Which means: *Look, Vicka, there's Our Lady.*

"What do you mean, *Our Lady*?" was my reaction. I turned quickly, threw away my shoes and ran back home straight away. I mean I ran away.

At that moment Ivan came along. I said, "Ivan, they are claiming that they see Our Lady. We do not have to see but at least let us go closer."

Ivan, who was carrying some apples said, "Let's go."

He was full of courage by saying that we would go, but as we drew nearer to them I turned around, and Ivan had run away. He was not there and I was alone.

At that moment I was alone and I could not go back or forward. Something stronger kept me there and then, my God, they were calling me. "Come Vicka, come!" (They asked me to come closer.) I was afraid. I must not even look at them especially not at the hill where *Our Lady* was. While I was standing there at the spot wondering where I would go, suddenly something very strong possessed me and, in a moment, I was beside them. When I came close to them I did not at first look straight to the hill. They were telling me, "Come on Vicka, look Our Lady is waving at us, while keeping something in her hand."

I was afraid. I was afraid to look towards the hill. Then suddenly, maybe with the grace of God, I looked at the hill, and Our Lady was there in front of us.

There are no words for man to descibe that day. It was happiness because I saw Our Lady but still we are all human and I wondered if she would come tomorrow.

On the second day in the afternoon the three of us, me, Mijana and Ivanka, went walking. We said that we would go and see if Our Lady was coming. We expected to see her but still wondered if she would come. We went along the same road to the same spot as the previous day. Ivanka was again first to see Our Lady.

I returned home to bring Marija and Jakov because after the first day they asked me, "Vicka, if you see Our Lady, come and get us. We do not have to see her but we would like to be with you."

So I went to bring the two of them but they were already on their way to the hill.

We had nothing on our feet and it seemed that we were not walking on the ground but gliding above it. Suddenly we found ourselves at the apparition site. On that second day those who were not so shy could ask questions but mostly we were praying with Our Lady.

On the third day I took a glass of holy water and sprinkled it at Our Lady, I said, "If you are Our Lady, stay with us but, if you are not, leave us alone."

The Lady smiled, and the water I threw just flowed off her dress.

Since the children's revelations on witnessing the apparition of Our Lady, thousands have made a pilgrimage to Medjugorje to pray, and feel the love of Our Lady.

After we finished our break in Medjugorje we continued our journey back to Split. En route we travelled on winding mountain roads. Norwegian Frank Karlsen was travelling behind my truck when, suddenly, over the radio I heard Frank's trembling voice say, "Oh my God."

I replied, "Frank are you okay? Over."

Frank, voice still trembling, answered, "George, I misjudged that bend, my wheels were right on the edge of the road. I thought I was going off the mountain. Shit, it's a long drop off that mountain road, over."

I replied, "Frank, do you want Christian to slow the convoy down? Over."

Frank answered, "No, it's okay, George, just a lapse of concentration on my part, roger out."

I am pleased to say that both convoys arrived back in Split without any further problems or incidents.

At the ICRC delegation in Split, negotiations were taking place with all the military authorities in that conflict. The ICRC delegates now had to consider if another attempt could safely be made to repatriate prisoners of war. While that was being considered we spent most of the afternoon kicking our heels. Swiss driver Alain Porchet received some bad news, from Zagreb, that his grandfather had passed away. Obviously Alain was very upset, it's not easy to hear sad news like that when you're on a mission in a war zone. As soon as possible, the ICRC was now making all the necessary arrangements to get Alain back to Switzerland.

At 1800 hours, the ICRC delegation in Split announced the cancellation of the mission to repatriate prisoners of war.

The ICRC delegation in Zagreb had arranged a flight to Switzerland for Alain. The only problem for Alain was the flight departed Zagreb at 1015 hours tomorrow morning, and there was no connecting flight from Split to Zagreb. The only way Alain could make that flight was to travel overnight by road. The ICRC would not let Alain make that journey alone in a war zone overnight. But if enough drivers volunteered to travel in a overnight convoy to Zagreb, Alain would have plenty of time to make the flight in Zagreb tomorrow morning, and there was no way we was going to let Alain miss his flight. Diego, Christian, Robin, Keith, Frank and I, all members of Alian's convoy, volunteered to travel overnight with Alain in order for him to catch his flight. Patrick Davis from the other convoy would also join our overnight journey: in total eight trucks.

That act of camaraderie demonstrated just how close we all where. It did not matter if you were from a different country or culture. When one of your colleagues were sad, you were also sad. We all shared the pain and joy on our mission, we were all one big-hearted family, and supported each other through good and bad times.

All our trucks had now been refuelled and checked, and we departed Split at 1950 hours. The convoy arrived in Pag at 2135 hours, with only one ferry operating from Pag to Karlobag, we had a thirty-minute wait. When the ferry arrived, only six trucks from our convoy boarded the first crossing. Frank Karlsen and Patrick Davis remained in Pag to board the next crossing, while we waited for them in Karlobag to rejoin the convoy. Christian, our Convoy Leader tried to make radio contact with Frank and Patrick, but Christian was not getting any reply. They could not have been in their trucks at the time Christian was trying to contact them. Some months ago, I remembered the fun we had with Dave T when I impersonated Patrick's voice; Dave T really thought he was talking to Patrick. I wondered if Christian would fall for it?

Moments later I heard Christian on the radio, he said, "Christian to Frank, or Patrick, over." There was a pause, and no answer. I thought that was my chance to have a bit of fun.

Again, Christian said, "Christian to Frank, or Patrick, over."

I replied, "That was Patrick receiving you Christian, over."

Christian replied, "Patrick, are you on the ferry yet? Over."

I replied, "Sorry Christian, we fell asleep and missed the ferry, over."

Christian replied, "Oh no, Patrick where was Frank? Over."

I replied, "He's still asleep, over."

Christian replied, "Shit!"

A few moments later the ferry arrived in Karlobag with Patrick and Frank's trucks on board. Christian was so relieved, but when they told him he'd been talking to me, and not Patrick, Christian started banging his head on the side of his truck.

Thursday 16th December 1993. At 0005 hours with the convoy reunited in Karlobag, we continued our journey back to Zagreb. Frank and Patrick were still laughing at the bit of fun we had at Christian's expense. Even Christian saw the funny side of it. The convoy successfully negotiated checkpoints, and arrived in Zagreb at 0625 hours.

We had been on duty for over twenty-three hours, and we all had eyes like piss holes in the snow. That convoy was expected to be occupied on the prisoner evacuation mission for the rest of the week. With no further relief convoys arranged for us, I refuelled my truck for the very last time, parked up, stopped the engine and blew the air tanks. I felt so sad, that truck had played a big part in my mission, as I started to walk away, I could not stop myself from looking back at my truck for one last time.

Before we all went back to our apartments to get some well earn sleep, Alain thanked us all for making it possible for him to go back to Switzerland today. At 1300 hours, with bleary eyes I woke up. I thought, a pot of tea, shower, shave and a long walk and I would soon be back in the land of the living.

Like so many towns and cities throughout the world, the Christmas atmosphere in Zagreb was very apparent with the sound of carols. No war could ever cancel Christmas.

In the evening I met the lads at Metor's Bar. It felt strange that I would not be on any more convoys with these special guys.

Friday 17th December 1993. Completed some last-minute shopping for souvenirs and gifts to take home. I came across Edit in the town centre, we were both surprised to meet. When I moved into my first apartment in August, Edit was the housekeeper. We went for a coffee and chat. I told Edit that one day I would like write a book on my mission in the former Yugoslavia. I asked Edit if she would like to tell the story of her evacuation from her home town of Petrinja. And would she mind if I include her story in my book? Edit promised to write her story for me, I thanked Edit for that, and for everything she did for us. Before we said our goodbyes, we exchanged addresses.

In the evening I arranged to met, and have a drink with my present housekeeper called Goga. It was just my way of thanking Goga for keeping the apartment clean, and doing all my washing and ironing. After a very pleasant evening, we also exchanged address and promised to write to each other. At that rate, I would be writing to so many people, would I have time to write a book?

Saturday 18th December 1993, the penultimate day in Zagreb; sadly no need to go to the drivers' meeting. I felt envious of the drivers who were about to receive their relief convoy duties for next week. I went across the road from my apartment, to the Bar Caffe for a coffee, and to say goodbye to the owner Zvonimir Papec, and his staff Jadriawka and Jva. I then arrived at Metor's Bar to say goodbye Metor, Mirra, Andréa, Goran and Nina, and to meet the lads hoping they were not going to talk about next week's convoy duties.

After a few *pivo*s with the lads, I accompanied Frank, Dragica and Zana to their parent's house. That gave me a chance to say my goodbye to Dragica and Zana's parents.

Back in July I was saying goodbye to my family and friends. In a positive way, I knew I would see my family and friends again when I returned from my mission in the former Yugoslavia. But saying goodbye to so many newfound friends in Zagreb was a lot harder because there was no guarantee that I would ever see them again.

Late afternoon, Frank, Dragica, Zana and I went to the Zagreb Christmas fairground. After what I would have called a moderate fairground ride, poor Frank's face was as white as a sheet, and he was feeling a bit sick. As a leaving present, Frank and Dragica kindly presented me with a beautiful clock and, yes, to this day it is still in working order. Fortunately, the night before I was leaving Zagreb, the ICRC delegation had arranged a Christmas party for all the ICRC staff. The venue had a disco and a bar, in fact everything we all needed to have a really good Christmas party. With the party in full swing Dragica was feeling unwell. Before Frank took her home, Dragica said, "George please promise me, you will make sure Zana gets home safely."

I told Dragica not to worry, and promised to make sure Zana got home safely.

Some months ago I mentioned going to Irena's eighteenth birthday party. While I was getting drinks at the bar, Irena came up to me and said, "George my little Devil Eyes, how are you?"

I replied, "I am fine, Irena. You are looking well."

Irena went on to tell me that Dave T had invited her to come to the UK. She asked for my address and telephone number so she could come and see me in the UK next summer. I gave Irena my contact details; little did I know that in six weeks time the beautiful and lovely Irena would loose her precious life in a freak swimming pool accident. I would never forget Irena, she was full of all the joys of spring, and had all the warmth of summers in her heart.

God Bless you, Irena, R.I.P.

I spent a good part of the evening on the dance floor. There was one particular girl who, every time I looked at her, she was looking in my direction and smiling. I had seen her several times at the delegation. But I had made a promise to Dragica to make sure Zana got home okay. So I never asked that girl for a dance, or to take her home. I have often wondered if I missed out on something special with that girl. But I believe the course of life composes of 50% destiny, and 50% in the choices make in your life.

Why does time go so quickly when you're enjoying yourself so much? I think we have all been there. James Alexandersson from Iceland had charge of a Land Cruiser, earlier in the evening, so he had promised to take a few us of home. That was until James had attempted to drink the bar dry, for James had now had far too much to drink and he could hardly stand, let alone drive. We tried everything to get the Land Cruiser keys off James, but he was not having any of that. I told the lads there was no way I or Zana would get in a vehicle with James driving in that state. I ordered a taxi for Zana and me. At Zana's parent's house I thanked her for a lovely evening, and wished her a good-night.

Sunday 19th December 1993. I finished some last-minute packing. Frank, Dragica and Zana arrived at my apartment. We went to the ICRC delegation in Zagreb. Met Dave T, Robert, Erik, Walter and the rest of the lads; I wished them all a safe mission. Robert Fenwick told me that, after last night's party, James Alexandersson crashed his Land Cruiser. He was not injured, but hearing that I was glad Zana and I did not travel with James. Dragica thanked me for making sure Zana got home safely last night. Beat Mosimann thanked me for a successful mission, and wished me well for the future.

After all the sad goodbyes at the delegation, Frank, Dragica and Zana accompanied me to the airport for the final goodbyes. One of the finest events of my life had now come to an end. I would treasure the memories of that adventure until the day I die.

CHAPTER TWELVE

Coming Home

It was a beautiful sunny day, with blue sky as far as the eye could see. On board the Croatian Airlines flight to London via Split, I had time to reflect on the last five months of my mission. As we flew over the former Yugoslavian en route to Split, I looked down at the countryside with all the shades of greens, browns and the red-top roofs, I wondered how much of that ground I have travelled on, over the last five months.

We didn't seem to be in the air for to long before arriving in Split, a far cry from the nine- to ten-hour journey to Split on convoy. In Split the passengers were required to leave the aircraft for just over an hour while the luggage and passengers in Split were being booked in. Before the Zagreb passengers could re-board the aircraft, we were required to have our passports checked.

The airport official looked at my passport, looked at me, looked again at my passport, and again at me, and said, "You are English?"

I replied, "Yes."

He said, "Your complexion is a lot darker than your passport photo, you look Bosnian."

I replied, "Lots of sunbathing."

He smiled, and stamped my passport and wished me a pleasant flight. Perhaps he thought I was trying to leave the country on a false passport. The food and service on Croatian

Airlines was excellent, and the flight from Split to London (Heathrow) only takes two hours. I arrived back in London at 1700 hours. Hard to imagine coming home from a war zone, in just two hours.

After I went through customs I got a taxi to a hotel, which was near the British Red Cross headquarters in London, where I would be required to attend my mission debrief tomorrow morning. At the hotel I had a refreshing shower before taking a stroll and getting a bite to eat. I had only walked about 500 metres from the hotel when I came across homeless beggars, sat on the pavement. That was a stark reminder to me that every city in the world has unfortunate people who have fallen on hard times. The only difference is that some cities have more destitute people than others. Thankfully, unlike Zagreb, we do not have beggars on our streets who are very young children, or young women with tiny babies in their arms. To quote an old cliché, 'There but for the grace of God, go I'.

Last July, at Felixstowe, just before boarding the ferry to Zeebrugge, my last meal in the UK was fish and chips. You could not get fish and chips in Zagreb. On my return to the UK, I was not prepared to take any bets on what my first meal would be. Come on, you can't blame me for wanting to get my fish and chips fix! After all, it's been five months. It was not hard to find a very good pub in London that also served excellent food. As I got stuck into my fish and chips, I thought about the lads in Zagreb, and what they would be doing at that moment in time. I guessed that, by now, that most of them would be at Metor's Bar. God, I was missing them already! All of a sudden I felt I didn't belong here, I felt like an alien in my own country. I don't want you to feel sorry for me, but I also was feeling quite lonely. Over the last five months I have never been alone until now. It felt so strange not to listen to banter from the lads in Zagreb. Yet I did not want to start drowning my sorrows in drink. So I finished my meal and drink, and went back to the hotel to phone my family, and Sandy. I let them all know that I was safely back in the UK and, depending on how long the de-brief would take at the

British Red Cross HQ tomorrow, I would either be home tomorrow night or sometime on Tuesday. Talking to them all lifted my spirits somewhat, and helped me to feel a little more at home. I guess it was going to take a little while for me to settle back into a peaceful enviroment.

Before attending the debrief at the British Red Cross HQ at 0930 hours, I enjoyed a very tasty breakfast at the hotel. On arrival at the British Red Cross HQ I was welcomed by Ann Kerr, the Overseas Personnel Officer; it was nice to see Ann again, and we had a pleasant informal discussion. To be honest, my mission's debrief did not take as long as I thought it might, and by 1100 hours, I was on my way back to the hotel to check out and get a taxi to Paddington Station. The next train to Plymouth was at 1410 hours, I had an hour to spare, which allowed me to call my family and Sandy to let them know that my train would arrive in Plymouth at 1735 hours. Unfortunately, when the train arrived at Taunton Station, there were railway line problems at Cullompton. All the passengers for Plymouth and Penzance were told to leave the train, and wait for coaches to take us to Exeter, where we would board another train to complete our journey. That delay meant that I would not arrive in Plymouth until 2000 hours.

When I finally completed my journey to Plymouth I was surprised to see Sandy, and her children Ryan and Adam on the platform. They had been waiting for me at Plymouth station for three hours.

I spent the next couple of days at Sandy's house. While I was away, my car had been written off in that accident. So I hired a car for two weeks, which allowed me to get around meeting my estranged wife Anita, my sons, Martin and Lee, my father and my sister, Shirley and brother-in-law, Peter.

With only three days left before Christmas day, I spent most of them meeting all my family and friends. Sandy kindly asked my father to have Christmas dinner at her house. As for me, I was still trying to get my head around being back home from a war zone. It felt so strange, and unreal. In Plymouth's shopping centre the streets were crowded with people doing their last-minute shopping. Every Christmas, people spending more money than they earn. So many people in Plymouth carrying more bags than they could manage. Unlike most of the people in Zagreb, Banja Luka, Bihać, Knin and many other places in the former Yugoslavia, who would lucky to have a Christmas dinner on the table, let alone buy presents for their children.

Originally I thought it was a good idea to come home for Christmas, but to experience a war zone country near Christmas, and then your own country full of materialism, made the transition just a bit more than I could handle. Hindsight would have been served well if I decided not to come home until after Christmas. On Christmas Day, after Sandy had served a wonderful Christmas lunch, my father and I sat in the lounge to allow our Christmas dinner to settle. Ryan and Adam sat on the floor in front of us. They had put all their selection box sweets into separate polythene bags. Adam kept looking at Ryan's bag of sweets, and asked Ryan why he had more sweets than himself. Adam then accused Ryan of taking sweets from his bag of sweets. All hell then broke loose over these sweets until Sandy intervened. I could not help myself thinking about the children in Tešanj; when I gave them sweets, I saw all the children sharing their sweets with some of the children who did not have any. Ryan and Adam's actions on Christmas Day just confirmed my feeling, that it was a big mistake coming home for Christmas.

On Boxing Day I had a long telephone conversation with Frank, Dragica and Zana; after I put the phone down I felt very emotional not to be out there with them. I told Sandy that I needed to go to my apartment to check the mail that had been sent to me while I was away. Sandy got a little upset, and in Sandy's words she accused me of retreating to my *Ivory Tower*. I reassured Sandy, and asked her to understand that I have been away for over five months, and that my son Martin, who had been looking after my apartment while I was away, told me I had a large pile of mail to get through at the

298

apartment. Sandy seemed to see reason when I told her I would be back tonight.

With Christmas now over, I spent most of next few days before the New Year looking for car. After the New Year, I would return to work for my employer Crown Berger Paints, and because of the unsociable working hours, I would need a car to get to and from work. Crown Berger Paints has been very good to me, especially allowing me to have leave to work for ICRC in the former Yugoslavia. I am also fortunate to have a job to come back to; many of drivers that finished their missions in the former Yugoslavia did not have a job, when they returned to their homeland.

Tuesday 4th January 1994. I returned to work in the UK. When I was in the former Yugoslavia, on a trip to Knin, I told Diego we don't get much snow in south-west of England. Guess what welcomed me back to work on my first day, in the south-west of England? Yes, snow! The roads of Cornwall had a heavy snowfall last night. Nowhere near as bad as the snow falls in the former Yugoslavia. But all the same a nice welcome back to my job here. I found my first day at work very strange; apart from one mission to Banja Luka, I always had the company of the lads on every convoy, or the company of passengers in my truck. Quite frankly I found my first day back to work very boring compared to the exciting adventures on the convoys in the former Yugoslavia. Every time I looked in my rear-view mirrors no longer did I have the view of Red Cross trucks in my convoy. Now and again I would drift into the memories of my mission in the former Yugoslavia. Always wondering what lads were doing now, and where their convoy was going today. I was beginning to feel like the boy in the *Home Alone* movies. It was obviously going to take me a while to settle back into my work in the UK. Hopefully once I get my first week out of the way, I could start putting my mission in the former Yugoslavia in the halls of history, and get on with my life.

Over the next few weeks I received letters from Vanja, Edit, Goga, Zana, Dragica and Frank, Kent, Ross, Stuart

(Skippy), Tony and Queenie, Eddie and Anita, Diego, Erik, Robert and Dave T. I was obviously going to spend a lot of my spare time answering all these letters. These letters kept me up to date with all the latest news from the former Yugoslavia and what was happening in their own lives when they went home.

At the end of January Dave T phoned me from Zagreb, with the heartbreaking news that Irena had died in a swimming pool accident. It took while to come to terms with that shocking news. Irena was so young and beautiful, she had so much to look forward to in her life. At the Christmas party before I came home, Irena asked me for my address and telephone number. Irena told me she was going to visit me in the summer. How fragile and short life can be, we all take so much for granted, and we look forward to our tomorrows. Unfortunately, at times, the tomorrows never come.

For the rest of the year the letters continued to arrive with the latest news. Dragica wrote, "I am pregnant, and would be going to Norway with Frank when he finishes his mission here. Frank is now a Convoy Leader. Dave T has already told you about Irena, it's so sad, and a very big shock to all who knew her. George, do you remember Irena and me always called you Devil Eyes? It was only because your eyes sparkled with lots of fun and laughter. George, it's not the same without you here. We all miss you so much."

In October 1994, I visited Dragica and Frank in Norway, meeting Frank's family and friends. Zana was also there paying them a visit, it was nice to see Zana again, and of course to see Dragica and Frank's baby called Thor-Daniel. What was not nice to see was how much Dragica and Frank had changed. In Zagreb, it was so apparent from their body language that they were both very much in love each other. But when I saw them in Norway, I could not believe that was the same couple that I saw in Zagreb. They both seem to be so unhappy with each other. Frank was always finding fault with Dragica. Was it love in a war that had turned sour, or the responsibility of a child? Perhaps it might be a bit of both. I remember Australian Tony saying, "George that was not the real the world in that war zone."

Sadly, a few years after my visit, Dragica and Frank separated. Frank went on another mission with the ICRC in Angola and met a girl from the UK. Dragica remained in Norway, and met a Croatian guy called Zoran.

From Australia Tony and Queenie wrote regularly. Tony was finding it difficult getting work in Australia, but both were happy and in good health.

Goga sent me some romantic letters and a Valentine's card. Goga wrote, "What does it mean when you have everything, but lose your soul? When you're sad and cry at night, don't worry. Just close your eyes and I would come to you."

Goga's words were very flattering, but unfortunately Goga was just a bit too young for me. In a quirky twist of fate, destiny led Goga to meet ICRC driver Kevin Webster in Zagreb. Kevin was also from my home town of Plymouth. In 1995, Goga came to the UK, and married Kevin in Plymouth.

I was receiving a letter about every three to four weeks from Vanja. Love was in the air, with a Swiss delegate called Phillppe Boschung. Phillppe had been to meet Vanja's parents. In the not to distant future, Vanja would return to Switzerland to marry Phillppe, and before they settled down to have children Vanja and Phillppe both served on another mission with ICRC in Peru. Vanja visited me in the UK in 1995 and 2003.

The last time I saw Edit in Zagreb she promised to write to me, and write her story for me to put in that book. Edit never broke her promise to me. I received regular letters from Edit, in one she wrote, "I wish you lots of happiness, love and joy, and may all your wishes come true. Often thinking of you, your friendly eyes and words, which helped me a lot through my bad times. I hope to see you again some time." Some months later, I received Edit's letter and her story, on how the conflict in the former Yugoslavia affected her family and friends in Petrina, Croatia.

That was my coming home story, not easy at the start, but in time you just move on. Having said that, even to that day in 2012, the memories of the wonderful camaraderie shared by so many, would never be forgotten. In 2013, on the 20th anniversary of my mission, I plan to return to the former Yugoslavia, and visit some of the areas that were badly affected by the conflict. It would be wonderful to see these areas vibrantly at peace.

CHAPTER THIRTEEN

Edit's Introduction and Letter

Edit Posavec Kolic was born in Sisak, Croatia, on the 10th January 1966. Later her family moved to Petrinja. Edit attended the primary and secondary schools in Petrinja and graduated in 1987 at the Department for Visual and Design Clothes and Textile Fabrics. Until 1991, Edit continued to work in Petrinja at the Visual Shaping Design of Authentic Weavers' Activities, and Souvenirs in the advertising department.

During the Serbian occupation of Petrinja from 1991 to 1995, Edit spent some time in Switzerland, and Italy, and returned to Croatia to work for the ICRC in Zagreb. Edit was an established artist in the watercolour technique. Her work has been given the seal of approval by experts in her field, including Sinisa Bozicevic, Professor Branko Cacic, Professor Juraj Baldani and Professor Tonko Maroević.

Edit was a winner of the acknowledgment by the Cultural and Educational Parliament of Croatia, for the participation at the republic meetings of fine arts in Varaždin, Karlovac, Zagreb and Split. Edit held exhibitions of her work in Petrinja, Sisak, Zagreb, Grožnjan, Virje and Varaždin in Croatia. Also at Ljubljana, Postojna and Brežice in Slovenia, and Eichenau in Germany. Edit participated in many group exhibitions in Croatia, Italy and Switzerland. She was a participator of numerous artists' meetings throughout the former Yugoslavia and Italy.

Edit somehow manages to find time for some charity work, with an auction of paintings to aid the building of a University Library in Zadar. Edit also aids the Anti-Cancer League in Zagreb, and the Association of the Blind and partially sighted people in Sisak.

When I look at Edit's resume, it seems a far cry from that talented young lady who was undertaking the housework of our apartment for the ICRC in Zagreb. Just before I completed my ICRC mission in the former Yugoslavia, and returned to the UK, I asked Edit if she would kindly write a story on the events that led to the Serbian occupation of her home town Petrinja, and how the Serbian occupation affected her life, and the lives of her family and friends. Edit sent me that letter, and tells her story in Chapter Fourteen:

Dear George,

My country Croatia was part of the Yugoslav states from 1918 to 1941, and from 1945 to 1991. While Croats lived in the Yugoslav states they suffered economic and national repression. We also lived in fear of the constant great Serbian aspiration to destroy the Croats.

As soon as the possibility of establishing non-communist parties in Croatia was announced, the result was a new atmosphere which spread, and was felt all over Croatia as early as the beginning of May 1989. That possibility meant the chance for Croats to make their centuries-old dream of forming their own country of Croatia come true. Always in the past, somebody tried to conquer our country, or steal our land. Croatia's coast with the Adriatic, and the Islands, plus the beauty throughout Croatia made my country a target for ambitious warlords. For decades Croats never succeeded to be independent, and decide their own destiny.

Croatia's history dates back to the seventh century. Croats on their own land, but never free from persecution. That natural and legally justified ambition was soon opposed by the aggressive aspirations of the Serbs, not only from Yugoslavia, but also the Serbs who lived in Croatia. Their aim was to establish a Greater Serbian nation, relying on the support of the Serbian JNA. A general atmosphere of tension was created in the whole of Bosnia, my hometown Petrinja was not spared.

The rebellious Serbs and the JNA took up arms against Croatia and the Croatian population, and attacked the Croats' homeland.

The Serb aggressors felt hatred for everything in connection with Croatia and Catholicism, and as a result they tortured, killed and persecuted Croats, who were forced to defend their homes and to save the lives of their families and themselves.

During the Patriotic War, my hometown Petrinja suffered extensive damages. As many as 121 patriot soldiers were killed defending Petrinja, six were recorded missing. For most of the soldiers who lost their lives, going by their place of birth sixty-seven came from Petrinja, thirty-four from Sisak, six from Glina and fourteen were from the rural areas in the district. The majority were Roman Catholics and Croat nationals, apart from one Serb and one Muslim who had chosen to fight the Serb aggressors to defend Petrinja. Seventy-one soldiers were married, of which fifty-one of them who lost their lives defending Petrinja had very young children. The recorded figures show that two soldiers had four children, five soldiers had three children, twenty-four soldiers had two children, and twenty soldiers had one child.

In order to defend its national state territory, as well as our culture and existence. Croatia was forced to form armed defence units. That was not suitable for some parts of the world or Serbia. The Serbian President Milošević had support from most of the Eastern Bloc countries, and some parts of Europe, because they did not want to see Yugoslavia fall apart and embark on a civil war. The Yugoslavian republic of Slovenia no longer wanted to be part of Yugoslavia, and declared Slovenia to be an independent state.

Milošević reluctantly let Slovenia seek independence from Yugoslavia, but planned to make Croatia and Bosnia Herzegovina into the Great Serbia. Milošević, as the main actor and antagonist in the Yugoslav conflict, orchestrated the Great Serbian ambition, and was prepared to use all the force necessary to achieve the Serbian dream.

My country feared the worst when Milošević gained the use of the former Yugoslav Army, and with that army Milošević anticipated that the conflict would be soon over. Croatia felt isolated, we could not understand how the rest of the world could allow the Serbian bullies to get away with such an act of aggression against a country ill prepared to defend itself. But the Croats, with God's help, decided to fight and defend what was rightfully their own land. We would not allow ourselves to become slaves to a tyrant. Croatian patriots not only from all parts of Croatia, but ex-pats from abroad returned to Croatia to defend their homeland. During World War Two, when the Nazis arrived in Croatia, many Croats left Croatia.

Others left Croatia in 1971 when the Communist regime was a big terror to any Croatian national. Many Croats have been expelled from the republic of Croatia because they refused to accept the Yugoslavian Brotherhood, at the expense of their Croatian nationality. Croats who did not support the brotherhood could find themselves in prison, many without blame or just reason, and many would never be seen again. Croatian boys from seventeen to eighteen years old have been taken from their families and loaded on to trains like cattle, they were never seen again. My late uncle lived in Podrasina, he had a son who was seventeen years old when he was taken away, and put on a train to an unknown destination, never to return.

Croats put their intellectual and physical capacities at the disposal of their own country and its people. In that respect the Croats from Petrinja and Bosnia were not inferior. They also formed army units whose patriot soldiers took action in that area and all other battlefields, and fought long and hard battles for their freedom and their homeland. One Croatian battlefield near Petrinja recorded the Croatian casualties as follows: sixty-six killed in subversive activity, twenty-seven soldiers died in POW captivity, twelve soldiers died from fatal wounds, six soldiers died from accidents in their own units, which included two suicides, and nine soldiers were killed by landmines. The twenty-seven Croatian soldiers who were held in the Serb POW, thirteen were executed by firing squad, eight were murdered or killed in other ways, and six soldiers died as a result of torture or illness while being imprisoned.

During the Patriotic War from 1991 to 1995 the Croats from Petrinja suffered a serious loss in the population. The records show that most of those who lost their lives defending Petrinja, were young people of a considerable intellectual capacity that had a lot to offer to Petrinja and their country. That meant an irrevocable loss for my town, and Croatia.

Soon after the liberation of parts of Croatia that were occupied by the Serbs, Croats started to rebuild the ruins caused by the war. The ravages of the war were huge; Serbs burnt and destroyed settlements, Catholic churches, Croatian cemeteries, hospitals, schools, factories, railways, airports, roads and bridges etc. And for years after the war we still had minefields all over the pre-occupied areas of Croatia. Because of these mines, many people and children were still losing their lives, or limbs.

With the help of the Croatian Government, the return of the exiles in the greatest number possible proceeded gradually. Some of them still didn't return for many reasons, as refugees some died from all kinds of illness, mostly from PTSP. Many who have successfully returned to their homeland bore the scars of war, invalids and sickness burden their lives. There are families with husbands, sons, brothers, uncles and nephews that are still missing! The Croatian Government, using its own funds and the financial support of the generous people from abroad, helped us to rebuild the destroyed parts of my country.

Croatia possesses strong national values, and Croats are very conscious and proud people. In honour of Croatia's Patriotic Soldiers, and all the many civilians, and children who have been killed or massacred during that war, I dedicate this testimony in memory of all the Croats who lost their lives. Petrinja lost 260 civilians. Some of them are registered as missing, along with the seventeen soldiers from Petrinja who are listed as missing. There was no information available that could help the Croatian Authorities to ascertain the fate of all those who were listed as missing. Most of the missing were captured when Petrinja fell to the Serbian aggression and occupation in September 1991.

In 1995 the military operation called *Storm* ended the conflict and many parts of Croatia and Bosnia were liberated. My family and I were able to return to Petrinja. It's a sad fact that the world sat in judgement, looking for all kinds of reasons to blame all the sides involved in the conflict. At times, the true facts were distorted to cover up the negligence shown by NATO. If NATO had acted sooner, many lives would have been saved. NATO failed to stop the Serbian aggression in the former Yugoslavia. We felt Lord Owen and the European Community had let us down, especially when they seem to think that nobody was to blame for all the killing of innocent civilians, and the needless destruction.

While ethnic cleansing was happening in the former Yugoslavia, the European Community hid its head in the sand. At first, they seemed to excuse these war crimes, because they felt that all the republics in the former Yugoslavia had been at one another's throats for centuries. Despite everything that Croatia had gone through in that conflict, certain European governments still judged and persecuted Croats. If fighting for freedom by defending our country from aggressors was a crime, then we are guilty! We have never attacked Serbia or had any ambitions to rule any country, apart from our own.

It was a well known fact that Serbia had aspirations to occupy a considerable amount of Croatia to achieve Serbia's quest for a greater Serbian nation. Serbia was prepared to stop at nothing in order to achieve superiority over the other Yugoslav republics. Serbian warlords marched against Croatia, occupying almost half of Croatian territory. Like a fire raging through a forest, the Serbs destroyed everything that belonged to the Croatian people. And the Croatian people themselves were not always spared the Serbian wrath of evil that pillaged Croatia. With the distortion of Croatia's past, Serbia violently disputed Croatia right to decide our own future. Croatia paid a heavy price for its freedom and democracy, and the right to be recognized as an independent country throughout the world. We asked the world to be fair, when they measured our sincerity, and honesty. These values our very much in tune with the majority of Croats.

We would never forget the defenders of Petrinja and Croatia; we also support the need to bring any perpetrator of war crimes to justice. Anyone who does not recognize a crime has been committed defends the crime. He who continually buries his head in the sand avoids the light of life, and sees only the darkness of death.

In the name of Milošević's Greater Serbia, there are crimes that took place that still remain unpunished. The Serbs' hunger for terror among the civilian population was fuelled by the way of ethnic cleansing, massacres, rape, torture and the destruction of property. The Serbs didn't know the meaning of the Geneva Convention. Croatia stood firm against Serbia, and resisted the inhuman actions of Serbia. The Croats didn't make war out of hatred to others, because of the love for our homeland, and the agonized Croatian people; we only fought against the persecution of Croats from the Serbs. Croats have three values that dictate the way they should live, and behave in their life. These are: God, Homeland and Family, these are the Christian values every child was brought up on.

After Croatia seceded from Yugoslavia we declared Croatia an independent country. We now live in peace, and pray that our future generations will live a better and more beautiful life. But we must never forget what happened to my generation near the end of the twentieth century, and the young people that died, because they were Croats. I went to school with friends who lost their lives, unlike me; they are not here to enjoy the freedom with their families. They all gave their lives for what they believed in, they died to give Croatia a future to look forward to. That sacrifice was made by so many Croats in the name of freedom for our homeland. And no matter what other people think, or say, that was our obligation to tell the truth about the Patriotic War.

George, you asked me to write and give you an account on how the war in the former Yugoslavia affected my family, myself and the people living in Petrinja. I pray you will understand why I write with so much passion for the Croats, and my country.

George, I must write everything for you to put in your book, but believe me, George, it was emotionally very difficult for me. It brings back so many unhappy memories, but I would persevere for the sake of my fellow citizens who died, and for those who survived, but went through so many bad things. I hope and pray that that would help in some way to prevent those terrible events ever happening to our country again, and to other countries in our world.

Today we have Croatia, and we must take care of our country, keeping our homeland safe from criminals and assassins who have always tried to take away our freedom, and the loved ones who mean so much to us. I pray such people would be caught, and face the rightful justice and punishment for their crimes against humanity. I know God would take care of us.

The most dishonourable action from the nations in our world was the lack of prosecutions and the time it takes to convict a large number of war crimes that was mainly committed by the Serbs, and remain unpunished. The accusations concerning war crimes in the former Yugoslavia came from many nations; many nations in our world were of the opinion that the Croats were just as bad as the Serbs. We all felt hurt and totally betrayed to hear such comments. How can people judge us in that way? We were only defending ourselves, and fighting for our freedom.

These accusations create a feeling of injustice among Croatians. Sometimes people are faced with the truth that was as clear as black and white, but ignore the true facts before them; they have already made their assumption. Rather than be proved to have got their opinions wrong, they decide to bury their heads in the sand. The true facts are Serbia attacked Croatia, and we had to defend ourselves in the best way possible. Croatia did not harbour any desires to have control over Serbia. We just wanted to live in peace on our own land, and God bears witness to that. For the sake of our children, I pray God would help us to prove our sincerity.

George, you may be surprised to read some of the comments that I have written in that letter, and the story I have sent to you. It was my duty to tell you the truth on how that terrible war affected so many good Croatian people, my family, my friends, and myself. It is your choice to decide if you want to use our story in your book, or think whatever you like about me. Wherever your life takes you, it was important to know who you are. George, I prayed to God for guidance before writing our story for you. I also prayed for all the people in our world, and for God's light to wash everything that was bad from our world, and to wash everyone who has committed evil acts against the innocent civilian population. I pray for the fire of remorse to pierce their hearts, making them aware of the pain and suffering they have caused.

George, I don't hate anybody, I love life, people, friends and nature, and they are all God's creations. For me, with God's help, only warm hearts and love can open the doors for peace. In all that story that I have written for you, I am nothing special, just a small part of life in Croatia, like a grain of sand, or a drop of water in that reality. But what is reality? It was all around you and me, in the people, and past events, and the way we live now, and in the future. We all share that moment in time, in mind, body and spirit. In our hearts we choose to laugh or cry, to be good or bad, and to love or hate.

311

These eternal feelings connects us with others around us, we all play our part through the journey of life.

CHAPTER FOURTEEN

Edit's Story

Until 1960, Petrinja was a typical Croatian town with very few Serbian families. About four families in total, but we never called them Serbs, we only call people Serbs if they live in Serbia. The Serbians who did live in Petrinja were accepted as part of the community in Petrinja and Croatia, along with their Orthodox Church, they had every right to their religion and education.

The ambitious Great Serbian Politics started much earlier than the war began. After 1960 Serbian families from Bosnia villages and Serbia started to settle, and heavily populate, Petrinja. They had every right to settle within the brotherhood of the former Yugoslavia. In my home town Petrinja, the Serbian population increased every year. Over a short period of time the Serbian population with the patronage of the Communist regime, got all the better jobs, and systematically ignored the equal rights of the Croatian citizens in Petrinja. The Croatian people of Petrinja are the true citizens of our town; my grandfather and father were born in Petrinja. Don't misunderstand me, I did not object to any Serbian families that wanted to live in Petrinja, until they gradually suffocated all the cultural Croatian national activities in Petrinja. Still we endured that, but when somebody thought differently, and stood up to the Serbian takeover, he or she would lose their jobs, and be forced to leave Petrinja, and find work elsewhere.

For example: at a famous grammar school in Petrinja, the Professor of Art was a citizen of Petrinja. He use to take his students to see and study the sacred motives in our ancient church of St Lovro in Petrinja, because that was part of the educational program to draw the sacred art motives and architecture in the church of St Lovro . The Serbian leaders in Petrinja accused the Professor of teaching his students Catholicism. The Professor lost his job immediately, and because of the pressure put on him, he was forced move to a town called Sisak.

The law in the republic of Croatia then and always states a right to religious belief guaranteed to any nationality, but it was in fact and reality refused to Croatians in their own town. There were Serbian spies who were checking on the movements, the feelings and the religious beliefs of the citizens of Petrinja. At the end of the sixties, and beginning of the seventies, unemployment among the Croatian population in Petrinja had doubled. Many of our citizens had to leave Petrinja because any prospects to earn a living, and raise their families, had been taken away from them.

I remember when I was going to the grammar school, we had a wonderful teacher of Physics, who held many credits from abroad. He attended a political rally, and raised his voice against communist politics and their poor record concerning human rights, he declared himself to be Croatian, Serbian leaders felt that he was not permitted to say that in public, but no matter what statute in law says, everyone should have the right and freedom to have an opinion. A few days later at school, I went to attend a Physics class, and he was no longer there. A Serbian principal informed us that he had to leave the school, because of his political views against Serbia.. Pupils and teachers revolted against that, because in our Physics class he was always teaching us about Physics, not politics. Surely in his private life as a free man, and by law, he had every right to do and think whatever he believes in? But there was another law which was created by the once minority, they wanted to be the majority. Nationalist who came from another republic wanted to rule among others. We never succeeded to bring him back to our school; he had to move to another town.

All the pupils who took part in the protest had to attend a meeting, we called it an 'informative' we had long and boring conversations about not getting involved in political demonstrations.. I think the purpose was to brain wash us of any mutinous thoughts. We all received black marks on our records and reports. I was sixteen years old, and we were all warned that if we continued our political aptness, we would find it difficult to find employment when we left college. You know what that means to a teenager who was looking forward to finding a job and earning some money to help your family. I was an excellent pupil, and later a hard-working student. I had an agreement with a local company that, when I finished college, the company would offer me employment.

Unfortunately the main chief in the company was a dictator and brotherhood nationalist. That company was the biggest in its field throughout the whole of Yugoslavia, and was established in Petrinja in 1821. Because the main chief in the company was a dictator and a brotherhood nationalist, the company was taken from private ownership and nationalised just before my graduation. Serbians and not Croatians had a major say in the running of that company in Petrinja. After my graduation in 1987, although the company had promised me a job, they did not offer me employment. I tried so hard to find work, but I was unsuccessful for over a year, until some honourable people at the company that had agreed to give me employment finally offered me employment. From the early sixties until the conflict in the former Yugoslavia, the increasing Serbian population in Petrinja was slowly imposing its will on the hard-working and diligent Croatian citizens in Petrinja.

Compared to their Serbian neighbours, Croatian citizens in Petrinja were getting poorer education, and were less likely to be offered employment. Many Croatian citizens in Petrinja were forced to leave their hometown to find work to support their families, or live under the big foot of the Yugoslav

Brotherhood and egoism. What the nationalist did with the company in Petrinja spread to other companies and landowners, everything around us in Petrinja went from privately owned to socially owned. Croatian citizens born in Petrinja lost their right to own a small piece of land. So if you wanted to build a house on the land you once owned, you had to get permission from the nationalist authorities. That resulted in many unsuccessful applications made by the Croatian citizens in Petrinja who wanted to build houses on the land now owned by the state. Serbian applications to build houses in Petrinja were met with a much more favourable response. That desperate situation among the Croatian citizens in Petrinja made some of them commit suicide. Serbian houses started to be built without a building permit on the land Croatians once owned.

That was a big injustice to our citizens. So day by day, the population in Petrinja started to change. By 1988/89 almost half of Petrinja's population was of Serbian nationality. The nationalist law was on their side, and they penetrated every Croatian pore, and infiltrated deep inside it to get what they wanted. Serbians were now creating every activity in Petrinja, and yet they still complained of being treated like second-class citizens by the Croatian citizens. In fact it was the other way round; the Croatians did not have any rights in the town they were born in. We were all starting to feel like strangers in our own town. We opened our arms to welcome all nationals as equals, who wanted to settle in Petrinja. We gave them thefreedom to be part in our community; we did not refuse them anything. In turn the Serbian community abused us with the rod of freedom.

Croatians felt that all the good will they had given to the Serbian settlers in Petrinja had now come back to destroy them, making us feel less worthy and inferior. We were loosing our pride and national identity.

The Croatian citizens were not prepared to heel like dogs to Serbian orders. We have had enough of being treated in that unjust manner, and were not prepared to take anymore. On

March 4th 1989, on Petrova Gora in Croatia, about 50,000 people from Kordun, Banorina, Lika, Krajina, Pokupje, Bosnia, Kosovo, Vojvodina and Serbia gathered at a big meeting to discuss *Brotherhood and Unity*. Serbians carried pictures of Milošević, and shouted slogans; "That was Serbia! Yugoslavia, we will kill Tuđman", Tuđman was our Croatian leader.

On April 22nd 1990, in Croatia, for the first time since the end of the Second World War, elections were held for free and democratic parties to serve in the Croatian Government.

On May 23rd 1990, in Croatia and Slovenia, the arms for territorial defence were taken away by the JNA. That was by order of the Federal Secretary for National Defence in Belgrade.

On August 10th 1990, in Petrinja, for the first time since the Second World War we devoted and celebrated *Lovreucevo* in Petrinja. This is a spiritual plebeian saint's day of Petrinja's Croats and Catholics. St Lovro was the patron saint of our town, and the main church of St Lovro dates from Baroc, and was protected by the European Convention for Cultural Monuments. St Lovro was built in the centre of our park.

On August 17th 1990, in Banovina, Croatia, news of the anti Croatian feeling in the town of Knin erupts and bursts into widespread violence against Serbs

On August 18th 1990, Petrinja's votive pilgrimage Marija Bistrica (Sanctary) took place.

On August 25th to September 3rd 1990, the pilgrimage of Petrinja's RC parish of St Lovro to Lourdes was held.

On September 27th 1990, after the well-known demonstrations in Knin, and the so-called beam revolution of Serbian nationalists, Serbia's screenwriters created disorder to destroy the Croatian state. In the very centre of Petrinja, just before midnight, Serbian residents started to cause trouble. On the main road to Sisak, Serbian rebels stopped and turned back a Petrinja special police vehicle, which conveyed weapons for Petrinja's public service security. On the main streets of Petrinja, Serbian rebels erected barricades and used their vehicles to block the road, stopping the entire traffic heading to Sisak.

The following morning, most of the citizens of Petrinja were surprised and in a state of shock that left them feeling very bitter towards the Serbian rebels. Buses that carried workers to Sisak were stopped and prevented from continuing their journey. Many of Petrinja's citizens could not get work, and were forced to return to their homes with anger in their hearts. In the streets of Petrinja, a number of people started to demonstrations, and hour by hour the demonstrations got bigger. Some of Serbian rebels attacked journalist from Zagreb and Sisak. They were demanding that weapons held by the Petrinja reserve police had to be surrendered to the Serbian JNA. They broke into the police armoury, and stole all the weapons.

That day, like every day of his life, my father was going to work. My father never had a day off because of sickness or anything else; he was a very honest diligent worker. My father was a quiet well-mannered man, and never looked for any trouble. All he ever asked for was to live in modesty, and support all his family. My father had to use the Sisak highway to get to work. When he saw the trucks blocking the road ahead, he was not exactly sure what was happening there. As my father approached the roadblock in his car, the men at the roadblock signalled to him to stop. The men had long beards. They were not from Petrinja, they came from Serbia, and had a special task. They asked my father where he was going. He told them he was going to work, and he would be late.

They told him, you cannot pass! My father told them, I go that way to work every day, why won't you let me pass? They insisted that he was not going to get to work today. When my father attempted to go through the roadblock, they dragged him out of his car. Many men started to rock his car, to turn it over. Some of the men twisted my father's arms up his back, others started to beat him.

A Serbian man who worked work at the same company as my father arrived at the roadblock. He was one of the minorities of honest Serbian people who knew and saw my father at work every day. He stood up to defend my father, and saved his life, he told the men who were beating my father to stop and let him go. He told them that my father was an honest and good man. Thank God they listen to him, if it wasn't for my father's Serbian work colleague, they would have probably beaten my father to death.

My father had just risked his life to go to work, a task he did every day without any problems. He had never experienced anything like that before. When my father came home that day, he was cut, bruised and in a state of shock. All day and night he broke down in tears. I have never seen my father like that before. When the hurt and emotions passed, my father felt angry, and could not understand how anybody could come to our peaceful town, and cause so much terror.

All day long, Serbian activist gathered in streets of Petrinja on Croatian land shouting, "That was Serbia! That was Serbia!" They said, "Wherever a Serbian lives, then that was part of Serbia." The Serbian activism had now started its campaign against the republic of Croatia. They raided armouries at police security stations in Petrinja, Dvor and Glina, and stole twenty-five machineguns, seventy-five rifles, 157 pistols, and 59,000 rounds of ammunition.

That was the beginning of the brutal and bloody future for the citizens of Petrinja and Croatia.

On November 9th 1990, in Sisak, at the rector of St Marija (Mary) Church, parish priest Antun Grahovar, was murdered in a vicious and brutal knife attack.

On December 16th 1990 Petrinja celebrated the anniversary of the first written documents of the town of Petrinja, also the parish of St Lovro, and the historical and spiritual life of our church from 1240 to 1990.

On December 21st 1990, in Knin, Serbian activists declared autonomy in the area of Krajina.

On December 22nd 1990, in the Croatian capital Zagreb, the Croatian Parliament declared a new democratic constitution for the Republic of Croatia, the so-called, 'Christmas Constitution'.

On January 26th 1991, in Petrinja, Croatian political parties organized a peaceful protest at the pubic park in the town centre. Our protest was to reaffirm that Petrinja as always been a Croatian town, and would continue to stay a Croatian town forever more.

Croatia was not prepared to allow the Serbian leaders Milošević and Rashovic '' to add Petrinja to their Serbian autonomy area of self-declared Krajina. (Greater Serbia).

On March 1st 1991, in Pakrac, a revolt of Serbs culminated in the disarmament of the National Croatian Police Force.

On March 22nd 1991, in Serbia the authorities ordered the extortion of Petrinja's company Gavnlovic. In its field, that was one of Croatia's largest companies. The top manager of that company was a Serbian Nationalist, and with his key men in the company they orchestrated everything in the company. He was also directed from the Serbian autocrats for the Greater Serbian cause,also known to be associatedwith the so-called Serbian backed JNA. March 31st 1991, in our Croatian National Park in Plitvice, an armed revolt by the Serbian population led to the death of a Croatian policeman called Josip Jovic. That happened during the Easter Religious Festival, later branded as 'the Bloody Croatian Easter'.

On April 6th 1991, in Knin, the president of the Serbian radical party Vojislav Sejely made an announcement to help the Serbian cause in Krajina. He offered to defend Serbian territory with the service of his 10,000 chetnik fighters.

On April 9th 1991, in Zagreb, on the first sitting of Croatia's Supreme State Council, under the presiding Dr Franco Tuđman, the Croatian National Guard was established with the primary task to protect the constitutional order and territory of the republic of Croatia.

On May 12th 1991, in Petrinja's main square then called, *the Square of Marshall Tito*, Serbs organized an illegal referendum, for the connecting of local communities in Banija

Serbian villages to the self-declared, and so-called, *Serbian Autonomy District* (Krajina). The referendum was signed by the majority of people with Serbian nationality which was now living in Petrinja. They were once our friends, neighbours and fellow citizens, but now they wanted to take our town and make it part of a Great Serbia. They said, "Wherever one Serbian lives, that was part of Serbia." That was their rule! Incidentally, the main square where the Serbs held their referendum in 1991 was now called, *the Square of Croatian Patriotic Defenders.*

On May 16th 1991, preparations were being made for the defence of Petrinja, and the coordinating council for defence had been established. The defence council did not waste any time arranging the lines of direction for the defence of Petrinja. All over our town the sound of explosions could be heard at night. With the arrival of experienced Serbian specials from Pancevo in Serbia, the explosions increased every night.

On May 30th 1991, in the church of St Lovro, Petrinja's RC parish priest Stiepan Levanic, held mass for our homeland, on the day we celebrated our statehood. That priest was special man of God to us, because he was an example of the story in the Bible, when Jesus brought Lazarus back to life from death. Our priest was murdered by Serbian Chetniks. At the hospital our priest was diagnosed as clinically brain dead, half of his head was missing, and he was just left to die. The doctors said there was no chance that our priest would survive with such horrendous head injuries, but Jesus can achieve everything that was not possible in our eyes. It was truly a miracle that only Jesus could do; he came to, our priest, and returned to life. Our priest made a full recovery, and his mind was perfectly healthy to tell everybody his story. As God was my witness, I tell the whole truth about that wonderful miracle.

On May 31st 1991, in Petrinja disturbances settled down for a while, local guards patrolled the streets and the main buildings. A great number of these Croatian guards were unarmed, a few were armed with their own hunting guns, and a very few managed to be armed with military automatic weapons.

My husband, who was at that time my boyfriend, with whom I wanted to marry and have a family, was looking forward to decorating the house that my grandmother had given to us. Daily we would excitingly plan and discuss getting new furniture for our home. That would be a new life and beginning for us both, we had so much to look forward to. But now, with our future so uncertain, we did not talk about our home or furniture so much. All we talked about was surviving that crisis in our lives.

My boyfriend joined the local guards. I worried so much for his safety, and he only had a revolver to defend himself. His duty was to guard the front of a police station at night; a short distance from his post was a large Serbian military barracks. Every night through dimmed light he could see a tank in the barracks with its guns pointing in the direction of the police station he was guarding, he was very scared for his life. There was clearly a relative difference of weaponry between the Croats and Serbs, and you can imagine what kind of force the Serbs had at their disposal, because there was also a military airport on the outskirts of Petrinja. The Serbs were prepared to use whatever force they could get their hands on, and use that military might against the Croatian citizen of Petrinja.

When first Serbian families settled in Petrinja in the early sixties we were their hosts, and we welcomed them as we would welcome anybody who came to settle in Petrinja.

June 25th 1991, in Zagreb, the Parliament of the Republic of Croatia proclaimed with a constitutional decision involving all the citizens of Croatia. Croatia was now an independent and sovereign state, and no longer part of Yugoslavia, ninety-four per cent of Croatian citizens voted in favour of our independence.

On June 26th 1991, in Glina, Chetniks attack the police station, and after a long battle the Chetniks capture it.

Casualties were three dead, ten wounded. Armed conflicts became a regular occurrence on Banija. From the military barracks in Petrinja a long line of tanks heading in the direction of Glina passed through the main streets of Petrinja. Serb propaganda stated the tanks were sent to Glina to calm the armed conflicts, but in fact the truth was to support the Chetniks.

On June 27th 1991, in Slovenia, the so called JNA threatened the territorial defences of Slovenia. On the same day, in the Croatian town of Osijek, the tanks of the so called JNA were crushing and destroying cars as they ploughed through the streets of Osijek.

On July 4th 1991, in Borovo near Vukovar, Croatia. Serbian irregular forces attacked guards and policemen, killing ten civilians and wounding ten others.

On July 5th 1991, in Gorufa in upper Budiclina a Croatian village near Petrinja, at about eight o'clock in the morning, Chetniks attacked and ambushed a family in the yard of their house. Josipa Kozic, a sixteen-year-old, was murdered, her sisters Vladu and Sufezana were wounded. I knew that family very well, their mother worked with me. The shock of that attack on an innocent family was heartbreaking; we just could not believe what was happening.

On July 7th 1991, near Banija, a meeting of representatives from the Yugoslav Government, the Republics of Croatia and Slovenia and the European Union was held. A declaration of intent was agreed by all parties at the meeting, to solve the Yugoslav crisis and ensure a peaceful outcome in the next three months.

On July 13th 1991, in Banovina, the forces of the ex-Yugoslav Army openly stood on the side of the Serbs, and were now known as the JNA or, to most Croatians, as the Serbian Army. They were helped by territorial forces, the so-called SAO-Krajina. With mortars and infantry fire, these combined Serbian forces attacked Croatian police stations in Kraljevac, Dragotinja, Prinjavor and Cuntic, as well as all Croatian villages around Petrinja. In these attacks thirty-seven

Croatian policemen were killed and seven were wounded. By July 21st 1991, 830 refugees from the nearby villages that were attacked came to Petrinja for shelter and to escape the Serbian attacks on the innocent, civilian population.

On July 27th 1991, in the nearby village of Cuntic, eight Serbian soldiers of the JNA attacked a Franciscan monastery. They doused the Church with gasoline and set it on fire, destroying all the valuable paintings, books, chalices and many holy mass vestments from the eighteenth century. That Church in Croatia was our first monument of culture to be attacked in the Croatian Patriotic War.

On August 25th 1991, in Petrinja, the police station was attacked in the morning. The Serbian forces then systematically attacked are destroyed many parts of our town. From our own military barracks, that was now in the hands of the Serbs, artillery and tank attacks destroyed the Church of St Bartol in Petriula, Hrastovica.

These attacks started a mass evacuation of citizens who were settled in Petrinja and Sisak. My parents were very worried and afraid of what might happen now our peaceful life was in ruins. They contacted my godmother and her sister, who lives Switzerland, and asked them if they would kindly let me stay with them in Switzerland until the situation in Petrinja was over. At the time I was lucky, or maybe it was just my destiny, that many of Petrinja's citizens did not have this get out of jail card to play. I travelled by train to Switzerland to avoid the horror that was happening in Petrinja, unaware that the worst was yet to come for the citizens of Petrinja.

On September 2nd 1991, in Petrinja, the Serbian JNA started their attack on the innocent citizens of Petrinja. They started with an artillery barrage, their infantry opened fire with mortars, heavy machine guns and grenades. The assault on Petrinja's residential area continued throughout the whole day, with sniper fire and short bursts of machine-gun fire. At about 1500 hours wounded children were airlifted to Zagreb Hospital. Street fights broke out all over our town.

Many important buildings and over 300 residential houses and flats were set on fire; even a kindergarten was destroyed, along with the Church of St Lovro Secondary School, a hospital, bars, restaurants, communal buildings, factories and the company that my father and I worked for. The Serbs had almost burnt every Croatian house in Petrinja, and their carnage did not spare our citizens if they tried to defend their families and property. Even the minority of honest Serbian families who had chosen to stay in Petrinja to protect their homes were not spared. They all suffered as we did, and some lost their lives at the hands of their own Serbian nationals. Never before in the history of Petrinja have its citizens witnessed so much destruction in our town.

At about 1600 hours just outside Petrinja the military barracks that the JNA had captured from Croats was protected from any attack with the activation of a minefield. The majority of the Serbian population had fled Petrinja in the wake of the forthcoming attack. Most of them went to the Serbian villages around Banija, or sought protection at the military barracks that was occupied by the JNA. Those who had remained, and survived the carnage, now found themselves to be refugees along with their Croatian neighbours.

I was in Switzerland when Petrinja fell into the hands of the Chetniks, but my parents and my boyfriend remained in Petrinja. I never stopped praying for them, I was so very afraid for their safety and their lives; back in 1991 we didn't have widespread use of mobile phones or the Internet like we have nowadays. I relied on a landline phone call, or the long-awaited letter. There were no guarantees that either of those forms of communications would be available, if the telephone lines had been cut, or letters were destroyed by the Serbian forces.

My boyfriend mentally suffered defending his hometown, and feared for his life and the lives of my parents. You can only imagine the constant tension that he, my family and the rest of the citizens of Petrinja went through. They also feared that their Serbian neighbours in Petrinja might betray them by helping the Chetniks to identify anti-Serbian Croats, and help them to make a killing list of Croatians who were politically anti-Serb.

Just before Petrinja fell to the Chetniks an artillery shell exploded in the yard, behind our family home. The explosion broke most of the windows in my parents' house and burnt the windows that did not break. Paintings and ornamental plates that hung on the internal walls to my parents' house, fell to the floor. Many were destroyed or badly damaged. We had a family collection of about 150 paintings and plates, all of them were the work of my father and me. We are both artists and proud of all our Paintings, we also had a collection of about 100 treasured sentimental gifts and paintings that were given to us both from friends who had died. These gifts meant a lot to us as a memorial to our very dear friends. Thankfully some of the paintings, plates and gifts were only slightly damaged.

My father salvaged what he could, and in case the shelling started again he stored them in boxes underneath the big wooden steps at the centre of our house. Unfortunately during my family's absences from Petrinja, the Chetniks destroyed half of our treasured possessions, the other half of our possessions that were not damaged were transported to Belgrade to be sold through the channels of the black market. During our time as refugees we tried to find many ways to locate our stolen possessions through humanitarian organizations. They could not help us because the lost of possessions did not come under any humanitarian umbrella. To be honest we understood that, rightly so, life issues are more important than possessions.

What we were not happy with was the way the UN forces sat on the fence when crimes against humanity took place. Their role was similar to a boxing referee keeping the fighters apart if they got to close for comfort. But many times they even failed to carry out and police these duties because they were simply out numbered by the warring factions. It even came across to many Croatians that the UN protected the Chetniks as much as they were supposed to protect us. There were unfounded rumours that some UN forces were overfriendly with the Chetniks and the JNA. These rumours did not help the Croats to have any confidence or faith in the UN forces.

While we were refugees in our own country, we had to pay for rented rooms to sleep, while the UN forces watched the Chetniks and the JNA destroy our houses and town. Through that all-day shelling in Petrinja, my father continued to report to his company for work. No matter for what reason or excuse, my father's company insisted that all employees must report for work. Any Croat employees who failed to report for work, would lose their job. That rule did not apply to the Serbian employees; the majority of Serbian families in Petrinja had fled to a safe area away from the shelling.

On September 3rd 1991. That night my father did not get any sleep, but he still made his way to work. En route he saw many houses destroyed and many more were on fire. He passed columns of frighten citizens fleeing Petrinja.

From the military barracks that was occupied by the Serbs in Petrinja, further heavy shelling was followed by machine-gun fire, and sniper fire directed at Petrinja and the surrounding villages. They bombarded a graveyard of the Holy Trinity Church, and the Waterworks.

From the 3rd to 16th of September 1991 every day the shelling and gunfire was directed at the civilian population in Petrinja and the outlying villages. There was no military objective in Petrinja or the nearby villages for the Serbs to continue that needless killing of innocent citizens, and the careless destrution of Petrinja's infrastructure. Churches, schools and hospitals were destroyed, many of them flattened to the ground. Many citizens, young and old, men, women and children who weren't able to escape, or too afraid to flee their houses, died in the ruins that buried them. None of them wore a military uniform. They were all victims of the murderous Serbian JNA and Chetnik forces.

My mother was in constant fear for her life and the life of my father. She was close to breaking point and could not cope with the situation in Petrinja for much longer. In a cry for help, my mother contacted friends in Slovenia; they very kindly asked my mother to stay with them until the situation calmed down. My mother left Petrinja with one small bag of essential belongings in September 1991, everything else that my mother and I owned was left behind in our house. She waited for the so-called calming down period that would take nearly four years before we could all return to Petrinja in the spring of 1995.

I was so relieved that my mother had managed to escape to the safe haven in Slovenia. But my anxiety continued because my father and boyfriend still remained in Petrinja to try and protect our property. So many of our young and old men were killed in the shelling, and sniper fire. The Serbs were systematically destroying everything in Petrinja, and forcing the people to run away from their town.

From the military barracks, artillery and mortar attacks continued daily on Petrinja and the nearby villages, even my father's company was hit. Brave employees helped firemen from Zagreb and Kutina to control the fires; they all fought so long and hard to extinguish the fire to prevent an ecological disaster. But the JNA went into the factory to start more fires, and prevent the firefighters from extinguishing the flames.

Sisak's hospital was inundated with over forty wounded Croatian defenders and citizens. Many other Croatian defenders were killed or captured, which resulted in a severe war crime. That day twelve Croatian prisoners of war were massacred or executed.

Among them was one man my age called Dejan Gregec, I went to school with him, he was my special friend. I loved him so much. A few men were never found, and are still listed as missing persons. Only one man very badly wounded man survived that massacre; God helped him to live, in order to tell the story of that horrific crime against humanity. Many other witnesses came forward with war crime information about

328

massacres that took place in Petrinja's streets, and the surrounding hills and villages.

My boyfriend suffered a lot, he was afraid for his life, and could not sleep. I begged him to leave Petrinja to take a break for at least a month, that way he would no longer be a target for our enemies and live to fight another day. Although my boyfriend was very scared he did not want to admit defeat, and run away from Petrinja. I told him that if he loved and cared for me, he would leave Petrinja, because I wanted him alive to have his children.

Finally I persuaded him to leave, and he left Petrinja with the clothes he was wearing and a little food to have on his journey to Switzerland to be at my side. I was so relieved and happy to have my boyfriend safe and well in my arms. But my worries were far from being completely over. My father still remained in Petrinja, he was a very proud and determined man. All his life he worked so hard building our family home, and he did not want leave the house that meant so much to him and our family. For the first time in our family's life, we were all separated in different corners of our world. My mother was in Slovenia, my father was in Croatia, and my boyfriend and I were in Switzerland, what a terrible mess my family was in!

On September 19th 1991 in Petrinja, a foreign journalist Pierre Blanchet was killed by an explosion, which also wounded fellow journalist Patrick Gigauti. They came to Petrinja to tell the world the real truth about all the war crimes against the innocent victims of that conflict.

During the shelling in Petrinja my father was always helping people to save their personal belongings, and he would use his car to help them escape. When my father was at work, and for the second time, his company came under attack from an artillery bombardment. Many employees were killed, my father was listed has missing. My mother and I were out of our minds with worry; we did not get any more news about my father for three days. Unknown to us at that time, my father was trapped in the ruins of the company's cellar, all the exits was blocked with rubble. When the shelling started my father had the common sense to seek shelter in the cellar, his action probably saved his life. But he spent the next three days trying to dig himself out with his bare hands. During that time he had no food or water, and he could still hear shells exploding above.

On the third day the shelling stopped and father continued to dig himself out with his bare hands, that were now cut and bleeding. As he moved some large rocks, daylight suddenly lit the cellar like a torchlight, and he started to feel an inner strength to shift the remaining rubble, and managed to squeeze through a small opening. My father sat in the rubble and listened for a while in case there were others trapped and crying for help. There was just a deathly silence, you could have heard a pin drop; my father continued to look for a way out of the ruins of his place of work. Now and then he would stop and listen, in case the Serbs or Chetniks were outside, but the area was deserted. Finally, and thank God, my father got safely back to our house to clean up, and get something eat.

Fortunately my father managed to find a phone that was working so he could let us all know he was still alive. When I heard his voice on the phone I could hardly speak to him because I was crying so much. My father told me that I was as bad as my mother, she could not stop crying either. My father was also going to let his sister in Zagreb know that he was okay. In the following years my father's stressful experience changed him so much, he never wanted to talk about the siege of Petrinja again, and we never asked him. At long last my mother persuaded my father to come to Slovenia; she told him that she was ill with worry for his safety. My father managed to leave Petrinja on the 20th September.

In the short time my father was in Slovenia with my mother, he was very restless worrying about our cousins, friends and our house. My father opened his heart to my mother, telling her all the reasons why he must return to Petrinja. After a very long heartfelt conversation, my mother could see that my father could not stay in Slovenia and wait for heartache to go away. Nobody could have stopped him, his mind was made up. So, reluctantly, she agreed to let him go back to Petrinja if he promised to be careful, and not do anything reckless.

Meanwhile in my father's absence during the last two days, Petrinja and the surrounding area suffered its heaviest attack which including an air strike from the so called JNA that was operated by the Serbs. At midday the JNA artillery, mortars and tanks opened fire on every position that was held by the Croatian soldiers that were defending Petrinja, and the surrounding villages.

Later that afternoon, a very fierce and hard battle took place at a big old bridge called Granmaa which spans river Kupa; that bridge connects the village of Brest to the town of Petrinja. Our Croatian soldiers were forced to retreat over the bridge in the direction of Zagreb, and regroup to organize a defence on the left-hand side of the river Kupa. The JNA had the third largest armed force in Europe, and they threw all their might at these few brave Croatian soldiers until their resistance collapsed under the level of strength from the JNA. Those who succeeded to escape from Petrinja were considered to be the lucky ones. The majority of Croatian defenders and civilians who did not escape were killed, massacred or captured, and then used as slaves to bury our citizens. Many more citizens suffered the trauma of every kind of physical and emotional tortures, many of them died as a result of their experiences, or suffered the consequences of not getting the required medical care for their injuries.

My father travelled back to Petrinja in his little Fiat 750. When he arrived at Brest and approached the bridge called Granmaa, he stopped his car and stared in a state of shock when he saw how badly that bridge was damaged. For a brief moment he felt paralysed, he stood at the north side of the bridge with tears rolling down his face. Everything he worked so hard for all of his life was over the other side of the bridge, all our possessions were in our house. Before that conflict, we had only happy memories in Petrinja; but now we can't be there, how was all that heartache possible? My father did not want to go to far away from Petrinja, because he always hoped and prayed that that nightmare in our lives would soon go away. He eventually turned his car around and stayed with some friends in Brest, Mala Gorica on the north side of the river Kupa.

My father had many friends in that village, he once help to save their lives during the bombing in Petrinja, and helped them in their everyday work. But even in small village of Brest and Mala Gorica, the Serbs continued to fire on the positions of the Croatian defenders. My father was sleeping in barns, and at the houses of our Croatian defenders and soldiers.

The towns of Petrinja, Glina and Dvor were all now occupied by the Serbian JNA and Chetnik activists. We always prayed that someone very soon would help us to return to Petrinja. I was born in Petrinja, and now Serbian Nationalists and Chetnik terrorists live and walk the streets of our town. They robbed every Croatian house, and set fire to most of the houses in Petrinja. The Serbs were very happy with their victory and their occupation of Petrinja. Through their new radio station called Free Serbian Radio Petrinja they made regular announcements to all the Croatian refugees, saying tThat "Petrinja is now part of Serbia Krajina, Croats will never come back to our Serbian town."

All my family and friends were now refugees, and we would remain refugees for nearly four years before we could all safely return to our Croatian town of Petrinja.

During the Serbian occupation they destroyed everything that was Croatian. Two RC churches, St Lovro and St Cathy, were destroyed along with the three churches, Holy Trinity, St Rok and St Benedict along with their graveyards around the hills of Petrinja. Any signs of Croatian history past or present, and all traces associated with Croatia, were destroyed. It was a Serbian attempt to erase Croatia from any existence on earth. They say without a past you have no future.

On November 18th 1991 the Serbian controlled JNA, and the various voluntary forces of the Chetnik terrorist groups from Serbia and the former Yugoslavia, occupied the town of Vukovar. The Serbian occupation inflicted their terror on the innocent civilian citizens of Vukovar. Numerous war crimes of torture and massacres against the sick and wounded took place against humanity, and all the Geneva Conventions that Serbia had signed to honour. During the conflict, the Vukovar citizens became the biggest exiles of Croatian people from their native town. Like so many hospitals throughout Croatia, Vukovar Hospital was overrun with civilian patients requiring urgent medical attention, as a result of gunshot and shrapnel injuries. Dr Vesna Bosanac was the head of medical care at Vukovar Hospital.

To try and prevent further suffering and genocide, she asked for help from all the humanitarian organizations, and the authorites in Zagreb. But that help never arrived in time, many civilians, men, women, and children, died needlessly. If it wasn't for Dr Vesna Bosanac and the miracle of God's help many others would not have survived their horrific injuries. During my time in exile, I had the honour and fortune to meet Dr Vesna Bosanac while taking part in an artists' convention. The famous Croatian professor of Art Anton Bauer, who was born in Vukovar, introduced me to Dr Vesna Bosanac. Everyone in the artistic field knows Professor Anton Bauer and the famous Vukovar collection of very valuable Paintings. That famous collection of paintings were stolen by the Serbian and Chetnik forces who occupied Vukovar; the paintings that were not destroyed were taken to Belgrade, and have still not been returned to their rightful owners in Vukovar. The main purpose of that convention was to demonstrate to the world for a free Vukovar, and tell the world about the injustice Serb occupation of Vukovar. At the same time all the artists present at the convention donated paintings to be sold, to raise funds for the Free Vukovar cause.

I stayed with my godmother in Switzerland until February 1992. During that time I worked in a hotel restaurant for most of the day until midnight. The long hours helped me to forget everthing ugly that had happened in our lives over the last year. I could also earn a little money to send to my parents, and buy a few essential things for myself, because when I arrived in Switzerland all I had was the clothes I was wearing, and a small bag containing very few summer clothes and a pair of shoes. My boyfriend, who joined me in Switzerland a little later, had less than me, all he had was one jacket and a pair of boots, and my mother and father was no different, we all had lost everything.

Our lives had completely changed, our family was divided, we lost our home and all our belongings, we lost the lives we were all used to, we have never lived or worked like that before. Every morning I woke up and I prayed that it was just a nightmare, a bad dream that was not happening to us. But with my eyes open and looking at the surroundings that I was not used to, my heart felt so low again, so depressed, so homesick for my beloved Petrinja. I remember one night after working so late, I was walking to the house where a friend let me stay. It was about midnight, maybe a little later, it was a very cold and foggy night, I only had one warm coat. I was walking slowly, so tired from a long shift at work.

While I was walking down that street, I felt like an alien in another world, another country, another town, another street. Why am I here? I don't belong here. I was thinking to myself whom can I help, what use am I, and for whom am I valuable?

I don't have any children because the time had been taken away from me, my future life, my hopes and dreams, my planned wedding, my house, my town, all gone! If God wants to take me now, in that very moment, let him take me, I don't care anymore! I was very sad, and emotionally destroyed. I was so worried about my parents suffering in Croatia, I felt helpless, unwanted, and that nobody truly understands what we were all feeling, because you have go through that heartache to really understand what it was like. I am sorry if I sound so ungrateful for being alive; try to imagine living life without your soul. I can only express that the way I felt, was like living without your soul.

Meanwhile back in Croatia, my mother finally persuaded my father to leave Brest, and come to Zagreb to live with her. Some of my mother and father's friends also came to Zagreb, but only stayed there for a short while. While my mother and father were in Zagreb they moved from place to place, sometimes living in cold damp rooms and wet cellars. They never stopped dreaming about our warm, light and beautiful house, or sleeping in their own bed. Oh, it's so horrible when you don't have your own bed to sleep in, and you don't know where you would sleep tomorrow, and you wonder why that has happen to you, and for what reason, what did I do wrong? All because we wanted to be left alone to live in our own country in peace. Is that such a crime that we deserve to be treated worse than you would treat any animal? Is that possible? Now, in the twentieth century? Yes, I am afraid and sorry to say the whole world stands back and lets it happen. I am an artist, and had lost the will to paint; every time I put brush to canvas, my paintings were without colour, and I could only paint with a cold blue colour. I was mentally blocked.

For all the help we received, we were truly grateful to all the European countries like Switzerland, with the exception of Germany. At first along with the other European countries, Germany claimed they were helping the refugees of the former Yugoslavia, and that they would take good care of them, giving the refugees permission to stay in Germany longer if they could not return to their homes in the former Yugoslavia. In fact the oppisite was the case, Germany did everything to make sure the refugees' stay was as short as possible, and by February 1992 the refugees had to leave Germany for a safe haven in the former Yugoslavia.

My boyfriend wanted to go back; we both felt that we could not stay in Switzerland much longer, when your heart was somewhere else. We had some great help in Switzerland from friends who gave us food, and collected money for us to return to Croatia. Before the conflict, you live and share your everyday life with the people from your own town. But like someone from a horror movie, overnight those same people became someone else. You thought you knew these people so well, but now they were a great disappointment to you, they were now like strangers that you have never met before. Then God brings other people into your life that you don't know so well, and from the first time you meet them, they do so much to help you.

It was these wonderful people that stopped me loosing faith in human kindness. While I was in Switzerland, I made some close friendships with the people that I worked with from all over the world, Lebanon, Ghana, Ethiopia, Italy and my own country Croatia, who shared the same experience and destiny as myself. It just proves one thing to me: it doesn't matter from what country or what was your destiny in life, what really matters was what's in your heart and soul, and for all the good things we can do for each other.

Before I left Switzerland and returned to Croatia to live in Zagreb, I bought some mountain boots for me and my boyfriend, and a couple of military sleeping bags that could be used in extreme temperatures, also a three-person tent. At that time we didn't know where we would be sleeping in Zagreb. We didn't even know what would be waiting for us in Croatia. We were preparing ourselves for the unexpected in Croatia, in case we have to go on the run again

February 25th 1992, my boyfriend and I arrived in Zagreb, Croatia. I stayed with my mother and father, but my parents did not have much room at their friend's house, so my boyfriend stayed at his brother's house, but his brother's wife did not like having him in their house, not even my boyfriend's mother or father. People like that don't understand what it was like to be a refugee, or your destiny. I can only explain in six words what it was like for me, "You don't exist or belong anywhere."

My boyfriend joined the Patriotic Defenders, and served on the unoccupied frontline borders of Croatia's defence on Zupic Hill, and later Nebofan, near Petrinja.

In order to keep the warring factions apart, the UN was stationed between our Patriotic Defenders and the Serbian borders of the so-called Krajina. Croatia's Patriotic Defenders were eager take back their soveriegn land that the Serbs were now occupying, but the UN would not let that happen. Many Croats felt the UN were protecting the Serbs from the wrath of our vengeance. I guess they were trying to keep us apart to avoid a bloodbath. What a paranoiac situation.

Later, when my boyfriend was off duty from the Patriotic Defenders, he also got a part-time job as an electrician and worked in the Zagreb area. All the money that we earned and saved in Switzerland was spent on rent for rooms to sleep and buy food. At that time the long awaited liberation of our home town Petrinja was never coming. My boyfriend felt unwelcome at his brother's house, so we decided to live together. At the same time my parents were searching for a bigger place that we could afford for us all to live together.

You would not believe or try to imagine what kind of holes, cellars and musty rooms that people in Zagreb rented out for an extortionate amount of money, and they always wanted their rent in advance. Landlords in Zagreb made a fortune out of the suffering refugees, they didn't seem to care that they were getting rich on the misfortune of their fellow Croats, and all that took place just fifty-nine kilometres from Petrinja.

My parents, my boyfriend when he was on leave, and I, moved from place to place eight times in Zagreb. Finally we settled at a large private house called Gospocali Reuiete. We paid rent for two rooms, one for my parents, and a small room for my boyfriend and me, we shared a kitchen and bathroom with the other tenants in the house. The landlady was a good person who understood our situation, she treated us the way every human being should be treated, and was very good to us. She would always have time to listen to our problems, and help us through good and bad times.

Not long after we moved into that house, I started to work for the ICRC in Zagreb. A beautiful blonde lady called Ivana Persjc who worked in the personnel welcome office helped me get the job, and because we had lost everything we owed in Petrinja, Ivana also helped my family with furniture, cutlery, glasses, cups and plates etc. Ivana's husband also worked for the ICRC, she now lives in Switzerland, but we have kept in touch, and she has become a very dear friend to me and all my family. Immediately after the military operation called *Storm*, which instigated the liberation of Petrinja in 1995, Ivana visited my family a few times.

I had only been working for the ICRC for about nine months when I met a guy called George, who later asked me to write that story. I remember going to that ICRC apartment to carry out my daily cleaning duties. Upon entering the apartment, I heard a noise that sounded like the clatter of china coming from the kitchen. When I investigated who was making that noise, standing there was George washing dishes. I introduced myself has Edit your housekeeper, I told George politely that he was not required to clean up dishes, that was my job, and I am paid to do that. George said, "On my days off I did not mind helping me out." I also remember that particular day as I felt sad, because my father was not well, and I was crying. George asked me sit down and have cup of coffee with him, I told George about my family's situation and all that had happened to us since the conflict began, and my worries that that situation was no closer to being solved. George kindly listened to all my family's problems with a sympathetic ear. He was one of the few people that seemed to understand and sympathized with plight my family and I were in.

We were refugees in our own soveriegn country, nobody, not even the Croats in Zagreb understood what we were going through. Most people in Zagreb considered us poor people, only fit to clean their streets and houses.

Little did they know that before the conflict in the former Yugoslavia, we were just like them, we had the same living standard as them. The only difference between us now was we had that living standard taken away from us in Petrinja. If the same had happened in Zagreb, then our roles would have been reversed. You could say that Petrinja and its citizens were sacrificed to stop the Serbs attacking the fuel industry in Sisak and Zagreb. Instead of helping us, many of our fellow Croats in Zagreb looked at us with disdain and disgust. Sometimes while I was cleaning their apartment, I have overheard the whispers behind my back. I have heard such things like, *They should go back to where they belong*, *What are they doing here?* When you try to tell them that we once had houses like theirs and the good life that they have now, they were not at all interested to hear how we came to loose everything we had, and how we nearly lost our lives. Many of Petrinja's Patriotic Defenders and citizens lost their lives for the freedom of the citizens in Croatia capital Zagreb. I guess when you have everything you want, you are not interested in people who have nothing.

Before the conflict in the former Yugoslavia you could get a bus from Zagreb to Petrinja. In fact you had a choice of two bus routes, the long route took you via Sisak to Petrinja, and the shorter more direct route took you via Brest. So many citizens in Zagreb did not know you could no longer get a bus from Zagreb to Petrinja, not even the lady in the kiosk who sells the tickets to the Croatian public. The bridge over the river Kupa in Brest was destroyed by the Serbs, that action cut Petrinja off from Zagreb and Croatia. If you were required to present, renew or replace documents that were lost or destroyed during your evacuation, the authorities in Zagreb would tell you to go to your place of birth to get new documents. When you tried to tell them the reasons why that was not possible, most of them did not seem to care for the impossible situation we found ourselves in. To be honest most of them never cared for anything in their boring self-centred lives. They only cared about themselves, and were just narrow-minded snobs. If these people had any common decency, they would think about how lucky they were to live in their peaceful surroundings with their children, and to sleep in their own warm bed at night having the security and wealth of the world. In their cosy lives, they go home to their houses, and take off their shoes, put their nice clothes neatly in the closet, shower in their bathrooms, and cook dinner in their kitchens. They can do all the things we use to do in Petrinja, nobody would take that away from them in Zagreb, they never gave refugees like us a second thought. It felt like they just did not want to accept that the Serbs were now occupying Croatian territory on their doorstep fifty-nine kilometres from their safe comfortable lives. That was now a sad part of a refugee's life in Zagreb, and that's why I suffered so much. Many of my relatives and friends were killed in the conflict, many more were lost or were scattered throughout Croatia and Europe. I prayed for them all every day and every night, and I always prayed that some day my family and I would safely return to Petrinja. I know our lives would never be the same again, and we could never forget that terrible time in our lives, but we had to be strong and support one another to move on.

During that time, medical data records from the senior medical authorities in the republic of Croatia showed that from August 17th 1990 to February 28th 1992, the Croatian casualty list resulted in 3,125 killed, and 16,719 wounded. All the time I was in Zagreb, I searched and tried so hard to get a better job. At first I did not think it would be a problem, after all I was highly educated, and graduated with second degree in Italian and English language.

The fact that I was a refugee seem to go against me whenever I applied for a new job. There were a lot of people working for the ICRC in Zagreb. At times, I felt that a lot of the foreign staff was working for the ICRC to futher their careers, and earn good money, at the expense of the Croats suffering. Some of the foreign staff didn't seem to care about honest and true people. Instead they cared about their own opportunities, benefits and profits. Nearly every week I was employed in the mornings to clean up after the foreign ICRC staff party. It was okay for them to get drunk and have a crazy party, while so many people suffered terrible hardship as a result of the conflict in the former Yugoslavia. I was considered to be good enough to clean up after people who enjoyed themselves at the expense of our misfortune, but not good enough to be given a job in line with my education and qualifications. Having said that, for me it was not really important what kind of work I did to survive. All kinds of work carry their own merits and rewards, it was more important for me to do the work to the best of my ability, and that's the standard I always set out to achieve.

Please don't misunderstand me; my opinions and comments are not directed at the ICRC drivers like George Budge. Most of the drivers like George already had jobs in their respective countries, and were not here for personal gain. I also found that while I was working for the ICRC, the best ICRC staff were the drivers like George. In a nice way they were common and simple people like us, who had left their country and families to truly help the victims of war who were suffering so much. I respected them so much, and it makes me very happy to know that we have kind and good people in our world and to know that not everyone was bad. George, you are one of the good people who understood my situation, and you felt my sorrow in your heart because you are a true humanitarian, who truly cares for the people in our world. I would never forget you George, and would always remember the Holy Mother statue with the sacred water and Bible at your bedside. God Bless you, George.

While I was in Zagreb I regularly attended the church of the Mother of God in Reuete. There was a priest called, Zdrarko who helped me through all my depression, and bad times. His words of comfort and advice gave me the strength and the will to live. I remember one of many days of feeling very low and sad, thinking about my town Petrinja, and all the citizens that were lost. Last night I was reading my Bible, the words said, "Blossom where you were sown." I asked the priest to explain. How can I blossom, when I was forced to leave the town where I was born and I cannot go back to Petrinja where I belong? The Priest answered, "If you take a dandelion from the place it was growing, and blow at the seeds on the stem, the wind will carry the seeds until they land at the place where they would grow again. Sometimes destiny takes people where they don't want to be, the Bible was telling you wherever your life takes you blossom and shine, give everything of yourself, the best you can give, nothing less will do." After I had talked to the priest, I felt so uplifted; his words carried me over the length and breath of all my problems. He taught me to eccept the events of my life that I cannot change, and to change the way I deal with those events. Later the priest left his monastery because he felt inadequate to serve the people; he felt God was calling him to help people like me.

In 1994 my boyfriend and I got married in Zagreb. Ivana who worked for the ICRC and had helped my family so much, attended my wedding after a short honeymoon; my husband had to return to his military unit. He served in the frontline defence, on the outskits of Petrinja. I worried so much for my husband's safety; I was feeling so helpless, and afraid of receiving bad news from his military unit. I contacted my friend Tanja in Italy, she was also an artist, and worked in a gallery there. Tanja asked me to come to Italy and help her at gallery. That opportunity would give me a chance to renew my enthusiasm in my work as an artist, and to ease the constant worry about my husband's safety. Tanja and God brought back a meaning to my life, and inspired the creativity for me to paint again; all the colours of a rainbow and more came into my heart. You hear people say, "I am a born-again Christian." In comparison, I was a born-again artist. That also helped me to cope with with all my worries, especially my fears for the safety of my husband.

I remembered the words and advice given by the priest at the Mother of God church in Zagreb. Like the dandelion seeds blown in the wind, God had directed my soul to Italy to blossom and shine, and give everything of myself; painting was the best gift I could give in return. No longer was I at the lowest ebb of my life, every day I lifted my spirit to higher levels. Now that the colours had returned to my heart, I was able to paint with such amazing energy that I have never felt before. Try to imagine what it would be like to be imprisoned in a cold dark room for three years, and then to be set free to feel sun and gentle breeze caressing your body. That was the only way I could explain to you how I was feeling at that time of my life. God had cleaned my soul of all the bad and negative thoughts that grew inside me. From now on, I looked forward in a possitive way towards today and the future. I decided to spend every minute of my life doing and giving the best I can to help others who had gone through the same darkness that I had gone through. Within reason, I felt the power to do anything in the world, but most important I wanted to spread God's light to comfort all those who suffer throughout our troubled world.

Not long after I returned to Zagreb in Croatia, the military operation called *Storm* started, in order to liberate all the Croatian territory that was being occupied by the Serbian forces. I did not get any news about my husband for twenty days; we searched the casualty lists in hospitals. I know they say, "No news is good news" but, like you do, I feared the worst. I prayed so hard for my husband to come home alive, I also prayed that we could all return to Petrinja to live our lives in peace.

The battle to liberate the Serbian-held Croatian territory in the Petrinja area was one of the most fiercely fought battles of the conflict. For four days our patriotic soldiers fought to free Petrinja and the surrounding area from the Serbian aggressors. Many patriotic soldiers were killed; they had given their lives for our freedom to live our lives in peace in Petrinja. Finally with the help of a NATO air strike on Serbian frontline forces, our patriotic soldiers broke through the Serbian frontline. Petrinja was liberated, but not without the cost of the many patriotic soldiers who sacrificed their lives. So many wives, mothers and children had lost their husbands, sons and fathers. News of Petrinja's liberation brought mixed feelings of joy, relief and fear for your loved ones who were involved in the fighting, and the uncertainty for what we would find when we all returned to Petrinja. The anguish I felt was intense, I have never cried so much in my life.

Thank God, the day after Petrinja had been liberated, I received the good news that my husband was alive. He was among the first patriotic soldiers to walk into Petrinja, and his unit was ordered to advance to liberate the villages that surround Petrinja.

With the battle now won, many of Petrinja's citizens were anxious to survey the damage to their town and property. Many houses had been severely damaged, or were completely destroyed; my husband's parents' house was burnt to the ground. Over 50% of Petrinja's houses had to be rebuilt, many others had to have extensive repairs. Without much money to hire builders to carry out the rebuilding and extensive repairs to houses in Petrinja, most of the work was carried out by the citizens themselves. At a time of so much heartbreak, the citizens of Petrinja organised themselves into working parties and started to repair our broken town. Bricklayers, carpenters, plumbers, electricians, painters and general labourers worked very long hours to bring Petrinja back to life again. My husband was a skilled electrician, and worked alongside my father and friends to repair our house and the houses of our friends. Walls, roofs, windows, bathrooms and kitchens all had to be built, or replaced. While my husband and father carried out that work, they had a hard and rough time living in a primitive way, sleeping on concrete floors, washing in bowls etc. while all the repairs to our house took place, my mother and I remained in Zagreb.

After a long period of time, most of the houses had completed all the necessary repairs to make them inhabitable for families. Slowly, day by day, the citizens of Petrinja returned to their houses, but even after they returned, the citizens of Petrinja still had to continue further work on their houses to bring them back to the standard they had before the Serbs had occupied and vandalised our town. Most of Petrinja's citizens had now returned to their houses and had started a different rebuilding project, the most difficult of all: to rebuild was their lives. So many of these citizens had lost husbands, wives, daughters, sons, brothers, sisters and even little children. How does anybody cope with such heartache? How can anyone ever forget and put all that tragedy in their lives behind them? They say, *Time is a great healer*, but that cliché does not apply to all, everyone has a standard cure for life's heartbreak and bereavement. But for the sake of our children, we must try to find everyway possible to make Petrinja a secure, safe, a more beautiful, and a better place to live in.

Apart from losing some very close friends that I had gone to school with, our family was some of the few lucky ones; every citizen had lost either a relative, neighbour or friend. It would take a generation to repair the psychological effects suffered by the citizens of Petrinja, and of course many other towns and villages throughout the former Yugoslavia. My husband was experiencing nightmares and flashbacks, and was feeling very insecure. My father's company had now been rebuilt, and were recruiting staff. My husband applied for work, and was successfully employed as an electrician at my father's company.

While I was in Italy I had a special dream. In my dream I was holding a golden medal inscribed with Jesus and the Holy Mother Mary. I was walking through the wet green grass, my feet and legs were getting very wet, but when I looked down at the grass, milk was flowing from the grass in small drops. With all my my strength I shouted out in a very loud voice, "We are saved, Jesus is coming!" Everyone I met in my dream, whether good or bad, had a changed in their heart, shaken from the Holy Spirit, they cried.

They all prayed for forgiveness. I was so happy in my dream, my heart was full of love for everyone in the world. In the morning, I told my friend Tanja about the dream; she said,

"The milk that flowed through the grass was the Water of Life, and you will soon go back to Petrinja." Later that day I asked Tanja what she meant when she told me the milk flowing through the grass was the *Water of Life*. Tanja could not remember that she said that or talked about my dream. I looked at Tanja with astonishment and disbelief, was I going mad? No! just a few hours ago, I clearly remember telling Tanja about my dream. When I again explained to Tanja about my dream. Tanja said, "If you are sure that I've already told me, then God must have been talking to you through me."

I telephoned my family, and all my friends in Croatia, to tell them about my dream and the beautiful news of what the dream meant. I did not care if they thought I was crazy, I know that God talks to us all during the desperate times of our lives. Perhaps there are some people that are to afraid or not ready to accept God in their life.

On September 11th 1994, shortly after my dream, news of the holy father Ivan Pavao the second visits Zagreb. I would never forget that day, and from that day, I was sure with God's help, my family and I would return to Petrinja.

In the Autumn of 1995 my family and I returned to Petrinja. A few weeks after we had returned to Petrinja, I was walking down our street and heard a familiar voice calling, "Edit, Edit!" I turned around to see the priest called Zdrarko, he who had given me so much help while I was staying in Zagreb. After we had asked about each other's welfare, Zdrarko told me why he left the priesthood and that he was now working and training people to deactivate landmines. He told me he was on his way to a minefield near Petrinja, in order to make the area safe for the people and children to walk without fear in Petrinja and the surrounding villages.

I told Zdrarko that the best mission he had on earth was when he was a priest, because he always helped lots of people with terrible problems, including me. I thanked him for everything he did for me. That day was the last time I would ever see Zdrarko again, one month later Zdrarko was killed when a landmine he was deactivating exploded. Just a few days before he was killed, Zdrarko had told friends that he was going to return to his priesthood. I feel his mission on earth was complete, God needed him to be a priest in heaven. George, in memory of Zdrarko, I dedicate my story to him. I pray the eternal light shines to him, and he rest in peace with God. Amen.

It's now been four years since the citizens returned to Petrinja. In 1999, I exhibited all my special paintings that were created with the help of God and the Holy Spirit from 1994 to 1999. When I first showed these paintings to my friend Tanja, she said, "Edit these paintings were created from your soul."

I told Tanja, "The paintings were created in a special way, I was deeply dedicated to God in prayers and, at times, I felt God so close to my heart. I held the brush, but it was free from my will and led by the Holy Spirit. The paintings mostly contained a spectrum of colours on a religious theme depicting Jesus and the Holy Mary. Every time I finished a painting I thanked God. The paintings were so different from my usual style of painting, in fact, I have never painted in that way before. I believe, and feel, that God's divine creative energy was around us and exist within us all."

Most of the people who came to my exhibition made comments about feeling God's love and positive energy when they looked at my paintings. These comments made me feel that I had achieved a link between these people and God, and that made me feel so happy and contented. If we are prepared to open our hearts to God, it would allow us to be happy and free from all bad and negative thoughts. Glory to our Lord, and Hallowed be thy name.

After everything that happened to my family and me, I consider myself to be lucky. Over a period of time possessions can be replaced, but people can never be replaced. A mother who has lost a child, or anyone who looses a loved one, faces the worst heartache that they would ever experience in their life. Throughout all that heartache and bad times, I have lived to tell my story. That experience has made me a stronger person, and I have met some wonderful people on that my journey. I have also learnt to value many things that I took for granted before the conflict. The most important of them all was LOVE. That was the only thing that should ever matter to all of us. If the world had more Love, it would be a far better place to live. We must try to love those who cannot love, or don't know how to love. Every day never forget to thank God for his mercy in our lives.

Finally, I give you part of the lyrics to one of my favourite Croatian songs:

Steady hand and honour, holy water and baptism.
Be a man that was proud, a reflection of your ancestor.
Do not give your own, do not take somebody else's, it's dammed.
Who passes away through life, and proudly stands before God.
Wherever life takes you, you must always know who you are!

All my love Edit, from Petrinja (now a free town).

CHAPTER FIFTEEN

'Serbia'

I had planned for the last chapter of my book to be written by a Serbian lady called Vanja, you might remember Vanja was mentioned a few times in Chapter Eleven, *The Convoy Diaries*. I emailed Vanja and asked her if she would like to write the last chapter giving a Serbian account of the conflict in the former Yugoslavia. Vanja thanked me for giving her the chance to write something for my book. Three months later I received an email from Vanja telling me that she was going to ask her sister-in-law to write something for my book. I got the impression that Vanja did not have the time or could not be bothered to write a Serbian account for my book.

A few more months went by. Once again I emailed Vanja asking her how her sister-in-law was getting on with Chapter Fifteen. A few weeks later I received a very disappointing email from Vanja, telling me that her sister-in-law had declined to write anything about the Serbian involvement during the nineties conflict in the former Yugoslavia. Vanja also mentioned that she felt she was not qualified to represent the Serbian people who had suffered during the conflict in the former Yugoslavia. I could not believe that that was the same lady that I had grown to respect over the last nineteen years.

Just when you think that you know that person, you realize that person was really a stranger to you. I find it sad when you ask a Serbian friend to write a chapter for your book on the suffering of the Serbian people during the conflict in the former Yugoslavia. You then wait for six months while they scratch their heads trying to think of something to write. Then to be let down, because she feels unqualified to represent the Serbian people. What? Excuse me! But Vanja played an important roll in Chapter Eleven, *The Convoy Diaries*.

I mentioned that Vanja worked for the Red Cross. During her service for the Red Cross, surely she was near the front line of operations to see, or hear about any suffering that might have been inflicted on the Serbian people as a result of that conflict in the former Yugoslavia. Perhaps Vanja or her sister-in-law did not witness or hear about any suffering by the Serbian people. After all Serbia was the main aggressor in that conflict, any hardship or suffering by the Serbian people was brought on by their own greedy ambitions to occupy the sovereign land of neighbouring countries. Maybe Vanja and her sister-in-law would have found it hard to write and compare their suffering against the suffering that Serbia had inflicted on the men, women and children in Croatia or Bosnia Herzegovina. Perhaps, Vanja and her sister-in-law are ashamed of what the Serbs did in Srebrenica, and many other towns throughout Croatia and Bosnia.

Serbian Leader Milošević and his Colonel Mladić wreaked a hostile wave of genocide throughout the former Yugoslavia. The Serbian butchers showed no mercy towards many innocent civilians. Thankfully the conflict ended in 1995, after NATO gave the Serbian asses a good kicking. All the cowardly Serbian leaders, including Milošević and Mladić, fled into hiding and the disgusting Serbs played their part in hiding and protecting their war criminals. Years after the conflict in the former Yugoslavia, Serbia wanted to be accepted as part of the European Union, and could only achieve that status if they handed over, or supplied information on the location of, their wanted war criminals.

When the Serbs want something so badly, they would betray their own nationals to get what they want from the European Union. Thankfully Milošević and Mladić and many other Serbs are now paying the price for their war crimes at The Hague.

Perhaps there are many people out there who may understand why Vanja and her sister-in-law might want to forget the suffering of Serbian people or the part Serbia played in the conflict in the former Yugoslavia. But I believe it's equally important to remember all the mistakes, and bad things of our past life in order to appreciate the comfortable lifestyle we have now. Yes, we must all move on from the trials and tribulations of our past life, but that does not mean to say we should forget the past hardships we faced in order to get where we are now. We must never forget the sacrifices that were made by so many, in order for us to enjoy the democratic lifestyle that most of us have in our world, today.

When I came home after my mission in the former Yugoslavia, Vanja and I kept in touch with letters and the odd phone call. Some of those letters in part described some of the hardship that she and her family were going through. Fortunately for me, and that book, I have kept all Vanja's letters and many other letters from friends that I served with on my mission. It is not my intention to establish who suffered the most in that conflict. I only wish to point out there are no winners in wars, only losers on all sides survive to pick up the pieces to rebuild their lives. Therefore, the following parts of letters from Vanja might indicate some of the Serbian suffering during the conflict in the former Yugoslavia.

Vanja's letter dated 20–01–94;

Dear George,

There are a lot of bad things happening, Banja Luka delegation was on standby since two days ago. On Monday 17th January in the morning Simon (Workshop Manager) Land

Cruiser was blown up by plastic explosive. It was completely destroyed, the roof of the Land Cruiser ended up in a nearby tree. All the windows on the houses near the Land Cruiser were broken. Also, about five evenings before that, nearly every evening the ICRC cars was broken in to and robbed and the ICRC staff houses too. So from now on we are on standby. I work that week, and next week I have to be on holiday and stay in Banja Luka in case that we start to work. Most of the ex-pats went to Zagreb. I told Rod that they were saving their own butts and leaving us here. That was not really fair of me, but anyway I don't expect any kind of protection from them. They say that most probably they would come back to Banja Luka. Last night the Geneva negotiations failed again.

I stayed in the whole evening in front of the TV with my parents watching the news from there. Nothing good, as I expected. Everybody says that that was the last chance for peace here. NATO said that they would bomb Serb targets in Bosnia. Of course nobody was that stupid to accept that their bombers would miss a few civilian buildings (remember Somalia). I really don't like Americans. I am not afraid, I am pissed off (excuse me). I would like it all to end one way or another. That we all go to hell, or that the nightmare stops. What was most expected now was that Serbs and Croats unite on wiping Muslims away. I think that they would because only Muslims didn't want to sign the peace treaty. Now enough of my moaning, I am sending you a few photos. Some were taken at a party we had with some drivers. I hope you like them? Drivers ask me how you are, and do you miss the convoys? They all wish to be remembered to you and send their regards. On Monday we were supposed to have a convoy for Zenica. We took another route from Zagreb via Sisak, because of a flood at the broken bridge. We were stopped, started to go, returned back, stopped again etc. In the end we had to stay overnight at the Danish UNPROFOR in Zeadgwarter. We had a party with the Danish that night. Later when I returned to the Banja Luka delegation everybody was asking me if I felt uncomfortable? I responded that I could not feel uncomfortable with my drivers with me, they even escorted me to the toilet, and waited for me. People became so jealous of me here, but I don't care.

We have strict rules about using the telephones for private use in the delegation, but I hope I would manage to call you from time to time.

I hope that you are fine, I am thinking about those plans for Norway and England. That was really my dream. I am thinking of you, and really appreciate our special friendship, and all the kind things you do for me. You would never know how much it means to me take good care of yourself, please stay in touch.

God Bless always yours,

Vanja.

Vanja's letter dated 22-03-94:

Dear George,

I hope that letter finds you in the best of health. I know it's been some time since you received my last letter. I always prefer to sit in peace and quiet, and write a nice letter to you slowly. Just lately I don't seem to have the time or right conditions to write to you.

I am okay, well! More or less. I have had a lot of problems lately, it seems one problem was followed by another. At times I don't know whether to laugh or cry. My grandma might lose her home, and my parents are so stressed about that situation. I was so worried that my father was going to have a heart attack, and my mum would freak out. Due to all that has been happening to us over the last 2/3 years my parents have become weak. I don't think losing your home was worth making yourself ill, I find some other things more important, but I was hurt because there was no justice! I guess things look different from their point of view. When something like that happens, nobody can protect you, it was all legal, but who cares?

Anyway, I managed to pull some connections, and got the problem solved. The authorities promised me that it would not be brought up again. My granma is here now, she had to travel 1,000 kilometres through two corridors, and she was eighty-one and my cousin from Sarajevo was here also. We had another refugee cousin with us for some time, but she as gone now. After that my mother got ill with a serious disease, but slowly she was getting better. Worst of all she was so lethargic and desperate, she thinks she has cancer. I try to help her, but I am finding hard to explain anything to her. At the moment I am not getting on very well with my sister, and I feel so bad about that. As for me I have had problems with my left hand. The doctor sent me for some blood tests, but they still don't know what was wrong with me.

From time to time it gets very warm and itches cause me some pain. There are more problems, not mentioning those that I have with myself trying to cope with the whole mess around me, and my life. My job with ICRC was not what it was. Most of the drivers are new, they are okay, but it would never be the same as it was when you were here. Last week forces started firing fifty metres behind the convoy near Komar. The security situation on the boarders was getting worst, especially near Türbe. On Thursday I am supposed to go to Tešanj, but nobody knows if we would get the clearance. You see, my life was great. Seriously, I am fed up. I have just been told Tešanj was confirmed. I hope it would be okay. I would give that letter to Frank today, he would post it for me in Zagreb.

That's all for now, take care love,

Vanja.

Vanja's letter dated 06-06-1994:

Dear George,

I don't feel very nice, actually I am quite down. It seems that I always write you a letter when I am like that. Which means most of the time I am usually in a good mood. Maybe I am bothering you with the situation here, but I have to say you are to blame for staying in touch with me, and wanting to have a friend from a country at war. I would not be able to write that letter for much longer, because there was no electricity.

The last seven days we have had six hours reduction per day in our electricity supply. You never know when your electricity would be cut, and from today we would have a reduction of twelve hours per day. I can hardly see what I am writing. Obviously its worst at night time, we have to use candles or oil lamps, but we are well trained in situations like that. I do miss TV and radio, sometimes the electricity was cut when you don't expect it. Can't see to put on my make-up, shower by candlelight, no ironing or washing clothes, no reading books to learn, though sometimes I did try to read books in candlelight, but the light was not good for reading or writing etc. I guess you get the picture. I can manage everything with that war, but no electricity! I know I would have to try and deal with that situation, and I know very well how to live without electricity, but it just freaks me out, and makes me feel like a savage. I can't imagine that we are going back to that situation, I did hope things were getting better. I will finish that letter later.

16-06-1994; here I am again, I called you last night, but you were not at home, so I left a message on your answering machine. I hope you would call me later, because I worry about you. It's been difficult to get a phone line lately.

Anyway as usual I don't feel good, I have had a very bad headache, and a very low blood pressure (85/65), so I am in bed.

I was in Prijedor today to attend high-level meetings, and we are now allowed to work there again, but it was a difficult area to work in.

Apart from that my life was very boring. When I am not working, I have not gone out for two weeks. At night, I don't feel like going back home alone without streetlights. Very rarely do I see my friends, there are only a couple of them left in Banja Luka. All I think about was coming to England, and you know I would like to go to London, but I like your home town Plymouth better. I would really like to come to England, I guess we would have to see what happens about that. Would you please check what requirements I would need to obtain a visa to come to England? I think I would need a letter of acceptance from you when I apply for a visa. Anyway if you would kindly check all the possibilities and all the possible problems that I might encounter with a view to avoiding them.

And you know I miss you, I miss talks with you, I miss the good feeling that you give me. You are a special person. So that was all for now, I have to go now to Gradiska. I hope you keep yourself well, drive carefully, and don't forget me.

Thinking of you Love,

Vanja.

Vanja's letter dated 08-08-1994:

Dear George,

I hope Vinko called you and told you about the news here. I don't want you to worry or panic, but I just want you to be prepared if that NATO action starts. I also want you to know what was going on, and why you cannot reach me on the telephone.

Serbia cut off all our phone lines from Serbia to the world, and we don't know how long that situation would last.

Personally, I am pessimistic, Serbia has also closed the corridor. Only people with luggage, medicines and food supplies can pass through the corridor. You know that was our only connection with the rest of the world, so that action was a complete disaster. It seems that the state of war would be announced and special measures taken. Today it was decided that everybody in Serbia has to work ten hours per day, with one day off on Sunday. Nobody can take a holiday until further notice. I told you how seriously ill my mother was, my father was sixty-one, and they cannot be expected to work like that. Probably everyone would be assigned to some kind of working unit, or called into military service. Also we would probably have a so-called 'Reduced Supply'. That means we would be told how much food or hygiene material we can buy, regardless of how much you have. There was no money coming in or out of Serbia, no export or imports, no raw materials,Serbia's economy is in ruins, and very little industry working. If that situation continued all industry would be brought a standstill. We are almost cut off from the outside world so after two or three days you can imagine how expensive it was to buy food or any other supplies

People had already started to panic buy huge stocks of food and supplies. We had all been trained and experienced to know how that would affect us. We had already accepted to go without butter and bacon, but I couldn't even find

357

margarine to buy. If war was declared, universities, shops and bars etc. would be closed, only a few shops would remain open. Concerning the working in a unit, or military obligation, I think (or hope) I can get away with an exemption of service, because so far local ICRC staff have been considered to be on a working obligation already. But that situation can change day by day, I am also worried for my sister, she was in nursing school.

We have very little electricity now, only three or four hours per day, two or three days per week. We also ran out of gas, and there was no more gas to buy. I don't know how we would manage to cook what little food we have or make coffee. Our water supply was rationed, and we ran out of water every day for several hours or more. The temperatures are about 36° centigrade, some days hotter still. I worry about my parent's health, old people dehydrate so easily if they don't have water to drink.

All that hardship because Serbs in the Serbian republic don't want to sign the peace plan of the 'Contact Group'. I would not make any further comment about it, because once I start, I would not be able to stop. I am full of anger, full of everything. I am so fed up and annoyed with our situation. I have a feeling we are all slowly going crazy. All that pressure we are all under, at one time we looked forward to a future that does not exist any more, but I try my best to find brighter moments to lift my spirits into a positive mode. All the people I talk to in the delegation always talk about the cases of people being ill-treated and beaten up, houses burnt, families being killed, prisoners being ill-treated. All these stories and my family and I are caught up in the middle of that nightmare, what a mess! Sometimes I wish I didn't exist. I hope we would all get over that nightmare. Damn Americans, Germans, Serbs, Muslims and Croats!

Next week I would go to Doboj to take those exams that I told you about. I am surprised they are letting me stay there for four days. A friend of mine in Doboj told me she would give me shelter, which made me feel a lot better. I don't know how this letter sounds to you, maybe angry or cold, or whatever, but please forgive me if I make you feel depressed.

I don't mean to, but I know you would understand me at that most critical time. I can't write any more. I hope you and your family are fine, I think of you often.

Love,

Vanja.

Vanja's letter dated 06-12-1994:

Dear George,

I've tried to write you a letter several times. However, it was not easy, I don't know what to say or feel anymore, how sad it was to be confused about my life. Still having said that, I would try to write and say what I feel now. I get so mentally blocked. Yet sometimes when I am alone I think and feel I could write you a long letter with so many things to say, telling you what I feel, but I don't like to write tasteless letters.

I am in the Banja Luka delegation, and have found some time to write to you before my working day ends. There was not much inspiration to write a letter in that office. We are almost completely blocked in here, the work I mean. Of course it's all due to the situation. It's not very motivating to come to work. We are trying to do something to get some results, but everything has gone too crazy. We have had a lot of incidents. At the end of September two colleagues, a nurse and a female translator, were kidnapped and ill-treated by their captors before being released. All that happened in my field, their Land Cruisers were also taken, but later on the police returned the vehicles. The perpetrators of that crime haven't been found.

Two weeks later, our Land Cruiser was stolen again, and the local driver was ill-treated, the driver and Land Cruiser were later returned, and once again the perpetrators were not found. Again two weeks ago, two ICRC teams in Land Cruisers were arrested and held overnight. Everyone was so worried for their safety, and was afraid what might happen to them. Thankfully, they were released on the following morning. So as you can see it was getting more and more difficult to work in that area. The electricity has just been cut, so I'll stop now, and continue this letter at a later date.

Vanja's letter continued 09-12-1994:

Here I am again. To continue about the electricity, we get six hours electricity after every 48 hours. That situation drives me crazy, now at that time of the year we have shorter daylight hours. I don't remember when I last got ready for work in the morning with electricity.

As I have already told you, the situation was very bad here. All you read and hear from the media are all lies, so don't believe them. All my friends are on the front line, and I don't have any friends here to talk to anymore. I worry like hell about them, I have friends in a town called Glamoc, that town is being destroyed by the Muslim army and Republic of Croatian Army, and nobody in the world's media mentions that. Dozens of civilians are killed there almost every day. In the world's eyes that doesn't exist. Anyway that war was so dirty and all that was happening are just war games and politics. The problem was Serb Krajina - former Croats also. Croats won't make any compromises (of course that's what was said in the media) and the Serbs would never ever give it back to the Croats. Serbs from Bosnian Krajina (that's the part where I live) would fight for those in Serb Krajina [in] former Croatia. I don't see the solution to that war. To me, it really looks that it won't end until Croatia and Serbia start a full-blooded war with each other, and finish it.

I really believe more and more that was the only way to end it. I have not been able to call you lately, but I have just got news that the phone lines are now open again. So please try to call me when you can. Maybe I would go to Belgrade next week to check about my visa, we'll see what happens. I would end now. Please give my regards to all your family. I hope to see you all soon. Take care of yourself.

Love,

Vanja.

Over a period of two years, Vanja had sent me fifteen letters or cards. Rather than bore you with the small talk you get in most letters, the letters you have just read go a little way to describe a little of the Serbian hardship and suffering caused by the conflict in the former Yugoslavia from 1993/95.

These letters, along with many other letters from friends and colleagues that I had met during my mission, were stored in a box for safekeeping. It was eighteen years ago when I last read Vanja's letters, and I am sorry to say that reading Vanja's letters again only confirmed to me that the lady who wrote these letters was not the same lady that I recently emailed, and who now lives a comfortable life in Switzerland.

From 1992 to 1995, Vanja was grateful to the Red Cross for work and their help at a very difficult time in her life. I asked Vanja to help me complete that book to raise funds for the Red Cross. You already know the answer I got, but that's life. She must have her reasons other than the feeble excuse Vanja gave me not to write that chapter.

Food for thought: I asked Vanja if she ever wondered what she might be doing now, if it wasn't for the conflict in the former Yugoslavia? Vanja would not have worked for the Red Cross and met her husband, a Swiss guy who was also working for the Red Cross in Banja Luka. That being the case Vanja would not be enjoying the comfortable lifestyle she has in Switzerland right now. And of course Vanja and I would never have met, and I would not be writing that book. Fate and destiny plays such a major roll in our lives.

At some time or another we all touch someone's life that leads us to share a moment in time, and sometimes our own actions can have mixed consequences that can either change another person's life for the better, or worse. Throughout history every nation and person in our world has played their part in orchestrating future events that could affect so many lives. Over many centuries Serbia and the Serbian people are no exception to that rule. In Chapter Fourteen, *Edit's Story*, she mentions the reasons for the Serbian Army occupying her town and many other towns throughout Croatia and Bosnia, fuelled by an ambition to create a 'Greater Serbia'. For over one hundred years, these words also appear in historic records.

Under the 1878 Treaty of Berlin, Austria-Hungary received the mandate to occupy and administer the Ottoman Vila yet of Bosnia, while the Ottoman Empire retained official sovereignty. Under the same treaty, the great powers (Austria-Hungary, Britain, France, Germany, Italy, the Ottoman Empire and Russian Empire) gave official recognition to the principality of Serbia as a sovereign state. Four years later Serbia was transformed into a kingdom under Prince Milan IV Obrenović who thus became King Milan I Obrenović. Serbia's monarchs at the time, from the royal House of Obrenović, maintained close relations with Austria-Hungary administrators and were content to reign within the borders set by the treaty.

That changed in May 1903 when Serbian military officers led by Dragutin Dimitrijevic stormed the Serbian royal palace. After a fierce battle in the dark the attackers captured the head of the palace guard General Laza Petrović, and forced him to reveal the hiding place of King Alexander I Obrenović and his wife Queen Draga. The King and Queen were forced to open the door to their hiding place. The King was then shot thirty times and the Queen was shot eighteen times.

The royal corpses were then stripped and brutally stabbed with sabres, before the attackers threw the royal corpses out of the palace windows, ending any threat that loyalist to the King and Queen would mount a counterattack. Head of the palace guard General Petrovic was also killed. Vojislav Tankosić organized the murders of Queen Draga's brothers.

The conspirators installed Peter I of the House of Karađorđevic as the new King of Serbia. King Peter I's dynasty was more nationalistic in the Serbian cause, friendlier to Russia, and less friendly to Austria-Hungary administration. Over the next decade disputes between Serbia and its neighbours erupted as Serbia moved to build its power and gradually reclaim its fourteenth-century empire. These conflicts included a customs dispute with Austria-Hungary administration beginning in 1906 (commonly referred to as the *Pig War*), the Bosnian crisis of 1908-1909, in which Serbia assumed an attitude of protest over Austria-Hungary's annexation of Bosnia-Herzegovina, ending in Serbia's acquiescence without compensation in March 1909, and finally the two Balkan Wars of 1912-1913 in which Serbia conquered Macedonia and Kosovo from the Ottoman Empire.

In 1913/14, Dimitrijevic and Tankosić figured prominently in the plot to assassinate Archduke Franz Ferdinand of Austria. Serbia's military successes and Serbia's outrage over the Austro-Hungarian annexation of Bosnia-Herzegovina emboldened nationalistic elements in Serbia and Serbs in the Austro-Hungarian Empire who were annoyed under the Austro-Hungarian rule. Serbia's nationalistic sentiments were stirred by Serbian cultural organizations. From 1909 to 1914 lone assassins, mostly Serbian citizens of Austro-Hungary, made a series of unsuccessful assassination attempts against Austro-Hungarian officials in Croatia and Bosnia-Herzegovina. The assassins received sporadic support from elements in Serbia.

In 1913 Emperor Franz Joseph commanded Archduke Franz Ferdinand to observe the military manoeuvres in Bosnia, which were scheduled for June 1914. Following these manoeuvres, Archduke Franz Ferdinand and his wife the Archduchess of Hohenberg planned to visit Sarajevo to open a new state museum.

Serbia considered the Austro-Hungarian dynasty a threat to Serbia's ambitions to create a 'Greater Serbia'. And to do that Serbia wanted control of Bosnia-Herzegovina. Danilo Ilić was a Bosnian orthodox Serb and a leader of a Serbian nationalistic 'Black Hand' terrorist cell in Sarajevo. In late 1913, Danilo Ilić attended a Serbian meeting in Užice. At the meeting he spoke to Serbian Colonel C. A. Popović who was at that time a leader in the Black Hand terrorist cell.

Ilić recommended an end to the period of building a revolutionary organization, and move to direct action against the Austro-Hungarian dynasty. Colonel Popović sent Ilić to Belgrade to discuss his recommendations with the chief of Serbian military intelligence, Colonel Dragutin Dimitrijevic, known more commonly as Apis. By 1913, Apis and his fellow military conspirators, drawn heavily from the ranks of the May 1903 coup, had come to dominate the Black Hand terrorist cell. Apis' right-hand man and fellow Black Hand member Major Vojislav Tankosić, who was in charge of guerrilla training, attended a meeting in January 1914 at Toulouse, in France. During that meeting various possible Austro-Hungarian targets for assassination were discussed, including the Archduke Franz Ferdinand.

In Mostar on the 26th March 1914, Ilić informed fellow Black Hand member Mehamed Mehmed about the plan to assassinate the Archduke Franz Ferdinand, and told Mehmed to be on stand-by for that new operation.

Shortly after Easter on the 19th April 1914, Ilić recruited Serbian youths Vaso Čubrilović and Cvjetko Popović, plus three Austro-Hungarian Bosnian Serbs youths Gavrilo Princip, Trifko Grabež and Nedeljko Čabrinović, who were all living in Belgrade. They were all eager to carry out assassinations to fuel the Serbian nationalistic cause. They approached a fellow Bosnian Serb Milan Ciganovic who was a renowned guerrilla fighter known to be well connected and with access to arms, and through him Major Tankosić reach an agreement to transport arms to Sarajevo for the planned assassination. while waiting for the arms to be delivered.

Major Tankosić gave his assassin recruits one pistol to practice with. The rest of the weapons were finally delivered to Sarajevo on 26th May 1914. Milan Ciganovic trained the assassins and provided maps, six hand grenades, four Browning pistols, ammunition and suicide pills.

Princip, Grabež and Čabrinović left Belgrade by boat on the 28th May 1914 and travelled along the Sava river to Šabac to meet Captain Popović of the Serbian border guard, who provided them with a letter to be delivered to a Captain Prvanovic in Loznica. They were given the identities of three Customs officials in order to receive discounted train tickets for the journey to the small border town of Loznica.

Princip, Grabež and Čabrinović arrived in Loznica on the 29th May 1914, where they met Captain Prvanovic and delivered the letter. They also discussed the best way to cross the border undetected with Captain Prvanovic and his three sergeants. At the meeting Princip accused Čabrinović of repeated violations of operational security. Princip was not happy to cross the border with Čabrinović and his cavalier approach to their mission. They finally agreed to cross the border via separate routes. Čabrinović made his way to Zvornik, and would met Princip and Grabež in Tuzla. Meanwhile Sergeant Budivoj Grbić led Princip and Grabež by foot and then boat to Isakovic's Island, a small island in the middle of the Drina River that separated Serbia from Bosnia. They and their weapons reached the island on the 31st May, 1914.

Sergeant Grbić passed the assassins and their weapons to the hands of agents from the Serbian Narodna Odbrana for transportation to Austro-Hungarian territory, and from safe house to safe house Princip and Grabež finally crossed the Austro-Hungarian border on the evening of the 1st June 1914. They and their weapons were passed from agent to agent until they arrived in Tuzla on the 3rd June 1914 for their rendezvous with fellow assassin Čabrinović. They left the weapons in the hands of a Narodna Odbrana agent, Mihajlo Jovanović.

Čabrinović's father was a Sarajevo police official in Tuzla, and Čabrinović accidentally came across one of his father's friends, Sarajevo police detective Ivan Vila, and struck up a conversation with him. By coincidence Princip, Grabež and Čabrinović boarded the same train to Sarajevo as Detective Vila. Čabrinović started talking about the proposed visit of the Archduke Franz Ferdinand to Sarajevo. Čabrinović asked Detective Vila, 'Do you think the Archduke's visit will take place?' Unaware he was talking to assassins, Detective Vila replied, 'Archduke Franz Ferdinand will visit Sarajevo on the 28th June.'

On arriving in Sarajevo on the 4th June 1914, Princip, Grabež and Čabrinović went their separate ways. Princip reported to Ilić, then visited his family in Hadzici and returned to Sarajevo on the 6th June 1914, taking up residence at Ilić's mother's home with Ilić. Grabež joined his family in Pale. Čabrinović moved back to his father's home in Sarajevo.

On the 14th June 1914, Ilić travelled to Tuzla to bring the weapons to Sarajevo. Agent Mihajlo Jovanović hid the weapons in a large box of sugar.

On the 15th June 1914, Ilić and Jovanović travelled separately by train to Doboj, where Jovanović handed the box of sugar that contained the weapons to Ilić. Later that day Ilić returned by train to Sarajevo, being careful to avoid police detection. Ilić transferred to a local train just outside Sarajevo, and then to a tram.

Over the next twelve days before the planned assassination of the Archduke Franz Ferdinand, the group of assassins spent a lot of time studying the proposed route that their target would be taking, selecting the best possible positions in order to successfully carry out the planned assassination. What they could not train or prepare themselves for was the nervous tension that would hit your stomach on the day of the assassination.

On the 27th June 1914, Ilić started to issue the weapons to the assassins. To avoid detection, or the risk of an informant in the Serbian Black Hand group, Ilić had kept the identities of the recruited assassins a secret.

On the 28th June 1914, Ilić supervised and positioned the assassins along the motorcade route, exhorting and praising his assassins en route.

Meanwhile, Archduke Franz Ferdinand, his wife Archduchess Sophie and his party proceeded by train from Ilidza Spa to Sarajevo. Governor Oskar Potiorek met the party at Sarajevo station. Six automobiles were waiting to transport the royal party to the military barracks, the Town Hall and then to the Museum. By mistake, three local police officers got into the first car with the chief of special security; the special security officers, who were supposed to accompany their chief in the first car, got left behind. The second car carried the Mayor and Sarajevo's chief of police. The third car in the motorcade was a Graf & Stift open sports car with its top folded down; that car carried Archduke Franz Ferdinand, his wife Archduchess Sophie, Governor Potiorek and Lieutenant Colonel Count Franz von Harrach.

The remaining three cars carried civic dignitaries and security personnel. The motorcade's first stop on the preannounce program was a brief inspection of a military barracks. At ten a.m. the motorcade departed the military barracks and headed for the town hall via Apple Quay. En route the motorcade passed the first assassins, Mehmed and Vaso Čubrilović. Danilo Ilić had placed them in front of the garden of the Mostar Café and armed Mehmed with a bomb, Čubrilović with a bomb and a pistol. As the motorcades passed, they both failed to act. Further along the route Ilić had placed his next assassin Nedeljko Čabrinović on the opposite side of the street near Miljacka River, arming him with a bomb. At ten ten a.m. the motorcade approached Čabrinović's position, and he threw his bomb at Archduke Franz Ferdinand's car.

The bomb bounced off the folded back convertible cover on the Archduke's car. The mistimed detonator caused the bomb to explode under the following car, wounding twenty people. Čabrinović swallowed his cyanide pill and jumped into the Miljacka River.

Čabrinović's suicide attempt failed as the cyanide only induced vomiting, and at that time Miljacka River was only thirteen centimetres deep. Police dragged Čabrinović out of the river, and he was severely beaten by the crowd before being taken into custody.

The motorcade sped away towards the Town Hall, leaving the disabled car behind. Cvjetko Popović, Gavrilo Princip and Trifko Grabež also failed to act, as the motorcade passed them at high speed.

Arriving at the Town Hall for the scheduled reception, Archduke Franz Ferdinand showed understandable signs of stress. Interrupting a prepared speech of welcome by Sarajevo Mayor Ćurčić, the Archduke angrily said, 'Mr Mayor, I came here on a visit and get bombs thrown at me, it's outrageous.' Archduchess Sophie then whispered into the Archduke's ear and, after a short pause, the Archduke asked the Mayor to continue with his speech. Archduke Franz Ferdinand then seemed to be calmer as the Mayor delivered his welcoming speech to the royal party. Following this, the Archduke's speech was delayed while his aides retrieved his written, bloodstained text from the car that was damaged in the assassination attempt. To his prepared speech the Archduke added a few remarks about the day's events, thanking the people of Sarajevo for their ovations. He went on to tell the crowd that he could see the expression of joy in their faces at the failure of his attempted assassination.

Security officials and members of the Archduke's party discussed the rest of the day's planned programme. The Archduke and -duchess wanted to change their planned programme in favour of visiting the wounded from the assassination attempt in hospital.

At ten forty-five a.m., in order to avoid the city centre, Governor Oskar Potiorek recommended that the royal car should travel straight along Apple Quay to Sarajevo Hospital.

However the royal driver, Leopold Lojka, accidentally took a right turn into Franz Josef Street.

After learning that the assassination had been unsuccessful, assassin Gavrilo Princip went to a nearby food shop, Schiller's Delicatessen in Franz Josef Street. Just as Gavrilo Princip emerged from the delicatessen the royal car passed the shop. The driver, realizing his mistake, suddenly stopped the royal car about 100 metres past the shop near Latin Bridge and began to reverse the royal car; in doing so the engine stalled and the gears locked. Call it fate, or destiny: that gave Gavrilo Princip his opportunity. Princip approached the royal car with a Belgian made 9x17mm (380 ACP) Fabrique Nationale model 1910 semi-automatic pistol in his hand. At a distance of one and a half metres Princip fired two shots. The first shot hit the Archduke in the neck, and the second shot hit the Archduchess in the stomach. The Archduke and -duchess remained upright, but died while being driven to the Governor's residence to receive medical treatment. Count Harrach stated Archduke Franz Ferdinand's last words were, 'Sophie, Sophie! Don't die! Live for our children!' followed by six or seven utterances of 'It was nothing'.

These utterances were followed by a long death rattle. Archduchess Sophie was dead on arrival at the Governor's residence; the Archduke Franz Ferdinand died ten minutes later.

At that point, I question why they decided to take the Archduke and -duchess to the Governor's residence for medical treatment. Why not the nearby hospital that they were en route to visit? Surely when someone suffers serious injury you don't take them to your home, you take them to hospital. That's assuming, you have got nothing to hide...

Gavrilo Princip was immediately arrested at the scene of the assassinations. The following days after the assassinations brought widespread anti-Serb protests and rioting broke out in Sarajevo and various places within Austro-Hungarian territory.

Archduke Franz Ferdinand and Archduchess Sophie of Hohenberg's bodies were transported to Vienna, and were interred at Artstetten Castle. Only the immediate imperial family was requested to attend their funeral.

Serbia's Ambassador to France Milenko Vesnić and Serbia's Ambassador to Russia Spalajkovic put out statements claiming that Serbia had warned Austro-Hungary of the impending assassination plot. Serbia's Prime Minister Pasic soon thereafter denied making any such warnings and also denied any knowledge of the assassination plot. Serbian Education Minister Ljuba Jovanović claimed that, at the end of May and the early part of June, Prime Minister Pasic and members of his cabinet had reviewed intelligence reports that contained threats of an assassination plot.

On the 18th June 1914 the Serbian ambassador in Vienna, Jovan Jovanović, received a telegram, lacking in specifics but ordering him to warn Austro-Hungary that Serbia had reason to believe there was a conspiracy to assassinate the Archduke Franz Ferdinand in Bosnia. On the 21st June 1914, Ambassador Jovanović met with Austro-Hungary's Finance Minister Bilinski and stressed in general terms the risk that the Archduke heir apparent was taking on his plan visit to Sarajevo, and to consider the inflamed public opinion in Bosnia and Serbia. Jovanović also expressed concerns that his visit might give rise to incidents and demonstrations that Serbia would deprecate, but that would have fatal repercussions on Austro-Hungary's relations with Serbia. Bilinski showed no sign of attaching any great importance to Jovanović's warnings and dismissed his warnings when saying goodbye, he thanked Jovanović for his concerns and casually said, 'Let's hope nothing happens to the Archduke'.

The assassination of the heir to the Austro-Hungarian Empire and his wife produced widespread shock and condemnation throughout Europe, and there was initially much sympathy for the Austro-Hungarian position. Within two days of the assassination, Austro-Hungary and Germany advised Serbia that it should open an investigation, but

Secretary General to the Serbian Ministry of Foreign Affairs Slavko Gruic, replied, 'Nothing had been done so far, because the matter did not concern the Serbian Government'.

An angry exchange followed between the Austrian chargé d'affaires at Belgrade and Gruic. After conducting a criminal investigation, and verifying that Germany would honour its military alliance with the Austro-Hungarian Empire, the sceptical Hungarian Count Tisza was persuaded to endorse a formal letter sent to the government of Serbia. This letter reminded Serbia of its commitment to respect the Great Powers' decision regarding Bosnia-Herzegovina and to maintain good neighbourly relations with Austro-Hungary. The letter also contained specific demands aimed at preventing the Serbian publication of propaganda advocating the violent destruction towards the Austro-Hungarian Empire, at removing the people responsible from the Serbian military and arresting the people on Serbian soil who were involved in the assassination plot and to prevent the clandestine shipment of arms and explosives from Serbia to Austro-Hungarian territory.

That letter became known as the July Ultimatum, and Austro-Hungary stated that if Serbia did not accept all of the demands within forty-eight hours, it would recall its ambassador from Serbia. After Serbia received a telegram of support from Russia, Serbia mobilized its army and responded to the Austro-Hungary letter accepting point #8 demanding an end to the smuggling of weapons and the punishment of the frontier officers who had assisted the assassins and completely accepting point #10 which demanded that Serbia report the execution of the required measures as and when they were completed. Serbia partially accepted, finessed, disingenuously answered or politely rejected elements of the preamble and enumerated demands #1–7 and #9. The shortcomings of Serbia's response were published by Austro-Hungary with complaints placed side by side against Serbia's response. That led to Austro-Hungary breaking off diplomatic relations with Serbia.

The next day, Serbian reservists were aboard tramp steamers on the River Danube and crossed onto the Austro-Hungarian side of the river at Temes-Kubin. Austro-Hungarian soldiers fired into the air to warn off that act of aggression by the Serbian troops.

The report of that incident was initially sketchy, but it was reported to Emperor Franz-Joseph as a considerable skirmish. Just one month after the assassination of Archduke Franz Ferdinand, on the 28th July 1914 Austro-Hungary then declared war on Serbia and mobilized sections of its army that would face the already mobilized Serbian army.

Under the Secret Treaty of 1892, Russia and France were obliged to mobilize their armies if any of the Triple Alliance mobilized. On the 1st August 1914, Germany declared war on Russia and France. Britain was allied to France on a much looser worded treaty, but like a moth drawn to light, on the 4th August 1914 Britain declared war on Germany. Italy although allied to both Germany and Austro-Hungary was able to avoid entering war by citing a clause enabling it to evade its obligations. In short Italy's treaty was committed to defend Germany and Austro-Hungary only in a defensive conflict. Italy argued that Germany and Austro-Hungary's actions were offensive, and declared Italy's neutrality. But in May 1915 Italy joined the conflict against her former allies Germany and Austro-Hungary.

While mayhem and the carnage of World War I spread throughout Europe, most of the assassins were eventually caught, and those in Austro-Hungarian custody would be tried together with most of the conspirators who had helped and smuggled the assassin's weapons to Sarajevo. The defendants faced indictments of conspiracy to commit high treason involving official circles within Serbia. Conspiracy to commit high treason carried a maximum sentence of death. The trial was held from the 12th October to 21st of October 1914, with the verdicts and sentences announced on the 28th October 1914.

Under Austro-Hungarian law, the defendants under the age of twenty years at the time of the crime could not receive the death penalty, and could only receive the maximum sentence of twenty years in prison. The court heard arguments regarding Gavrilo Princip's age, there was considerable confusion and doubt over his true date of birth, but the court concluded that Gavrilo Princip was nineteen years old and twenty-seven days short of his twentieth birthday when he assassinated the Archduke Franz Ferdinand and his wife the Archduchess Sophie of Hogenberg. At the trial, the adult defendants facing the death penalty portrayed themselves as unwoulding participants in the conspiracy.

Under the examination of defendant Veljko Čubrilović, who helped to coordinate the transport of the weapons to Sarajevo and was a Narodna Odbrana agent, Čubrilović stated to the court that Princip glared at him and very forcefully said, 'If you want to know, it was for that reason and we are going to carry out an assassination of the Austro-Hungarian heir and if you know about it, you have to be quiet. If you betray us, you and your family would be destroyed.' Under further questioning by the defence council Čubrilović described in more detail the basis of his fears that compelled him to cooperate with Princip and Grabež. Stood behind Princip at the trial, Čubrilović explained that he was afraid of a revolutionary organization capable of committing great atrocities, he therefore feared his house would be destroyed and his family killed if he did not comply and explained that he knew such an organization existed in Serbia. When Čubrilović was asked why he risked the punishment of the law, instead of asking for protection from the law against the threats, Čubrilović responded, 'I was more afraid of terror, than the law.'

The conspirators from Belgrade, Gavrilo Princip, Nedeljko Čabrinović, and Trifko Grabež, who were all under the age of twenty years, and would not face the death penalty if they were found guilty. During the trial, in order to refute the charges they focused on putting the blame on themselves and deflecting any blame from Serbia. Under cross examination, Princip said, 'I am a Yugoslav nationalist, and believe in the unification of all South Slavs in whatever form of state that they be free of Austria.' Princip was then asked how he intended to achieve his ambitions? He responded, 'By means of Terror.'

Nedeljko Čabrinović testified that it was political views that motivated him to take part in the assassination. These same views were held in many circles that he travelled in throughout Serbia. The court did not believe the defendants' stories claiming to hold official Serbia blameless. The court felt this was proved by the evidence that both Narodna Odbrana, and circles within Serbia in charge of the espionage service, collaborated in the assassination.

Death sentences, prison terms and acquittals were as follows:

Danilo Ilić, Veljko Čubrilović and Mihajlo Jovanović, death by hanging on 3rd Feb 1915.

Jakov Milović, death sentence, commuted to life in prison by Kaiser Franz-Joseph.

Nedjo Kerović, death sentence, commuted to twenty years in prison by Kaiser Franz-Joseph.

Mitar Kerović, sentence to life in prison.

Gavrilo Princip, Nedeljko Čabrinović and Trifko Grabež, twenty-year prison sentences.

Vaso Čabrinović, sixteen year prison sentence. Cvjetko Popović, thirteen year prison sentence.

Lazar Đukić and Ivo Kranjčević, ten year prison sentences.

Cvijan Stjepanović, seven year prison sentence.

Branko Zagorac and Marko Perin, three year prison sentences.

Nine other defendants were acquitted.

At the trial Nedeljko Čabrinović had expressed his regrets for the murders. Following sentencing Čabrinović received a letter of forgiveness from the three young royal children the assassins had orphaned. Throughout our lives we all have regrets of something we have done or said, yet for Gavrilo Princip there was no indication of any remorse to the cold-blooded crimes that he had committed. While Princip was serving his prison sentence, I wonder if he ever got any news of World War One, the war that was mainly caused by his crime?

If so, I wonder if there might have been just a little sign of remorse for all the lives lost on both sides in the battlefields of Flanders, Ypres, the Somme and many more battlefields in World War One.

Due to the cold and damp prison conditions, Gavrilo Princip and Nedeljko Čabrinović contracted tuberculosis and died in prison during the early years of their prison sentence. Ironically they died just before the end of World War One, the war that had started as a result of the assassinations of Archduke Franz Ferdinand and his wife, Archduchess Sophie.

In 1920 Gavrilo Princip's body was exhumed and brought to Sarajevo to be buried at St Mark's Chapel with the heroes of Vidovdan. The Chapel was built to commemorate for eternity the heroes of Serbia.

That I just cannot comprehend. Gavrilo Princip a hero? Princip a hero my ass! Don't Serbs have any common decency or shame? That animal caused death and suffering to thousands human beings during World War One. Do you think Germany would honour Hitler in the same way? No chance. Why? Because most decent German people are ashamed, and want to forget what Hitler did to their country in World War Two.

Back to World War One: in late 1916 and the early part of 1917, secret peace talks took place between Austria-Hungary and France. Austria-Hungary's key demand was for returning Serbia back to the control of the Serbian government in exile, and that Serbia should provide guarantees that there would be no further political agitation, emanating from Serbia, against Austria-Hungary.

For some time the Serbian regent Alexander and the military officers loyal to him had planned to get rid of the military clique headed by Apis, as Apis represented a political threat to Alexander's power in Serbia. The Austro-Hungarian peace demand gave impetus to Serbian plan. On the 15th March 1917, Apis, and the officers loyal to him, were indicted on various false charges unrelated to the Austro-Hungary royal assassinations that took place in Sarajevo in 1914. Apis and his officers were tried by a Serbian kangaroo court martial on the French-controlled Salonika front. On the 23rd May 1917, Apis and eight of his conspirators were sentence to death, two other conspirators were sentenced to fifteen years in prison.

One defendant died during the trial, and the charges against him were dropped. At the appeals, the Serbian High Court reduced the number of death sentences from eight to seven. Serbian regent Alexander commuted four of the seven remaining death sentences. Apis, Colonel Ljuba Vulović and Rade Malobabic were executed by firing squad on the 26th June 1917. As the three condemned men were driven to the place of their execution, Apis said to the driver, 'Now it was clear to me and clear to you, that I am to be killed today by Serbian rifles solely because I organized the assassinations in Sarajevo.'

Among those tried, four of the defendents had confessed their involvement in the Sarajevo assassinations in 1914. In the late 1915, Apis' right-hand man Vojislav Tankosić died in battle, and was therefore never brought to trial. Muhamed Mehmed's basic fifteen year prison sentence was commuted, he was released in 1919.

In 1953, the Supreme Court of Serbia retried all the defendents involved in the Serbian kangaroo court on the 15th March 1917, and all the defendents were exonerated. Nationalistic action from Serbian conspirators in Sarajevo in 1914 bears some similarities with the conflict in the former Yugoslavia from 1991 to 1995. For more than 100 years Serbia harnessed ambitions to create a 'Greater Serbia' in the

Balkans. That ambition started World War One, and not so long ago the conflict that broke up the former Yugoslavia in the nineties.

Every nation in our world has played their part in writing the pages in our history books. People of every nation can only be as good and honest as their leaders and governments. Some leaders and their governments represent their people for the good of their own nation, but the great leaders and governments of nations represent all the people in this world no matter what colour, or creed. Unfortunately many Statesmen and Political Leaders are misrepresented, they can only act on the information given to them by their security advisors. Whats the cliché used? "Don't shoot the Leaders, shoot the messengers".

We all know that most nations in our world have signed the Geneva Convention, but how many nations actually honoured all the statutes written in the Geneva Convention? Try to imagine what kind of world we would all live in, if every nation adopted as part of their constitution, or the Fundamental Principles of the International Red Cross and Red Crescent Movement with their principles of Humanity, Impartially, Neutrality, Independence, Voluntary Service, Unity and Universality. These principles could only serve to make that world a better place for us all to live in. Okay, I am a dreamer, but if you want somethings bad enough, and you are a believer, then nothing is impossible.

Finally, during my mission on one of my early convoys in the former Yugoslavia, I remember the blue sky as far as you could see and the sun shining on the red roofs of houses that had escaped destruction from shelling. For a brief moment in that peace and tranquillity, you could forget you were serving in a war zone; that was until I had a radio call from my Convoy Leader, Dave T, he said, 'George what do you think of Yugoslavia?'

I replied, 'Dave, Yugoslavia is so beautiful, what a shame that conflict is destroying communities and lives of so many innocent people.'

Will we ever learn from the mistakes of the past? We can only hope and pray that we will wake up, smell the fresh air and be grateful for every day that we can live our lives in peace, and free from the destruction of war.